A History of Mass Communication

Six Information Revolutions

D0073814

A History of Mass Communication
Six Information Revolutions

Irving Fang

Focal Press
Boston, Oxford, Johannesburg, Melbourne, New Delhi, Singapore

Focal Press is an imprint of Elsevier Science.

Copyright 1997, Elsevier Science USA.

∞ This book is printed on acid-free paper.

Library of Congress Cataloging-in-Publication Data
Fang, Irving E.
   A history of information revolutions / Irving Fang.
      p.   cm.
   Includes bibliographical references and index.
   ISBN 0-240-80254-3 (pbk. : acid-free paper)
         1.   Communication-History. I. Title
P90.F26   1997
302.2'09-dc20   96-36527
                                                    CIP

British Library Cataloguing-in-Publication Data
A catalogue record for this book is available from the British Library.

The publisher offers special discounts on bulk orders of this book.
For information, please contact:
Manager of Special Sales
Elsevier Science
200 Wheeler Road
Burlington, MA 01803
Tel: 781-313-4700
Fax: 781-313-4802

For information on all Focal Press publications available, contact our World Wide Web homepage at http://www.focalpress.com

10 9 8 7 6 5
Printed in the United States of America

Contents

Acknowledgments   xiv

What Are Information Revolutions?   xv

Defining an Information Revolution   xv
Six Information Revolutions   xvii
Shared Characteristics   xviii
The Power of Information   xix
Highway and Village   xx
Sorting Media from Content   xx
Replacing Transportation   xxi
Shaping and Being Shaped   xxi
Difficult Beginnings   xxii
Life Is Different   xxii

Political Tools and Weapons   xxiii
Arresting Gorbachev   xxiv
Tiananmen Square   xxiv
The Infection of Mass Communication   xxvi
Terrorism and the Media   xxvii
Clandestine Radio   xxvii
Middle Eastern Examples of Media's Force   xxviii
New World Information Order   xxviii
Cultural Imperialism   xxix
Economic Freedom with Political Controls   xxx
Altering American Politics   xxxi
The Gulf War   xxxi
Notes   xxxiii

1   Writing
The First Revolution   1

The Invention of Writing   1
Writing on Clay   1
Advancing Knowledge   2

Skin and Bones and Papyrus   3
Papyrus in Egypt   4
Papyrus in Greek Hands   5
Parchment   6
Other Writing Surfaces   7

The Greeks   7

The Alphabet   8
Out of the Dark Ages   8
A Time of Turmoil   10
Supplementing an Oral Culture   11
The Warning of Socrates   12
From Greece to Rome   12
The First Libraries   12
The Lamp of Reason   14

Carrying the Message   14
Notes   16

2   Printing
The Second Revolution   18

Turbulent Europe   18
Sources of News   19
Reformation and Renaissance   20

A Gift from China   20
Origins   21
No Information Revolution   22
Paper Moves West   22
300 Sheep Skins for One Bible   23

Books and Universities   23
The First Universities   24
The New Book Culture   25
Censorship   26
Punishment for Publishing   27

Mail in the Middle Ages   28
Postal Services for Town and Gown   28
Postal Service as a Business   29

Here a New, There a New   30
Forerunners of Newspapers   31
The First Newspapers   31
Unintended Consequences   32

Printing and Literacy   32
Vernacular Printing   32
Why Bother to Read?   33
The Engines of Printing and Literacy   34
Literacy and Equality   34

Did Gutenberg Know About China?   35
European Ferment   36

What Did Gutenberg Know?   36
Movable Type in China and Korea   38
Gutenberg's Achievement   38
Notes   41

3   Mass Media
The Third Revolution   43

The Turmoil of a New Age   43
The Shift to Cities   43
It Also Brought Misery   44
Three Revolutions   44
Child Labor   45
Social Changes   46
Mass Dependencies   46

Printing for Everyone   47
Printing Changes   47
Stereotyping   48
Setting the Type   48
Offset Lithography   49

Paper for Everyone   49
A Continuous Sheet of Paper   49
A Lesson from a Wasp   50

The Information Pump   51
The Business of Newspapers   51
The Penny Press   52
Reporting   52
The Birth of Objectivity   53
Improvements in the Composing Room   54
Photographs in Newspapers   54
Free Presses   55
Controlled Presses   55

The Muckrakers   56

Women Can Type   57
Helping to Bring Women Out   57
The Old Office   57
Inventing a Writing Machine   58
The Sholes Machine   58
Women Mean Business   59
QWERTY   59

"If Anyone Desires..."   60
Creating Demand   60
Origins of Advertising   61
The Word Is "Advertising"   61
The Advertising Agency   62
Catalogs and Patent Medicines   63
Brand Names   63
More Advertising Tools   64

      Radio Advertising 64
      Televising Advertising 64
      Setting Standards 65
   Solving Postal Problems 65
      Postmasters and Publishers 66
      Postal Services for Newspapers 67
      Transporting the Mail 67
      International Agreement 68

   Photography 69
      Ancient Roots 69
      The Chemical Basis of Photography 70
      Daguerre and Talbot 70
      Wet-Plate Photography 72
      Photographing the World 72
      The Muckrakers' Photos 74
      Photoengraving 74
      The Copier 75
      Looking Ahead 76

   Current News 77
      Newspapers Change 77
      Ancient Signals 77
      The First Telegraphs 78
      "What Hath God Wrought?" 79
      Western Union Takes the Lead 79
      Its Role in Transmitting News 80
      News Agencies 81
      Changes in Service 82

   Voices on a Wire 83
      Intruder and Rescuer 83
      "Mr. Watson, come here. I want you." 84
      Can the Lower Classes Use It? 86
      The Telephone As an Early Radio 86
      Telephone Operators 87
      Into the Twentieth Century 88

   Signals in the Air 89
      Some of Radio's Societal Effects 89
      Origins of Radio 90
      Marconi 90
      Competition 91
      The Titanic 92
      Voice 92
      Hobbyists Tune In 93

   Movies Are Born 95
      Movies As a Communication Medium 95
      How Movies Began 96
      Edison Orders an Invention 97
      Motion Picture Projection 97
      Projected Movies Come to America 98

The Earliest Films   98
Notes   99

4   Entertainment
The Fourth Revolution   101

Public Recreation   101
  Money from the Poor   102

Entertaining Newspapers   103
  Adding Color   103

Magazines for the Fragmented Public   104
  English and Colonial Beginnings   104
  Plagiarism Was Common   105
  The Nickel Magazines   106

The Novel   106

Entertainment on a Plate   107
  The Start of Recorded Music   107
  Nothing Ever Like It   108
  Phonograph Parlors   109
  The Phonograph as Furniture   109
  Dancing and Jazz   110
  High Fidelity   111

Portable Recording   112
  The Story of Audiotape   112
  Germans Move Ahead   113
  A Tool for Journalists   113
  New Formats   114

Broadcasting   114
  Isolating Listeners   115
  The Radio Act of 1927   116
  Commercials   117
  Broadcasting Policy in Other Countries   118
  Networks   118

Owning Cameras   119
  Technical Improvements   119
  The Kodak   120
  More Improvements   121
  Pictures that Lie   121
  Holograms   122

Movies Tell Stories   123
  Nickelodeons   123
  Fear of Revolutionary Ideas   125
  A Market for Simple Stories   126
  The Actors   127
  Assembly Line Production   128
  Motion Pictures in Other Countries   129
  The Coming of Sound   130

The Coming of Color   131
The Stars and Their Films   132
Censorship   133
Political Issues   133
The Drive-In   134
Enter Television   134
The Distribution Schedule   135
Making Movies Cheaply   136
Notes   137

5   The Toolshed Home
The Fifth Revolution   138

The Communication Toolshed   138
What Makes a House a Home?   138
Contacts Decrease   139
Extending the Toolshed Home   140
Problems with Heavy Media Usage   141

Home Mail Delivery   142
Free Home Delivery   142
Parcels, Catalogs, and Junk Mail   143
Changes   144

New Uses for Phones   145
Telephone Company Reorganizations   145
Cellular Phones   146
Pocket Phones   146
The New Picturephones   147
A Variety of Uses   147
Reach Out Without Touching   148

"Free" Entertainment   148
Political Broadcasts   149
Cultural Influence   149
Improving the Sound   150
Radio Reinvents Itself   150
Citizen's Band   151
Looking in Radio's Crystal Ball   151
The Benefits of Broadcasting   151

Pictures in the Parlor   152
Time Spent Watching   153
The Scientific Roots of Television   154
Electronic Television   154
The Public Is Introduced to Television   156
The Fight Over Standards   157
HDTV   158
The Commercial Basis   158
Programming   158
Settings and Plots   159
Soap Operas   159

    The Sitcoms   160
    What Is for Children?   160
    Talk Shows and "Infotainment"   161
    Paying for Programming   161
    The Decline of Broadcasting   162

Tragedy in the Parlor   162
    Radio News   163
    Two Roots of Television News   164
    Kennedy Assassination Coverage   165
    The Civil Rights Movement   165
    Anti-War Demonstrations   166
    "The Living Room War"   167
    Not Newspaper Journalism   168
    Sometimes a Global Village   168

Wiring the Toolshed   169
    Two Trojan Horses   170
    How Cable Began   170
    CATV Pioneers   171
    Originating Programming   172
    Cable's Early Growth   172
    City Franchises   173
    Pay-TV Without Cable   174

Videotape, a New Book   174
    Advantages of the Home VCR   174
    Trying to Record Television   175
    The First Videotape Machines   175
    Electronic News Gathering   176
    Going to the Movies at Home   177
    The Near Future   178
    Spreading Worldwide   179
    Broadening the Video Journalist Base   180
    Video Piracy   180
    "Cultural Imperialism"   181
    Video Production Diffusion   181

Setting New Records   182
    Radio and Recording   183
    High Fidelity   184

We Still Have Books   185
    Notes   187

6   The Highway
The Sixth Revolution   189

Heavy Traffic   189
    Choices   190
    Interactivity   191
    Separated by Communication   192
    Distant Connections   193

Computer at the Wheel   194
   A Tool of Communication   194
   How It All Began   195
   Desktop Publishing   195

Magazines Target Their Readers   197

Multimedia, a Newer Book   198
   What Is Multimedia?   198
   CD-ROM   199
   CD-ROM Zines   200

Cable Narrowcasting   201
   Ted Turner Moves In   201
   New Channels   202
   Home Shopping   203
   Cable Franchises   203
   Pay Cable   204
   Wireless Cable   205
   Fiber Optics   205
   Programming Through Optical Fibers   206

Footprints on the Globe   207
   Geopolitical Considerations   207
   A Split-Second Apart   208
   Changes in News Reporting Structures   208
   The Beginnings   209
   INTELSAT   210
   Video Teleconferencing   211
   Direct Broadcasting   211
   C-Band and Ku-Band   212
   Scrambling the Signal   213
   Teleports   213
   A Limit to Infinite Space   213

Electronic Commuting   214
   Who Works at Home?   215
   Advantages of Working from Home   215
   The Telecenter   216
   Where Will We Live?   216
   What Will Happen to Cities?   217

The Internet   217
   Who Owns the Internet?   218
   The World Wide Web   219
   Electronic Cash   220
   Bulletin Boards   220
   Exercising Control   221
   Knowlege Groups   222
   Advertising   222
   Chat Lines   223
   Social Implications   223
   Radio on the Internet   224

Mailbox in the Computer   225

Faxing   226
>   *Speed of Facsimile   227*
>   *"Fax" Is More Than a Noun   227*
>   *Facsimile's Origins   227*
>   *A Variety of Uses   228*

Going Up the Highway   229
>   *The Qube Experiment   230*
>   *Teletext and Videotex   231*
>   *Online Services   232*
>   *Other Interactive Operations   232*
>   *Interactive Possibilities   232*
>   *Manipulating Television Programs   233*

News Online   234
>   *The Electronic Newspaper   234*
>   *Telcos, Newspapers, and Newscasts   234*
>   *Selling News Instead of Newspapers   235*
>   *The Computerized Newspaper   236*
>   *National Distribution   236*
>   *Notes   237*

A Summing Up   239

Revisiting the Six Information Revolutions   240
>   *Communication in Three Eras   241*
>   *Notes   243*

Bibliography   244

Communication Timeline   255

Index   268

Acknowledgments

This book is an attempt to find common themes in the long and complex history of communication. It endeavors to show how the means of communication grew out of their eras, how the tools were developed, how they influenced the societies of those eras, and how they have continued to exert influence upon subsequent generations.

The book is divided into six periods that are identified as information revolutions, recognizing that the events that constitute an information revolution defy neat categorization. For example, motion pictures are both mass information and packaged entertainment. Placing certain events within a particular movement became a necessity for the sake of clarity and narrative flow.

Because the author has not found it possible to have a sufficiently detailed knowledge of the entire sweep of history covered by this volume, he has relied on the exper-

tise and the kindness of others. Among them are Hyman Berman, Ken Doyle, Mark Heistad, Nancy Roberts, Phillip Tichenor, and William Wells, all of the University of Minnesota; documentarists R. Smith Schuneman, Niels Jensen, and Peter Hammar; William Cologie, National Cable Television Center; George Potter, Pennsylvania Cable & Telecommunications Association; Martin Collins, National Air and Space Museum; Haney Howell, Winthrop University; Scott Bourne, net.radio; David Glitzer, *Blender*; Steve Yelvington, Minneapolis *Star Tribune*; Bernard Finn, Kay Youngflesh, and E.N. Sivowitch, Smithsonian Institution; Thomas Volek, University of Kansas; Steve Blum, USSB; and James Bruns, National Postal Museum.

Special thanks are due to Cheri Anderson and Erin Labbie for their research assistance, and to Annie Singer for her drawings.

What Are Information Revolutions?

Year by year more people are saying more over more channels on more topics to a bigger total audience. The Internet is exploding. The talk in cable television is of 500 channels. Videotape stores sell used tapes to clear their crowded shelves. Desktop publishing pours out newsletters, self-published books, magazines, and multimedia presentations, with no end in sight. New computer software arrives every day. In free industrial nations, bookstores and magazine stands are jammed with product. Libraries hardly know what to do with all their books. It has been true for decades that anyone can own a book. Now, in industrial societies, almost anyone can own a movie. Meanwhile, more movies are being shot than ever. And desktop video is bringing a budget version of Hollywood to Main Street. Meanwhile, home computers expand information use in ways only recently undreamed.

Even if it were nothing else, our Information Age is the latest in a series of social revolutions that define and span recorded history. A desire to produce communication as well as to consume it has been present in every generation. Venturesome souls have risked personal freedom, savings, reputation, even life and limb to create and distribute information. In the present generation, when technology has merged the computer and other connective media like cable and satellite with end-user media like books and television, opportunities have arisen that find their closest comparison in the fifteenth century, when printing began in Europe and the old limits crumbled.

Defining an Information Revolution

The wish to remember something by writing it down led over the course of millennia to the start of the first information revolution. It and the revolutions that followed would shape humankind more than any wars or any kings ever did or could. With a few scratches, our inventive ancestors set in motion the never ending story of recorded information, the communication and storage of knowledge outside the brain. Here broke history's long dawn.

What would constitute an information revolution? The word *revolution* implies a sudden and often violent change, but revolutions can be more subtle, evolving over decades, even centuries.[1] In the general parlance, *revolution* is an overwrought description of any societal developments. The word long ago became a cliché. Consider it here in the sense of profound changes involving new means of communication that permanently affect entire societies, changes that have shaken political structures and influenced economic development, communal activity, and personal behavior. Unlike so many of our wars and switching of rulers, information revolutions create changes, intended or not, that stick. The new media of information become part of the changing society.

It appears evident that for an information revolution to succeed, media that will provide new means for communication must be disseminated within societies already undergoing change. Communication technologies by themselves are not enough. The media both aid and are aided by whatever has shaken the existing order, for those who seek change will reach out to grasp whatever means become available to gain support for their opinions. This is not a new idea. A Chinese of the T'ang dynasty (7th to 10th centuries A.D.) wrote, "When customs change, writing changes."[2] As those opinions spread, so does awareness of the media themselves. From awareness comes use by other hands. The interwoven cause and effect relationship between social change and media development has continued since the beginnings of recorded history. The argument may be stated this way: if you build a better mousetrap, the world will not beat a path to your door unless the world can be shown that there are mice to be caught. That has been the story of the tools of communication, the "better mousetraps." They have affected much in our lives, but inventions by themselves do not change society. When people want change enough to take action, an invention helps. In the industrial nations throughout the century that we are now completing, change has been constant and constantly desired.

Social revolutions—those that permanently affect the lives of most inhabitants—do not emanate from royal edicts. They grow from disturbed soil, an openness to change, at least at some societal levels. Media join the turbulence, fastening means to purpose. The tools of communication become weapons in some hands, while in others they serve to extend humankind's knowledge and the richness of intelligent life.

The social turbulence that provides the necessary basis for an information revolution leads to independence of thought and the capacity for growth. Graham Greene played a bit fast and loose with history, but made at least a discussable point in *The Third Man*, when his amoral character Harry Lime said, "In Italy for 30 years under the Borgias they had warfare, terror, murder, and bloodshed, but they produced Michaelangelo, Leonardo da Vinci, and the Renaissance. In Switzerland they had brotherly love. They had 500 years of democracy and peace. And what did they produce? The cuckoo clock."

One or more new communication technologies arriving in the midst of social change can lead to an information revolution that adds to the turmoil and, more importantly, leaves permanent marks on the society. Indeed, the world is in the midst of an information revolution now, a period identified with capital letters as the Information Age, a product of the information revolution of the second half of the twentieth century. Yet, the second half of the fifteenth century, following Gutenberg's invention of printing, deserves as much as our own half century to be called the Information Age. A strong claim as the Information Age could also be made for the second half of the nineteenth century, following the inventions of photography and the telegraph, a half century that gave birth to the phonograph, telephone, typewriter, motion pictures, and radio, plus significant changes in printing and early experiments in television and in recording tape technology. Each of these communication technologies was born in the midst of the Industrial Revolution, a time of tension across all layers of contemporaneous society.

Of course, changes in communication occurred during quieter periods as well, but those identified here took a role in creating a qualitative difference in society. The change has always led toward an equalizing of the status of members of society, the road toward democracy. That there has never in human history been true equality should not detract from an appreciation of genuine improvement in human affairs.

Six Information Revolutions

This book identifies six periods in Western history that fit the description of an information revolution. The periods range in time from the eighth century B.C. to the near future.

The first of the six information revolutions may be characterized as the Writing Revolution. It began primarily in Greece about the eighth century B.C., with the convergence of the phonetic alphabet, an import from Phoenicia to the east, and papyrus, an import from Egypt to the south. With writing used to store knowledge, the human mind would no longer be constrained by the limits of memory. Knowledge would be boundless.

The second information revolution, the Printing Revolution, began in Europe in the second half of the fifteenth century, with the convergence of paper, an import originally from China, but proximately from the Arab and Moorish cultures, and a printing system that the German goldsmith Johannes Gutenberg assembled, perhaps from a variety of sources. With printing, information spread through many layers of society. Printing lent itself to massive political, religious, economic, educational, and personal alterations. We have called these changes the Reformation, the Renaissance, humanism, mercantilism, and the end of feudalism. Printing marked the start of the modern world.

The third information revolution, the Mass Media Revolution, began in western Europe and the eastern United States during the middle of the nineteenth century, with the convergence of advances in paper production and printing press methods, and the invention of the telegraph, which changed the way information was conveyed. For the first time, newspapers and magazines reached out to the common man with news about events near and far, and packaged goods for sale. Photography spoke to his heart. Public schools and public libraries dotted the countryside and the growing cities. For the masses, literacy came within reach.

The fourth information revolution, the Entertainment Revolution, started in Europe and America toward the end of the nineteenth century with such technologies as stored sound, affordable cameras, and motion photography. Stories were printed and sold cheaply. Like the pots and pans coming off the assembly lines of the Industrial Revolution, entertainment could now be infinitely replicated and canned. In the coming decades, it would be seen in the nickelodeons and heard on the radio. The whole world would come to love the entertainment products. At the start of the Entertainment Revolution, no one could have imagined the number of hours that we would spend entangled with this love.

The fifth information revolution, the creation of the Communication Toolshed Home, evolved during the middle of the twentieth century, transforming the home into the central location for receiving information and entertainment, thanks to the telephone, broadcasting, recording, improvements in print technologies, and cheap, universal mail services. The century has, of course, been a period of unrelieved political, cultural, and psychological turmoil and shifting. That the media of communication have become inseparable from our lives is a matter that has been written about in countless worried articles, books, and research papers.

The sixth information revolution, the Information Highway, is now being constructed out of the convergence of computer, broadcasting, satellite, and visual technologies. Communication is shaking off transportation for work, study, and play. Yet, if the information-elite can live anywhere, doubt arises about the future of our cities, which grew with the centripetal demands of the Industrial Revolution coupled with sharp population increases.

If economies depend upon information, what does the future hold for vast areas of the globe that are not fully plugged into the information streams? What will happen to our interdependent world of instant communication and weapons of mass destruction if these areas continue to respond with economic stagnation, environmental destruction, and overpopulation? Can we afford to let the Information Highway bypass any communities?

The pace of information revolution is speeding up. The second revolution arrived 1,700 years after the first crested. The last four, each quite distinct, have overlapped during the last two centuries.[3]

Shared Characteristics

Each information revolution appears to share certain characteristics with the others:

- Each is based upon the invention of more than one tool of communication, such as papyrus and the phonetic alphabet, paper and printing, or television and satellites. Their convergences have had powerful effects.
- Each took place where change of a different sort was stirring the society and where a social structure existed that enabled change to occur, such as those in modern Western democracies.
- The tools of communication gave social and political changes added dynamism and were themselves given a forward thrust by those other changes, a symbiotic relationship of cause and effect.[4]
- Information revolutions tended toward some leveling of conditions for those who participated in them. Their results tended to be egalitarian. They pointed toward a greater degree of democratization or sharing of influence than previously existed. Where the use of the tools has been limited, both in ancient times and now, human beings have been less free.
- The changes wrought by these dispersions led toward a greater sharing and

more specialization of knowledge than previously existed. They also led to an overloading of information and to an increase in misinformation.

- As each information revolution has run its course, which was based on the widening availability of the tools of communication, content broadened. More producers sent a greater amount of information on a greater variety of subjects over more channels to more and more receivers.
- The spread of media production, emanating from a multiplicity of independent thought, led to increases in what postmodernism identifies as *decentering* and *fragmentation*, with a widening of the expression of points of view, frames of reference, experiences, and histories. Although by definition *postmodernism* followed *modernism*, elements of a distinctive pattern have been a characteristic of every information revolution.[5]
- Each new communication technology has displaced some other means of communication or behavior that had been satisfactory until the new technology became available. When something was gained, something of value may have been lost.
- All tools of communication have had one or more hardware components and at least one software component; that is, physical tools and methods or systems. As the tools reached more hands, both hardware and software became more complex, but they became simpler to manage. Their unit costs dropped and they were also likely to shrink and to transmit data faster.
- The need for physical transportation to send information has been reduced as communication replaced transportation of messages.
- The tools of communication have been diffused, or distributed, across most of the societies into which they were introduced, or at least that portion of each society that gave—or gives—direction to the whole of that society; in short, the tools were in the hands of each society's movers and shakers. In fully open de-

mocracies, many of the tools are available to those who want them.

- Changes in communication encountered opposition from those who, for political or financial reasons, disliked the changes taking place. Reaction was inevitable from those who must surrender a share of influence and power. They responded both by using the media themselves and by trying to control their use by others. However, given enough time media availability has continued to spread.

- New literacies have arisen to accommodate the new communication technologies, from the phonetic alphabet of the first information revolution to the computer codes of the latest. With each new language has come a new class of experts fully aware of the advantage emanating from the hoarding of their knowledge.

- As to the belief that the average citizen lies increasingly helpless under the heel of political and economic tyrants who dominate the media and suppress freedom of thought, history tells the opposite story. The dissemination of the tools of mass communication has increased the potential for social protest, and to that extent it has made humankind more free, not less. Their limitation has the opposite result.

- Tools of communication were influenced by marketing considerations. Within the boundaries of available technology and scientific possibility, communication tools ultimately have become what their users wanted.

- The technology has changed markedly, but not people's tastes or interests. The old wine is poured into the new bottles.

- Use of communication media, their effects multiplied by their convergence, led inevitably to the separation of their users. Herein lies a dilemma. The tools have given us communication without transportation, yet we still possess a human need for face-to-face contact.

- Heavy personal use of the tools of communication has been accompanied by less social activity. The more time spent with mass communication, the less time has remained for face-to-face communication and group activity. In extreme cases, a social dysfunction has resulted.

- Unlike political revolutions, the dates of social revolutions, including information revolutions, do not lend themselves to pinpointing. All the information revolutions had more or less identifiable beginnings. None has truly ended.

The Power of Information

Communication media intrude into our lives more than most of us realize. They influence our daily activities. We cannot ignore them or abandon them. When we use them judiciously, we harness their strength.

At a national level they have assisted in overthrowing governments. The tools have worked quite efficiently in the hands of those who would sell us every known form of government from democracy to fascism, communism to theocracy. From Tom Paine's *Common Sense* pamphlets to Mao's little red books and the Ayatollah Khomeini's audiotapes, media have been used as tools of revolution. Lenin's smuggled writings promoted the Bolshevik revolution and the underground *samizdat* of writers living under communism promoted its end.

Electronic tools have now joined the printed tools to bring added breadth to revolutionary fervor. Our age has also witnessed successful media use by those who have no apparent ideology, no political agenda other than to grow rich or influential.

Even if control of information does not always include responsibility, it does bring influence by journalists and other writers for the popular media, whom Witold Rybczynski calls the "ragmen of information."

> While secondhand experience still depends, to a certain extent, on personal contact—rumor and hearsay—the greatest single source of most people's secondhand experience is neither education nor conversation, but the media: newspapers, magazines, film, radio, and television. Nowhere is the influence of these ragmen of information

felt more than on the public perception of technology.[6]

Highway and Village

Much consideration will be given in this book to what is called the Information Highway. To abuse an overworked metaphor, let us note that highways have directions, and their travelers have points of departure and destinations. As the telephone companies, cable companies, and broadcasting companies pour the cement, there are strong indications that this new highway is not coming from the public library or the news office despite the publicity releases, as much as it is coming from the cinema, the shopping mall, and the video arcade. What we, the audience, want is oftentimes the stuff of dreams.

And where is this information highway going? It is not heading toward the "global village." Marshall McLuhan was correct in foreseeing the technological possibility of a "global village" in which most of humankind could share information.[7] However, his metaphor of a village, where folks normally communicate by talking face to face, presumes that radio and television are returning us to an oral culture; for example, "...the electric implosion now brings oral and tribal ear-culture to the literate West."[8] Yet, broadcasting although it strikes the ear, has not returned us to an oral culture, which is based upon a two-way, limited scale of information on a human dimension. Instead, one-way radio and television, plus their content of recordings and motion pictures, are oral versions of the limitless quantity of information that identifies a written culture that no single human being can absorb in its totality.

A further reality has been that only on rare occasions, such as a lunar walk, the Olympic Games, or the Gulf War, do we venture together into the shared space of a global village. Mostly, we prefer to retreat into our homes, where we now spend so much of our time with so many communication media that our homes can be thought of as *communication toolsheds*, which is another focus of this book. It is to

these individual toolsheds that the Information Highway will have its offramps.

The information will be cheaper, enabling larger segments of the population to ride on the Highway and dwell in communication toolsheds. At the turn of the century, the cost of renting a telephone for a month represented about two weeks wages for an average workman. The first commercial television sets sold for half the cost of a new car. Just a few decades ago the thought of self-publishing anything except via mimeograph was almost out of the question for middle-class Americans. Today, even making a movie is not beyond a middle-class purse.

Sorting Media from Content

Why do we believe what we believe? What are the sources of our opinions and attitudes? Although the answers to such broad questions are complex, it is obvious that almost everything we know about present events beyond our limited horizons comes from media. In this we are different from ancestors who learned most of what they knew through direct experience. If not from such current events media as newspapers, radio, and television, our information has come from books, the storehouses of human memory. At times our information is mediated through other people who derive their information from communications media and may distort it in the process.

It is a highly arguable point, but in relative terms of societal good, what we are watching, the content, may not matter as much as the way we shape our lives around media. The medium, Marshall McLuhan told us, is the message. The effects of content are quite independent of the effects of using the medium carrying it. For example, the effects on a child of watching violent cartoons and junkfood commercials on a Saturday morning are quite distinct from the effects of spending the entire Saturday morning watching television, no matter what is on.

It has been argued that the problem with television, a justifiable focus of irritation, is that society, especially producers and educators, has not fully marshaled its resources to use the television medium wisely, or in fact to consider this medium the way we regard the medium of books as existing for more than financial gain. Yet, a visit to the paperback racks of any drugstore will remind us that books are not always used as means of acquiring knowledge. It is useful to distinguish content from the carriers of content, media.

Replacing Transportation

Through recorded time, most communication depended upon transportation. Information was bound by human limitations, the sound of a voice, the time it took a pair of feet, or a horse, or a ship to reach a destination. Communication technology changed that. Human limitations fell away.

The promise of the Internet and the rest of the Information Highway is even more replacement of transportation. Shopping by electronic catalog, working and learning at home via computer modem and facsimile, video teleconferencing in place of business travel, acquiring specialized education, and receiving computer-assisted diagnostic medical care are all reporting success.

If significant parts of one's work, marketing, education, entertainment, and well-being can be accomplished without leaving home, will more people choose to live in the countryside instead of in cities or suburbs? Will they choose San Francisco and commute electronically to Omaha instead of living in Omaha? Such a pattern could lead to a further decline in cities.

Population transfers resulting from technology are not new. The Industrial Revolution shoveled people out of the countryside into cities. The post-World War II shift of middle-class families from the city to the suburbs, a move encouraged by the technologies of cars and highways, altered American life. A new population shift based on the emerging communication technologies promises to shake up life as much as these earlier mass movements did.

Shaping and Being Shaped

As we spend time with the tools of communication, we spend less time with one another. Fewer Americans attend town or school meetings. Voter turnout has declined. At the same time, distrust of government has grown. Memberships in the PTA, the League of Women Voters, and labor unions is down, while social distrust is up. Fewer volunteers turn out for the Boy Scouts, Red Cross, Lions Club, Shriners, and Jaycees.[9] The nation has drifted from De Tocqueville's observation in the early nineteenth century that Americans liked to form civic associations. In organizations whose membership has increased, like the Sierra Club, the National Organization of Women, and the American Association of Retired Persons, people do not normally attend meetings.

McLuhan observed that not only the media are shaped. As the technology is shaped for and by its users, the technology shapes the users. It shapes our lives and our views. When enough people adopt a new means of communication so that people change the way they go about their daily activities, the society itself is altered.

> …in operational and practical fact, the medium is the message. This is merely to say that the personal and social consequences of any medium—that is, of any extension of ourselves—result from the new scale that is introduced into our affairs by each extension of ourselves, or by any new technology.
> …the "message" of any medium or technology is the change of scale or pace or pattern that it introduces into human affairs.[10]

For example, the ways that we use a computer changed because the technology changed. Because it is more efficient than it used to be to work on an airplane or even in a taxi weaving through traffic, people now work who once relaxed while traveling by reading a magazine article about something unrelated to their work, or staring out of a window and thinking, or chatting with a seatmate. Now the traveler works. We changed the media and then the media changed us.

Difficult Beginnings

Many tools of communication began with quite limited ownership. For the centuries when books were hand produced by monks and booksellers, most people lived out their lives not knowing that such a thing as a book existed, let alone ever seeing a book. For a half century after its invention, the still camera was a complicated piece of equipment for the serious hobbyist and the professional. Even though ordinary people aspired to own photographs they did not think of owning a camera. The videotape recorder and the video camera were not initially designed for untrained hands. Scientists alone worked with the first computers. In 1943 IBM chairman Thomas Watson said, "I think there is a world market for maybe five computers."

Some familiar means of personal communication began as tools of government and business, but achieved success in personal use. The world's postal systems, a real communication technology, belong to this category. In the last quarter of the nineteenth century, the typewriter, the telephone, the phonograph, and the radio all saw the first light of day as aids to the world of commerce. In the twentieth century, audiotape, videotape, and the computer evolved with no idea that millions of ordinary people would take them into their homes. Those familiar business and government tools, the fax machine and the copier, are in the process of joining them in the home.

Not all technologies showed immediate promise. The telegraph and the computer went through periods of government support and little public acceptance. In time, they altered our world.

New technologies found acceptance when their superiority over existing technologies for specific uses was recognized, but diffusion required an infrastructure that extended far beyond an invention, bringing together elements of business, finance, engineering, and government regulation. Businesses and individuals adopted the telephone because it offered an attractive alternative to communication by mail and telegraph. Then structures grew in support of the technology to that end. Before the turn of the century, Bell's telephone company, formed soon after the telephone's invention in 1876, had become AT&T. By 1920, a web of telephone wires provided long distance service for much of the country, and conducting business by telephone had become a norm of American business.

Some common tools of communication may have begun their public existence as novelties beyond most people's understanding of how they could possibly have any meaning to daily life, yet as they were diffused into society, the public found that meaning. Public feedback led to further refinement, which in turn led to new uses by yet more people. Photography, for instance, had value for almost no one except hobbyists until a steady stream of improvements led first to a demand for family pictures and later to a rush to own simple cameras that required only the push of a button. Market driven, photography flowed into art and journalism. It spread to printed media and, in motion pictures, photography spawned a new medium of arguably greater impact than its own.

As the quality of communication tools improved and their advantages became known, they spread throughout their potential market. Their costs dropped in the pattern of the so-called "calculator syndrome" that has affected the entire electronics industry. Engineers also improved designs to make the equipment easier to operate. The "buttons" went inside. Video cameras and decks, once limited mostly to television stations and industries, metamorphosed into camcorders, a hot selling item for the home. As a result, for a growing number of families, spoken words and pictures have replaced words written on paper. A letter to a distant loved one is sent in the form of a video. In high schools, the video yearbook joins the familiar bound version.

Life Is Different

The success of the means of communication in becoming almost transparent to the user has the unintended effect of leading us to overlook their individual and collective impact on the society.

For example, consider the percentage of our lives devoted to watching a television screen. The set is on in the average American home for more than seven hours a day. Our general sense that life is different than it was only a few short years ago—more comfortable or more dangerous, more under our control or more beyond it—may fail to lead us thoughtfully to consider that among the reasons that we regard life as different is the time we spend looking at phosphor dots. It is just a step from regarding life as different to regarding life as strange. That may raise some concerns and unease that can affect our attitudes about the world around us. Heavy television users, for instance, tend on the whole to be more fearful persons than non-users. As a result of our concerns, we may hesitate to go out at night, we may buy a deadbolt lock or a large dog, and we may vote for a law-and-order candidate for mayor, all without the attendant recognition that our attitudes can be traced to one of the tools of communication in the toolsheds that we call our homes.

Recent telephone technologies like cellular phones and facsimile machines have affected some occupations, such as selling real estate and the lunch trade of some city restaurants. In the late 1980s and the early 1990s, *cellular* and *fax* were hot items in news stories and full page ads, so they got a lot of attention, but telephone answering machines, based on a simple technology, never were exciting. Yet, when we arrive at home each evening, because of its time-shifting advantage the answering machine may be our first stop after opening the front door. It liberated us from the need to be physically near the telephone if we awaited an important call. It will remain an important tool of communication until the telephone itself shrinks to a cellphone that is as convenient to carry as a wallet, and we are always "at home."

It is the communication tools themselves and their effect upon the societies into which they were introduced that compose these chapters, the communication tools that we all pick up as comfortably as a Saturday sweater.

Political Tools and Weapons

Russian television carried the horrors from Chechnya, of hungry dogs circling the corpses in Grozny. For decades such scenes, neither photographed nor transmitted, did not disturb the Kremlin's rigid control. No longer. Russia and the rest of the world are far different places now that television cameras see, videotape records, satellites transmit, and television sets in living rooms show. Even if the Kremlin had the power it once had to block broadcasts on Russian media, CNN would beam the signals from the border of Finland to Vladivostok. Jamming a satellite TV signal is considerably more difficult than jamming radio. With 24-hour-a-day financial transactions and the penetration by global news agencies, we live in what is becoming a borderless world.

The power of the tools of mass communication first to shake and then to shape national policy was evident on the streets of American cities during the Vietnam War. It became clearer in the Soviet Union just a few years ago.

> ...while it once appeared that the new media would enhance the power of governments (as, for example, Orwell argued in *1984*), their effect recently has been the opposite: breaking state monopolies of information, permeating national boundaries, allowing peoples to hear and see how others do things differently. It has also made richer and poorer countries more aware of the gap between them than was possible a half century ago, and stimulated legal and illegal migration.[11]

Arresting Gorbachev

In 1991, a cabal of old-guard Communist leaders tried to overthrow the more liberal government of Mikhail Gorbachev. The Soviet President, his family, and aides were placed under house arrest in a villa on the Crimean peninsula hundreds of miles south of Moscow. The plotters did their best to shut down telephone, radio, and television communication. But something went wrong. The plotters were either not aware of the Internet, the globe-girdling network of computer networks, or they did not worry about it. They should have. Boris Yeltsen knew about the enormous network and was tapping it to plot counter strategy with experts at NATO. Some of his statements, relayed back to the Soviet Union by the Voice of America, rallied public support. At the same time, shut off from what was going on, Gorbachev and his aides rummaged around in the basement and came up with some old radio sets in working order. They were able to pick up signals from the BBC, the Voice of America, and Radio Liberty. Reports of the coup and its collapse made it easier for Gorbachev to act quickly to resume power.

The coup failed and, in the days that followed, a stunned world listened as the Soviet empire fell apart. That world of listeners included the people of the Soviet Union themselves, who were denied local radio.

"They have closed the papers, but that's not so important," said Vladimir Sluzhekov, a reporter, as he stood by a surging crowd of demonstrators. "The radio—that's what hurts. Without the radio, no one knows what's going on except the people who are right here."[12]

However, through glasnost, the policy of openness, they were getting access to worldwide radio and television sources from the streets of Moscow.

I think the histories of these incredible three days will focus heavily on Radio Free Europe and the Voice of America and the BBC, for relaying back to the Russian people what Boris Yeltsin was saying.[13]

On just one data network between Moscow and Helsinki, 13,000 messages were counted. Fax machines and cellular phones carried reports to distant corners of the empire, emboldening those who opposed the coup. Self-printed samizdat were augmented by the electronic magnitizdat. In the end, the plotters of a return to the tyranny of the past were undone, at least in part, by the tools of the Information Age. Nowhere have the effects of the information revolution of the twentieth century been more evident than in nations where information clashed with autocratic rule.

"If it hadn't been for television—and radio, too—none of this would be happening." Those were the words of a friend who has long experience of Russia and Russians. We were watching news reports of jubilant crowds in Red Square as tanks retreated. Only a few years ago, she said, all of the dirty business of the coup could have been carried out in secret. But now, "because of television, nothing can be hidden." Or, as a State Department official told the Washington Post, "The bottom line is, you can't lie to people any more. You're going to get caught."[14]

Tiananmen Square

An earlier round of communication wizardry came to widespread public attention in China, a millennium and more ago the wellspring of such communication technology as paper and printing, but now its recipient. The events in Tiananmen Square are further evidence that the tools of communication can make life difficult for even the most determined dictatorships by sending out text and pictures where the government preferred silence and darkness.

Early in the summer of 1989, taking advantage of an influx of foreign reporters covering the state visit of the Soviet leader Mikhail Gorbachev, a thousand university students in Beijing occupied Tiananmen Square and began a hunger strike as a protest against the rigid government of China. An estimated 300,000 protesters supported them in Beijing as demonstrations erupted in cities across China. Some students in Tiananmen Square sculpted their own version of the Statue of Liberty, the "goddess of freedom and democracy." The world watched, stunned, as television news stories and pictures were beamed out by satellite day after day.

At first, Deng Xiaoping's government appeared just as shocked. Then it unrolled an intense campaign of disinformation while it tried to put an end to the western coverage by pulling the plugs on the satellite feeds, but its efforts at censorship were circumvented, mostly by now familiar tools of communication, but partly by a new piece of equipment, the Pixilator, an electronic device that broke an individual video frame into bits for transmission over an ordinary telephone line. The government's efforts to limit what the camera was able to photograph were also frustrated by small, low-light 8mm cameras which, in the hands of one resourceful photographer, was hidden in a shoebox tied to a bicycle.

The flyaway portable satellite uplink found effective employment in Beijing. Brought there by a CNN crew to supplement the overworked Chinese uplinks during the visit by Soviet President Gorbachev, a flyaway uplink was transmitting video pictures accompanying television news reports when the student demonstrations began. The Chinese government could not "pull the plug," for in this case it was not their plug. The CNN signal traveled a complex route. Its transmission frequency was converted from Ku-band to C-band as it moved from Beijing to a satellite to a relay station in California to another satellite to the CNN news center in Atlanta, then was returned to Beijing two seconds later as part of a satellite newscast, a trip of 200,000 miles. The pictures were sharp, dramatic, and so damaging to the Chinese government that the CNN crew was commanded to stop the transmissions. As the city was under martial law, the journalists had little option but to comply. Yet, they had accomplished much because the entire world was witness to the protests.

When the Chinese government-run television broadcasts did not reveal the truth about the demonstrations which spread rapidly from city to city, people across China turned to overseas radio broadcasts.

Meanwhile, renegade Chinese students abroad mobilized telephones, facsimile machines, audiotape, the mails, and the Bitnet telecommunications network to keep abreast of the latest news.

> The fax machines are, in a way, the fuel of the (Chinese) revolution. The faxed materials inform, encourage, embolden the young revolutionaries. They have become the wall posters of this generation. Never has there been anything like it.[15]

Newsweek reported:

> The students collected about 1,500 fax numbers in China from anyone who knew them. They posted the numbers on their computer bulletin boards and sent their messages without any idea who was at the other end—the electronic equivalent of a note in a bottle. In China, students, hotel waiters or office workers retrieved the messages; then they were reproduced by the hundreds in photocopiers and put on public display.[16]

They fed back into Chinese cities outside Beijing what was happening in their own capital city. Faxes, multiplied by copier machines, sometimes ended up as wall posters, a simple but effective news distribution system. In at least one city, Nanjing, large crowds gathered around boom boxes tuned loudly to the Voice of America. Elsewhere the direct-dial telephone and the photocopier spread the news.

> Now from China comes the news that the police are guarding the fax machines. What comes next, house arrest for the telephone? Interrogation for the portable computer and its modem? Will we see a cellular phone in manacles?
>
> There is something horribly appropriate about the attempt by this government to take back the fax. It is not just the student leaders who are being held responsible for protests this time. Nor is it just reporters who are being expelled for spreading the word. It is the demon of communication technology itself...
>
> In China, days of protest and repression have shown the relationship between information and freedom, technology and democracy. Between fax and facts.[17]

A *Wall Street Journal* article added this:

> Can the (Chinese) government keep news reports from making their way back to China? Fax machines in this country have been speeding photographs and newspaper articles across the Pacific ever since the protests began. International phone lines are humming...China's 40,000 students in the U.S. write letters home. Hong Kong television is picked up in Canton. The Voice of America...is reportedly ready to transmit from a jam-proof site in the Philippines. China's days as an isolated empire are definitively over.
>
> The Chinese may call their country the Middle Kingdom, but it's really just a billion-citizen suburb of McLuhan's global village.[18]

The government at last put an end to the protests by brutal repression at night, at an hour when the camera's eye saw only dimly, then began a public relations campaign by all its available means of mass communication to create a different reality. Meanwhile, the satellite pictures from the West were examined by government authorities to identify protesters to be arrested. Some of those pictures were shown on Chinese television to enlist public help in locating protesters who otherwise might have gone into hiding to form an underground movement.

From the start, the events of May and June in China were not only reported by the tools of mass communication, they were altered by them. Never had more dramatic evidence been offered of the power of communication technology to alter the course of history.

The Infection of Mass Communication

To stop the infection brought by free access to mass communication, governments take whatever steps they can get away with short of engendering revolts in the streets. ABC's Ted Koppel saw at first hand how easily the contagion can spread.

> When I was in China last year at this time, the Chinese students over there did much of what they did because they had seen on television what Solidarity had done in Poland. When I was in Romania, I learned that the revolution over there began in the small city of Timasoara because Timasoara happens to be on the border with Yugoslavia and Hungary, and it was there that they—as distinct from the rest of the Romanians and the rest of the country—saw CNN broadcasts at one o'clock in the morning on Romanian television explaining to them what was happening in Hungary.
>
> In other words, the interaction that exists, exists on such a level that it is producing revolution in the world today. It is producing changes, the substance of which is absolutely indisputable.[19]

Some version of media-aided uprising could be found from Chile, where banned movies, documentaries, and protest music were circulated on videotapes, to the Baltic countries, where videos of protest demonstrations were shot. In the Philippines, a "living room video" of news reports of the assassination of President Ferdinand Marcos' political opponent Benigno Aquino was among the videotapes widely copied and shown to groups of people gathered in living rooms. Spliced-together newsreels were available as video rentals. Massive mailings of news clippings added fuel to the fires of anger that eventually toppled Marcos and brought Aquino's widow, Corazon Aquino, to power.[20]

Governments have proven virtually powerless to stop determined underground exchanges of media. In many developing countries, television sets and videotape recorders set up in villages to carry government-approved material were being diverted to whatever videocassettes the villagers found more interesting. Some government agencies supply and advertise entertaining tapes just to attract villagers, hoping they'll stay for their own tapes. People tune out state television to view a wide selection of cassettes.[21]

> If VCRs and videocassettes had never done anything but alleviate the oppressions of censorship, they would have earned an important place in history. Their powers have not stopped there, but have extended in innumerable directions. Videotaped press releases, home made videotapes of hostages

passed to the mass media by terrorist groups, and individual purchases of satellite and cable TV time to show specially pre- pared videos, are a few of the new means of individual political expression made possi- ble by this medium.[22]

Terrorism and the Media

That we live in the midst of an information revolution is not by itself a cause for cele- bration. If one component of revolutionary fervor is the demand to be heard, then the wish can be granted without overthrowing a government. No one knows this better than the modern terrorist who neither knows nor cares to know his fellow air or ship travelers, through whom he can achieve the heady experience of reaching a global audience.

> The terrorist operating within (a liberal) society knows that his acts of terrorism will be instantly publicized by the television, radio and press and that pictures of a really sensational attack or outrage can be relayed round the world with the aid of TV satel- lites.[23]

Another comment on the same subject:

> The terrorists and the TV executives cooper- ate in raising terror and ratings. There would still be terrorism without TV, but it wouldn't have much impact on us.[24]

Beirut and Iranian hostage takers sporadi- cally issued photographs and videotapes of their American and European victims that American and European journalists eagerly featured on the front pages of their newspapers and played and replayed on television newscasts. As anticipated, public opinion, pricked by hostage relatives, was aroused by their cries to their governments to *do* something. Thus, the forceful political tools of media were employed to generate the emotions essential to undergird foreign policy shifts in democracies. What lasting effects they had is arguable, but they cer- tainly augmented the general impression that Jimmy Carter was an ineffectual presi- dent. The disastrous helicopter effort to rescue the hostages in Tehran grew out of a public demand, inflamed by those pictures, to *do* something.

All this the journalists reported, for jour- nalists and terrorists, pursuing parallel paths for what Margaret Thatcher called the "oxygen of publicity,"[25] act out of dis- tinctly different motives, but share the goal of seeking maximum drama from the tak- ing of hostages.

Clandestine Radio

Unapproved, clandestine radio stations have been broadcasting for decades, fre- quently from a transmitter outside the tar- get country's borders, so its government cannot shut them down. Often an opposing government supports the clandestine sta- tions, a fact ignored in the broadcasts, which claim to be "The voice of a free...... (name of country)." Where conflict exists, either civil war or strife between nations, clandestine radio has become a weapon. During the Cold War, such radio stations were scattered across Europe, Asia, and Africa.

It should have come as no surprise that the end of the Cold War brought an increase in the number of clandestine stations. Al- though it seemed to be time to sign off the air, many stations that had existed because of the hostilities between the United States and the Soviet Union did not do so. They kept broadcasting because the new free- doms and halting movements to democ- racy unleashed nationalistic fervor and demands for change. The numbers of pro- ducers of media have increased because there was influence to be had.

Opposition television may not be far be- hind. A report from the laboratory prom- ised direct broadcast satellite reception to anyone with a receiver the size of a dinner napkin.

Censorship does not block news flow as it once did. Shepherds now receive news as quickly as national leaders do. Goat herd- ers in Siberian villages now watch their republic's news each night and they're talk- ing about it.[26] Bedouins on their camels listen to radios as they cross the Sahara.

Middle Eastern Examples of Media's Force

In the Middle East, the rapid spread of transistor radios was credited with having contributed to the resurgence of Arab nationalism.[27] In Iraq, Saddam Hussein banned typewriters for years, perhaps recalling his own use of a typewriter and a mimeograph machine as he plotted to seize power. In remote Balochistan, deep in the mountains of Pakistan, radio made the difference:

> ...illiteracy here was ninety-five percent but everyone seemed to have a radio, and in the most isolated villages tribesmen were agile in discussing world affairs. Undeveloped Balochistan certainly was; backward it certainly was not.[28]

Meanwhile, Israelis and Jordanians continued to watch each other's television programs. Pakistanis watched Indian movies while their armies sniped at one another.

An interesting if perverse example of the power of tools of communication arose in Iran during the 1970s, where the government of Shah Reza Pahlevi, an absolute monarch, used communication extensively, but did so counterproductively. His regime rapidly acquired a formidable arsenal of broadcasting equipment and computers for information storage and retrieval.[29] Books and films were censored or refused publication. *Macbeth* and *Hamlet* were prohibited because they showed the murder of a king.[30]

> At the same time, with effects that were more subtle but no less real, the TV portrayal of upper and middle-class standards of living must have augmented the sense of injustice, envy and outrage felt by the poor and the devout.[31]

Countering the government's control of television and other "large media," a communication network of "small media" arose across Iran, centered on 90,000 mosques supplemented by meetings in lecture halls and private homes where audiotapes carrying religious messages were either played or read in mimeographed transcripts. The Ayatollah Khomeini sent fiery pronouncements from his Paris exile on audiotapes that were transcribed and either Xeroxed or mimeographed. A Tehran University professor commented, "We are struggling against autocracy, for democracy, by means of xerocracy."[32] Clandestine radio stations located outside Iran pumped in more messages. When the call to revolution came, the masses responded. The opposition made itself felt in the streets in 1978 with strikes and demonstrations, astonishing observers with well orchestrated demonstrations of as many as three million people.[33]

> Through centuries of war, battle plans were roughly the same: secure the main garrison or palace. When the new flag went up, it was all over. High ground is now the transmission tower; the new flag is a different face in the anchor's chair.[34]

For would-be revolutionaries, the tools of communication have the decided advantage of privacy over public rallies as a way to spread the message.[35] Messages of hate and calls to revolt can be received in the privacy of the home, where no stranger intrudes and where virtually no danger exists of the policeman's billy club.

New World Information Order

The U.N. was at the center of a controversy about transmitting information that governments did not like across their frontiers. UNESCO, the United Nations Educational, Scientific, and Cultural Organization, was the forum of bitter debates about the worldwide flow of information. The argument of many Third World countries was that the principal news agencies, controlled in the industrialized West, distorted what was going on in the developing nations by emphasizing natural and man-made disasters, dictatorship, government corruption, and backwardness. The spread of such stories around the world, it was argued, accomplished little more than to humiliate the developing countries and harm their efforts at improvement.

It was further argued that, because of the diffusion of the tools of communication, like inexpensive shortwave portable radios in the huts of peasants, the power of Western-based media, with their Western culture and biases, had become too great, poking into the countries being examined and undermining them. The flow of news between First and Third World nations was deeply imbalanced. Direct broadcast satellites posed an even greater threat as their signals spilled over into many countries with televised entertainment, carrying information and culture beyond the power of national governments to counter.

Censorship and jamming cannot halt the communication flow across porous borders. What Third World countries proposed was a New World Information and Communication Order of international agreements about communication. If Western journalists chose to ignore a basic tenet of public journalism—that journalism should serve to improve society—then they should be pressed to do so.

Needless to say, proponents of freedom of information bitterly opposed the idea of a New World Information and Communication Order, convinced that much of the opposition stemmed from the fear by these regimes that the media could be a crowbar that pried out their entrenched dictatorships. Opponents argued, among other things, that the proposal was nothing more than a wish to expand from national to international censorship, the purpose of which was to perpetuate corrupt governments and hide the misery and poverty of the majority of their populations. Opponents of the NWICO argued that the fancy phrases were doubletalk to maintain authority in the hands of dictators who already controlled their nation's presses and microphones. Look, they said, at the record of journalists either murdered or silenced by death threats against their families or simply the threat of being deprived of the relative prosperity permitted by their livelihood.

The argument may never end. At present, it is less heated than in the past, and the New World Information and Communication Order has yet to be established, but the issue has not disappeared. Whatever the outcome, the quarrel has shown the influence of modern tools of mass communication on life in even the most remote of villages.

Cultural Imperialism

Entertainment supplies another form of information, so it came as no surprise when governments of smaller nations around the globe sounded the alarm at what they defined as the "cultural imperialism" of Western, especially American, fictional television fare. American attitudes, at least those displayed by Hollywood and the television networks, toward the family structure, government executives, the police, sex, and religious values are by no means uniformly shared around the world. In addition, what struck American viewers as innocent fun was viewed with alarm by political leaders in some less developed nations because of the potential of situation comedies, soap operas, and adventure shows to make the people of their countries dissatisfied with their own lots when they saw unattainable levels of freedom and opulence. The potential of mass media as an agent of social change has not escaped notice beyond our frontiers. For example, a dispatch from Reuters:

> China's television minister called Thursday for vigilant control of programming. Minister of Radio, Film and Television Ai Zhisheng, writing in the People's Daily, urged broadcast officials to keep a tight grip on the flourishing satellite TV market, which over two years has virtually slipped from government control....
>
> "Keeping a firm grip on the direction of public opinion is an important responsibility of television as the mouthpiece of the party and government," he wrote in a long commentary.[36]

Media cultural imperialism, sometimes dubbed "Coca-colonization," has been a familiar subject of debate in international forums.

> "A lot of us really admire Americans' way of living: better houses, better education. I

want CNN," said Muhammad Ishgi, a Chamber of Commerce official in the Red Sea port of Jidda. "But there is what you might call an American cultural danger to us, because they show us another way to look at things. They tell us we might do things differently. You must know that education is a weapons system. It can go either way."[37]

Before the Berlin Wall crumbled and the two Germanys were locked together, a survey showed that Dresden area residents were five times as likely to seek permission to leave as other East Germans, grumbling that life under communism was intolerable without the consolation of television from West Germany. The city was too distant from the border of West Germany to receive its television signals over the air. After discussion, local authorities in the East German city of Dresden brought West German signals in by cable. Likewise, in Canton, China, observing that rooftop antennae were pointed toward Hong Kong, the communist authorities allowed dubbed versions of an American police adventure program and a Mexican soap opera. Anecdotes like this can be found in other places where television is sharply controlled.

Economic Freedom with Political Controls

A fundamental question facing countries that want economic development along with dictatorial political control is whether they can have both in the Information Age. The dictators and oligarchs who run countries want the latest electronic communications in order to compete in today's global marketplace, but they don't want the thoughts that pour through them. Exiled dissidents from safe havens in western democracies are sending home all the subversive material they can by all the media they can, especially these days over the Internet.

Dictators who acquired power by subversive means complain of western-sponsored subversion. They also complain of cultural imperialism and fret that their populaces are being ruined by what they are seeing and hearing via television, radio, computers, and telephones, but they can

only slow the process; they cannot stop it. That does not, however, keep the oligarchs from trying, as the Iranian government did in 1994 by restricting use and ownership of an estimated 250,000 satellite dishes as a means of keeping Western influence out. Some dish owners risked heavy fines, so they disguised the rooftop dishes as air conditioners.

As an editorial put it, "Tyranny cannot survive in a nation equipped with fax machines and video cameras, the high technology of free speech."[38] Other comments:

In the long run, a country can't have a modern economy or society without its megabytes and modems, its phones and fax machines. It cannot conduct research or business without the ability of communicate easily, directly, personally.[39]

From *The Economist*:

The telephone, the calculator and the personal computer are gradually outflanking the thought-police. Only places that cannot yet afford those gadgets, plus the North Koreans and Albanians which still manage to control every corner of life, are immune to the effects of this new wave of self knowledge.[40]

To this short list of media-controlled countries can be added the pieces of what once was Yugoslavia. In Slovenia, Croatia, and, especially, Serbia, rigid controls came down on television, radio, and print. Their somewhat isolated populations heard a propaganda storm of hatred and lies directed at their neighbors. The mutual vilification by what someone called *media gangsters*, unchecked and untempered by other voices, allowed the mutual slaughter to proceed.[41]

"Always we first protected the typewriters, then the printing presses, and then ourselves," recalled the editor of a Polish underground weekly newspaper.[42] Once free, the Polish people continue to use media, but far differently:

Consider a Polish family settling into the Friday night TV lineup with remote control in hand, a cable box atop the color set and a satellite dish outside the window.

They can flick between lowbrow and high, new American or classic, MTV or the Simpsons. They can tune in CNN or European or Polish stations for news or political discussion. There is the wildly popular satire, "Polish Zoo."...

Poland, a country of some 10 million television sets, all dutifully tuned to propaganda during the 40-plus years of Communist rule, is being wired for almost anything these days.[43]

Asked what caused the fall of communism in Eastern Europe, Polish president Lech Walesa pointed to a TV set. "It all came from there," he said.[44] He also said it was "especially radio (which) brought information prohibited in our country. It raised our spirits, strengthened faith and hope. It created a feeling of togetherness and international solidarity of free people."[45]

Altering American Politics

It is not only outside the borders of the United States that mass communication technology can alter governments. News and commentary have been credited—or blamed—for helping to bring down Senator Joseph McCarthy and President Richard Nixon.

In 1995, Lamar Alexander of Tennessee began a campaign for the Republican presidential nomination by announcing it on the Internet. "No bunting, no pretzels, no beer," said his media adviser, Mike Murphy.[46] Vice President Al Gore and Speaker of the House Newt Gingrich were among leaders who carried politics into cyberspace. There they were joined by everyone from highly organized groups to angry loners across the entire spectrum of issues.

Each new communications medium in America elevated leaders who could use it. FDR was radio itself. JFK and Reagan thrived on television. But these were unifying mediums, at least when there were only three networks. The nation assembled, literally, in front of them to hear and see real-time theater. But who could possibly lead a nation of cybertribes in a time-shifting world with no center stage?[47]

If mainstream politicians could use the media, so could political extremists. It is not necessary to be a political leader to disseminate opinions. At least one pro-Nazi computer bulletin board managed to surface on the Prodigy network. A racist talk show, *Race and Reason*, turned up across the United States on public access cable channels where it could be taped for later group viewing.[48] Its producer, Tom Metzger, hardly a household name, could thus extend his unpleasant opinions far and wide, visible testimony not only to the First Amendment, but to the democratic effects of the tools of communication.

The Gulf War

The Gulf War was characterized by high-tech weaponry and a public glued to their television sets for what came to be labeled the *CNN syndrome*. No amateur at manipulating media, the general in charge of the coalition forces was moved to remind everyone that real blood was being spilled. War, said General Norman Schwarzkopf, is "not a Nintendo game."

Yet, it seemed so. The war may have appeared unreal to some of the hundreds of millions of people around the globe who watched the bridges and buildings blowing up, seeing it through the camera lenses of the very missiles that struck the targets. A science fiction unreality accompanied the Gulf War. It was not only the Stealth airplanes, the missiles that intercepted missiles, or the smart bombs, but the *cleanliness* of a Buck Rogers war. We all knew, of course, that this war like all wars was not clean, but was filled with pain, misery, and death. Yet while we knew it, most of us did not see it or hear it, so we did not feel it, as one should feel wars, in our guts. Instead, we were treated to the glossiest presentation to date of the glossiest war to date, at least from the Western perspective.

The wizardry of mass communication technology effortlessly sent the audience ping-ponging from videotape of missiles landing to actual live views of incoming missiles in Saudi Arabia, from statements by officials in Washington to interviews in Amman, from a few moments at a ruined house in Israel to a walk through a ruined neighborhood in Baghdad.

With these instant images and on-the-spot reports burning in their minds, yet with virtually no knowledge of events other than those supplied by modern mass communication, people in scores of cities around the world took to the streets to support one political course of action or another. Government leaders heard them and, in many instances, after seeing and hearing the same mass mediated reports, added their own voices. The full consequences of this public action, informed and inspired by mass communication reporting, may not be known for years, but the likelihood that consequences result from mass media is certain, just as consequences followed news coverage of the Vietnam War a generation before. General Schwarzkopf at a military briefing sardonically thanked reporters who were fooled into believing the fully revealed plans for a seaborne invasion of Kuwait, a disinformation strategy that kept Iraqi guns pointed in the wrong direction.

A review of what might be called the top 10 technologies of coverage during the Gulf War may be instructive, evidence of the current pace of communications technology:

1. E-mail links connected reporters at newsworthy scenes with producers at distribution centers in spite of the turmoil.

2. Still pictures of high quality destined for newspapers and magazines could be sent in either analog or digital form by radio and ordinary telephone lines.

3. The ability to transmit pictures from the scene of events was matched by frame capture equipment that received them in newsrooms thousands of miles away.

4. Portable facsimile machines could move reporters' stories and other documents quickly from any telephone.

5. Even when bombs demolished the Baghdad telephone exchange, a special satellite uplink permitted by the Iraqi government only to Cable News Network served

as a long-distance intercom to carry reports, notably those of foreign correspondent Peter Arnett, who concluded, "I was having an impact on what was happening."

6. Remote-sensing technology enabled ABC News to show pictures taken from a satellite of such scenes as the Kuwaiti oil well fires. (A French commercial satellite had alerted the world of the Chernobyl disaster.)

7. Laptop computers carried by reporters were linked by modem with central news bureaus. That simplified and expedited the news dispatches.

8. Flyaway satellite uplinks, relatively easy to transport, let television correspondents send live video from remote locations on short notice.

9. The correspondents did so via international data transmission networks, a complex of satellites, uplinks, downlinks, and transmission facilities that could focus the world's attention on a patch of desert sand. Wire service reporters could call in their stories via portable satellite telephones.

10. Computer graphics added a high-tech glitter to the on-air reports of this high-tech war.

Watching the televised Gulf War or the more recent tank shelling of the Russian parliament building, we were now living in the world of "Imagine that!" Thanks to communication technology it may have seemed that we had awakened inside an arcade game. Small wonder that, by an overwhelming percentage, Americans at home supported and applauded the Gulf War, whereas the Vietnam War two decades earlier brought riots into our city streets.

Journalists in Vietnam were enviably free to roam about. Less enviable were the logistics of television reports. The black-and-white 16 millimeter film traveled by truck, car, and then airplane to the United States for processing in a West Coast film lab, after which an edited segment was transmitted to New York at considerable cost over leased wideband telephone company lines for showing to the American public two or three days after the film was shot. Compare this with the instantaneous live switching from Baghdad to Dhahran to Tel Aviv to London to New York, and so forth, sometimes accompanied by videotape shot moments earlier or even by those pictures transmitted by a bomb as it closed in on its target. The black-and-white film of World War II and the Korean War, neither of them so very long ago, appeared only in movie theaters many days after the events shown. The tools of communication are themselves smart bombs, but they have an even greater range.

Let us now turn to the beginning of the story of humankind's development of the means of communication. The first information revolution was writing.

Notes

1   In his study of the means by which society controls significant shifts in activity, James Beniger accepts revolutions that occur over decades. See James Beniger, *The Control Revolution* (Cambridge: Harvard University Press, 1986), 7.

2   Henri-Jean Martin, *The History and Power of Writing*. Trans. Lydia G. Cochrane (Chicago: The University of Chicago Press, 1994), 25.

3   Alvin Toffler makes a similar point in *The Third Wave* (New York: William Morrow, Democracy (January 1995): 65-78.

4   For a fuller discussion of this concept using the example of Meiji Japan, see T.R. Lakshmanan, "Social Change Induced by Technology: Promotion and Resistance," in Nordal Åkerman, ed., *The Necessity of Friction* (Heidelberg: Physica-Verlag, 1993), 135-158. See, especially, 154-55.

5   There has been little agreement on the meaning of these terms. Barry Smart writes, "The terms 'modernism' and 'post-modernism' are not only notoriously lacking in specificity, in addition they appear at times to carry very different connotations for continental European and American critics." In Bryan S. Turner, ed. *Theories of Modernity and Postmodernity*. (London: Sage Publications, 1990) 22.

6   Witold Rybczynski, *Taming the Tiger: The Struggle to Control Technology* (New York: The Viking Press, 1983), 26-27.

7   Marshall McLuhan, *Understanding Media: The Extensions of Man* (New York: McGraw-Hill Book Co., 1964), 50.

8   Ibid.

9   Robert D. Putnam, "Bowling Alone: America's Declining Social Capital," *Journal of Democracy* (January 1995): 65-78.

10   McLuhan 7-8.

11   Paul Kennedy, *Preparing for the Twenty-First Century* (Toronto: HarperCollins Publishers Ltd., 1993), 333.

12   Report on the coup attempt in the Soviet Union, *New York Times*, 20 August 1991.

13   George Washington University Professor William Adams, quoted by Gannett News Service, 22 August 1991.

14   Jonathan Yardley, Washington *Post*, 5 September 1991.

15   Michael Gartner, *The Wall Street Journal*, 8 June 1989.

16   *Newsweek*, 19 June 1989, 29.

17   Ellen Goodman, Minneapolis *Star-Tribune*, 23 June 1989, sec. A18.

18   Melanie Kirkpatrick, *Wall Street Journal*, 26 May 1989, sec. A10.

19   Ted Koppel, during discussion on the PBS program, "Culture in the Communications Age," taped 19 May 1990.

20   Gladys D. Ganley, *The Exploding Political Power of Personal Media* (Norwood, NJ: Ablex Publishing, 1992), 29.

21   Ganley, 31.

22   Ganley, 33.

23   Paul Wilkinson, *Terrorism and the Liberal State* (New York: New York University Press, 1986), 103.

24   Otis Pike, *Newhouse News Service*, 6 August 1989.

25   Speech to the American Bar Association, London, 1985.

26   Georgetown University Professor Harley Baltzer, quoted by Gannett News Service, 22 August 1991.

27   Alvin Toffler, *Future Shock* (New York: Bantam Books, 1971), 437.

28   Mary Anne Weaver, "A Reporter at Large: Balochistan," *The New Yorker*, 15 January 1990, 90.

29   Majid Tehranian, "Iran: Communication, Alienation, Revolution," *Intermedia*, (March 1979): 9.

30   Tehranian, 10.

31   Tehranian, 11.

32   Ibid.

33   Ibid.

34   *Newsweek*, 8 January 1990, 25.

35 Daniel J. Boorstin, *The Americans: The Democratic Experience* (New York: Random House, 1973), 476.

36 Minneapolis *Star Tribune*, 4 November 1993, sec. 13E.

37 Minneapolis *Star Tribune*, 12 October 1990, sec. 11Ae.

38 Rochester, NY, *Democrat-Chronicle*, 22 August 1991, sec. 12A.

39 Ellen Goodman, *The Boston Globe* syndication service, 23 June 1989.

40 *The Economist,* 15 October 1988, 19.

41 Letter by Karolina Udovicki, *The New Yorker*, 23 May 1994, 12.

42 Helena Luczywo, editor-in-chief of *Tygodnik Mazowsze*, reported in *Kontakt*, No. 6/86, 1989.

43 *The New York Times*, 26 November 1993.

44 *The Economist,* 13 February 1994, 4.

45 Speech to Freedom Forum, Columbia University, April 1993.

46 *Newsweek,* 27 February 1995, 30.

47 Op. cit.: 33.

48 Ganley, 29.

1

The First Revolution Writing

The Invention of Writing

With the cultivation of grains and the domestication of animals, tribes of hunters, fishers, and gatherers could put down roots in stable communities, expecting to be able to feed themselves from year to year. In alluvial valleys and deltas, the nomads settled down to the more certain life of farmers. So it was in the Nile delta of Egypt, along the banks of the Indus in northwest India, the Yellow in China, and the Tigris and Euphrates in the part of Mesopotamia that is now Iraq, where the Sumerians once dwelled. Communities grew, conquests united them, governments followed, and commerce spread. Priests required tribute to the gods and tax collectors came calling for much of what was left. All of this getting and giving required writing and record keeping.

On what medium were kept all these records, these calendars and contracts, these land deeds and calculations? To be practical the medium had to be transportable, storable, reasonably permanent, readily made, and cheap. The writing had to be fixed, so a contract, government document, or religious proclamation could not be altered. The writers of documents would

get what they needed, for even at this early stage of history, the requirements of the users were driving the technology. Writing would be the foundation of progress. The tools themselves were ordinary, humble things. What ancient peoples eventually did with them was not.

Primeval Chinese *ku-wan—gesture pictures*—preceded pictographs, the picture symbols that first appeared in Western Asia. Native American tribes notched or painted sticks to convey messages. In South America, Incas knotted colored *quipu* cords to keep complex records. Aside from portability, however, these media were of limited use.

Writing on Clay

The Chauvet cave paintings recently discovered in France are 30,000 years old and those of Lascaux and Altamira perhaps half that old. But we must look to the Fertile Crescent, particularly to Mesopotamia, for the long trek to reproducing and storing spoken language, which began about 8,000 B.C. in Sumer. Small clay triangles, spheres, cones, and other tokens were molded to

1

represent sheep, measures of grain, jars of oil, and other trading goods. These tokens served a community as a means of keeping track of goods for the purpose of pooling and redistributing the community's resources.[1] As status symbols for the elite members of the community, they were sometimes placed in burial sites. The tokens also indicated gifts brought to the temple for the gods, or brought to a ruler as tribute, or yielded with the best possible grace to the tax gatherer.

The shape of the token carried its meaning. Dozens of different clay tokens aided the accounting over an astonishing period of 5,000 years.[2] Starting about 3,700 B.C., the tokens were placed in hollow clay balls, a kind of envelope, for storage. It may have been frustrating that, once the tokens had been sealed inside the ball, there was no way to determine what was inside without cracking the ball open. Sumerian accountants figured out that they could identify the contents of the ball either by fixing an identical token set into the ball's soft clay surface or leaving an impression by pressing each token against the surface before it hardened. The next step toward writing was taken by scratching a *representation* of the token in the clay instead of impressing the actual token. In surviving specimens in the world's museums, the shapes of the representation do not match the tokens, indicating an important step toward abstract thinking.[3] Because the outside markings carried the meaning, there was really no need to stuff the actual tokens inside a hollow ball, nor was there really any need for the ball itself. Without the tokens, the ball could be flattened to the shape of a tablet that bore all the information anyone needed.

Sumerians also engraved pieces of stone or metal to make seals that, when pressed on the clay of a wine jar, announced its ownership. The stamped seal gave way to the cylinder seal, which was rolled over the wet clay. As it rolled along it reproduced a pattern, a forerunner of the cylinder press of our own era.

Advancing Knowledge

About 3100 B.C., the Sumerians invented numerals, separating the symbol for sheep from the number of sheep. So, some researchers believe, both writing and mathematics evolved together. The earliest Sumerian writings were pictographs, simple drawings of objects. Archaeological diggings at Uruk showed that the Sumerians advanced to ideographic writing, in which an image or symbol might stand for one or more objects; a symbol could also represent a concept. Writing developed into a tool that was able to communicate ideas. About the time that the Sumerians invented numerals, they advanced an additional step with *phonetic* writing, where the symbol meant the sound of a consonant and a vowel, thus combining the written and spoken language. The Sumerians had invented syllabic writing, somewhat like the modern Japanese *kana*, not yet an alphabet.

Babylon carried its predecessor Sumerian and Akkadian cultures to new heights. Writing, as the Sumerians and the Akkadians did on clay tablets with cuneiform script, plus a syllabary (each symbol is a syllable, usually a consonant and a vowel) that they interspersed with ideographs,[4] the Babylonians recorded abstract religious and philosophical thoughts. They classified plants, animals, metals, and rocks. They advanced knowledge in mathematics, astronomy, and engineering. However, unlike

Figure 1.1   Pictographs carved into clay tablets enabled peoples of the ancient Near East to keep records.

the analytical thinking of the later Greeks, the Babylonians mixed logic with superstition and myth.[5]

The most famous of all documents in Mesopotamian history, Hammurabi's legal code, written during the eighteenth century B.C. in the Semitic Babylonian language, was carved on stelae and placed in temples. Among the nearly 300 laws by this "Mighty King of the Four Quarters of the World," was a reformed, standard writing system for the lands he had conquered, extending from present day Syria to Iran.

Writing that began in Sumer was later adopted by Egypt. How it traveled there is not known. Perhaps it moved along the trade route that had existed since prehistoric times.[6] *Hieroglyphics*, serving mostly for sacred writing, were inscribed on Egyptian tomb walls and on pottery. Hieroglyphs were used also for recording each ruler's version of history, not as a way for ordinary mortals to communicate with each other. Egyptian priests formulated a second written language, *hieratic*, for relig-ious writing. From hieratic, a secular version, *demotic*, was conceived for daily use such as record keeping and correspondence. It was a combination of picture and phonetic writing, yet still not an alphabet. With demotic writing, the Egyptians had developed a writing system that brought written communication to a slightly wider segment of society, but it was still complicated and difficult to master, and it was by no means mass communication.

The next step up the evolutionary ladder of writing beyond the symbolic ideographs would be an integrated system of symbols for both written and spoken language. In a word, an alphabet. Neither the Sumerians nor the Chinese nor the Egyptians, for all their innovations in the uses of writing, had produced the simple, practical system in which one written symbol stands for one spoken sound, so a combination of visible symbols represents what is spoken aloud. The next step would be the *phonetic alphabet*.

Skin and Bones and Papyrus

Animal skins and bones, palm leaves and oak tree bark, wood and wax, metal and stone, seashells and pottery, silk and cotton, jade and ivory from elephant tusks have all been used to store humankind's memory.

Other writing media included brass tablets and sheets of leather. Homer's *Iliad* speaks of messages written on wood. In Roman times, wax coated the wood. That permitted reuse, as the wax could be warmed and smoothed over, an early recycling program. The reply to a letter might be written on the same letter while the messenger waited. Officials in Julius Caesar's government used such wax tablets to provide a daily bulletin exhibited in the Forum; the *Acta Diurna* was a precursor to newspapers.

The familiar vocabulary of the written word began to take shape. Pliny speaks of early writing on leaves and tree bark. From the practice of writing on palm leaves comes our use of *leaf* as a *page* of a book.

The Latin word *liber*, referring to the inner bark of trees, gives us *library*. From the Anglo-Saxon *boc*, also meaning *bark*, we get *book*. The word *volume* derives from the Latin word for *revolve*; papyrus scrolls were read by unrolling them. The word *paper* itself comes from the word *papyrus*. The Greek word for papyrus was *byblos*, after the Phœnician city of Byblos, home of sea traders who carried the bales of papyrus to the Greek cities. From *byblos* comes the word *bible*, meaning *book* or *books*.

Across the ancient Near East from Sumer to Egypt, common, familiar clay was finding use as a writing medium. The clay was sometimes shaped as flat tablets, sometimes as octagonal cylinders. Moses received the Ten Commandments on "tablets of stone," which some scholars think were actually sun-dried clay. Historical records might be preserved in *books* consisting of a series of tablets varying in size from one to twelve inches square.

Figure 1.2 Bone inscribed with questions and answers was used to tell the future during the Shang dynasty in China, 1760-1122 B.C.

Ink and inking tools had evolved for untold centuries. Common soot such as collects on pots was mixed with water and some vegetable gum like plant sap to produce a serviceable ink. A reed cut to a point or a brush of hair from a braying animal served as a pen.

Systematic written language began with the Sumerians, who used reeds to scratch marks on tablets of clay. To solve the sticky problem that a reed scratching into wet clay will pull the clay up as it is withdrawn, they designed a writing tool with a wedge tip, resulting in the writing we know as *cuneiform*. Hardened in fire or the sun's heat, thousands of these clay tablets have survived to this day, more durable than paper.

Although the medium of clay offered permanent writing and record keeping, plus widespread availability, its disadvantages of inconvenience and weight limited its value. The makers and keepers of records required something different, a medium that ideally was plentiful, cheap, lightweight, and reasonably durable in the short run.

Papyrus in Egypt

Ancient Egyptians found it in the Nile river delta, the reed called *papyrus*, growing 10 feet high along its banks. From it, peasants constructed boats and huts. It would also prove to be what Durant whimsically termed "the very stuff (and nonsense)" of which civilization was made.[7] Workers split the reeds into thin strips, placed one layer crosswise over another in close-set rows, hammered them gently for a couple of hours, and let them dry in the sun. A seashell or a piece of ivory was used to smooth the resulting sheets. The product of this effort weighed little, but lasted for years. Glue fastened the sheets end to end to make a scroll. It could be rolled up for convenient transport and storage. Scribes could fasten the papyrus sheets to form a single piece 30 feet or more in length, which they rolled around a cylinder of wood, metal, or ivory. Scribes also tied smaller sheets together by passing a string through holes along one margin, an early form of bookbinding.

Figure 1.3 Stylus used in the ancient Near East to write on soft clay.

When we recognize that even in our own time those who can understand certain kinds of symbols such as computer programming languages have an advantage in a computer-dependent society, we can appreciate without difficulty what happened in Egypt with a shift of writing from priestly control to its widespread use. Egypt under the pharaohs around 2000 B.C. underwent a transformation from absolute monarchy to a more egalitarian system of organization that coincided with a shift to papyrus as a medium of communication.[8] The flow of power from a tightly organized class, the pharaohs and the priests of the Theban temples, led to a decentralization of command. A government that depended upon absolute and centralized control, such as that of the pharaohs, weakened as Egyptian minor officials far from Thebes discovered the ease with which they could communicate with each other.

> The shift from dependence on stone to dependence on papyrus and the changes in political and religious institutions imposed an enormous strain on Egyptian civilization. Egypt quickly succumbed to invasion from peoples equipped with new instruments of attack.[9]

The invaders were the Hyksos, sometimes called the *shepherd kings*, who proceeded to rule Lower Egypt for a century and may have been the predecessors of the ancient Hebrews, who would leave meaningful writing of their own centuries later.

It was not only that the Egyptians recognized the administrative benefits of papyrus. The increased writing was accompanied by secularization of writing and also of increased thought and activity. Writing on papyrus was quicker and more relaxed, even hasty, compared to the stiff and formal stone chiseling. Thought gained lightness.[10] At the same time, new religions emerged in Egypt, including the monotheism of the pharaoh Akhnaton. Humankind was at the dawn of recorded history, yet evidence shows that a means of communication had already strengthened its users.

The concepts of time and space reflect the significance of media to civilization. Media that emphasize time are those that are durable in character, such as parchment, clay, and stone. The heavy materials are suited to the development of architecture and sculpture. Media that emphasize space are apt to be less durable and light in character, such as papyrus and paper. The latter are suited to wide areas in administration and trade. The conquest of Egypt by Rome gave access to supplies of papyrus, which became the basis of a large administrative empire.[11]

A civilization using clay, like the Sumerian, would be limited in area and would be concerned with religion and morality, which change little. On the other hand, a civilization using papyrus, like the Roman, would be encouraged to build a vast empire and would be more concerned with changing values, such as those of law, administration, and politics. The introduction of writing undermined the magic of the spoken word and the authority and tradition of the elders, leading toward science and secularism.[12]

Reeds gathered along the Nile would make Egypt a paper mill to other civilizations for an estimated 3,000 years, an astonishing span. Ships leaving the port city of Alexandria carried bales of papyrus to Athens, Rome, and hundreds of other cities as literacy spread.

Papyrus in Greek Hands

Papyrus widened Greek influence because the Greeks were the source of so much of the Mediterranean world's teaching. The Ptolemies who ruled Egypt and controlled the papyrus industry were of Greek origin. The Egyptian queen Cleopatra was descended from one of Alexander's generals. Papyrus saw increasing use in the Hellenic world. As Greek influence dominated Egypt under the Ptolemies, the Greek-controlled port city of Alexandria in Egypt became the leading source of book publishing. With papyrus and the phonetic alphabet as the carrier of thought, knowledge and ideas traveled the Hellenic world and returned enriched.

In Egypt and Mesopotamia, the scribes, those programmers of the ancient world, enjoyed a high social status because the writing was complex and took much study to learn. The scribe's craft even attracted recruits from the privileged classes.[13] For slave and freeman literacy became a skill worth achieving, a path to a better life. The literate, those who could write and read contracts, oversee commercial dealings, and engage in exchanges of diplomatic notes, achieved a measure of influence. Illiterates hired scribes if it was necessary to conduct written business.

Among the Greeks and Romans, perhaps because phonetic simplicities dispelled the mysteries of the writing craft, slaves were trained as copyists, readers, and, in Rome, librarians. For literate household slaves, the scribe's life was infinitely better than an existence of toiling in the fields, and no doubt longer. The scribe kept the family's accounts, noted what was bought, what was sold, how much was paid or received for this and that. The scribe counted the sheaves of wheat and the sheep going to market, recorded the tribute given to the tax collectors and to the priests. Egyptian scribes, whose trade was literacy, considered themselves superior to others, a persistent delusion of the literate. Observing the statue of the nude Egyptian scribe in the Louvre, Will Durant surmised:

> He is sedulously attentive and mechanically industrious; he has just enough intelligence not to be dangerous. His life is monotonous, but he consoles himself by writing essays on the hardships of the manual worker's existence, and the princely dignity of those whose food is paper and whose blood is ink.[14]

Parchment

Papyrus had its limitations. Manuscripts made from the reeds growing along the banks of the Nile eventually turned brittle and disintegrated. Only a very few papyri still survive in libraries, carefully preserved. A further limitation, papyrus came from one source, Egypt. Something more durable and more universally available was also manufactured.

That was parchment, made from the skin of a sheep, a calf, or a goat. The skin was scraped clean to remove the hairs, rubbed smooth with pumice stone, then dressed with chalk and lime. Ancient writers also used vellum, the thin and supple skin of unborn lambs or kids.

Like papyrus, parchment was rolled up as books, with their edges fastened, page after page, or folded into books, their pages cut and bound for turning. Both papyrus and parchment loaned themselves to collecting and archiving. Both were relatively cheap and easily transported. Parchment had some advantages. It could take writing on both sides. It was sturdy and durable, which schoolchildren and travelers appreciated, but less so the scribes, for writing on parchment took some physical effort. It was actually recyclable, because the ink could be removed and the parchment written on again. Perhaps its greatest advantage was that it could be fabricated anywhere there were sheep. Papyrus grew only in the Nile Valley. Parchment also resisted time better than papyrus. Old parchment documents still exist, but almost no papyrus from ancient times.

Both were to continue in use for centuries, interchangeable as writing media. Which would be used depended upon political, economic, and cultural conditions. Use of the parchment *codex*, the cut and folded pages written on both sides that made up a book, expanded at about the same time that Christianity spread. By the second century A.D., Christianity had developed a strong written tradition with the publication in Greek on books of parchment codex of the four Gospels, making them accessible across the known world in a familiar language.

The written tradition was strengthened in the third century as scholars tried to find a synthesis between Hebraic religious beliefs, which were at the base of Christianity, and Greek philosophy, which was at the base of intellectual life in the Roman empire. In this period, the new practice of writing things down overcame the continuing oral tradition of the Hebrew and Greek peoples.

From the Greek phonetic alphabet, so essential an element of the first information revolution, came the Roman alphabet, and from that came other alphabets of Western civilization, including English.

Other Writing Surfaces

Papyrus would prove to be less enduring than the alphabet it carried across the Greek and Roman civilizations. Half a world away, another culture, older and more firmly established than the Greek, had long ago learned to rely upon a different, non-alphabetic writing, and upon paper, a medium much cheaper to produce, which would one day sweep into history papyrus, parchment, and all other writing surfaces. Yet China, where paper and printing with movable type were invented, would never give rise to an information revolution.

Paper would not be made from trees until nearly two thousand years passed, but in their experiments with materials Chinese and Japanese paper makers used mulberry bark for paper that has remained in perfect condition to this day.

Indian civilizations from Mexico to South America used the inner bark of certain trees. Their books survived the elements, but not the missionaries. A Spanish missionary in the Yucatan peninsula wrote in the sixteenth century, "We found a great number of books written with their characters, and because they contained nothing but superstitions and falsehoods about the devil, we burned them all."[15]

With the fiery charge of Islam in the seventh century across the Middle East and North Africa, exports of papyrus from Egypt to Europe dropped sharply. Marshall McLuhan has argued that this led to declines in bureaucracy, uniform roads, and cities.[16]

In Europe, now began centuries of monastic responsibility for knowledge and information. As monasteries were built in Europe during the Dark Ages of western civilization, monks, chiefly Benedictines, took up the profession of scribe. Among their tasks, they were charged with the duty of transcribing the crumbling old papyrus manuscripts in the libraries onto fresh parchment that was prepared in or near the monastery. To be a scribe was no longer a mean calling. It was to do the work of God.

The Greeks

The Greeks took the alphabetic building blocks of their neighbors to the east and with them built a soaring edifice. The Greek historian Herodotus tells us that the Phœnicians introduced writing into the Hellenic world.[22] The date was somewhere between 1100 and 800 B.C. The Greeks added vowel sounds and both expanded and contracted the Phœnician alphabet to create the uniquely Greek alphabet.

The Greeks broke speech down into its individual elements. What one community could do, others could also. Copied inexactly and altered locally, the alphabet took unique forms wherever it settled. The alphabet could serve any language, any dialect. Until the end of the fifth century B.C., almost every Hellenic state had its own

alphabet.[23] At first the Greeks shaped their letters like the Phœnician letters. According to Herodotus, King Cadmus, the legendary inventor of the alphabet, may have actually been a Phœnician immigrant.[24]

They expanded the use of writing well beyond the trading of Canaanite shepherds and Phœnicians sailors to embrace philosophy, metaphysics, history, science, mathematics, medicine, politics, and the arts, using it even for comedy and tragedy. The Greeks would seek the abstract visions of pure truth and pure beauty. The Greek genius for abstract thinking, for logic, analysis, rationality, and plain common sense would light up Western civilization. By separating humankind and its works from the world around it, they conceived

THE ALPHABET

The invention of the alphabet, about 1700 B.C., fell to the relatively unlettered Semitic people in the Sinai and Canaan of modern Israel, perhaps the Midianites or Kenites of the Bible. A simplified rendering of the difficult Egyptian writing for their own spoken language, it transcribed their spoken language so efficiently that it was adopted by one tribe after another, each modifying what they received to suit the sounds of their own language[17]

A version of the Canaanite alphabet was adopted by the Phœnicians, living along what are now the coastal strips of Syria, Lebanon, and Israel.[18] Famous as seagoing traders, their ships plied the Mediterranean, establishing colonies in Greece and at Carthage on the North African coast. It should not seem at all odd that such a wide-ranging and commercially active people would formulate a unified language system, for the alphabet met the needs of trade. Nor is it surprising that such an advance came from this relatively free society on the Mediterranean coast instead of the controlled and centralized empire of Persia, or that other equally controlled empire spreading from the banks of the Nile.

With the alphabet, speech itself could be stored. Human communication was now no longer restricted to the temporary sound of a voice. Additionally, the alphabet's simplicity permitted more of the populace to figure out how to use it.[19]

Organized religion that was founded upon written scriptures set, for the societies that accepted them, enduring values, but underlying many of the religions, an oral culture breathed. The stories of the Old and New Testaments were told and retold for centuries before someone committed them to writing. So were the god-drenched stories of the Trojan War, which was fought 500 years before someone set down on papyrus the Homeric version of the events.

As the use of the alphabet widened, it was copied and inevitably changed. Derived from the Phœnician alphabet were the Hebrew alphabet, beginning *aleph, bet*, and the Greek alphabet, beginning *alpha, beta*. To a Phœnician, *aleph* and *bet* meant, respectively, *ox* and *house*. Invert a capital A and you may see the face of an ox. The original *bet* was in the shape of a square, a typical house.

Robert Logan has argued that "the phonetic alphabet, monotheism, and codified law were introduced for the first time to the Israelites by Moses at Mount Sinai in the form of the Ten Commandments."[20] This hypothesis, startling in its breadth, falls in line with a basic argument of this book, that for an information revolution to succeed, there must be new communication technology reaching people who are in the midst of profound change. For the illiterate slaves who followed Moses out of Egypt, these conditions were certainly met by laws written "with the finger of God."[21] And that their history, their myths, and their monotheistic beliefs would be documented in book after book of what would become the Bible, certainly meets any test of an information revolution that succeeded.

of nature as something separate, an entity worthy of study, and that increasingly meant committing to papyrus as well as communicating orally.

Out of the Dark Ages

The gathering of knowledge in a way that might be characterized as an information revolution had its faint beginnings in the Hellenic world during the eighth century B.C., when the Phœnician alphabet took root in Aegean soil. It was the period after the Greek emergence out of the Dark Ages.

Because of the alphabetic script and the availability of papyrus, the *Iliad* and the *Odyssey*, the epic poems of Homer, recalled and repeated orally for the previous four centuries by storytellers, were at last written down.

The information revolution gathered strength over the next century as the first readers came into being.[25] During the following three centuries, there would be an outpouring of intellectual, artistic, and political ideas such as the world had never seen before and has scarcely known since. By the seventh century B.C., the Greeks must have had papyrus.[26] Throughout the Mediterranean world, words on papyrus led to a knowledge explosion as scrolls reached isolated scholars. Aristotle could not have gathered the body of known knowledge without the means of creating a permanent record on a storable medium. Science and medicine could not have advanced as they did without ideas, conclusions, and reports of experiments written on a transportable medium. By the time of Aristotle in the fourth century B.C., the Greeks, especially the Athenians, had a reading public, some collections of books, and of libraries.

The burst of Greek lyric poetry has been attributed to cheap papyrus.[27] Access to supplies of papyrus brought the copying of books and perhaps the first private collections. By the fifth century B.C., in Greece a book market existed.[28] In the cities, free people could read and write. Athens created a public depository of books in 330 B.C., during the lifetime of Aristotle, who according to the Greek historian Strabo, was the first book collector; it was Aristotle who taught the kings of Egypt to set up proper libraries instead of mere collections of books, and it is from his collections that we have the word *museum*.[29]

With Aristotle the Greek world passed from oral instruction to the habit of reading.[30] Aristotle classified as much of the world's knowledge as he could acquire. (He also observed that writing was useful for making money and managing households.)[31] Others made great strides in mathematics, medicine, astronomy, geography, and biology. Style was introduced to written and spoken communication. After Aristotle, the Hellenic world had a new reality, a written culture functioning alongside its oral culture.[32] Life would no longer be the same. In a sense, the first information revolution had ended, and had been a success, although virtually by definition a successful revolution never ends.

Not everything the Greeks did was perfect by any means. The principal weakness in Greek thought was a reliance on deductively derived logical conclusions in preference to observation, experimentation, and inductive reasoning. It left them trying to explain a static world existing under an unchanging heaven. Pure deduction based upon incorrect premises would hamper Western science past the Middle Ages.

Yet, written symbols to objectify speech and codify information aided the Greeks and eventually other peoples to govern themselves, to trade, and to express a religious faith. Fixing the spoken word changed the human condition.[33] Writing added to humankind's ability to think abstractly.

The invention of written language developed over a period of centuries, advancing sporadically in different locations toward modern alphabetic systems. Creating an additional mode of communication, writing came out of practical need, probably with little experimentation.

Examination of most communication technologies shows a pattern of slow progress that is illuminated occasionally by a sudden sharp advance. Early Greek civilization advanced in a similar manner, a laborious crawl that exploded in revolutionary political, social, and economic changes, interlinked changes in virtually every field of life, of which the information revolution was a small but integral part.

It is reasonable to assume that the diffusion of writing sped through society because it was a sensible way to communicate and archive information. A slave bore orders from a ruler to a provincial governor, a fellow slave carried messages of eternal affection between a general in the field and his mistress, and a third slave ran between two merchants clutching orders to sell at a certain price, with the written instructions remaining as a record of the transaction. Commerce beyond the village would come to rely heavily on the diffusion of writing. And government officials surely learned early to love written documents, a love that has withstood the erosion of the centuries.

The Greek city-state evolved over several centuries to the limited democracy that was Athens, limited because only a portion of its residents could become citizens.[34] Writing and political freedom were the roots for the extraordinary growth of what Hegel has called *the civil society*, a domain distinct from government. The spread of democracy may have owed something to the spread of literacy that soon.

> Even to ostracize (banish) an undesirable person from Athens for ten years was only possible if 6,000 men each wrote his name, simultaneously, on individual pieces of *ostraca* (potsherd). Writing, far from being a (semi-) secret art practiced by a specially trained elite, was an essential element of Greek democracy.[35]

"We who dwell between the Phasis River and the Pillars of Heracles," wrote Plato quoting Socrates, inhabit a small portion of the earth, "living around the sea like ants or frogs around a marsh."[36] The Greeks dwelt mostly in coastal communities stretching from the eastern edges of Asia Minor and the Black Sea to the western edges of the Mediterranean, where it meets the Atlantic Ocean. Athens may have been a leader of culture, but by no means was it the only center. Away from Athens, in the thousand colonies that constituted the Hellenic civilization, were born Greek poetry and prose, history, philosophy, mathematics, and oratory.[37]

Importantly, the Greeks shared a language, both spoken and written, that remained stable for a thousand years.[38] To appreciate what this means, consider how much English has changed in the six centuries between us and Chaucer, or even the four centuries since Shakespeare. Although Greece never had an empire like those of Egypt, Persia, or Rome, there was a far-flung Hellenic world traversed by ships on the Mediterranean Sea, the highway of a remarkable people. For the knowledge that it carried on papyrus and in the heads of travelers, the Mediterranean deserves to be recognized as the world's first information highway.

After schooling in the academies of Athens and other cities, students returned to the corners of that wider Hellenic world. The amount of communication that continued among them can only be guessed at.

Most Greek scientists worked in isolation.[39] That they maintained some written contacts and read each other's books seems obvious, for the alphabet was known to them and papyrus was available. It seems natural that they corresponded.[40] Greek scholars wrote extensively and their writing was meant to be read by their contemporaries or to be read aloud in public.[41]

With democracy in Hellenic society came a growth in schools for freeborn boys and girls.[42] Learning was by rote, but it led to a widening basic literacy. That led in turn to a greater capacity to acquire information, and the inescapable thrust toward egalitarianism that accompanies communication.

A Time of Turmoil

As with all revolutions, the seeds of information revolutions, when they are scattered in disturbed soil, plant roots most deeply to send forth both their flowers and their weeds. So it was in Athens, the first among the Greek cities, for its economy and politics suitably churned the ground of ancient Attica centuries before the height of Greek civilization.

The landowners, the aristocratic Eupatrids, were citizens who took power into their own hands and reduced the king to a figurehead. These oligarchs, living in luxury in town, sent freedmen and slaves to till their fields. Next in wealth, a middle class of professionals, craftsmen, traders, and other free men were pushed down by the aristocrats and, in turn, pushed down the poorest free laborers. At bottom were the slaves.

Add to this feudal mix the hard scrabble harvests of the stony Greek soil. Coinage was introduced to replace barter, which proved a great calamity for many. It precipitated an economic revolution.[43] Money shook up the Aegean world. Commerce offered an effective means to disturb the feudal society, much as it would prove effective nearly two millennia later in feudal Europe. The bread one earned by trade has always tasted richer than the bread earned by sweat. Commerce freed men from dependence on the land of the nobility, on herding and farming. Across cultures and centuries, people have ventured into unknown lands to better their lives. No matter what their luck, those who survived returned home more worldly. If they had not actually moved toward democracy, they had at least taken steps toward leveling the aristocrat's advantage.

Commerce by sea and land over long distances promoted the use of writing. It could not have been the case that all wealthy merchants accompanied all the goods they traded to distant ports. Inevitably, partnerships formed, goods were consigned, and documents were drawn up to keep traders relatively honest.

Sending men off to fight added to the economic dislocations. Sporadic wars erupted among the city-states and with the powerful empire of Persia to the east. From the late seventh century to the late sixth century, five great empires collapsed, those of Assyria, Medea, Babylonia, Lydia, and Egypt, plus several Greek tyrannies. At home, there was the cruelty of Draco's code, which brought the word *draconian* into the language. The reforms of Solon pointed the way toward the democracy that was established by Cleisthenes in Athens in 507 B.C., and later in other cities.[44] A clue that literacy entered into the managing of affairs was the Athenian requirement a century later that magistrates could not apply "an unwritten law."[45]

Sparta refused to embrace written communication with the enthusiasm that Athens showed, contending that literacy by itself guarantees no cultural superiority. Lycurgus, reputed founder of the Spartan constitution, among his reforms actually forbade writing. He had his reasons.

The long history of its praise in the Western tradition is the self-interested product of those who write, but there has always been a party, less audible by the nature of its doctrine, opposed to writing. The Spartan believed that the unrecorded good behavior of citizens, though lost to history, was worth a book full of unrealized ideals.[46]

Supplementing an Oral Culture

Pre-literate societies preserved their histories in what Eric Havelock called "the living memories of successive living people who are young and then old and then die."[47] They did so through their oral culture, enriching their lives and enhancing memory with the verbal and metrical patterns of epic poetry, story, and song.

Because they did not require such a technology as writing, many oral cultures did not adopt it, as Durant pointed out:

Simple tribes living for the most part in comparative isolation, and knowing the happiness of having no history, felt little need for writing. Their memories were all the stronger from having no written aids; they learned and retained, and passed on to their children by recitation, whatever seemed necessary in the way of historical record and cultural transmission.[48]

Writing supplemented, but by no means supplanted, the predominantly oral Greek culture. The early writing in the new Greek alphabet was meant not to be read but to be heard, either sung or spoken to the accompaniment of the lyre and other musical instruments.[49] Rhetoric, so important to political affairs, was taught as a spoken art. Reciting on public occasions was commonplace. It is true that Plato wrote his *Dialogues*, but they were, after all, written as conversations. How much the Greeks learned orally and how much from written sources is not clear. We are certain only that much knowledge was, for the first time, written, and therefore it was meant to be read by contemporaries. Writing encouraged reflection and critical thinking, unlike memorization, which the rhythms of poetry served well.[50] Recitation was suited to poetry, writing to prose.

In the Greek historians, we see the shift from oral to written communication. Herodotus, Thucydides, and Xenophon, preferring spoken eyewitness accounts to documents, used only a few written sources, but they themselves wrote their accounts. Thucydides was able to transcribe some letters, inscriptions and treaties, but, like Herodotus, preferred oral to written evidence.[51]

The Warning of Socrates

Legend has it that when the ibis-headed god of magic, Thoth, told the Egyptian pharaoh Thamos of Thoth's invention of writing, Thamos denounced it because students, "now that they possessed a means of storing up knowledge without trouble, would cease to apply themselves, and would neglect to exercise their memories."[52] Recalling this venerable tale, Socrates, the old conservative, used it to bemoan writing:

> For your invention will produce forgetfulness in the souls of those who have learned it, through lack of practice at using their memory, as through reliance on writing they are reminded from outside by alien marks, not from inside, themselves by themselves: you have discovered an elixir not of memory but of reminding. To your students you give an appearance of wisdom, not the reality of it; having heard much, in the absence of teaching, they will appear to know much when for the most part they know nothing, and they will be difficult to get along with, because they have acquired the appearance of wisdom
> instead of wisdom itself.[53]

Socrates correctly foresaw that memory would be weakened by our reliance on writing. Many oral-aural societies, past and present, nourish memory skills that are beyond our technological cultures.[54] For the Greeks, there occurred, besides memory skill losses, some reduction in the oral tradition itself. Disseminated across the educated populace of the Hellenic world, writing gradually sent the oral tradition into a decline that affected everything, even the tellers of tales and the schools of rhetoric. Nevertheless, although the Greeks are credited with inventing literacy and the literate basis of modern thinking, their tradition remained predominantly oral.

From Greece to Rome

Spoken thoughts hover about the speaker. The words never quite leave their source. Writing, on the other hand, stands apart from the writer. Through writing the Greeks fashioned the idea of objectivity, the separation of the knower from what is known. It was the beginning of objective thinking, of the scientific method.[55]

The Greek language would be the language of education, diplomacy, literature, and science in the eastern Mediterranean for another thousand years. Romans conquered the Greek city-states, but adopted their culture. Rome replaced the Greeks in power and eminence, building a large standing army and a large bureaucracy. They ruled a dominion beyond the dreams of any Greek city-state tyrant. Caesar's conquest of Egypt assured a steady supply of papyrus for the administration needed to run their empire.[56] Romans wrote things down and kept records.

> ...And what was that mechanism of (Roman) law and administration based upon? Paper, or more exactly, papyrus... Engraving in stone is for the priests; they have an affinity for spanning eras. But soldiers are no-nonsense managers. They need to deal with the here and now. The alphabet and paper create armies, or rather the bureaucracies which run armies. Paper creates self-contained kingdoms at a distance.[57]
>
> After the population attains a certain size, for example, government cannot expand without written records. Human messengers, relying only upon their memory, impose a severe limit on the power of the state. Only so much of resources can be allocated to communication before military and economic sectors begin to suffer.[58]

The First Libraries

Ancient Egyptian temples held collections of writing principally about religion, liturgy, and rituals. The temple libraries were called *houses of life.* What little we know of their holdings we learn principally from Greek writers.[59] These were archives, not true libraries.[60] The Egyptians did not consider literacy a part of general education, but rather specialized training for government or temple bureaucracy.[61] Temple priests had a monopoly on papyrus, but some of the writing may have been on parchment, too. Nothing remains.

We know more about Assyrian and Babylonian libraries because their books were on clay tablets that have survived the centuries. The oldest extant catalog of books is Sumerian, listing the titles of 62 literary works.[62] The first library of significance was built in Ninevah by kings of the 8th and 7th centuries B.C., begun by Sargon, continued by Senacherib, and expanded by his grandson, Assurbanipal, who undertook a systematic collection of Assyro-Babylonian literature, neatly divided and each book numbered according to its location. It was the world's first book collection library, estimated at 20,000 to 25,000 tablets. The Assyrian conquest of Babylon improved the collection considerably, because the conquered territory was ransacked for clay books on grammar, poetry, history, science, and religion.[63] The library was designed to serve church and state, to advance scientific knowledge, and to promote the fame of the king. Assurbanipal's library kept copyists, a library staff, and a cataloguing system to register its religious, historical, and scientific documents.[64] The question of access is unclear, for this was a private royal reference library. Those highly placed at court could probably have gained access, but it was unlikely that this privilege was extended to scholars.[65]

Beyond this remarkable venture, we must look to the Greeks.[66] At Pergamum, a Greek city-state in what is now western Turkey, a city known for its devotion to the arts, its grand library figures in an interesting tale involving Cleopatra's ancestor, the pharaoh Ptolemy. It seems that Ptolemy grew jealous of the library assembled by King Eumenes II, and blocked further shipments of papyrus to him. Eumenes, so the story goes, encouraged the mass production of treated animal skins, and that is how parchment came to rival papyrus and, later, paper.[67]

The greatest of the Hellenic world libraries, established by the Ptolemies at the start of the third century B.C., was the Alexandrian, which served as a university, a research center, and a publishing house employing a cadre of educated slaves as scribes. Ships docking at Alexandria were searched for manuscripts that were not in the library. At its height in the first century A.D., the library, ambitiously intended to hold a copy of every book in the world, generated dictionaries, concordances, and encyclopedias.[68]

By the fourth century A.D., Rome could boast at least 28 libraries with 20,000 or more rolls each, divided into Greek and Roman sections. Throughout the empire, collections grew in municipal libraries and the private libraries of the wealthy.

The Alexandrian Library was partly destroyed in 48 B.C. during street fighting in an uprising after Julius Caesar captured the city. As compensation for the lost Museum library scrolls, a collection numbering some 200,000 scrolls, Antony made a gift to the Alexandrian Library of the library of Pergamum, which was Roman state property. Antony's accusers charged that he gave away Roman state property illegally as a further expression of his affection for Cleopatra.

All tales of how the Alexandrian library was eventually destroyed are in dispute. According to one version, the famed library was demolished by a mob of infuriated Christians in the fifth century. In the twelfth century, a story was spread that this library had been destroyed by Moslems.[69]

Figure 1.4   An Egyptian scribe, usually a slave, kept the household accounts and wrote letters for his master. Scribes also copied books.

The Lamp of Reason

In a world of darkness, Greece lit the lamp of reason. Writing allowed that lamp to shine for all the generations to come. The first information revolution, the Writing Revolution, slowly moved the Hellenic world—and subsequently Western civilization—from an exclusively oral culture to one that left its tracks by means of writing. During this period, approximately the 8th through the 4th centuries B.C., the world's first democracies formed in the Greek city-states. By the third century B.C., writing was accepted throughout the educated segment of the Hellenistic world as a means for learning and for communication. Reading was taught in schools. It had reached a large segment of Greek society.[70] Papyrus books were gathered into libraries. The first information revolution had succeeded.

The invention of writing made it possible to encapsulate information and send it winging across space and time to be pored over by other minds in different places and different centuries, continuing to benefit our own minds today. Political and communication changes would continue to intertwine across continents and eras.

With writing used to store knowledge, the human mind would no longer be restricted by the limits of memory. Knowledge henceforth would have no boundaries. To the Greek writers who went beyond mundane communication into the sciences, philosophy, and religion, there was allowed, far more than simple pictographs on walls, a means of surviving their own life span by leaving behind their mortal years a detailed legacy of their thoughts, satisfying the unspoken, but ever present, human need to be remembered.

CARRYING THE MESSAGE

Like most communication technologies, the postal system was not invented by any individual, but changed over time, with the unenviable distinction of backsliding during the Dark Ages. The European merchant in 1400 probably did not feel as safe in entrusting a dispatch to the mails as an Assyrian merchant did some four thousand years earlier. The history of postal service describes not an information revolution, but a slow, erratic information evolution as old as writing itself.

Yet, postal service shows a history of improvements that have widened public access, a definite trend toward equality of access to information. Speed of delivery also improved despite setbacks. Today, with fax and E-mail, both of them existing outside of government-managed service, the delivery of letters is virtually instantaneous. The Post Office system, managed by governments in every nation, is dismissed as *snail mail*.

For most of recorded time, the history of communication was a history of transportation, with postal service serving as a common carrier of writing. Since transmission before the telegraph required physically carrying the written page, the quality of communication remained a function of the available transportation technology. When what was being mailed was a newspaper, magazine, or book, the mails were transmitting forms of mass communication, just as they were when the parcel being mailed was a news story, a manuscript, or photographs destined for publication. Only by improving transportation did the information get out more quickly to more people at greater distances and at less cost.

The postman through history followed two trails, the path of the government and the path of the private citizen. In only the past few centuries, a fraction of postal history, have they merged.

The beginnings of communication by post are lost in the fog of antiquity. It is useless to ask, "Who wrote the first letter?" Like language, postal service was not invented. It grew.[71] Letters are extant in ancient Egyptian characters and there is reference to a regular postal service; in an ancient papyrus someone advised, "Write to me by the letter-carrier."

Continued

Carrying the Message *(continued)*

The Egyptians had a relay system that helped maintain central control of their empire. Museums also have letters from the kingdoms of Babylon and Ninevah. Both the Old and New Testaments contain ample references to letters, such as King David's letter to the battlefield that sealed the fate of Bathsheba's unlucky husband and Paul's letter to the Romans.

In China an organized postal service existed in the tenth century B.C. Probably all such services until recent centuries were for government use, although no doubt business correspondence and love letters were carried along. Japan's postal system was limited to government use until a private courier service began in the seventeenth century.

In the New World, lacking horses, Incas and Mayas employed relay stations of runners. Perhaps at the same time in the Old World the Assyrians allowed merchants to send letters by government post. These were small clay tablets encased in clay envelopes bearing addresses.

Persians under Cyrus, Darius, and Xerxes established relay stations of horses throughout the empire. They could not have been popular because the public was forbidden to use the service, yet nearby communities were forced to support each station with horses, food, and labor. It was said that the burden of supporting the larger stations was so crushing that people fled nearby farms and villages. It was of the Persian postal service that Herodotus wrote, "Neither snow nor rain nor heat nor gloom of night stays these couriers from the swift completion of their appointed rounds."[72]

Ancient Greeks employed runners. The most famous, we know, was the youth who ran so hard to carry the news of the victory at Marathon that he fell dead after delivering the message "Nike!"—"victory." His feat is celebrated in the modern marathon races. Private messenger services also existed in the Greek city states. Using homing pigeons to carry messages may have begun either in Greece or China. Both literatures refer to them.

The Romans, rulers of the Mediterranean World south into Africa and north to the British Isles, ran a much larger postal system, the *cursus publicus*, for papyrus and parchment letters. Those famous Roman roads have been credited, in part, to the wish to improve the mails. Roman emperors wanted to receive intelligence and send out orders quickly. A simple alphabet written on easily transportable papyrus and parchment encouraged communication, which was later discouraged by the walled towns and city-states that rose as Rome fell.[73] Walled towns would flourish during the Dark Ages when literacy and writing were at their nadir.

By the fourth century A.D., the Roman postal service included officials called *curiosi*, whose duties included keeping an eye out for fraud involving the posts and also government spying, probably including opening letters. In the *Phillipics*, Cicero rails against spying on private letters. So indeed, 1,500 years later, would Martin Luther, who wrote, "There is no greater forger of letters than he who intercepts a letter."

Ordinary citizens of the Roman Empire, forbidden to use the government *cursus publicus*, devised their own means of communication. For long journeys, the writer had to rely upon traders and ship captains. Over short distances, private messengers or servants, usually slaves, carried letters. It was a dangerous duty, for a slave risked loss of limb or life if he was caught by his master's enemies but, if he failed to deliver the letters promptly, faced a similar fate at home.

Notes

1   Denise Schmandt-Besserat, *Before Writing* (Austin: University of Texas Press, 1992), 178+.
2   Schmandt-Besserat, 198.
3   Schmandt-Besserat, 128.
4   G.R. Driver, *Semitic Writing: From Pictograph to Alphabet* (London: Oxford University Press, 1948), 196.
5   Robert K. Logan, *The Alphabet Effect: The Impact of the Phonetic Alphabet on the Development of Western Civilization* (New York: William Morrow and Co., 1986), 73.
6   Leonard Cottrell, *The Quest for Sumer* (New York: G.P. Putnam's Sons, 1965), 86.
7   Will Durant, *Our Oriental Heritage,* vol. 1 of *The Story of Civilization* (New York: Simon and Schuster, 1935), 171.
8   Harold A. Innis, *The Bias of Communication* (Toronto: University of Toronto Press, rev. ed., 1972), 15.
9   Innis, 19.
10 Innis, 16.
11 Innis, 7.
12 Innis's arguments on communication, dense with historical references, are not always easy to follow, but *The Bias of Communication* and *Empire of Communication* reward the patient reader. For a lucid exposition of Innis's main points, as well as those of Marshall McLuhan, see James Carey, "Harold Adams Innis and Marshall McLuhan," *The Antioch Review* 27 (1967): 5-39.
13 Albertine Gaur, *A History of Writing* (London: The British Library, 1987), 150.
14 Durant, 161.
15 Diego de Landa, of the Monastery of Izamal, Yucatan. Reported in Dard Hunter, *Papermaking: The History and Technique of an Ancient Craft* (New York: Dover Publications, 1978), 26.
16 McLuhan, Marshall, *Understanding Media: The Extensions of Man* (New York: McGraw-Hill, 1964), 100.
17 Logan, 33-36.
18 W.M. Flinders Petrie, *The Formation of the Alphabet* (London: MacMillan & Co., 1912), 5.
19 Jack Goody, *Literacy in Traditional Societies* (Cambridge: Cambridge University Press, 1968), 3.
20 Logan, 82.
21 Exodus 31:18.
22 Herodotus, *The History* 5:58.
23 William A. Mason, *A History of the Art of Writing* (New York: Macmillan Co., 1920), 343.
24 Herodotus 5:57ff.
25 Will Durant, *The Life of Greece*, vol. 2 of *The Story of Civilization* (New York: Simon and Schuster, 1939), 206.
26 Henri-Jean Martin, *The History and Power of Writing* (Chicago: University of Chicago Press, 1994), 46.
27 Innis, 7.
28 M.I. Finley, ed., *The Legacy of Greece* (New York: Oxford University Press, 1984), 16.
29 Goody, 55.
30 Frederic G. Kenyon, *Books and Readers in Ancient Greece and Rome*, 2nd ed. (Oxford: Clarendon Press, 1951), 25.
31 Aristotle, *Politics* viii.3.1338a 15-17.
32 Innis, 58.
33 Schmandt-Besserat, 1.
34 Chester G. Starr, *The Origins of Greek Civilization: 1100 - 650 B.C.* (New York: Alfred A. Knopf, 1961), 337.
35 Albertine Gaur, *A History of* Writing (London: The British Library, 1987), 156.
36 Plato, *Phaedo*, 109B-C, trans. & ed. David Gallop (New York: Oxford University Press, 1993), 69.
37 Durant, 174.
38 Finley, 3.
39 Lloyd, G.E.R., "Science and Mathematics," in Finley, 262.
40 William V. Harris, *Ancient Literacy* (Cambridge: Harvard University Press, 1989), 56.
41 For example: "Herodotus's Histories were composed in writing to be read in public." Kathryn Payne, "Information Collection and Transmission in Classical Greece," *Libri* 43.4 (1993): 278.
42 Henri-Jean Martin, *The History and Power of Writing* (Chicago: University of Chicago Press, 1994), 69.
43 Bush, Wendell T., "An Impression of Greek Political Philosophy," *Studies in the History of Ideas*, vol. 1 (New York: Columbia University Press, 1918), 52-53.
44 Durant, 109-24.
45 Marti Lu Allen, *The Beginning of Understanding: Writing in the Ancient World* (Ann Arbor: Kelsey Museum of Archaeology), 4.
46 Robert Pattison, *On Literacy* (New York: Oxford University Press, 1982), 57.
47 Eric A. Havelock, *Preface to Plato* (Cambridge, Mass.: Belknap Press, 1963), 42.
48 Will Durant, *Our Oriental Heritage*, 76.
49 Starr, 263.
50 Gaur, 14.
51 Arnaldo Momigliano, "History and Biography," in Finley, 160.
52 Gaston Maspero, *The Dawn of Civilization: Egypt and Chaldæa*, trans. M.L. McClure (London: Society for Promoting Christian Knowledge, 1922), 220.

53 Plato, *Phaedrus*, 275, trans. C.J. Rowe, 2nd (corrected) ed. (Warminster, England: Aris & Rowe, 1988), 123.

54 Walter S. Ong, *The Presence of the Word: Some Prolegomena for Cultural and Religious History* (New Haven: Yale University Press, 1967), 23.

55 Logan, 107.

56 Innis, 7.

57 Marshall McLuhan and Bruce Powers, *The Global Village* (New York: Oxford University Press, 1989), 137.

58 Mark Poster, *The Mode of Information: Post-structuralism and Social Context* (The University of Chicago Press, 1990), 7.

59 James W. Thompson, *Ancient Libraries* (Berkeley: University of California Press, 1940), 2.

60 Thompson, 15.

61 Steven Shubert, "The Oriental Origins of the Alexandrian Library," *Libri* 43. 2(1993): 163.

62 Samuel Kramer, *From the Tablets of Sumer* (Indian Hills, CO: Falcon's Wing Press, 1956), 254.

63 Thompson, 11.

64 Alfred Hessel, *A History of Libraries*, trans. Reuben Peiss (New Brunswick, N.J.: The Scarecrow Press, 1955), 2.

65 Shubert, 163.

66 Thompson, 17.

67 Durant, *The Life of Greece,* 600.

68 Shubert, 143.

69 Thompson, 23.

70 Harris, 46.

71 Alvin F. Harlow, *Old Post Bags* (New York: D. Appleton, 1938), 7.

72 Herodotus, *The History* 8:98.

73 McLuhan, 90.

2

The Second Revolution Printing

Turbulent Europe

Despair is the mother of renewal. The Dark Ages of European civilization had lasted for almost a thousand years, but by the middle of the fourteenth century, changes were clearly afoot. A Little Ice Age began at the start of the century. It reduced crops and left the population prey to starvation and disease. Gossip spread of people taking the flesh of hanged corpses for food and even eating their own children.

Starting in India or China, the bubonic plague swept across Asia and into Europe. Black swellings the size of an egg appeared in armpits and groins, oozing blood and pus, followed by spreading boils and black blotches, fever, much pain and, within five days, death. Between 1348 and 1350, the *Black Death* killed an estimated one person in three. Perhaps 20 million people died in Europe alone, but no one can ever know. As the death carts rumbled by, the cities emptied. Paris, Florence, and Vienna had the most victims. Entire villages were wiped out. Almost everyone expected to die.

The stunned survivors fell into social and economic turbulence, bedeviled by all the deadly sins that sloth, avarice, and debauchery could assemble. The bubonic plague was borne by the omnipresent rats

and fleas, but ignorant of this, the survivors reached for other explanations. The Devil was blamed and, as usual, the Jews. Massacres followed, unchecked by the few reasoned voices who pointed out that all were dying of the plague together. Then, as if the slaughter of the previous Crusades and the devastation of the plague were not enough, Europe embarked on the Hundred Years War and still another failed Crusade.

There was more. Food ran short. So did ore deposits from easily worked mines. A money economy was replacing the old feudal service arrangements, which worsened economic conditions for many. Across France and Italy, lawless bands of knights spread terror. A decade after the first wave of the bubonic plague subsided, a second wave followed, less deadly but no less dreadful. It suffused Europe with a profound sense of doom. A third wave of plague began in 1373.

A schism saw rival popes in Avignon and Rome. The Vatican was weakened by corruption that reached from the papacy to monasteries with a reputation for promiscuity. The licentious behavior of priests and nuns led to the closing of convents in England and to scandals elsewhere.[1] This

18

was also the century of the fanatical Flagellants, the Peasants Revolt in England, and the oddity of a dancing mania that led people in the Rhineland, Holland, and Flanders to dance themselves into exhaustion accompanied by leaps and screams and religious visions. Everything seemed to be falling apart.

> The ills and disorders of the fourteenth century could not be without consequence. Times were to grow worse over the next fifty-odd years until at some imperceptible moment, by some mysterious chemistry, energies were refreshed, ideas broke out of the mold of the Middle Ages into new realms, and humanity found itself redirected.[2]

In fourteenth century England, John Wyclif preached man's direct communication with God, and his Lollard disciples painstakingly copied and recopied an English translation of the Bible, knowing they risked the cruel death meted out to heretics.[3] Not long into the next century came the voices heard by Joan of Arc, the peasant girl who combined the old religious fervor with the new force of national patriotism and strength on the battlefield that shook France. The Holy Roman Empire was declining, to be replaced eventually by nation-states.

Pope Boniface VIII issued a papal bull, "It is necessary to salvation that every human creature be subject to the Roman pontiff."[4] In smaller territories, many nobles were no less arrogant in asserting their own primacy over the Third Estate, which consisted of everyone who was not a member of the clergy or nobility.

But commerce was beginning to demand attention and there were stirrings in the establishment of towns, cities, and universities, in banking and invention, and in brave ships that ventured into unknown seas. The Mongol horde sweeping to the eastern gates of Europe opened a window to China that had been blocked by Arab and Persian middlemen who had always taken their cut of trade.

At home, nobles built themselves houses with a new feature to replace the simple hole in the roof for escaping smoke. Chimneys along the walls opened onto fireplaces in private rooms. For the first time, the noble family members separated themselves from their servants in the common hall, where all had come together to be warm. It was a small, early step to meet a human desire for privacy. For most people, privacy was unknown.

Sources of News

News from afar came at third and fourth hand from itinerant monks, soldiers, peddlers, couriers, and the pardoners who traveled from town to town selling absolution from sin. For the most part, people neither knew nor cared how the rest of the world fared. For the few common men who were fortunate enough to be literate, not much was available to be read, and what literacy existed was held in low regard. Most nobles, even kings, could neither read nor write. Medieval bishops encouraged civil illiteracy.[5] The Bible could not be translated into the vernacular, and only the clergy could possess copies, in Latin. Yet, the ranks of those with some measure of education had expanded.

Most information reached the brain through the ear, via gossip, morality plays, sermons, narrative ballads and tales, but here, too, technology was bringing change. Cheap, locally produced paper was replacing papyrus. The invention of spectacles aided old and weary eyes to read more.

By the end of the century, literacy was being considered a test for intelligence. Limited as it was, the mass of writing had multiplied considerably.[6] For the scholar, there were, in addition to the Bible, books on the various arts and sciences, plus romances and other diverting topics. The monastic rotula, the university couriers, the merchants' messenger services, and the new Tasso family postal system planted the roots of European mail services.

Centuries of struggle between Christian and Moslem forces deeply affected the spread of knowledge, not always negatively. The fall of Toledo, a center of Moorish and Jewish culture, to El Cid in the eleventh century had opened its libraries to western

Europe. In the fourteenth century, the Ottoman Turks overwhelmed Byzantine rule in Gallipoli, a vestige of the Roman Empire, and stood poised at the doorway of Europe. They would capture Constantinople itself at about the same time that Gutenberg was printing the 42-line Bible. Fearing Ottoman control even more than they disliked Roman orthodoxy, Byzantine scholars brought out classical Greek and Roman manuscripts of whose existence Western European scholars had been largely unaware. This began a search through lands under Byzantine control for manuscripts, statues, and other artifacts of the ancient cultures. The church supported the hunt for ancient treasures provided that any report about classical learning would be written in Latin or Greek, languages that were meaningless to the common people.[7]

In the fourteenth century, Dante wrote *The Divine Comedy*. Petrarch showed the Latin and Greek classics to a new age. The age of humanism is said to have been born in 1348 when Petrarch discovered letters written by Cicero, writings unknown in all the intervening centuries.[8] Boccaccio's tales laid the foundation for modern literature.

Reformation and Renaissance

Here was fertile ground for change, for the reform of the church, Reformation, and for rebirth, Renaissance, sparked by discovery of classical Greek and Roman manuscripts. This is not to say that they went hand in hand. They did not. Martin Luther denounced Desiderius Erasmus, the most brilliant humanist of his age, as a dreamer. The humanists, while they favored reforming the church, saw the Protestants, with their talk of hell, as reactionaries bent on a return to medievalism.[9]

Their quarrel continued for many centuries under many names, and continues today between secular humanism and religious fundamentalism. With all of this and more, the medieval world crumbled. Not since Rome fell had change been so deep, so complete. Princes who wished to attract humanists to their entourage scooped up precious manuscripts from abandoned monasteries and anywhere else they could be found to create libraries. All viewpoints would turn to Gutenberg's invention for their expression and dissemination.

Printing had not disturbed the monolithic Chinese empire. The introduction of printing in mid-fifteenth century Europe might also have made little headway if Europe were not ripe for change. As it turned out, because fifteenth century Europe was what it was, the ingenious system devised by the German goldsmith acted as a catalyst for forces that staggered the world. The world's second information revolution was printing.

A Gift from China

Paper is the most common, the most homely of things, hardly worth mentioning alongside the computer, digital compact discs, and satellites in geostationary orbit. Yet, with all these electronic wonders at our command, to imagine a world suddenly without paper is to plunge us into the midst of the Dark Ages, when the head of the Holy Roman Empire, Charlemagne, who never learned to write, and surely had never heard of paper, standardized writing to secure his empire.

Paper dispersed the Renaissance through Europe. Paper fueled the flames of the Reformation and the Counter-Reformation and every religious, political, and social upheaval since.

To understand paper's impact is to be aware of the force that communication technology exerts on our lives. It would take an effort to consider what the economy, religion, or our personal lives would be like without it, let alone what education, science, or medicine would be today. Paper has unobtrusively served as the hand-maiden of literacy. Because literacy and printing have fed each other, paper continues today as a fundament of freedom of thought, for it is most available in democratic nations, least available in the most repressive tyrannies. It is not by chance that some governments, while trumpeting freedom of the press, retain tight control over the newsprint supply.

To be aware of how important paper is to our lives, yet how transparent it is to our sight, it is necessary only to look up from the paper page on which these words appear and to glance around. Its applications are almost infinite. A goal of our late twentieth century technology includes the *paperless office*. The goal itself is written on paper. It is still "ten years away," as it has been for decades although there has lately been movement in that direction, especially in record keeping and databases.

Origins

The ancient Chinese incised animal bones and tortoise shells for messages and sometimes as a tool for fortune telling. Early Chinese emperors recorded messages on jade tablets, while nobles and high government officials did so on ivory, but obviously none of this was economically practical for sustained or widespread communication. What the Chinese needed was something readily available and less difficult to acquire than polished jade or ivory. They found a better writing surface in bamboo, from which they made tablets on which they wrote with a pointed bamboo or wooden stylus dipped into a black varnish. Bamboo had its limitations, too. A lot of records were a bulky load for a government functionary to carry around.

The Chinese also invented the camel's hair brush, gently writing on silk and on a type of silk paper. These writing surfaces, though expensive, had the advantage of convenience, for they could be carried and stored in rolls. Chinese writing, the oldest written language still in use, is pictographic and ideographic, each character a separate word derived from one or more modified pictures. The Chinese have not to this day

developed a phonetic alphabet. The advent of their written character words is dated to about 2700 B.C., nearly 3,000 years before paper.

The invention of paper in China is credited to a eunuch, Ts'ai Lun, the emperor's minister of public works, in 105 A.D., although he may have been given credit for someone else's invention.[10] In view of his important position, it is not unreasonable to infer that the government welcomed the invention because paper met an obvious need. It is hard to imagine that any government ever existed that didn't wish for more substances on which to record information and send out orders.

The clever inventor may have observed the wasp, which chews plants into a moist pulp and presses them into layers for its nest. The inventor tore rags apart into fibers, soaked them in water and beat them into a pulp, then pressed the pulp flat in a screen, and allowed the thin sheets of pulp to dry. The resultant paper held together, could be cut to any size, and could be written upon. Further experiments showed that linen, hemp, even fish nets and tree bark could be used to make paper. A hair brush served as the writing instrument, with ink from lamp black.

No doubt exists that the Chinese invention of *paper* eventually reached Europe. How much of *printing* the rest of the world owes to China is a matter to be taken up later. Cheap, plentiful, and flexible in use, paper turned out to be indispensable to Chinese religious elites, bureaucrats, and scholars. Paper helped to establish Confucianism in classical literature. Buddhist priests found paper of value to propagate their faith just as Christians would find parchment and then paper worthy for their faith. The Chinese carved word characters into wooden blocks that they inked and printed on pieces of paper sold as charms.

Other employment for paper included shoes, hats, belts, wrapping, wallpaper, napkins, curtains, toilet paper, and even military armor that protected against an enemy's arrows. The Chinese discovered the delights attendant upon printing paper money, which fascinated Marco Polo, whose usual curiosity about everything he witnessed in China did not extend to the printing methods. He wrote only about the banknotes. Unfortunately, the successive Chinese governments also paid a great deal of attention to paper money. After several waves of inflation, they discontinued its use in 1425, not to be resumed until the mid-nineteenth century.

No Information Revolution

The inventive Chinese are also credited with, among many things, the first uses of cast iron, steel, the mechanical clock, the umbrella, porcelain, the compass, wheelbarrows, spinning wheels, the parachute, kites, playing cards, the magic lantern, the chain pump, the fishing reel, the suspension bridge, whiskey, gunpowder, and printing. Some of these inventions shook Europe. Gunpowder, for example, helped to blow feudalism apart and raise citizen armies, for a horsed knight could not stand against cannon or musket. And the compass pointed the way to new worlds. China also gave Italy the noodle.

Approximately during the same period that the ancient Greeks were wrestling with political ideas along with a great expansion of knowledge in several fields, the Chinese were also advancing in medical theory, mathematics, philosophy, and technology generally far ahead of anything in the West.[11] Yet, in China there was no possibility of radical change. Free debate in an open society did not exist. Dynasties might change, but imperial rule remained untouchable.

For 500 years after its invention, paper was made only in China. Then Buddhist priests carried the secrets of paper and ink making to Korea and Japan, where the papermaker's art developed in unique ways. Some of the finest handmade paper in the world today is Japanese, fabricated by centuries-old methods. The Japanese adopted the Chinese characters, too, but the Japanese expanded their own written language by adding two additional sets of characters based on syllables to produce what is widely regarded as the world's most complicated system of writing. Their three distinct written forms often appear in the same sentence.

Paper Moves West

Paper craft also began its long journey west. When the Arabs captured Samarkand in 751, they discovered among their prisoners several Chinese papermakers. According to one version the men voluntarily gave up the secrets of their craft; another version claims they did so only under torture.[12] From them the Arabs learned the papermaker's art. A large industry of papermaking grew in Samarkand, then traveled the Silk Road to Baghdad and Damascus, which was to supply Europe with paper for several centuries. Islamic civilization was at its height. Its famed love of learning was well served by this new art. Paper replaced papyrus even in Egypt. A ninth century polite letter of thanks closes with the words, "Pardon the papyrus." It seems as if the writer is apologizing for not using the new and obviously more stylish paper.[13] In a macabre footnote to paper's history, mummies were being disinterred for their wrappings.[14]

When the Moors brought papermaking to Spain in the twelfth century, they anticipated the machine age by attaching stampers to the shaft of a water wheel. Except in Holland, which preferred its abundant windmill power, the water wheel continued to be an integral part of papermaking until the introduction of steam power in the nineteenth century.

The first paper factory in Christian Europe was reportedly established in France during the twelfth century by Jean Montgolfier, a crusader who escaped his Saracen captors in Damascus, where he worked as a prisoner in a paper mill. The art of papermaking established itself in mills near Fabriano, Italy, and eventually spread across Europe. Medieval paper, though more fragile and with a rougher surface than parchment, took ink better.[15] Neither product was cheap by modern standards. Much more significant was the amount of available rags compared to the available sheep and calf skins. Parchment and vellum continued to be used for luxury editions and for the production by monasteries of missals and breviaries.

A commercial expansion began in Europe toward the end of the thirteenth century, aided by Arabic numerals and paper for contracts, insurance, bills of lading, and bills of exchange.

> Paper production served the needs of merchants, bureaucrats, preachers, and literati; it quickened the pace of correspondence and enabled more men of letters to act as their own scribes.[16]

To the more conservative mind, paper was suspect, the product of a pagan culture. Attitudes about this were by no means uniform and many in the church welcomed paper as they would printing, but Emperor Frederick II decreed in 1221 that documents written on paper had no legal validity.[17] By then parchment had been well established for centuries. It served the needs of church and state and was for the most part under their authority, notably under the monasteries, large users of parchment.

In any event, paper did not find wide use in Europe until printing was invented. Low literacy kept demand down. If paper made printing effective, it was printing that introduced paper to most Europeans. Ultimately, the printing press won the day for paper. Parchment was too expensive for mass production. It was also not porous enough to absorb printing ink very well.

300 Sheep Skins for One Bible

Of the 210 printed copies of the first Gutenberg Bible, 30 were on parchment, 180 on paper. Each parchment copy required, it was estimated, the skins of 300 sheep. Not surprisingly, parchment for book printing did not survive to any extent beyond 1500. As for the 180 bibles printed on paper, the quality of the paper was so good compared to today's bleached and treated paper that 500 years from now a Gutenberg Bible, made in 1455, will probably look better than a Bible manufactured in 1997.

> The greatest pressure of all for literacy, however, was caused by the sudden availability of paper... As the paper mills spread, so too did the spirit of religious reform... As the price of paper continued to fall, the development of eye-glasses intensified the pressure for literacy. Glasses had first appeared in the early fourteenth century, and a hundred years later they were generally available. Their use lengthened the working life of copyist and reader alike. Demand for texts increased.[18]

In Nuremberg in the fourteenth century, the man who built the first paper mill in Germany, Ulman Stroemer, to assure himself a monopoly, demanded a vow of secrecy from his employees and a pledge never to work for anyone other than himself and his heirs. What followed was the first recorded labor strike in history. Stroemer broke the strike by imprisoning his workers until they gave in. It is likely that we know about this because someone wrote it down on paper.

Books and Universities

During the centuries of the Roman Empire, not many people even knew what a book was, but the riches of classical verse and prose were available to the small percentage of the populace of the far-flung empire literate in Greek or Latin and able to afford the hand-written copies. They could read the epic poetry of Homer and Virgil, the tragedies and satires, political speeches, philosophical questions, religious thought, and a gathering of scientific knowledge.

In the depths of the Dark Ages, these volumes disappeared, hidden away or lost forever. Scattered points of light shone in the European literary darkness in the scriptoria of monasteries as monks huddled over their painstaking illuminations on vellum of the Bible, religious commentary and, in

Figure 2.1
The fourteenth century Stromer paper mill, Nuremberg, the first paper mill in Germany.

some orders, perhaps a copy of a work from classical Greece or Rome. The book production of the monasteries was almost exclusively limited to church scholars and the schools that the monasteries kept for their novices and sometimes also for boys who were not destined to become monks. For nearly a thousand years, from the fall of Rome to the introduction of the printing press, the monasteries kept the sputtering flame of knowledge.

Monks, hunched over their scriptorium desktops, painstakingly hand lettered and painted manuscripts magnificently to reproduce books, *incunabula*, for libraries and cathedrals. The monks customarily mumbled or read aloud, not silently; monastery scriptoria resonated to a medley of oral communication accompanying the scratching of pens on parchment.

The First Universities

Establishment of European universities from the twelfth century onward marked the end of the 700-year-old Monastic Age. The more secular age that followed saw the emergence of a literate middle class and a rising demand for books of all kinds. Nobles may have known literature from hearing it read aloud, but those members of the new middle classes who were more familiar with reading and writing wanted books. Inevitably, errors crept into the copied and recopied books. Not until Gutenberg were books consistent from volume to volume.

The founding of universities, beginning in Bologna in 1158, shook the monopoly of the monasteries over the production and distribution of books, knowledge, and information. That monopoly would be badly weakened by the winds of change blowing

Figure 2.2   In a monastery scriptorium monks copied books onto parchment, a prepared animal skin, usually from a sheep or a goat.

through university towns where private booksellers and the secular copyists known as *scriveners* were to be found.[19]

As the centers of intellectual life shifted from the monasteries to the universities, private book dealers and copyists plied their trades, encouraged by teachers and students. The university booksellers were licensed and considered to be university officials. They enjoyed such privileges as exemption from certain taxes and the right to be tried in university courts, in exchange for which they accepted strict control by the university. They also had what amounted to a franchise, because outsiders could not compete. The university fixed the sale price of books, setting it cheap enough for a number of students to afford. Booksellers were not so much retailers as custodians of books through successive generations of teachers and students. Booksellers found a greater profit in renting them. Poor students shared books or copied them by hand.[20] Elizabeth Eisenstein drew a comparison between early printing and modern times:

> ...there are irreversible aspects to the early modern printing revolution. Cumulative processes were set in motion in the mid-fifteenth century, and they have not ceased to gather momentum in the age of the computer printout and the television guide... Commercial copy centers, for example, have begun to appear within the precincts of modern universities, much as stationers' stalls did near medieval universities.[21]

Early university students read little outside of theology and law. It was the age of scholasticism, with its attempt to prove faith by reason. Many monasteries produced few books outside of theology. In fact, the monks may have been forbidden to do so, although at a few monasteries the secular writings of Roman authors were considered fit to be copied, for which later ages have been grateful.

With scholarly texts once so rare now rippling out of printers' shops, wandering scholars had less need to go afield in order to consult a variety of texts, nor did they find it necessary to pore so long over a single work. And they finally had the opportunity to cross-reference among texts.[22]

Reading in the medieval monastery did not always mean what we mean today. Reading, or *lectio*, usually meant that the master read to the students. Books of the period were meant to be read aloud. The cost of books and the limited number of readers permitted no other choice. A school manual of a later period summed it up:

> "Are you a scholar, what do you read?"
> "I do not read, I listen."
> "What do you hear?"
> "Donatus or Alexander, or logic or music."[23]

With the rise in book production, literature could be absorbed in privacy instead of by sitting in an audience to hear it, an example of mass communication's pattern of separating people from one another.

The New Book Culture

Besides religious works, printers were turning out texts for schoolchildren and books on a variety of subjects for adults, among which guides and manuals to a well regulated family life seemed to be popular. Whether these were read aloud or perused privately, the result was a collective morality emanating from the shops of printers.[24]

Demand grew gradually for many kinds of books, especially for classical literature and for books on the sciences, many from India and the Arab cultural centers. Collections were small. A fourteenth century French bishop owned what was regarded as a large library of 76 books.[25] Authors covered a range of topics. England's first printer, William Caxton, chose the English language, not Latin, to publish the romances he turned out for the upper classes, and he found a ready market.

> Books of universal knowledge, mostly dating from the thirteenth century and written in (or translated from the Latin into) French and other vernaculars for the use of the layman, were literary staples familiar in every country over several centuries. A fourteenth century man drew also on the Bible, romances, bestiaries, satires, books of

astronomy, geography, universal history, church history, rhetoric, law, medicine, alchemy, falconry, hunting, fighting, music, and any number of special subjects.[26]

Even before Gutenberg, the availability of paper helped to spread literacy to the new merchant class, which was ready to read books on topics ranging from bawdy tales to religious works.[27] Xylographic printing, which impressed an entire page from an engraved block of wood, preceded movable type. Sheets of cloth or vellum or paper, printed on one side and folded over or bound back to back were assembled into "block books." The earliest block books were only of pictures, mostly religious. Later, text was added.[28]

People who could afford books treated them as liquid assets because they kept their value more than other personal items, to be sold when cash was needed. Bibles were family treasures to be mentioned in wills and passed down along the generations. In the absence of public libraries, literate people loaned books to one another.[29]

Authors who were not born to the nobility remained poor. Without copyright laws they did not dream of royalties, but depended on the protection and the purse of a wealthy patron unless they sold a manuscript outright to a bookseller. Milton parted with the manuscript of *Paradise Lost* for £5, with the promise of an equal sum if the printing sold out. The Middle Ages saw a gradual shift toward the recognition of authors that is part of the shift from an oral to a written tradition.

> In the Middle Ages authors had had little interest in attaching their name to a work, Printers were led to seek out, or have sought out, the true identity of the author of the works they printed—where, that is, they didn't invent it . . . But standards soon changed. Contemporary writers who had their names attached to hundreds and thousands of copies of their works became conscious of their individual reputations.[35]

The reading of books during the Renaissance may have had as much to do with a struggle for power as with a love of learning. The passing of the old medieval order reduced the need for military expertise, in which the nobility excelled, in favor of logical thinking, administrative skills, and a knowledge of the law. For some gentry, the change came hard. Wrote one sixteenth- century English gentleman:

> I swear by God's body, I'd rather that my son should hang than study letters. For it becomes the sons of gentlemen to blow the horn nicely, to hunt skilfully and elegantly, carry and train a hawk. But the study of letters should be left to the sons of rustics.[36]

The change came hard, but it came.

A sign of later times was the founding in 1665, with the encouragement of the French government, of the *Journal des savants*, the first periodical to review books.

Censorship

With the printing of books in Europe came severe censorship as to what could be printed. Publishing lay fully under the thumb of authority. Printers feared originality by authors, for it could cost printers their lives in the usual horrible ways devised by Church and State. New books, usually in the vernacular, were sometimes shunned.[30]

Before printing, few people in Europe other than scholars were literate, so the Church was not especially concerned about heresy in books, which were considered the working tools of scholars. Yet the danger of new ideas was that those in authority might themselves be swayed.

> Curiously, the threat print posed to authority was not that the masses would become voracious readers of incendiary tracts but that the authorities and exegetes from whom they habitually took their opinions would themselves become infected with new ideas.[31]

Church leaders were much more worried about what passed the lips of preachers who spoke to the masses in the common language.[32] That changed about 1478 with the publication of a handsomely illustrated Bible in Low German. Here was a direct challenge to the power of the church as the sole interpreter of God's Word. Rome responded by ordering the chastisement of all printers, buyers, and readers of heresy. In Mainz, where printing was born, the archbishop established a commission to grant permission for the printing of any book.

Governments were quick to discover that printing is easier to control than speech, for presses can be taxed and seized, paper can be rationed, newspapers can be censored, and books can be burned. Printing arrived in lands that had already known spoken heresies, and so government officials were not unprepared for the new heretical messages set before them in ink on paper.

The church was particularly suspicious of printing in any language but Latin. Church opposition to printing itself was minimal; in fact, except for some pockets of worry about its potential for mischief, printing was generally encouraged. Printing in the vernacular caused greater concern, for that cut into the exclusive domain over written communication of the ecclesiastic authorities. Printers encountered no problems when they restricted themselves to folk tales and similar entertaining fare, but both the religious and civil authorities cracked down upon printing in the vernacular that challenged authority. As for scholars writing in Latin or Greek for other scholars, there were relatively few complaints, so long as the common people were not troubled.

Punishment for Publishing

Burning books has proved a durable, if not always effective, means of control that has continued into this century. Writing confers too much influence to be ignored by the already powerful. As writing spread, so did its shadow, controls of writing. In many cultures across many centuries, writing has been restricted and invested with magical force, access granted to only a few. Such action inevitably led to turmoil. The most famous reactions of all, adding tinder to the fires of the Reformation, were the restrictions during the Middle Ages on reading the Bible and on printing it in anything but

Latin. Not the least of the responses were the book burning and the publishing of the index of forbidden books. A papal bill of 1502 ordered the burning of all books that questioned the authority of the Church. In 1516 the Fifth Lateran Council set forth *De impressione liborum*, forbidding any printing that lacked Church approval.

Before the invention of printing, a fourteenth century English religious sect, the Lollards, translated the Bible into English on the theory that God speaks directly to people in their own tongue, and that everyone can interpret God's message. This anticlerical heresy undercut the argument for hierarchy, was opposed by Church and State with burning by the former and hanging by the latter.

Church and State did not shrink from a policy of publish and perish. When William Tyndale, a humanist, printed an English translation of the New Testament, he aroused the furies. Captured, he was imprisoned, tried for heresy, and garroted. Then his corpse was tied to a stake and burned. Sir John Oldcastle, who has been identified as Shakespeare's model for Falstaff, was first hanged and then burned, both Church and State again getting their due.[33]

In Spain, as Columbus was getting ready to sail across the ocean to the Indies, the Inquisition burned books. Across Europe, the powers of Church and State cracked down hard on printers to assure that unapproved pamphlets and books were not distributed. Fines, prison, whippings, and death sentences were meted out to disobedient printers. By the time the Bastille fell in the French Revolution, more than 800 publishers, writers, and booksellers had been imprisoned there.

An exception to the dark cloud of censorship was Holland after it freed itself from Spain in the seventeenth century. Booksellers and intellectuals fled other countries for the freer air of Dutch cities, where they prospered, publishing banned books that they at times smuggled into the countries that banned them.[34]

Mail in the Middle Ages

During the Dark Ages and the early Middle Ages, when knowledge and literacy in Europe were the dominion of the church, little if any postal service existed. Few people could read, and nobles took pride in their illiteracy, believing that a strong memory would be weakened if the mind began to rely too much upon the written word. Few peasants journeyed even a few leagues from the place they were born. If they had, they might not have been able to return to it, for those who lived in these nameless hamlets had little perception of what lay beyond the next hill or the next turn in a rutted path. The land beyond their reach consisted at least as much of fantasy as reality. It was a flat world with heaven in the sky above and hell in the earth below. Dragons patrolled the edges of a world shared with races of gryphons and pygmies.

Unless their lord took them off on a crusade, the peasants married, raised their children, and died where they were born, for they belonged to the land. No doubt they enjoyed gossip as much as we do today, but they seldom if ever received news from afar. They could not have identified the country in which they lived, what the year was, or even the century. Life revolved around the seasons for planting and for harvesting, and religious festivals. For almost everyone, independent thought did not exist. The notion of freedom to choose a government would have been as bewildering as choosing a religion. You were what you were.

When the Roman Empire collapsed, so did the efficient Roman postal system. Peasants certainly had no need of a postal service. Hardly anyone else did either.

> One must try to conceive an age when there were no colleges nor even common schools, when rulers and even many of the clergy were immoral, filthy and ignorant. Nobles and knights were illiterate, and proud of it. Reading and writing were for churchmen, clerks (a rather despised profession), and perhaps a few highbrow women. A real upstanding man scorned such things.[37]

By the twelfth century, monasteries were communicating with one another. A favored means of swapping gossip and information was the *rotula*, a round-robin news letter on a parchment scroll. The abbot of a monastery would impart some news on the scroll, which was borne to the next monastery, whose abbot might comment on this news and add a fresh item or two about actual events, although the reader also found such entries as "Common report has it that Antichrist has been born at Babylon."[38] As the *rotula* made the rounds, it could grow quite long.

Postal Services for Town and Gown

The establishment of universities and the growth of towns and mercantilism expanded written communication. Merchants, peddlers, pilgrims, and crusaders carried news and private messages as they traveled more or less regular routes across Europe and the Near East. At the University of Paris, a system arose in the thirteenth century that helped lay the foundation of a national postal service. All university teachers and students were fortunate to be regarded as ecclesiastics. As such they enjoyed royal protection, including safe conduct when they traveled, exemption from military duty, and exemption from the taxes that other citizens had to bear. However, royal favor did not prevent students from sporadically writing home for money, one medieval tradition that survived the centuries. Subject only to the laws of the king and not to local justice, students lived a clamorous and penurious existence, cheated by the good townsfolk who blamed them for robbery, rape, and general debauchery.

To carry letters and money between the students and their parents, the University of Paris decided to set up a system of messengers, extending to them the same royal guarantees and exemptions that faculty and students enjoyed. As a result of this generous gesture, the inconsequential job of messenger became a coveted position despite the wages, or, to put it more precisely, the franchise to employ messengers was greatly coveted. To obtain their appointments, the messengers and their managers swore an oath of office and put up a bond. As the years passed, they supplemented their incomes by carrying along dispatches from outsiders. Ignoring restrictions, some messengers extended their routes to meet this growing, profitable demand. University administrators clambered down from their ivory towers to make sure that the university, too, derived considerable income from the mail service.

The spreading commercial interests of cities and towns led to arrangements to protect their trade with the outside world, particularly against bandits and feudal lords who taxed and sometimes seized goods crossing their lands. Arrangements included postal service between the towns. The prospering towns also set up a court system that required a separate messenger service to coordinate their decisions. Many of the powerful guilds of craftsmen and merchants wanted their own exchange of dispatches. In sum, what was hardly thought of during the illiterate feudal age of Europe became a necessity during the mercantile age that followed.

> The safe way, indeed the only way, to travel was in groups. In the Middle Ages, a lone traveler was a rare figure. He was usually a courier on the king's business, trained to repeat long messages word for word. Such a message could not be forged or lost.[39]

Postal Service as a Business

It might be expected that an ordinary citizen wishing to speed a letter to another ordinary citizen in another place, say a lover to the object of his or her desire, would search out anyone from a monk bearing a *rotula* to a messenger for the Butchers Guild willing to carry a perfumed letter along for a silver coin.

Regular couriers were appointed to carry mail for their organizations. They added outside letters, at first secretly and then openly with the permission of their organizations. Finally, this outside business became a part of their duties; the organizations they worked for profited from the courier's mail business sideline. During the fourteenth century, commercial letters were flowing among the port cities of the Hanseatic League. By 1500, letter routes open to the public crisscrossed Europe.

The quality of service was often a matter of luck. While some routes were overserviced, large areas of the continent were ignored. Postal fees soared, sometimes to the point of real personal sacrifice, with most of the fees paid by the receiver of the mail. If writing to a distant loved one might plunge him into debt, the lover did not write such a letter casually.

> When Patience Breton's letter arrived, if it did, her brother would no doubt be happy to have it. But he would be stunned at the fee he would have to pay. It would certainly help him to understand why the various postal systems were anxious to render him service.[40]

Rival postal systems emerged. Sometimes there were too many postmen, and competition grew nasty. Competition led to royal court intrigues and to violence on the highways.

In the fourteenth century, an extended Italian family named Tasso developed a private courier service that over the years fanned out across Europe. *Tassi* is the Italian word for *badgers*; as a symbol of authority the courier tied a badger skin over the forehead of his horse. Later, the couriers wore blue and silver uniforms. As the business prospered, the family became better known by the German name of *Taxis* and through marriage as *Thurn and Taxis*. Operating under charters of the Holy Roman Empire, the firm built a swift and dependable postal system across central Europe, a kind of pony express serving emperors, military officers, and merchants.

Because a postal service could be established in a country only with the permission of its ruler, it became the practice of a king to appoint postmasters not unlike the way a city today grants a franchise to a cable television company. In Britain, the franchise was called a *farm* and the franchisee a *farmer*. Besides these new private services, the government services continued. Eventually, most of them merged into a single State Post, a practice that began in France in 1627. However, some private services continued. The historic antecedents of UPS and Federal Express run deep.

In 1627, it became possible to send money by registered mail, the first arrangement of its kind. Soon after, a parcel post service began. A privately run city mail service for Paris was permitted in 1653. Letters were put into postage-paid envelopes, an early version of the postage stamp, and collection boxes were placed around the city. The project, however, proved to be a failure.

In 1682, one William Dockwra began a private postal service in London with penny postage and five hundred collection boxes, hourly collection, and six to ten deliveries a day.[41] Miffed, the government put Dockwra on trial, convicted him, and took over his business, promptly ending its efficiency and low prices. Another Londoner tried to set up a similar private service a generation later and met a similar response from the government. The service was quickly suppressed. After that, no one else anywhere in Europe tried competing with his or her government for two centuries.

In the early history of the United States, some private delivery services carried letters within cities for a penny apiece and advertised that they could beat the government mail between Boston and Philadelphia; in 1851 the Supreme Court ruled against the practice on the grounds that private carriers deprived the government of income from postage stamps.[42] Congress enforced the monopoly by declaring all roads to be post roads. Efficiency was not at issue.

Time would bring change. At the effort to keep competition away, the postal service would not always be so fortunate.

In the Moslem nations, pigeons were employed extensively to carry news. Thousands were used during the Crusades. In Europe, too, until this century, pigeons carried correspondence, especially business information. Nathan Rothschild, who headed the London branch of the banking family, reportedly made a killing on the stock market when a pigeon brought him the first news of Napoleon's defeat at Waterloo. Others used pigeons to learn which horse won a race. Julius Reuter started the international news service that bears his name by using pigeons to fill a gap in the telegraph lines between Berlin and Paris.

Here a New, There a New

At first, no one considered that the public had a *right* to know, but apparently they *wanted* to know. Julius Caesar ordered that a record of official government news and announcements should be posted around Rome. It was called the *Acta Diurna* (*Daily Transactions*), a gazette of what happened at the Senate plus other matters the government thought the public should know. Newsletters that included items from the Acta were copied by scribe slaves to be privately circulated throughout the vast Roman Empire, which at its height of power stretched from Scotland to Egypt, a level of news dissemina-

tion that would not be matched for a thousand years.

In China, a few centuries later a similar gazette, known as *tipao* (*palace report*), carried official announcements and news from the far-flung provinces to a readership of bureaucrats, not for ordinary people, most of whom were illiterate in any case. Publication of these *tipao*, at first written by hand or printed with wooden blocks, continued until the end of the Manchu empire in 1911. Although the *tipao* had not been published frequently or widely, in one form or another they survived for about a dozen centuries!

Forerunners of Newspapers

When mercantilism in Europe replaced the feudalism of the Middle Ages, literate merchants and government officials sought reliable and prompt tidings from distant cities relating to trade, political events, or the outcome of battles. By the middle of the fifteenth century, about the time that Johannes Gutenberg began printing Bibles, handwritten newsletters appeared once again in Europe, where they had apparently been absent since the days of the Roman Empire. They were sent irregularly at first and then on a regular basis, at times coinciding with a weekly mail delivery.

The occasional *printed* pamphlet or broadside was published when someone wanted a piece of news or an announcement distributed widely. Fifty years after Gutenberg's invention, political newsletters, some in ballad form, were being distributed either printed or as handwritten manuscripts where printing was unable for one reason or another to meet the new demand for information. *Broadsides* at times carried their reports in the form of a rhyming ballad, following the tradition of balladeers who went from town to town earning coins by songs that included news in rhyme. Thanks to the printed pamphlet, there existed for the first time the means of reaching a large and scattered public quickly with information in each subsequent copy exactly as accurate as the information in the first copy. Some pamphlets, called *canards* in French, reported devilish actions, miracles, monsters, catastrophes, and the arrival of comets.

Later, the literate were able to read printed *newsbooks*, a compilation of several pages, usually on a single topic, occasionally illustrated with woodcuts and including the text of letters. Likely as not, the topic of a newsbook was a situation or event that someone in power wanted to bring to the public's attention, such as victory in battle or a planned royal wedding.

From Venice came the more current *newssheets*. They supplemented the town crier and the coffeehouse gossip with short political and military news items from various European cities—except Venice.[43] The earliest newssheets, a single sheet of paper slightly smaller than a modern sheet of 8 1/2 x 11-inch office stationery folded in half, was usually printed on one side of a piece of paper. In Italy, a small coin called a *gazetta* paid for a copy. In time, many of the early newspapers came to be known as *gazettes*.

The popularity of these newssheets, published sporadically, sometimes anonymously under changing names either under the government's watchful eye or a step ahead of the police, led to the concept of the *newspaper*, a publication that would be published under the same name on a regular schedule, a source of the latest news and a variety of news, a private enterprise not dependent upon the government or any other organization for its information. It was a wonderful idea, if not altogether safe. By the seventeenth century, newssheets began to expand into newspapers.

The First Newspapers

Scholars disagree as to which was the first newspaper. It may have been the Latin news periodical Mercurius Gallo-Belgicus printed in Cologne starting in 1594.[44] Both Holland and Switzerland claim the location for the world's first newspaper. What is agreed is that the idea of the newspaper soon spread across western Europe. It reached the American colonies in 1690, when Benjamin Harris produced a single issue of *Publick Occurrences* in Boston before colonial authorities shut him down. Harris was not unaccustomed to such treatment, for he had fled to Boston from London, where authorities took exception to his politically inflammatory publications.

Printers in eighteenth century America had a hard time surviving until they discovered the newspaper as a source of income.[45] A printer starting up in business made sure that a newspaper was part of his output, even though he might be the only contributor of articles. Borrowing from other newspapers became commonplace. It saved wear and tear.

The emergence of the daily newspaper enlarged the public's appetite for new information. Here a *new*, there a *new* added up to *news*.

Unintended Consequences

A growing commercial press, whose pages included not only news of commerce, but advertisements, was matched by a growing political press. The spreading of literacy, which printing made possible, led during the 17th and 18th centuries to news about public affairs and the establishment of a base of public opinion that governments ignored at their peril. In Europe, nation after nation saw the Divine Right of Kings fall before a public crying for reform and a voice in their governance, and willing to go to the barricades to achieve them. In the American colonies, the Stamp Act of 1765, which laid a heavy duty on newsprint, exacerbated the agitation preceding the Revolution.

> If it seems farfetched to relate the French and American and British revolutions to the 42-line Bible that came off the press in Mainz in 1455, it is less farfetched to relate them to news sheets, newspapers, and political tracts.[46]

An unintended consequence of the printing of news, whether by newsbook, newsletter, newssheet, or newspaper, was that it chipped away at authority. News printing helped to undermine the concept of the Divine Right of Kings. As so often recurs in the course of human affairs, the diffusion of a means of communication distributed political power, too. The printing of news was awaited so eagerly, even by illiterate commoners who listened to reports read aloud, that those in power found themselves obliged to publish in order to assure support. So it was that King James I of England felt it necessary, though extremely distasteful, to "descend many degrees beneath Our Selfe" and print his decision to dissolve Parliament. At least his statement stood in splendid isolation. No opposing viewpoint was permitted printers' ink.

A new tool of communication may replace something useful or pleasurable. Newspapers, the new tool of communication, replaced some measure of oral communication. Given the opportunity, people preferred to read their information than to hear about it. Instead of at church, gossip could be picked up by reading a newspaper at home. Private life expanded as communal activities and neighborly relationships shrank.

> Complaints about the "sullen silence" of newspaper readers in seventeenth century coffeehouses point to the intrusive effects of printed materials on some forms of sociability.[47]

Printing and Literacy

Printing spread literacy. Literacy spread printing. Together they created the modern world. In Europe, for more than one thousand years, Latin was the international language and the language of diplomacy, just as Chinese was in the Far East and English is today all over the world. Latin was the language of scholars and schoolboys, the language of books, the language used to communicate with God. It was a pillar of the unchanging medieval world. Then came printing, and with it the publication of books in the vernacular, in the several languages spoken on the streets of Europe.

Vernacular Printing

Less than fifty years after Gutenberg introduced his printing system some 10 million copies of books had been printed in Europe, an astonishing number in light of limited literacy. The number would rise to between 150 million and 200 million by the end of the next century.[48] Books printed in some of the European vernaculars codified those languages. By neglect, other vernaculars, like Gaelic and Provençal, were consigned to being spoken but rarely written. With the shift to printing in vernaculars, over a period of centuries Latin itself, along with those other classical languages whose knowledge once signified the scholar, Greek and Hebrew, fell into disuse except for formal prayer.

Vernacular printing also gave rise to standards of spelling and rules of syntax. When words were spelled at all they first appeared as they sounded, which could be as different as the shape of the ears of the printers who struggled for a visual equivalent of what they heard, unlike the precision of Latin. In time, English and other vernacular languages would develop the orthographic and syntactical structures that have been the despair of generations of schoolchildren ever since.

As books became available, literacy was fostered. As literacy expanded, so did the call for even more books. It is a tale that would recur through history.

> The new presses…probably did not *gradually* make available to low-born men what had previously been restricted to the high born. Instead, changes in mental habits and attitudes entailed by access to printed materials affected a wide social spectrum from the outset. In fifteenth century England, for example, mercers and scriveners engaged in a manuscript book trade were already catering to the needs of lowly bakers and merchants as well as to those of lawyers, aldermen and knights.[49]

Commoners steeped in book learning were now sitting in the highest councils of government. When the ability to read and write conferred a measure of authority, aristocrats who had expressed contempt for literacy began to treat books and learning with a bit more respect so they could resume what they regarded as their rightful, God-given places of power. Accompanying the change in behavior toward reading came the sometimes surprising discovery that reading could be enjoyable; indeed, the acquisition of knowledge could be a pleasure!

Vernacular printing also led French readers to think of themselves as being part of France, and English readers to regard themselves as part of England. This national consciousness hardly existed when literate people read only Latin and the spoken language was a babble of unrecognizable dialects.[50]

Why Bother to Read?

Printing and its accompanying literacy represent one of the greatest, if not the greatest of the watersheds of human history. In the Middle Ages, most people were illiterate. Someone who needed to locate an unfamiliar shop would look for a picture over the door. A hatmaker painted a hat on a sign. Why bother learning to read? And without something to read there was little reason to learn the difficult art.

> For over five hundred years this achievement (to be able to read and write) was rare in Western Europe. It is a shock to realise that during all this time practically no lay person, from kings and emperors downward, could read or write. Charlemagne learnt to read, but he never could write. He had wax tablets beside his bed to practise on, but said he couldn't get the hang of it.[51]

What literacy existed was mostly for men. Women were not expected to be schooled and just a modest percentage could read.[52] Among women of the poorer classes, literacy probably did not exist. But for both sexes printing was something to *listen* to when a book was opened by someone who would read aloud.

With religious and political tracts in the vernacular instead of Latin, to say nothing of the Holy Bible itself, making the heroic effort to decipher the words on a page now became for some a worthwhile endeavor. The astonishing dispersion of printed materials, matched by the spreading literacy, in turn increased the market for books and other written material, an ever widening circle. Literacy also brought a measure of independent thought to its possessors, even the means to power and wealth in a world where centuries of feudalism had blocked personal advancement. In a few cases, a desire may have been born to use the printing press to say something to others.[53] Peasants also discovered what the

Gospels really said about the poor and oppressed.

> The monopoly position of the Bible and the Latin language in the church was destroyed by the press and in its place there developed a widespread market for the Bible in the vernacular and a concern with its literal interpretation... The effect of the discovery of printing was evident in the savage religious wars of the sixteenth and seventeenth centuries.[54]

The Engines of Printing and Literacy

Printing and literacy were engines that helped to fuel the religious Reformation, the secular Renaissance, a spirit of nationalism, and the growth of mercantilism. An evangelical impulse powered the early presses with rapid, spectacular consequences.[55] Bibles, tracts, and sermons were held in roughened hands newly washed. Over several centuries the presses broke down the feudal system of kings and barons. Priests lost the exclusive prerogative of interpreting the Bible. The rigid social structure that determined a man's fate from the day of his birth crumbled as men empowered by literacy dared to reach out in new directions. Printing gave a boost to public excitement over ocean exploration just as, in our own day, television fired the public imagination for exploring space.

> As the presses disgorged new printed matter, the yearning for literacy spread like a fever; millions of Europeans led their children to classrooms and remained to learn themselves.[56]

Caught up in the ideas of humanism—with its focus on life, not on eternity—and the rediscovery of the learning of ancient Greece and Rome, fueled by the books made by paper, movable type, and presses, scholars and students came together at new universities. Within six decades of the publication of the 42-line Bible, more than a dozen additional universities were established. In just the two decades between 1496 and 1516, five additional colleges were founded at Oxford and Cambridge.

All this ferment led to that rarest of cultural phenomena, an intellectual movement which alters the course of both learning and civilization. Pythagoreans had tried it, four hundred years before the birth of Christ, and failed. So, in the third and fourth centuries A.D., had Manichaeans, Stoics, and Epicureans. But the humanists of the sixteenth century were to succeed spectacularly—so much so that their triumph is unique. They would be followed by other ideologies determined to shape the future—seventeenth century rationalism, the eighteenth century Enlightenment, Marxism in the nineteenth century, and, in the twentieth, by pragmatism, determinism, and empiricism. Each would alter the stream of great events, but none would match the achievements of Renaissance humanists.[57]

Curiously, and perhaps by coincidence, modern handwriting was born shortly after printing came to Europe and the handwritten book died.[58] Credit is given to the inventor of italic type, the printer Aldus Manutius of Venice, the possessor of what is still referred to as *a fine Italian hand*. The art of penning a charming letter in a flowing style of penmanship grew to be an accomplishment admired among the literate.

Literacy and Equality

As printing spread at the close of the Middle Ages (more accurately, the spread of printing *closed* the Middle Ages), so did written communication, but oral communication obviously did not disappear as a resonating source of information. Preaching continued, as did traveling plays and the news-peppered ballads of itinerant minstrels. Oral and written cultures have, in one expression or another, existed side by side up to the present moment.

The diffusion of printing across the world, like the diffusion of so many other tools of communication where they have not been restricted by a power elite, led to the equalizing effects of an increased number of producers delivering information of ever greater variety to a widening pool of users. In short, diffusion led to a decentralizing of authority and influence. Here was an early version of what in the late twentieth century would be termed *postmodernism*, as scholars and other writers brought a variety of backgrounds and perspectives to what had been a limited, rigid view of the world and challenged accepted views. With printing and literacy feeding one another, literacy itself served as a tool of communication.

Did Gutenberg Know About China?

Francis Bacon said printing, the compass, and gunpowder were the three inventions that changed the world. Each was Chinese.

We tend to think of printing only in terms of typography, the printing of words with the single letters of movable type. Actually, printing flourished long before typography. The Chinese printed books using carved wooden blocks. Fêng Tao, who improved the art of block printing, or *xylography*, is regarded in Chinese history

Figure 2.3   A sketch of the reconstructed workshop of Johannes Gutenberg in the Gutenberg Museum in Mainz, Germany.

much as Gutenberg is in the West.[59] Carving a pageful of characters and drawings into a single wooden block for inking was the basis for block printing, which existed for centuries before the invention of movable type in China. Although the Chinese invented movable type, they made little use of it.

Inked seals had been used in the ancient Mediterranean civilizations as far back as 4000 B.C. Alexander the Great may have brought them to India during his invasion. Merchants traveling between India and the Orient may have introduced them to the Chinese, who restricted the number of copies of the books they printed, unlike the Western practice of finding wider audiences.[60]

Romans in the first century B.C. discovered that printing stamps could be aligned for the efficient production of tablets or texts. However, the idea went nowhere. No suitable ink was available and papyrus and vellum were expensive and not ideal for printing. Also, little demand existed for large numbers of copies of books or documents. Literacy was not widespread; scribes could reproduce by hand all the written material needed.

It is instructive to compare Europe with China, which had known little but strong central governments, where paper manufacture and printing had been born, but where printing had languished. Monolithic government control must be taken into account. In China, from earliest times, printing was associated with either religious belief or government. Chinese ideographic characters were stamped on bamboo strips, many characters on a strip, to be worn as amulets to keep tigers and wolves away, and to cure illness. Bamboo strips were also stamped with such identification of the traveler as name, age, and appearance. Since stamps and ink were officially sanctioned, the government could use these early passports to regulate movement, like permission to enter a city gate.

European Ferment

Europe added several elements essential to the continent's rapid absorption of printing. As noted, it was a Europe in ferment, at the dawn of religious and secular change, its knights home from the Crusades, its cities pulsing with new ideas. Unlike China, mired in imperial rigidity, fifteenth century Europe was wrestling with change. From the twelfth century onward, there were the universities, whose scholars needed books.

There was religious ferment. By translating the Bible into the German vernacular, the Augustinian monk Martin Luther allowed people to do something astonishing—to read the Word of God for themselves in the language they spoke daily and to respond as individuals. To enlist a broader audience, including much of the nobility who knew no Latin, he wrote in the German that all those around him had spoken since childhood. The printing medium placed this vernacular Bible in their hands.[61] Europe also added an increasingly literate population among the elite. No sooner had Luther nailed on the church doors his propositions against indulgences than a campaign of posters, pamphlets, and caricature drawings began first across Germany and then across the rest of Europe. The available presses could not print pamphlets and books fast enough.

Bound up with the Reformation's almost insatiable appetite for religious books, printing presses were also tied to the Renaissance, with its great appetite for copies of the newly discovered Greek classics, and indeed for learning of all kinds. These hungers could not be satisfied by the slow pen of copyists in the monasteries and the back shops of the booksellers.

The convergence of printing with the religious impulses of the Reformation and the humanism of the Renaissance fractured a medieval structure that had stood for centuries. A turning of attention from medieval attitudes and alchemy to the newly rediscovered literature, morality, and politics of classical Greece separates the Renaissance from the Middle Ages.[62]

What Did Gutenberg Know?

What of printing was known to Johannes Gutenberg before he assembled the system that produced the famous 42-line Bible? Specifically, how much of what the Chinese had invented, if anything, was known to the German goldsmith who is credited with one of the world's most earth-shaking inventions? When Gutenberg produced printing, he may not have heard of far off Cathay. The real question is, was he aware of the printing that had been done there for centuries? The answer will probably never be known, but one of history's great mysteries tantalizes us with its clues.

Oriental technology and products traveled west from China by way of traders journeying along the Silk Road through fabled cities like Samarkand, Baghdad, and Damascus. It is not at all clear that the invention of typography—movable type and the casting of type—had ever reached Europe from the Orient, but block-printed books could well have found their way to Europe before Gutenberg's first impressions in the fifteenth century, for great numbers of books had been printed in China. Some block printing had also been done in Europe.

The oldest book surviving today is, in fact, a religious work dated 868, the Diamond Sutra, on a roll 16 feet long, a Chinese version of Buddhist scripture. Two copies have been found, one printed from stone, the other from wood, discovered undisturbed amid thousands of Buddhist texts stored in a subterranean chamber in the desert of western China, where the dry conditions minimized decay.

In imperial China, a book was a rolled manuscript of silk or paper until the tenth century, when the first folded books appeared, a precursor to the stitched book. A book was folded from a single sheet of paper, but like all block prints it was printed on only one side of the paper. The folds were pasted together so the book could be read by turning the pages.

The contents of all books must have been known to government officials because censorship was a known fact of life among Chinese scholars, hundreds having been buried alive by the first emperor of the Chin dynasty, who also burned all the books he could find.

As for other printed material that traveled west along the Silk Road, we can only speculate. With active commerce, it is likely that decks of block-printed playing cards and religious images moved freely between Europe and the Far East. Perhaps some trader took along a religious picture to comfort his hours along the route. The earliest known European block prints are religious images. Surely other traders packed decks of playing cards among their possessions to while away the hours at campsites far from home. Playing cards are known to have been in Europe by the fourteenth century, because a moralist of that era complained of card playing during sacred festivals and the hawking of obscene pictures in church.[63]

Block printing, although an active art across the Far East, had been unknown to the Europe of the Dark Ages, where monks patiently copied manuscripts. Between China and Europe lay the Islamic world, which refused for religious reasons to print its literature. The first mention in European literature of the Chinese invention of printing comes in 1546, a century after Gutenberg's 42-line Bible was printed, from the Italian historian Jovius, who examined printed books brought from China by Portuguese travelers and concluded that European printing was derived from China.[64]

The known history of paper hints at the way that printing technology may have traveled. Missionaries and other travelers relayed information that the Chinese invented paper, played with printed cards, spent printed paper money, and treasured printed religious pictures. It would be reasonable to conclude that the missionaries also shared the knowledge that a great number of books were printed in China.

Before Gutenberg no less than eight European travelers, Marco Polo among them, described printed paper money.[65] Pope Innocent IV sent an emissary, John of Plano Carpini, to the Grand Khan in the mid-thirteenth century. He returned with a letter sealed in the Chinese style, ink printed upon paper two centuries before Gutenberg. At the same time, several European prisoners, both men and women, were living in the Mongol capital. Yet, the trail remains cloudy.

> No positive documentary evidence has yet been found to show that…European block printing came from the Far East at all. But strong circumstantial evidence leads to the conviction that either through Russia, through Europeans in China, through Persia, or through Egypt—perhaps through several or all of these routes—the influence of the block printing of China entered the European world during the time of the Mongol Empire and the years immediately following and had its part in bringing about the rise and gradual development of that activity which in turn paved the way for Gutenberg's invention.[66]

In the thirteenth century, Genghis Khan and his Mongol army ripped down the Islamic blockade and brought the Orient to Europe's door for one century, until the Mongols fell. What Europe did not realize in its terror was that the Mongols had cleared away the impediments to direct communication with a highly civilized kingdom to the east, China.

The Mongols were an unlettered people when they swept out of their remote kingdom. As they relentlessly galloped westward, they conquered people who printed, including the Buddhist priests who used the art mostly to duplicate *sūtras*, which are religious manuscripts comprising narrative text and charms.[67] The Mongols adopted what they wanted of the cultures of the vanquished. Content to patronize Chinese literature in the East and Arabic literature in the West,[68] they even printed Chinese literature in their own Mongol language.[69]

Movable Type in China and Korea

For material such as documents and books, the East Asian written languages were at a distinct disadvantage for printing, especially when compared with Western languages. Each Chinese character and most Japanese characters represented a word, of which there were many tens of thousands. Western languages were based on alphabets of little more than two dozen letters that were combined to make words. The Chinese printer worked under another disadvantage. He did not use a press. Instead, his brush pressed the paper against the inked blocks, probably a single block at a time.

In the eleventh century, one Pi Shêng, a blacksmith and alchemist, invented movable type, molding characters out of baked clay—pottery type that he placed in an iron frame. He made several copies of each word character and 20 or more of the most common words so he could print a whole page at once. Unfortunately, success eluded Pi Shêng. No ink behaved well with pottery type and the sheer volume of Chinese word characters worked against his idea, so it was easier just to engrave wooden blocks. He had translated an ingenious idea into an invention, but he could not complete a printing system and move it to the innovation stage, where it would find a use. Pi Shêng was a man with an idea ahead of his time. His invention was not, however, completely forgotten. In 1313, about twenty years after Marco Polo returned to Venice, a historian, Wang Chên, wrote a detailed account of movable type, so it stands as part of the history of communication.[70]

Although typesetting failed to take hold in China, which was wedded to block printing, it was used in Korea decades before Gutenberg printed Bibles in Germany. Located where it was, the effect on the world of Korean publishing appears to have been modest, yet it should not be discounted. In that remote corner of the world in the early fifteenth century, King Sejong encouraged book production "so as to satisfy reason and to reform men's evil nature."[71] The royal Korean government even created a Department of Books.

The far-seeing king also ordered his scholars to create a simple alphabet for the common people. They produced *hangul* ("Korean letters"), a phonetic system based on Sanskrit with eighteen consonants and ten vowels. Sejong's enlightened attitude was quite at variance with the cramped, suspicious policies of Chinese emperors of the era. It was used to further literature and education.

The type used was the Chinese character set of perhaps 8,000 word characters instead of the much simpler Korean phonetic alphabet, because Chinese was the language of literacy, just as Latin was at the same time in Europe. Sejong's government type foundry cast copper type. The pieces of type were inferior to the kind that Gutenberg would invent a half century later. The type molds enabled Korean printers to cast identical character after character in small flat squares, a system that worked, but must have made binding in a form difficult. By 1434, a book had been printed in movable type, with both Chinese pictograph characters and their corresponding Korean phonetic symbols apparently joined on the same type mold.[72]

> It is a strange fact that China, Korea, and Japan, whose languages present the most difficulties to the typographic printer, should have been the first nations to invent and develop the art of typography.[73]

Gutenberg's Achievement

What Gutenberg produced that did not exist in Asia was a printing *system*. Most obvious among its elements were controlled, exact dimensions of alphabet type cast from metal punches made of hardened steel. These were not unlike the dies, stamps, and punches that were well known to European leather workers, metalsmiths, and pewter makers. Gutenberg invented the type mold. All of Gutenberg's individual casts of letters were of the same height and could be set in rows. A wooden frame held the page of type firmly in place for the handpress, which

Figure 2.4   Type was chosen from a job case and set by hand.

was a familiar item in fifteenth century Europe as both a linen press to remove wrinkles from clothes and a grape press to make wine. Perhaps borrowing from artists who were using oil as a base for their paint, Gutenberg added a linseed oil-varnish ink that was suitable for making legible impressions from metal type upon paper.

A few efforts had been made to produce books by block printing, but carving a page-sized block of wood for each page was plainly unsatisfactory. Gutenberg found a better answer by molding individual letters that could be used again and again. The idea may have come from the goldsmiths and silversmiths in the region around Mainz who used distinctive punches to impress their hallmark in the soft precious metals.

We know little about the contribution of Johann Gutenberg, an inventor whose name is associated with the achievement of printing with movable type. Many of the references to him in history are forgeries, and his name appears nowhere in books claimed to have been printed by him. The evidence that he invented printing with movable type is scanty, consisting mostly of a lawsuit against him which describes the nature of the printing that went on in his Mainz, Germany, establishment.[74]

A lawsuit in the year 1444 refers to two steel alphabets, and it is known that Gutenberg printed with movable type about 1450 to publish what is known as the 36-line Bible; that is, 36 lines per page. He refined his method over the next several years to print—around 1457-1458—the more famous 42-line Bible of 1,282 two-column pages, of which 48 copies are still in existence. Victor Hugo would state, "The Gothic sun set behind the gigantic printing press of Mainz."[75] It was a turning point of history.

To print a page, a sheet of damp paper was pressed down on the inked type. Then, the sheet was hung up to dry, after which it was dampened again for printing on the other side. Printing caught on immediately. When apprentices learned the secrets of their masters, they moved on to their own establishments.

The cousinly art of paper making, some three centuries earlier, had coursed through the cities of Europe the same way. When Mainz was sacked in 1462 by the army of Adolphus of Nassau, printing moved to Italy, where wealthy nobles patronized the arts and liberal churchmen encouraged learning.[76] In England, presses were set up at Oxford and Cambridge. A press was set up in Rome, 1464; Paris, 1470; Holland, 1471; Switzerland, 1472; Spain, 1474; England, 1476; Denmark, 1482; Constantinople, 1490.

The thousands of scribes at work throughout Europe did not disappear overnight. Hand copying continued for decades, but as it is today, handmade goods were more expensive. In Paris in 1470, a manuscript Bible fetched five times the price of a printed Bible. A curious riddle in Middle English about a book, describing how parchment is made and then written on with a quill, goes as follows:

A foe deprived me of life, took away my bodily strength; afterwards wet me, dipped me in water, took me out again, set me in the sun where I quickly lost the hairs I had. Afterwards the hard edge of the knife cut me, with all impurities ground off; fingers folded me, and the bird's delight sprinkled me over with useful drops... If the sons of men will use me they will be the safer and the more victorious, the bolder in heart and the blither in thought, the wiser in mind... Ask what my name is, useful to me; my name is famous, of service to men, sacred in myself.[77]

Sometimes a new edition of a printed book that had been sold out was hand copied when only a few copies were demanded because copying by hand was cheaper than resetting all the type. But the sun was setting on the honorable profession of scribe. It was estimated that a printer could on average produce in two days what a copyist produced in one year.[78]

Because the amount of type was limited and because stereotyping had not been invented, book printers could set up just a few dozen pages at a time. As a result, a single edition of a book was apt to be studded with variants, for harried authors were able to correct their texts only in the midst of the printing process.[79]

The phrases *upper case*, meaning capital letters, and *lower case* were born at this time. The early cases in which printers kept their type were divided horizontally, with the capital letters stored in the upper case and the small letters in the lower case. Anyone who is aware of the measurement of type sizes determined in *points* may also be interested to learn that one point was 144th the size of the foot of King Louis XVI of France, who died on the scaffold.

The many printing presses established by the Roman Catholic Church were part of the reason that the supply of books, which changed within a few decades from handwritten script to mostly print, changed also from scarcity to glut.[80] Each of the states of western Europe had at least one major publishing center. The numerous small states, towns, and bishoprics that existed in place of a strong central authority had created a fragmented political power in Europe. The consequent political competition and active evangelism set up diverse and competitive islands of power. This encouraged printing, for in every age of history people who compete with others will use the means of communication at their disposal.[81]

Gutenberg's little press in Mainz would be a pebble dropped into the pond of history, spreading ripples in an ever widening circle. Just as the phonetic alphabet on papyrus dispersed knowledge two thousand years earlier, so now did printing. By the sixteenth century, printing had expanded specialization and an even wider distribution of information and ideas.

In inventing printing, Gutenberg had also invented industrial repetition. The information revolution that he began in the fifteenth century would flower in the industrial revolution of the nineteenth century. That era would bring into being yet another information revolution, one marked by William Fox Talbot's invention of the repeatability of images and Thomas Edison's invention of the repeatability of sounds.[82]

Figure 2.5   The printing press changed little in more than three centuries.

Notes

1 William Manchester, *A World Lit Only By Fire: The Medieval Mind and the Renaissance* (Boston: Little, Brown, and Company, 1992), 130.

2 Barbara Tuchman, *A Distant Mirror: The Calamitous 14th Century* (New York: Alfred A. Knopf, 1978), 581.

3 Tuchman, 339.

4 His second bull, *Unam Sanctam*, in 1302.

5 William A. Mason, *A History of the Art of Writing* (New York: The MacMillan Co., 1920), 454

6 Stanley Morison, *Politics and Script* (Oxford: The Clarendon Press, 1972), 247.

7 Manchester, 182.

8 Morison, 265.

9 Manchester, 182.

10 Thomas F. Carter, *The Invention of Printing in China and Its Spread Westward*, 2nd ed. (New York: Ronald Press, 1955), 3.

11 G.E.R. Lloyd, "Democracy, Philosophy, and Science in Ancient Greece," in John Dunn, ed., *Democracy: The Unfinished Journey, 508 BC to AD 1993* (New York: Oxford University Press, 1992), 55.

12 Albertine Gaur, *A History of Writing* (London: The British Library, 1987), 46.

13 Carter, 136

14 Harold Innis, *Empire and Communication* (Toronto: University of Toronto Press, revised ed., 1972), 129.

15 Lucien Febvre and Henri-Jean Martin, *The Coming of the Book: The Impact of Printing, 1450-1800* , trans. David Gerard (London: Verso Editions, 1984), 16.

16 Elizabeth L. Eisenstein, *The Printing Revolution in Early Modern Europe* (Cambridge: Cambridge University Press, 1983), 17.

17 Douglas C. McMurtrie, *The Book* (New York: Dorset Press, 1989), 67.

18 James Burke, "Communication in the Middle Ages," in David Crowley and Paul Heyer, *Communication in History* (New York: Longman, 1991), 75-76.

19 Robert Pattison, *On Literacy* (Oxford: Oxford University Press, 1982), 95.

20 Febvre, 20.

21 Eisenstein, 274.

22 Elizabeth Eisenstein, "Some Conjectures about the Impact of Printing on Western Society and Thought: A Preliminary Report," *The Journal of Modern History*, (March 1968), 7.

23 Charles H. Haskins, *Studies in Medieval Culture* (Oxford: The Clarendon Press, 1929) 83. Also, F.M. Powicke, *The Christian Life in the Middle Ages*, (1935), 88.

24 Elizabeth Eisenstein, "Some Conjectures," 40.

25 Tuchman, 156.

26 Tuchman, 60.

27 Tuchman, 453.

28 Mason, 456.

29 Natalie Davis, "Printing and the People: Early Modern France," in *Literacy and Social Development in the West: A Reader*, ed. Harvey J. Graff. (Cambridge: Cambridge University Press, 1981), 85.

30 Febvre, 153.

31 Pattison, 113.

32 Henri-Jean Martin, *The History and Power of Writing*. Trans. Lydia G. Cochrane (Chicago: University of Chicago Press, 1994), 266.

33 Will Durant, *The Reformation*. Vol 5. of *The Story of Civilization* (New York: Simon and Schuster, 1957), 117.

34 Febvre, 196-97.

35 Febvre, 261.

36 Lawrence Stone, "The Thirst for Learning," in Norman Cantor and Michael Werthman, *The History of Popular Culture* (New York: Macmillan, 1968), 279.

37 F. Harlow, *Old Post Bags* (New York: D. Appleton, 1938), 25.

38 Manchester, 61.

39 James Burke, "Communication in the Middle Ages," in David Crowley and Paul Heyer, *Communication in History* (New York: Longman, 1991), 70.

40 Laurin Zilliacus, *Mail for the World* (New York: John Day Company, 1953), 18.

41 Daniel C. Roper, *The United States Post Office* (New York: Funk and Wagnalls, 1917), 10

42 United States v. Bromley, 12 How (US) 88, 13 Led. 905.

43 Mitchell Stephens, *A History of News* (New York: Viking Press, 1986), 153.

44 Anthony Smith, "Technology and Control: the interactive dimensions of journalism," in *Mass Communication and Society*. James Curran, et. al., eds. (London: Edward Arnold, Ltd., 1977), 178.

45 Febvre, 208-211.

46 Wilbur Schramm, *The Story of Human Communication* (New York: Harper & Row, 1988), 128-9.

47 Eisenstein, 93.

48 Febvre and Martin, 242.

49 Eisenstein, "Some Conjectures," 5.

50 Benedict Anderson, *Imagined Communities: Reflections on the Origin and Spread of Nationalism* (London: Verso, 1991), 44.

51 Kenneth Clark, *Civilisation* (New York: Harper & Row, 1969), 17

52 A study of social groups in the diocese of Norwich, England, 1580-1700, estimates 89% illiteracy among women of all classes. See David Cressy, "Levels of Illiteracy in England, 1530-1730," *Historical Journal*, Cambridge University Press (1977): 1-23.

53 Davis, 72-73.

54 Harold A. Innis, *The Bias of Communication* (University of Toronto Press, 1951), 24-9.
55 Eisenstein, 262.
56 Manchester, 98.
57 Manchester, 106.
58 Mason, 436.
59 Carter, 32.
60 Robert Pattison, *On Literacy* (Oxford: Oxford University Press, 1982), 88.
61 Clark, 159-60.
62 R.R. Bolgar, "The Greek Legacy," in M.I. Finley, ed., *The Legacy of Greece* (Oxford: Oxford University Press, 1984), 452.
63 Nicolas de Clamanges in his tract *De Ruina et Reparatione Ecclesia* (*The Ruin and Reform of the Church*), reported in Barbara W. Tuchman, *A Distant Mirror: The Calamitous 14th Century* (New York: Alfred A. Knopf, 1978), 485.
64 Carter, X.
65 Carter, 112.
66 Carter, 174.
67 Carter, 49 + .
68 Carter, 88.
69 Carter, 157.
70 Carter, 213 + .
71 Febvre and Martin, 76.
72 Walter S. Ong, *The Presence of the Word: Some Prolegomena for Cultural and Religious History* (New Haven: Yale University Press, 1967), 49.
73 Carter, 233.
74 Frank J. Krompak, "Communication Before America," in *The Media in America*. William Sloan, et. al., eds. (Worthington, OH: Publishing Horizons, 1989), 16.
75 Tuchman, 594.
76 Mason, 468-69.
77 *Anglo-Saxon Poetry*, trans. R.K. Gordon (London: Dent., 1954), 297-98.
78 Ithiel de Sola Pool, *Technologies of Freedom*. (Cambridge: Harvard University Press, 1983) 14.
79 Febvre, 60.
80 Febvre, 186.
81 Elizabeth L. Eisenstein, lecture, "The Fifteenth Century Media Revolution," Macalester College, 22 September 1993.
82 See Alvin Toffler, *The Third Wave* (New York: William Morrow, 1980), 135.

3

The Third Revolution Mass Media

The Turmoil of a New Age

Beginning around the time of the American and French revolutions and the Enlightenment, which elevated reason above faith, the Industrial Revolution would create mass society. It would bring much to improve life: cheap cotton for clothing, cheap pottery for dishes, mass produced furniture, cheap coal to fuel factories, cheap transportation for people and goods. The Industrial Revolution at last would give most people the chance to live as only a few had lived. The centuries of dependence on handicrafts or of doing without were swiftly passing.

The Industrial Revolution put print into unaccustomed hands. It created books and magazines, which it shelved in city libraries, and it trained minds to read them. It printed newspapers for everyone and filled them with the kind of news and advertising to which everyone could respond. And as it did all these things to open people's minds, it led them into mental seclusion, for reading is not so often a collective activity in a family setting or a literary salon as it is solitary and silent.

The Shift to Cities

With the invention of steam power, Europe and the United States shifted from an agricultural to an industrial economy. Villages racked by disease, malnutrition, and drunkenness were cleared out as men, women, and children trudged with empty bellies to cities, where factories arose to produce goods in mass quantity. They crowded into squalid urban communities. The world of the former villagers in their own country was disrupted almost as much as that of the immigrants to the United States who abandoned not only home, but homeland. Yet, bad as life was in the city slums, it was an improvement over the miserable food and housing, and too often the whips of their masters and landlords.[1] Contrary to what Marx and Engels concluded, the working classes saw the Industrial Revolution as an opportunity to break free, a chance for wealth and social advancement beyond the dreams of their parents.[2]

Starting in Great Britain and spreading across western Europe and the American colonies, the Industrial Revolution created much more than grimy factories and air choked with coal soot. It built the farm machinery that plowed the soil and harvested the crops to bring a rich variety of food to the tables that were assembled in factories. It carried chilled meat and fish never tasted by an earlier generation to be eaten with knives and forks made in other factories. It brought medicines to children who once had only home remedies. Now they had a better chance of surviving. They would live to be adults, and grow taller than their parents.

The Industrial Revolution brought a variety of clothing to those who once had only make-do. It would bring sheets and shoes and shotguns, pins and pipes, envelopes and engines, furniture and phonographs, magazines and movies.

It added choices to life and a cash economy. It extended the span of human years. It established universal compulsory education in assembly line schools that widened literacy. The reading of books spread in the nineteenth century with the free mass education movement, led in the United States by Horace Mann, and the free public library system, which had its origins during pre-Revolutionary times in the subscription library started by Benjamin Franklin in Philadelphia. Unlike hereditary landowners who wished to keep the laborer uneducated and in his place, the no-nonsense cotton masters preferred that their employees could read and write.[3] That was one of the few nice things one might say about the factory owners of the period.

The Industrial Revolution spun off information revolutions that brought knowledge and mass entertainment undreamed of in pre-industrial times, and all of it would be built from mass media technology.

It Also Brought Misery

The Industrial Revolution also brought the misery of grueling labor, often for longer hours than in pre-industrial times, the breakup of families, machinery accidents, job insecurity, employers who cared for machines not workers, sudden spurts in food prices, and the lack of any cushion for illness or aging. Cities dumped untreated sewage into rivers to flow alongside the chemicals dumped by factories. In some cities the smoke was so thick that midday appeared like dusk. A legend circulating in Pittsburgh held that the smoke was actually beneficial because it kept down the germs.[4]

In the village a man and a woman knew *their place*, in all the senses of that term, but in the city the Industrial Revolution made life impersonal and transitory. What little leisure existed centered on the tavern, where workers drank away their pay. A growing bourgeoisie of shopkeepers and entrepreneurs joined the classes of owners and workers, but unlike the two traditional classes, upper and lower, which had little daily contact with each other but shared ideas about life, the emerging middle class was in frequent contact—and frequent conflict—with workers.

For all classes, the social disruptions of the industrial age changed courtship patterns because, where families were no longer together, arranged marriages were less possible and less desirable. Yet, the rates of marriage went up in western Europe during the nineteenth century because, hard as life was, more people could hope to support a family.[5] Nuclear families of a father, mother, and two or three children replaced the traditional extended families of an earlier age. Also in this century women entered factories and, later, offices.

With the invention of the electric light, night turned into day for work and leisure, further disrupting what had once been an even flow of the pattern of life.

Three Revolutions

The Industrial Revolution, centered in England, coincided approximately with the French Revolution, which was political, and the American Revolution, which saw the emergence of a new force in modern world history, the colony that broke free to become a nation. All contained elements of class consciousness. The French Revolution poked its fingers into every class of society all across Europe as few events have in human history. Yet, in ways unintended by the framers of the legislation it made industrialization easier by laws abolishing guilds and prohibiting worker combinations, which reduced labor's capacity to organize.[6] Belgium, Germany, and England approved similar laws. In the English countryside, the enclosing of common land that peasants had used to graze their animals and gather their fuel drove them into the teeming city slums, the factories, and the collieries. The nineteenth century writer Thomas Carlyle described the "half-frightful scene" of an iron and coal works:

> A space perhaps of 30 square miles to the north of us, covered over with furnaces, rolling-mills, steam-engines and sooty men. A dense cloud of pestilential smoke hangs over it for ever, blackening even the grain that grows upon it; and at night the whole region burns like a volcano spitting fire from a thousand tubes of brick. But oh the wretched hundred and fifty thousand mortals that grind out their destiny there! In the coal-mines they were literally naked, many of them, all but trousers; black as ravens; plashing about among dripping caverns, or scrambling amid heaps of broken mineral; and thirsting unquenchably for beer....Yet on the whole I am told they are very happy: they make forty shillings or more per week, and few of them will work on Mondays.[7]

Child Labor

Children were not coddled or romanticized, but from an early age were regarded as incomplete adults. It was not unusual before the Industrial Revolution for children to work, but the new age made them particularly attractive for factory and mine because they were for hire cheaper than their fathers, cheaper even than their mothers, and expendable. Children also worked, as they had always done, in agriculture and craft manufacturing. Child labor and female labor had existed for untold centuries, and were depended upon. A German elector in 1543 specified that parents renting rooms from others could not keep children above the age of nine, but had to send them out to work or the parents would be punished.[8]

Harsh as the lives of children were in the pre-industrial era, the Industrial Revolution worsened the lot of some who were recruited in gangs from orphanages, poorhouses, and the city slums. Because their fingers were small and nimble, little girls were sought for cotton spinning mills. Because their bodies were small, little boys could crawl into narrow coal slopes. They were sometimes beaten to spur production twelve to fourteen hours a day. In this Dickensian England, the 1833 Factories Regulation Act prohibited employment of children under nine, and for children between nine and twelve, a maximum of nine hours work a day. The employers also had to pay for two hours of schooling daily. Until governments enacted child labor laws and regulated factory conditions, suicides were reported among children driven to despair in a sunless world.[9]

As for working women, as unpleasant as life was in the factories, it was usually better than the drudgery of domestic service and the sweated labor of women in pre-industrial times. Some observers expressed alarm at the growing independence of factory women.[10]

Women were valued by the number of children they bore. Populations exploded, doubling in England between 1750 and 1800 and rising in France during this same period by 50 percent. Yet, the rise in the birth rate was a minor contributor to population increase compared to the sharp drop in the number of Europeans who died young.11 War, accidents, and violence harvested their share then as now, but a larger portion had been demanded by those other horsemen, disease and famine.[12] Now the Industrial Revolution brought cheaper soap, iron to cook in, pottery to eat from, more food, and a greater variety of food to people whose standard of living had risen. Despite the great crowding of the cities and the greater sanitation problems, the better-fed, better-clothed, and actually better-housed population had new means to resist disease.[13]

In England at the start of the Industrial Revolution, the multitude of the lower classes subsisted on little more than bread and potatoes. One letter writer described the daily fare as "oat bread, a little milk or tea, in the morning; potatoes, and sometimes a little flesh, but not often, at noon, with potatoes for supper."[14]

Well into the Industrial Revolution the diet improved. Friedrich Engels noted that among better-paid workers meat could be enjoyed every day, with bacon and cheese for dinner.[15] Although potatoes, brought from the New World, were for a long time suspect, by the end of the eighteenth century European peasants were growing them as a food staple in place of wheat and oats because they produced more calories from smaller, less fertile plots of land. Until the blight wiped out the crops, the potato was an ideal crop to plant to feed the growing number of mouths.

Social Changes

When a member of a family moved to a distant city, every element of personality departed forever, except possibly something special mentioned in a rare letter home for those who had the skill and the means to write. So a young woman marrying and moving away or a young man going off to seek his fortune was in a way a personal grief as well as a time of joy. Most folks did not leave for distant places. Most lived out their lives within 50 miles of where they were born. The Industrial Revolution changed that pattern of behavior just as it changed so much else in people's lives.

Violence sporadically attended the Industrial Revolution. Food riots erupted as factory workers attacked bakeries for raising bread prices. Mobs of workers attacked competing workers, such as the uprising of Philadelphia weavers against Irish immigrants. British textile workers between 1810 and 1820 attacked and destroyed the new machinery that threatened their jobs. These British *Luddites* were followed a decade later by Luddites in France. Industrial strikes, sometimes accompanied by rioting, followed economic slumps when employers tried to cut wages. Efforts to form labor unions brought swift and bloody police response. The American Civil War itself was fought not only over the familiar issues of states rights, national unity, and slavery, but also over such economic issues as tariffs on manufactured goods and where cotton would be sewn into shirts.

War, the greatest violence of all, had markedly changed to sweep up civilians into citizen armies. Warfare no longer limited itself to professional soldiers. The French Revolution gave birth to a national patriotism that altered the scale of war as French civilians became army conscripts. In Napoleon's battle of Borodino on the road to Moscow, 77,000 died. Industrial Revolution factories turned out guns with increased killing power. Rifled musket barrels improved accuracy. The Maxim machine gun spewed 600 bullets a minute. By the start of the twentieth century, peacetime conscription had led to national mobilizations. The means of mass communication helped to stir nationalistic feelings. World War I would replace setpiece engagements with trench warfare that allowed soldiers to fight without letup. And with military goods flowing steadily from cities to the front, civilian populations became natural targets of the new total war.

"Watch and ward" has medieval roots, but the modern city police force is another product of the Industrial Revolution, for city crowding invariably raises the level of city crime. In London, Sir Robert Peel's "bobbies," the metropolitan constabulary, became the prototype for uniformed city police everywhere, although not always with the same benign results.

Mass Dependencies

Demand grew for more workers, not only in industry but in agriculture, to feed the swelling cities. Industrious rural families made do by mixing farming with off-season and household manufacturing tasks to provide themselves with furniture, clothes, and tools, and perhaps to turn out something extra to barter in the local community. The poor who did not own farms survived on whatever meager wages they could acquire. Country people often did not have occupations like farmer or carpenter as such; instead, they managed a shifting assortment of tasks.[16] Before the Industrial Revolution, farm households practiced mixed farming, not the more efficient production of one or two crops or types of livestock. People produced much of what they consumed, or bought what was made not far from where they lived. Goods were at times exchanged for labor in a cash-poor barter economy.

The Industrial Revolution replaced this self-sufficient economic system with a chain of mass dependencies. Mass quantities of raw materials were shipped by organized transportation to factories fueled by dependable supplies of the fossil fuels of coal, oil, or gas. The mass production by machines of identical finished goods were distributed by organized transportation to urban centers, and marketed by means of mass advertising in mass media, the means of mass communication. In time, the identical goods—light bulbs and automobiles and corn flakes—would be sold to consumers who no longer could or would provide for themselves. The system of interdependency worked, and continues to work, because each element functions.

Visiting the industrial city Manchester, England, that keen observer Alexis de Tocqueville wrote, "Civilized man is turned back almost into a savage."[17]

It was among these people in western Europe and the United States, sometimes torn from their roots into a world of both deprivation and choices, sometimes trembling with fatigue, that communication technologies would insinuate themselves to make life even more different. These communication technologies influenced the era of *modernism* that was given a big push by the Industrial Revolution, but they would also mark the *postmodernism* that followed.[18] The world's third information revolution was mass media.

Printing for Everyone

The French Revolution depended on the printed word to get out the message of liberty, equality, and fraternity. To seize power the revolutionaries had to fortify a lower class enfeebled by centuries of misery. Most peasants were illiterate, but they could look at posters and they could listen to others read.

Most people in Europe and North America could not read, let alone write. Beyond the few who were educated, most skilled craftsmen knew their letters, while most women, unskilled laborers, and peasants did not.

The printing methods themselves had not changed. It would seem reasonable that the burst of technology that gave western Europe and then the world a system of printing would continue its pace of invention and innovation to meet the excited demand. Yet, between 1450 and 1800 surprisingly little changed in the printing industry. Printers continued to set type by hand. A typical screw press impressed no more than 100 to 150 sheets of paper an hour. At the start of the Industrial Revolution, printing was done much as it had been accomplished in Gutenberg's day.

Printing Changes

After 1800, swiftly changing technology in the printing industry helped to alter the entire fabric of society. Religion on both sides of the Atlantic had been the major impulse to teach men and some women to read,[19] but printing further encouraged literacy, broadened knowledge, and involved ordinary people in public affairs to a greater extent than ever before as they tried in a more complex world to go through life adequately.

> The effects produced by printing may be plausibly related to an increased incidence of creative acts...Thus we need not invoke some sort of "mutation in the human gene pool" to explain an entire "century of genius"...we may also make room for the new print technology which made food for thought much more abundant and allowed mental energies to be more efficiently used.[20]

The Industrial Revolution brought to printing the advantages of mass production—a greater output of printed material at a far lower cost. First came the Fourdrinier machine, which made paper in a continuous web and increased papermaking capacity tenfold. Paper supply however, would remain a problem for decades more, because it still depended on rags.

Iron presses, easier to operate and making better impressions, replaced wooden presses around the turn of the nineteenth century. The lever press replaced the ancient method of pressing pages by twisting a screw. A steam press was operating in 1810. Richard Hoe's rotary cylinder press, making use of the rolls of newsprint from the Fourdrinier machines, replaced the flatbed press, multiplying newspaper production manyfold and increasing circulation. Pages came off the presses at the rate of 1,100 sheets per hour per side. Friedrich Koenig hooked two presses together, so that they printed both sides of the sheet at once. By 1827, output on the most modern presses was 7,000 sheets an hour, although this technology was spreading slowly and flatbed newspaper printing presses still required muscles and patience.

Society had changed, too. An emphasis on basic education for all brought literacy to many of the common folk of Europe and the United States for the first time in history. In Britain, Parliament passed the Compulsory Education Act in 1870. Other European nations and the United States soon followed. Now the printing press would have a mass market for its mass production capability. By the end of the century, huge Hoe presses were printing 72,000 copies an hour.

Paper was not the only commodity in short supply. Printers were forever running out of lead type. Smaller publishers could not afford all the type needed for an entire edition. That meant printing a few pages at a time, then tearing apart the page form to reset other pages. Even worse, the lead type eventually broke down from the punishing pressure of the repetitive printing process.

Stereotyping

Stereotyping solved many of the type problems. An impression of the page of type was taken on a cardboard-like flexible paper mâché mat. From the mat, one or more lead casts of the page were pressed. The lead type that made up the page, used once only and no longer required, was reused or remelted for employment elsewhere.

Introduction of the stereotyping process during the last half of the nineteenth century also provided multiple copies of a cast page, further expanding speed and capacity. It laid to rest the restraints of the *tombstone* style of page makeup, dreary single vertical columns whose column rules held the type in place during press runs. Now multi-column headlines, wood-block or metal engravings and, later, photographs could enhance the page's appearance. The curved stereo plate, developed in 1854, was coming into wide use, the pages cast so they could be placed in pairs around a cylinder, to be printed by a rotary press.

During the 1880s a new method, electrotyping, improved the quality of printing, especially of photographs, which were reshot through a fine mesh screen onto a sensitized copper plate that was then etched in acid. It created a pattern of dots known as a *half-tone*. The problem of how to put photographs in newspapers and magazines was solved and would get better with time. The public loved seeing pictures with their news. Because photographs and line drawings also appeared in ads, the advertisers joined the happy chorus.

Setting the Type

Due to the increasing automation and speed of the presses, the slowest part of printing was now the setting of type, letter by letter from a job case. Many inventors tried to design a machine to do the job. Mark Twain lost a fortune investing in one inventor's design. The first successful mechanical composing machine was built in 1886 by a German immigrant watchmaker, Ottmar Merganthaler. The machine was called a *Linotype* because it extruded one line of hot lead type at a time. The brass matrix for each letter in that line of type was then carried automatically back up to its original position.

In other advances, two cylinders printed on opposite sides of the sheet at the same time, a knife cut the rolls into newspaper sheets, a mechanical folder sorted and folded the sheets, and a binder wrapped wire around bundles of finished newspapers for efficient delivery.

This classic system of printing is known as *letterpress*. Raised letters are inked, then pressed onto paper, leaving an inked image.

Offset Lithography

A different system started with printing from the surface of a specially prepared stone. Lithography grew in popularity until today it has replaced letterpress in most applications. Based on the fact that oil and water do not mix, a photographic image is made on a metal plate—a *picture* of the typeset page. The plate is coated so those portions where there is type (or lines of a

graphic) will accept ink; the background portion (normally the white part of the page) does not accept ink. In the most common form, *offset lithography*, the inked image is transferred onto a rubber roller, which then rolls the image onto the paper. In this photographic-based printing system, the photo-typesetter replaces the Linotype.

Over the course of a century that began with the Industrial Revolution, the American Revolution, and the French Revolution, the Western world underwent a tremendous alteration. Printing played a significant role in all three revolutions, and was itself part of an information revolution. As we shall see, printing helped sell the goods produced by the Industrial Revolution. Pamphlets such as Tom Paine's *Common Sense* spread the revolt that led to the American Revolution. And printing awakened France and shook all of Europe with its *Declaration of the Rights of Man*[21]

Paper for Everyone

At the end of the seventeenth century, when the wage of a papermaker was between two and three shillings a week, a ream of writing paper—500 sheets—sold for 20 shillings, about two months wages. That kept what was printed on paper costly. To spread literacy, the price of paper would have to drop.

During the Colonial period most American newspapers got their stock from Europe. Colonial mills were small and inefficient; three men labored one day to manufacture 3,000 small sheets of poor quality. The irrepressible Benjamin Franklin, while a Philadelphia printer, is credited with having a hand in building more paper mills, although the interruption of paper delivery caused by the American Revolution led a number of newspapers to suspend publication.

A Continuous Sheet of Paper

Paper was made in small batches everywhere until, in 1798, Nickolas Robert, the manager of a mill in France, thought of making a continuous sheet of paper on a single machine using a web to pick up the

Figure 3.1   The first papermaking machine, invented by Nicholas Robert, 1798.

wet pulp. He got financial backing in England from two brothers named Fourdrinier. The invention, known as the Fourdrinier machine, could accomplish in two days what took three months of hand labor. After two decades of improvement, the Fourdrinier papermaking machine was turning out newsprint in an endless sheet. Newspaper reliance on small hand-made batches of paper had ended. Separate paper making processes were combined into a single machine. With steam-powered printing presses, newspapers could reach for large circulations. In another decade, the era of the *penny press* placed paper into hands unaccustomed to receiving information like this.

In Europe and the American colonies, the need for paper to print books and newspapers outstripped the supply of rags. Curiously, some help came from an unusual quarter. A sharp increase in the population of western Europe led to a great demand for clothing, which was met during the Industrial Revolution by new textile machinery and, in America, by Eli Whitney's cotton gin. This in turn increased the supply of worn-out clothes. Rags were still the source of paper, and this chain of events led to a slightly improved supply of paper by the turn of the nineteenth century.

> To clothe this new population (explosion) would have been impossible...had it not been for the perfection, in the county of Lancaster in England, of cotton spinning and weaving machinery, shortly followed in the 1790s by the invention in America of the cotton gin...Another consequence of cotton production was...an immense increase in worn-out clothes, or rags. Rags were the raw material of the papermaking industry... By 1839, publishing had been revolutionized. Printed matter was now cheap—for the first time in human history literacy could be massively extended through all levels of the population.[22]

Yet, demand grew. But where was the paper to come from? Demand outstripped the supply of rags. American papermakers, pushed by newspaper publishers, scoured Europe. Prussia and Rome followed France in prohibiting the export of rags. As prices soared, Americans turned to Asia for rags, buying from China, Japan, and India, but the problem continued to bedevil publishers.

> Aside from the introduction of the printed book, the demand for paper was felt in many new fields: teaching spread, business transactions became more complex, writing multiplied, and there was a growing need for paper for non-literary uses by tradesmen, haberdashers, grocers, chandlers. A whole new species of trades was created which depended on paper: carriers, boxmakers, playing-card makers, bill-posters and related trades whose precise duties were never exactly demarcated, despite endless lawsuits between the rival Guilds.[23]

A Lesson from a Wasp

A chlorine bleaching process gave mills the use of colored rags plus rope and other fibrous scraps, but it still was not enough. Something new was needed. That something new had actually been discovered more than a century earlier. In 1719 a French scientist, Rene de Réaumur, advised papermakers to learn from a type of wasp that built its nest out of dry wood that it mixed with its saliva to form a paste. The wasp smeared the paste in thin, overlapping strips that strongly resembled paper. Little was done with this idea of using wood pulp until German papermakers eventually picked up the concept. The first wood pulp paper machines were manufactured in the 1840s, and by the end of the nineteenth century, after processes were developed to separate the wood fibers and to *cook* the pulp with chemicals, wood pulp was the basis for papermaking. Prices plummeted. Wood pulp that brought 8 1/2 cents a pound in 1875 could be bought for 1 1/2 cents in 1897.

The world at last had a cheap, renewable source of raw material for paper. The advance in mechanical production and an abundant supply of material added impetus to the first mass medium in history, the penny press.

The Information Pump

Because of political and religious sensitivities at home, many early newspapers limited their news to what was happening in other countries. A publisher landed in jail if he was not careful, which might have meant being on the wrong side when a new government came to power. Publishing news was always risky. There were 350 newspapers in Paris alone during the French Revolution, but only four newspapers during the later period of the Empire. Yet, change was coming.

Not long after newspapers were introduced into an England torn by factional strife, around the time when King Charles I was beheaded, they were telling news of political events in England itself. England's newspapers could boast of having not just editors in the office, but reporters, including at least one woman, who went out to ask questions and gather information. These seventeenth and eighteenth century newspapers might also feature woodcut illustrations, and headlines piled up on the front page. London newspapers were sold mainly in the coffee houses, where it was relatively safe to engage in political disputation in public. There were also street hawkers, both boys and girls.

> The advanced stage coach, improved roads, and the train helped to expand the lines of distribution of the press and release it from the dependence on the coffee-house which had been the chief means of circulation since Cromwellian days.[24]

Sweden in 1766 passed a press freedom law. Later, in the new United States the First Amendment to the Constitution guaranteed freedom of the press. Other nations over the next century matched, to a greater or lesser degree, these promises of independence from government wrath.

Printers like Benjamin Franklin agitated against the government of the crown, often slipping into another colony just ahead of the redcoats. John Peter Zenger, a printer, was tried for seditious libel after he criticized the colonial governor. Stirred by Zenger's attorney, Andrew Hamilton, the jury disregarded instructions that only the judge could decide whether a publication was treasonable and found Zenger innocent. Newspapers would now, more than ever, be a force for freedom. It should not be surprising that the concept of a printing press unfettered by government leads the Bill of Rights, nor that Thomas Jefferson, who once wrote that if forced to choose he would choose newspapers over government, eventually grew heartily sick of newspaper agitation.

The Business of Newspapers

A printer turned out newspapers, books, and periodicals as a means of keeping his workers and equipment fully occupied. By the middle of the nineteenth century, the shift to larger presses and news by telegraph led to greater infusions of capital to produce the newspapers and greater income from them. In the New World, publishing newspapers helped to keep printers in business.

> Printing did not really develop in America during the eighteenth century until the printers discovered a new source of income—the newspaper. Far from their homeland, in sparsely populated areas, the pioneers felt cut off from contact with the rest of the world; probably that is why the newspaper developed more quickly in America than elsewhere.[25]

Newspapers in larger cities detached themselves from general printing houses and, more than ever, news was a commodity that could be manufactured from the raw material of facts and sold at a profit.

> With the diffusion of literacy, the technology of printing, and the development of the modern newspaper, there was, then the development of the modern notion of "news" itself. Indeed, between, say, about 1780 and 1830, the growth of journals, newsletters, and newspapers was so great in Europe that a fundamentally new social phenomenon

came into being—the "news"-reading public.[26]

The early decades of the nineteenth century saw two types of newspapers thriving. The commercial press was about trade. The party press promoted a set of views plus the candidates who adhered to them. A single copy of a newspaper cost about six cents and a subscription might be ten dollars a year, so dear that the average person did not see a copy of a newspaper and possibly might not have even been aware of the existence of such a thing as a newspaper.

The Penny Press

The *penny press* added a third type, a newspaper for the workingman. For a penny the popular press competed not with the older type of newspapers, but rather with the small cakes and apples that sold on the streets for a penny. Copies of the New York *Sun* were hawked on street corners as early as 1833. The effect on newspaper readership was immediate and astonishing. Between 1830 and 1840 the number of daily newspapers more than doubled and the number of weeklies nearly doubled. The total circulation of daily newspapers rose fourfold. Population was also rising, but not nearly as fast.

A penny or two brought news about people in unusual circumstances to masses of ordinary people who lacked a deep, abiding interest in either commerce or partisan politics, but were able to read and had a curiosity to satisfy. Popular journalism delighted in scandal, crime, and other *human interest* news.

Income came principally from the sale of individual copies and from advertising, not from the political party subsidies and subscription fees that sustained the existing party press. The penny press reached people whom the schools equipped with an ability to read, but did not endow with a burning thirst for knowledge. The urban gentleman regarded these popular newspapers with a contempt, possibly like that accorded today's supermarket tabloids, buying a copy now and then to amuse his family.

When the *Sun* first appeared on the streets of New York the combined circulation of the eleven newspapers in the city was 26,500. By 1835, the *Sun* alone was selling 15,000 copies a day at a penny apiece, thanks to the new high-speed printing presses. Two penny press rivals, the *Evening Transcript* and the *Herald* quickly followed, with a total daily sale of the three newspapers of 44,000.

To catch readers, they published a new kind of information, the unimportant but interesting item. The publishers did not quail at accusations of vulgarity and sensationalism. Beneath that news item appeared another new kind of information, equally trivial by itself, but equally significant when seen in its totality, namely the advertisement that could be addressed to a mass audience. Mass communication made possible mass advertising that created the appetites leading to mass consumption, which in its turn gave purpose to mass production.

> (In the penny papers) Advertising, as well as sales, took on a more democratic cast… advertising in the established journals, which heretofore had addressed the reader only insofar as he was a businessman interested in shipping and public sales or a lawyer interested in legal notices, increasingly addressed the newspaper reader as a human being with mortal needs.[27]

Modern newspapers reflect all three types: the commercial press, the partisan political press, and the popular press.

Reporting

The coming of the railroads and other improvements in transportation expanded circulation. Better transport founded new towns and with them came local newspapers. Alongside the railroads ran the telegraph wires, humming with fresh reports daily from distant places to towns up and down the line.

For the most part, previously published information received from outside sources filled the columns of newspapers. Newspapers printed old news stories and opinion articles from other newspapers sent through the mails in the system set up by Benjamin Franklin for a free exchange of newspapers among editors. Before the last half of the nineteenth century, news gathering by reporters was little known. Then the telegraph came along, providing the means for fresh reports from distant places. These reports whetted the public's appetite for more and still more news.

News itself would increasingly come to have value as a commodity instead of merely supplying the basis for a piece of political partisanship. Like a bushel of oats or a yard of silk, news had become a product, and in a newspaper, ink upon paper, it had the means to be packaged.

Then as now, reports had more value when the reporter was at the scene of events, sending back dispatches based on personal observation and answers to questions posed to the important players of each drama, even generals at a battlefield or diplomats at a foreign court. The practice of active investigation soon followed and so did a rise in the circulation of newspapers willing to pursue news actively. In response—or in self-defense—organizations from police to government to private business learned a myriad of ways to cope with the reporter's questions, ways that ranged from creating a public relations industry to these organizations actually improving what they were doing.

Cooperative news gathering began before the advent of the telegraph, but these ventures were brief agreements; for example, to share the cost of a boat. By removing the barrier of time for the transportation of news, the telegraph extended each newspaper's reach to wherever the telegraph poles ran, but rates were steep, which made cooperation the only sensible means of collecting news. The decades following the diffusion of the telegraph saw the independent *telegraph reporter* try to establish a foothold, only to be overwhelmed by the news agency, notably the Associated Press in the United States, Reuters in England, and Havas in France.

The Birth of Objectivity

Because a cooperative news agency existed to serve client newspapers and thrived by acquiring still more clients, it followed that the agency would try to please all its customers, or at least as many as possible, which covered a multitude of political leanings on every conceivable issue. Pleasing as many customers as possible translated itself into transmitting facts that were colored as little as humanly possible by the agency reporter's point of view. *Objective reporting*, something rather new, was born. In a profession that prided itself on the brilliant essay, it took some effort of will to hold facts high and opinion low. Yet, it had to be done if full advantage were to be taken of the transmission of news dispatches by electricity.

> The penny press wanted to appeal to everyone's interest and thus, logically, it stood opposed to anyone's 'special' interest—except of course its own interests, which presumably corresponded to its expressed policy of indifference.[28]

Modern journalism school arguments over whether objectivity is ever possible can be traced back to its emergence as a desirable goal, a product of the news agency and the telegraph. The source of newspaper efforts to strive for objectivity lay in the argument propounded by John Milton that truth would win in an encounter with error; therefore all viewpoints should be allowed free expression.

> Give me the liberty to know, to utter, and to argue freely according to conscience... So truth be in the field, we do injuriously, by licensing and prohibiting, to misdoubt her strength. Let her and falsehood grapple. Who ever knew truth put to the worse in a free and open encounter.[29]

Over a period that was measured not in months, but in decades, most newspapers taught themselves to follow the Associated Press's neutral, uninvolved reporting style, leaving opinion to the editorial page. Today, considerable controversy continues over whether objectivity can exist or is even desirable.

Improvements in the Composing Room

Technology never occurs uniformly across an industry. While New York newspapers were oiling up Hoe rotary presses, loading huge rolls of paper, and squeezing out stereo mats, publishers in small towns across America were still inking one page of type at a time before laying a sheet of dampened paper over it and turning a hand crank to roll type and paper under a platen that was lowered to meet it. After a few hours of this the publisher-editor-printer had, besides a tired arm, enough copies of a four-page or eight-page newspaper for his circulation.

Mechanical limitations as late as the early decades of the nineteenth century kept most newspapers to four small pages. Editorial copy was crowded into narrow columns framed by vertical rules; ads were printed want-ad style in agate type, illustrated at best with thumbnail woodcuts. Although handbills bore larger woodcut illustrations, newspapers seldom printed such large woodcuts. In 1820, the London *Observer* published a page of pictures, a rare effort. The problem was that the combination of poor paper and poor ink made a botch of illustrations. Newspapers actually refused to accept illustrated advertising, large type, or multiple columns long after improvements in printing processes and engraving would have allowed such modernization. Eventually, the desire for advertising revenue overcame that rather pointless tradition.

The penny press was from its outset a creature of the latest in printing technology. It could not have been born without the Fourdrinier machine that spun out a continuous web of paper or without Hoe's rotary press that could lay words of ink on that paper quickly and cheaply. It is unlikely that it could have grown as much as it did without stereo mats that could free up lead type and make multiple copies of a page for even faster production.

By the 1870s, newspapers were buying *boiler plate* and *ready prints* from syndication services. The former were stereo mats (impressions ready for transfer to lead for the presses) of individual stories, columns, or illustrations and the latter were mats of entire pages. Both cut down the space that a publisher would have to fill with local material. They also cut down the original, distinctive look of individual small newspapers, creating a sameness that still exists.

Joseph Pulitzer, a Hungarian immigrant, established the first newspaper art department at the New York *World* in the 1880s. His generous use of pictures led to a sharp increase in circulation. Etched line engravings and halftones of actual photographs replaced the woodcuts for both news and advertising. Magazines began using the modern illustrations sooner than newspapers because the higher quality magazine paper stock was kinder to photographic reproduction. England had an illustrated newspaper as old as photography itself, but its pages were filled for decades with woodcuts, for there was no way to reproduce a photograph in a newspaper.

Photographs in Newspapers

That problem was solved at the end of the nineteenth century by the halftone process, in which a photograph was itself photographed, this time through a glass scored by a mesh of fine lines onto a coated zinc plate. The plate was etched with acid to separate dark and light areas. The light areas, eaten by the acid, did not capture the ink. Photography and printing were now fully merged. The art of photojournalism soon followed.

In a few short years, the newspaper was totally changed. By the new century, Linotype machines replaced the handset type in the composing room, the *back shop*, of large city newspapers while the typewriter replaced the reporter's pen in the front. And on the reporter's desk, beside the typewriter, stood a telephone. On a nearby shelf, a camera may have rested. A quarter of a century later, behind a door, a teletype chattered with distant news.

The late nineteenth century also saw the expansion of newspaper chains. Family-owned newspapers were sold to newspaper corporations, and these sometimes became part of media empires that would in the course of a century encompass a variety of print and electronic forms of communication preparing to ride the information highway.

In the decades after World War II, newspapers switched over from letterpress printing to offset lithography. Today, no major newspaper and hardly any small newspaper still relies on hot lead. The simplicity, convenience, and lower costs of photocomposition are all too obvious.

At first, paper tape chinking out of teletypesetters was used to carry text produced by wire services and local reporters. These, too, have been consigned to the junk heap. Now computers send text to other computers.

Technological advances during the nineteenth century in printing presses, stereotyping, typesetting, photography, and lithography combined to change the daily newspaper from a product that even Gutenberg might not have found strange to a product not too dissimilar from what now lands on front steps each morning. Other inventions have contributed to the modern newspaper, importantly among them the telegraph and the telephone, which transmitted news reports; early facsimile, which transmitted pictures; the railroad, the automobile, and the airplane, which transported newspapers themselves; the typewriter, the computer, and that vital aid to transferring information, the electric light bulb, which not only allowed newspaper staffers to work through the night, but also gave readers an easier means of reading the newspaper after the day's work was done.

Free Presses

More than technology was responsible for the flowering of the penny press, which defined for the mid-nineteenth century the spirit of the mass communication revolution. A new and expanding nation infused with the fresh air of individualism and political independence as a result of free market capitalism and Jacksonian democracy provided the spirit that underlay the new

journalistic enterprises. Largely absent in the United States was a climate of political fear that could have impeded newspaper growth.

In the late nineteenth century, the extending of free, compulsory education, the growth of free libraries and, with them, a rising rate of literacy stimulated newspaper and magazine sales, even if the readers preferred simple fare. It may be as accurate to say that a growing literacy fueled the growth of newspapers as to say that the availability of cheap, unsophisticated newspapers increased literacy.

> The penny papers…transformed the newspaper from something to be borrowed or read at a club or library to a product one bought for home consumption.[30]

In the three decades from 1870 to 1900, the number of newspaper copies sold daily increased sixfold. The number of daily newspapers in the United States doubled, then doubled again.

It is not merely the gray columns of news reports that have shaped attitudes toward political issues and personal standards. Bylined viewpoints ranging from political columnists to *Dear Abby* have affected public thinking. So have the choices of photographs and editorial page cartoons. So indeed have the comic strips, from the conservative *Orphan Annie* to the liberal *Doonesbury*.

Controlled Presses

Newspapers have been an information pump for the world. They appeared in South America and Asia during the eighteenth century, and in Africa by the end of the nineteenth century. Many of these would become powerful, important voices, not only informing an ever more educated public increasingly hungry for news, but influencing leaders of finance and government, affecting the course of history. Technology must always be part of the equation.

> The method by which newspapers are manufactured and distributed, for example, has always had profound implications for what might be called the moral condition of journalism.

...information media shape the realities of a society, they interact with the processes of government, and provide the terms of the relationship between governors and governed, even (perhaps especially) in totalitarian societies.[31]

In countries with authoritarian governments, whether right wing, left wing, or *sui generis*, a different type of newspaper developed. These newspapers were—and are—heavily political, expressing only the views of their governments. In controlled societies, newspapers, along with radio, television, magazines, and books, have always been regarded as too important and too potentially dangerous to be allowed to report or comment on whatever its publishers, editors, and writers choose. Means of communication are regarded as an arm of government just like the educational system or, for that matter, the ministry of agriculture.

The adversary relationship between press and government, prized in democratic societies, is anathema to a government that views the press as a means of guiding the masses. News, *per se*, is not particularly important to a controlled press. How news is understood has always been of vital importance to suspicious rulers.

THE MUCKRAKERS

Just as the penny press in the early and mid-nineteenth century reached out to a much broader audience than newspapers had ever commanded, a new type of popular magazine, fueled by the national advertising for mass-produced goods, broke tradition in the late nineteenth century as the United States expanded from a rural, agrarian society to an industrial nation. In their pages, they carried something new. Today it goes by the approving phrase, *investigative journalism*. Then it was called *raking muck*.

Articles by the *muckrakers* appeared regularly in popular magazines, awakening the nation to governmental corruption, the greed of industrialists, and the need for pure food laws and child labor laws. Newspapers, limited in space and prey to community and advertiser pressure, were inferior to magazines as a medium to carry the sensational messages of the muckrakers that many people, including small children, lived and toiled in misery while a few politicians and industry leaders grew fat. Racial injustice, diseased meat coming out of packinghouses, and insurance fraud on a national scale were exposed. An Irish immigrant, S.S. McClure, used his *McClure's Magazine* during the first decade of this century to carry articles by Ida Tarbell, Lincoln Steffens, Ray Stannard Baker, and other muckrakers. Several magazines followed McClure's example as the public eagerly bought up copies.

Tarbell's series on John D. Rockefeller's Standard Oil led to a federal investigation and, ultimately, to a U.S. Supreme Court ruling to break the oil monopoly. Laws regulating meat inspection, the railroads, and over-the-counter medicine were initiated by muckraking exposés in magazines, newspapers, and books. Following an article in McClure's Magazine, "Daughters of the Poor," Congress passed the Mann Act, making it a federal offense to transport a woman across state lines for immoral purposes.

Congress extended low-cost mailing privileges to magazines in 1879, enabling entrepreneurs to revise or create magazines in order to reach a mass audience largely bypassed by existing periodicals. The last decade of the remarkable century saw the emergence of a strong cadre of national magazines. In the 1890s, national advertising and the mass circulation newspaper also became firmly established on the American scene, and so did the Associated Press. They spoke to people regardless of who they were or where their parents came from. They spoke to everyone as Americans. And from time to time the braver publications continued to rake muck.

Women Can Type

The battered typewriter that served us so well for so many years now gathers dust in an office storeroom or the family attic. Where it once resided there now sits a computer, appearing much more modern and quite different except for the sort-of-familiar keyboard. It is hard to image the old typewriter as part of any kind of social change, yet it was the catalyst of several significant changes in the way we live. The typewriter led to the restructuring of the business office. It can be said to have begun modern business communications. It made spelling and grammar important, and it sold dictionaries.

Helping to Bring Women Out

Much more significant, the typewriter helped free women from financial dependence on the men in their family, their fathers, brothers, husbands, uncles, and in-laws. It did much to bring them out of the home and into the office. Other factors were also at play. It has been argued that the demand for clerical labor, and not the typewriter, brought women into offices.[32] Gas lighting, which made the streets safer for women to take evening classes, also had a part in creating independence for women. Whichever was the more significant cause, the feminization of clerical labor roiled the waters of the late nineteenth century, and still roils the waters as humankind prepares to enter the twenty-first century. The invention and spread of labor-saving household appliances such as refrigerators and washing machines continued what the typewriter began. The typewriter was present at the start of the women's movement that unlocked the door of advancement to half the population. The door is far from being fully opened, even in the United States, but the lock has been broken.

The diffusion through the world of commerce of the typewriter, requiring a dependable supply of operators who at first were themselves known as *typewriters*, led to a social revolution with unimagined consequences. Arguably, nothing that was typed from the period of its introduction in the last quarter of the nineteenth century to the present day was as significant as the fact of a woman sitting in front of a typewriter. The medium was—and is—the message.

The Old Office

The business office in the 1870s looked considerably different than it does today. Lacking adequate illumination in the age before electricity, the dark wood helped to mask the accumulation of dirt and the smudge from kerosene lamps. Rolltop desks were standard appointments. Cuspidors graced the corners. There were no machines and, most likely, no females except for the scrubwomen who toiled invisibly through the night. Businessmen and male clerks wrote letters and filled ledgers with pens dipped into bottles of ink. Before carbon paper became widely available, they copied letters by dampening them with a wet cloth and pressing them against a blank sheet of paper. Office boys delivered the letters to other offices or to the post office.

The typewriter would one day relieve the dreary work of writing everything by hand. It would also replace illegible handwriting. But because it was frustrating to find young men willing to study for low-paid typing careers, young women were finally able to break the barrier of women working in offices. The arrival of the female office worker helped to change the rest. Out went the cuspidors. Out went the dark wood paneling that hid the dirt.

When the first wave of female typists hit the business office in the 1890s, the cuspidor manufacturers read the sign of doom. They were right. More important, the uniform ranks of fashionable lady typists made possible a revolution in the garment industry. What she wore, every farmer's daughter wanted to wear, for the typist was a popular figure of enterprise and skill. She was a style-maker who was also eager to follow styles. As much as the typewriter, the typist brought into business a new dimension of the uniform, the homogeneous, and the continuous that has made the typewriter indispensable to every aspect of mechanical industry.[33]

Inventing a Writing Machine

In 1714, an English engineer, Henry Mill, received the first patent for a machine that impressed letters one after another on a sheet of paper, although there is no record that he ever built the machine. More than a half century later several people actually built crude writing machines. Among them were an Austrian, a Swiss, a Frenchman, and an Italian.

A noble impetus lay behind the creation of these early machines: embossing letters on paper so the blind could read through their fingertips. Development of functions useful to the business world—like composing speed or ease of operation—were largely ignored for a century. The machine's use as a business device was fully appreciated only after it could outrace a pen that cost a penny.

Pressure to produce a more efficient writing machine came partly from the rapid extension of telegraph lines, a symbol of the quickening pace of the Industrial Revolution. While a good telegrapher could send a message at a fast rate of speed and could understand an incoming Morse Code message just as quickly, he couldn't write

it down fast enough. Ideas sprang from other ideas as inventors read or heard through the improving communications network about attempts to build a machine that would impress letter type directly on paper. Many inventors tried their hand at it, but either the designs were bad or the workmanship was. None of their inventions worked well.

A Frenchman in 1833 patented a writing machine in which the paper remained stationary while the machinery moved, an idea ahead of its time, one that IBM would revive more than a century later with the type ball. A few years later, another Frenchman invented a writing machine that resembled a piano, followed by a Russian invention that looked like the old fashioned drier fitted over the head of a customer getting a permanent wave.

The Sholes Machine

The 52nd writing machine to be patented was different. Inventor Christopher Sholes, a Milwaukee printer and editor, is credited as the *father* of the modern typewriter, although several friends assisted him in producing the first working typewriter in 1867. Their idea was to cut a type face on the side of a short bar that could strike a piece of paper much like a piano hammer hitting a string. The piece of paper was pressed against a glass plate with a sheet of carbon paper behind it, with each key striking upward from behind to make the impression. A clockwork mechanism pushed the paper along. Sholes called his machine a *type-writer*. Before they were done, he and his friends fabricated some fifty different models of the type-writer.

By 1873, the machine that the Sholes group continued to improve began to look like the modern typewriter. It had a keyboard of four rows with the letters, numbers, and punctuation in nearly the same arrangement that exists today. A tin black case covered the machinery. The paper wrapped around a cylindrical carriage that moved back and forth. The principal difference from more modern typewriters was that the type bars hit upward against the bottom of the roller inside the machine;

Figure 3.2   This 1857 typewriter was called a literary piano.

hence, the operator could not see the printing point and could not be sure of what was being typed until three or four lines later.

Western Union ordered so many machines that Sholes and his backers turned to the Remington company, which manufactured firearms, sewing machines, and farm tools, all products requiring finely machined components. Remington mechanics improved the Sholes design, placed the typewriter on a sewing machine stand, and adapted the foot treadle for a carriage return. Among those who became fascinated with the typewriter was Mark Twain, whose *Tom Sawyer* became the first novel ever typed.

For the next 25 years, the typists themselves were called *type writers*, just as the machines were. Because the future of the typewriter (the machine) seemed bleak and wages of typists were overly modest, not many young men were interested in embarking on this career.

Women Mean Business

In 1881, a branch of the YWCA in New York City came up with the novel idea of teaching eight young women to type for the purpose of entering the business world. Some criticism was expressed of such a bold step, for it meant that women would be required to work all day near men to whom they were not related. None of the eight backed away from the rigors of a six-month typing course. All were promptly hired to work in business offices.

This new technology, the writing machine, opened an employment floodgate. It offered higher wages than other jobs open to women and pleasanter working conditions. It was one of the few types of employment for women requiring literacy. Women poured into offices across the land. They became not only typists, but stenographers and secretaries, two careers limited to men. Some women, seeing that they could make even more money with their newfound typing skills as entrepreneurs, went into business for themselves as public typist-stenographers; their presence encouraged the twin concepts of women and machines in the business office.

Now typewriter sales boomed. Typewriting in the 1880s reached out first to Europe and then to the rest of the world. China and Japan lagged behind because of the difficulty of building a typewriter with perhaps 10,000 characters suitable for their languages.

The typewriter continued to improve incrementally. Remington designed a key shift for upper and lower case. John T. Underwood developed a typewriter with a front-strike design, so the typist could see the printing point. In 1906, the Royal Typewriter Company produced its first typewriter, which was superior to anything on the market. Its print strike area was totally visible. By the time of World War I, about one hundred typewriter companies had been started.

Other tools and business machines followed the typewriter into the office: carbon paper, inked ribbons, stencils, the dictating machine, the mimeograph, adding machines, accounting machines, envelope addressing machines, check writing machines, and postal meters. Rather than an oddity, the ability to clearly communicate on paper through typing became the standard for business. Schools to teach typing opened, public high schools offered typing classes, and contests were held for the fastest typist. By 1941, the record on a standard manual typewriter was a machine-gun 142 words a minute.

It was inevitable that the typewriter's versatility would be combined with the telegraph's speed at sending messages to distant places. The practical result in the 1920s was the teletypewriter, so familiar to generations of journalists. Although the facsimile machine and the computer printer hooked to a wide-band data line or a modem have set new standards, the ubiquitous teletype can still be found throughout the world, not only in newsrooms, but in government offices, police stations, commercial banks, brokerage houses, shipping agencies, and weather departments.

QWERTY

The subject of the typewriter should not be left without mention of the familiar arrangement of its inefficient keyboard. Typewriters and the computer keyboards that followed use what is called the *QWERTY* arrangement of letters and numbers, named for the letters on the left side of the third row of keys. Many of the earlier keyboards were set up in alphabetical order to facilitate learning. Before the invention of the shift key, separate keys were needed for capital letters.

Inventor Christopher Sholes and his brother designed their keyboard to *slow* the arrival at the printing point of frequently used letter pairs. In 1873, the type bars pivoted upward and easily jammed. The QWERTY keyboard was arranged so that the bars holding the letters that often turn up in combinations (such as *ie, ti, th*) or appear frequently (such as *the, of, or, and*) would come to the printing point from op-

posite directions. Further, this keyboard arrangement favors the left hand although most people are right handed; for example, the frequently used *a* must be struck by the weakest finger, the left pinky, while the seldom used *j* lies directly under the strong right forefinger.

Today, fast electric typewriters and electronic computer keyboards obviate any arrangement that slows typing speed. More sensible organizations have been proposed, notably the Dvorak keyboard, but the public, accustomed to the existing layout, seems to be stuck with it.

The typewriter may be on its way out as a significant tool of communication, but in a number of meaningful ways its legacy will remain.

"If Anyone Desires…"

If ever a means of communication existed that enabled multitudes of people to send an infinite number of messages by a variety of means to even greater multitudes of other people, it has been advertising. Among those messages are advertisements promoting the quality of candidates for political office and the delights or perils of the controversial issues before the society. Anyone who doubts its egalitarian thrust should imagine the opposite of what exists in free and open societies. Imagine a society in which very few people are allowed to advertise to a selected few a highly restricted number of goods and services, certainly not including candidates competing for office or the political issues of the day.

Creating Demand

The Industrial Revolution, which brought an unimagined variety of goods to the working classes, needed more than mass production and mass distribution. The next step in the chain, mass marketing, required advertising not only to announce the availability of goods, but to convince prospective buyers to part with their money. Advertising had to create demand.

Before advertising, which is mostly a means of moving mass produced goods, the uniqueness of an item was a distinct selling point, as exemplified by the cartoonish dismay of a woman who discovered that another woman was wearing the same hat. Now, several generations later, her great granddaughter and great grandson won't be caught dead in jeans or sneakers that don't carry the brand name all their friends wear. Advertisers talk of brand *loyalty*.

The advertisement has displaced the sales agent, but the ad is more than a helper.

> The primary argument of the salesman was personal and private: this hat is perfect for *you* (singular).… The primary argument of the advertisement was public and general: this hat is perfect for *you* (plural)… The advertisement succeeded when it discovered, defined, and persuaded a new community of consumers.[34]

The *drummer* with a battered case of wares represented a human element in the relationship of buyer and seller that dissolved with the centrifugal force of the advertisement. In the early nineteenth century, advertising lacked a human face. Instead, agate lines of single column type explained what the prospective buyer needed to know. After the stereotyping process brought in display ads, some advertisements supplied a human dimension with sketches of happy consumers or the friendly *Betty Crocker* and *Aunt Jemima*. Radio added a voice and television added a face plus a voice plus movement so the customer, shorn of direct communication, had a reference group, however distant or fictitious.

Origins of Advertising

As the old saying puts it, the more things change the more they stay the same. The first advertising was oral, delivered in ancient times by barkers in the marketplace shouting the wares of merchants. Some of the latest advertising is similarly oral. Just tune in television at night to watch and hear barkers shouting the wares of automobile dealers.

Outdoor advertising can be traced to posted notices on papyrus in ancient Egypt for runaway slaves. Instead of something for sale, notices of runaway slaves and bond servants, with rewards offered, may have been the first written advertising. Such notices were posted during all the centuries of slavery for the logical reason that these valuable pieces of property did not enjoy their life's condition, and possessed both the brains and legs to do something about it.

Testimony to the antiquity of advertising were the public crier in ancient Greece, shouting his wares to a nonliterate public in an oral age, and the sandwich man who carried his picture message on the front and back of his shirt, possibly an invention in Carthage. Archaeologists at the ruins of Pompeii unearthed walls that may have been controlled by an early version of an ad agency, filled with notices of theatrical performances, sports events, and contests of gladiators.

Few references exist to advertising during the Dark Ages, when literacy was regarded of little worth; in fact, to advertise a product might bring bandits as well as customers to the door. The growth of mercantilism during the Middle Ages changed that attitude. Notices called *siquis* were posted in public places, the term coming from the Latin *si quis* ("if anyone") because so many began "If anyone knows..." or "If anyone desires..."

Shortly after the invention of movable type in Europe in the mid-fifteenth century, printed notices began to appear. News sheets of the sixteenth century sometimes carried advertising, such as an ad for a book extolling the medicinal virtues of a mysterious herb. By the seventeenth century, tradesmen distributed handbills with not only printed words, but woodcut illustrations, hand lettering, and fancy borders.

A French *Journal of Public Notices*, a medium for want ads, was published in 1612; now called *Les Petites Affiches* (*Little Notices*), it is still published as a carrier of want ads and legal notices. It holds the distinction of being the world's oldest, continuous periodical. In England, a series of advertising newspapers called the *City Mercury* were distributed free.

Printed advertising at this time was often for the sale of books (printers, after all, printed not only the ads, but the books), auctions, houses for rent, spices for sale, and other merchandise just arrived by ship, plus rewards for runaway horses or runaway apprentices. Groceries at the consumer level, clothing, or household goods were generally not things to be advertised in print, although near miraculous cures might be. Requests for the return of lost articles were posted then as now.

The Word Is "Advertising"

The word *advertisement* began to show up in the latter half of the seventeenth century, replacing *advices*, which had replaced the older *siquis*. The word *advertisement* appears in the Bible and in the plays of Shakespeare in the sense of *warning* or *notification*.

From Roman signposts to eighteenth century English bill postings, the outdoor sign carried announcements of wants and offering, and identified places of business. The first commercial billboard, known in

Britain as a *hoarding*, is credited (if that is the appropriate term) to a London clothing merchant in 1740.

The Industrial Revolution of the nineteenth century led to a sharp increase in advertising as manufacturers sought outlets for the goods produced by their factories. Town criers had become less active, but now advertising bills were posted on walls everywhere, sometimes pasted up in the dead of night before police or property owners could stop them. No lamppost was safe. The sandwich man was back, sidewalks were stenciled, and billboards went up, for it became essential to use the tools of communication to market the goods coming out of the factories.

> Mass production and distribution cannot be completely controlled, however, without control of a third area of the economy: demand and consumption...The mechanism for communicating information to a national audience of consumers developed with the first truly mass medium: power-driven, multiple-rotary printing and mass mailing by rail.[35]

The Civil War ended the practice by many American newspapers of placing advertising on the front page. War news was too significant to be consigned to inside pages. After the war the news-filled front page, its columns led by multiple-deck headlines, remained. Simply, it increased circulation. For a time one or two front-page columns continued to contain ads, but in most newspapers, these eventually were relegated to the inside. Elsewhere in the world, front page advertising still continues, but the practice in the United States is sharply curtailed.

By the mid-nineteenth century, advertisers had found a new means of distributing their circulars—the postal system, supported by that new revenue device, the postage stamp. This direct mail allowed advertisers to use large display type and woodcut illustrations, both still barred from most newspapers until the end of the nineteenth century. Printers of circulars were not slow to take advantage of their opportunity.

By the close of the nineteenth century, the magazine advertisement had become a principal national vehicle for the distribution of the standardized goods. Selling the public on the bicycle as an ideal form of transportation was the first national ad campaign. Its success led to advertising for a new form of transportation, the automobile. The magazine publisher was now as much concerned with consumer groups as with editorial content.

The Advertising Agency

Another new facet of advertising in the late nineteenth century was the advertising agency, an American phenomenon which spread to Europe and then around the world. The agency concept began earlier in the century in France, where newspaper publishers regarded the acceptance of ads directly from advertisers as beneath their dignity. Instead, they sold space in bulk to contractors who retailed the space to those with goods to sell. Something like this concept was later adopted by American agencies. In the United States, the first version of the ad agency was the independent entrepreneur or newsdealer who, as a sideline, accepted ads for newspapers. Except for brokering space, the first agencies offered no service.

The next step taken by these space broker agencies was to offer lower rates to advertisers of nationally sold goods who agreed to buy space in dozens or hundreds of newspapers for each ad. The agency pointed out that by setting up a page of ads only once, a savings could be passed along to the advertiser. Agency owners emphasized their own knowledge of the media they dealt with, especially the actual circulation, a figure that was not likely to agree with the publisher's inflated numbers.

Some magazine publishers refused advertising; others accepted it reluctantly. Most resented the intrusion of questions about their circulation figures. When one advertising agent, George Rowell, asked the executives at *Harper's Weekly* about their circulation, they responded by rejecting his advertising.

As time went on, agents offered other activities such as copy writing and campaign planning until the full-service advertising agency so well known today was in place. Lord & Thomas, N.W. Ayer & Son, and the J. Walter Thompson Company were among the pioneer agencies that offered more than just what the advertiser requested. Among the largest advertisers in this period were Sears, Roebuck; Quaker Oats; Eastman Kodak; H.L. Heinz; and the National Biscuit Company, all giants of industry today.

A sharp rise in the number and circulation of magazines aided a phenomenal growth of advertising during the late 19th and early 20th centuries. Halftone engraving was a boon to advertisers. Many products, identified in the public's mind by trademarks, were usually outline figures until the halftone photograph breathed life into them.

> Advertising got into high gear only at the end of the last century, with the invention of photoengraving. Ads and pictures then became interchangeable and have continued so...For both the pictorial ad or the picture story provide large quantities of instant information and instant humans, such as are necessary for keeping abreast in our kind of culture.[36]

Catalogs and Patent Medicines

The direct-mail catalog provided another means of advertising goods. Montgomery Ward & Co. in 1872 issued the first mail-order catalog that was larger than a leaflet. The Sears, Roebuck & Co. catalog and others that followed were eagerly awaited in rural hamlets and hollows where they brought touches of comfort and civilization to lives that had little enough of these. They have become an important part of America's collective memory.

Chances on lotteries and patent medicines were among items offered for sale, which helped to give advertising a reputation for fraud, yet they did some good. Yale and Harvard, for example, owed construction of some of their buildings to widely advertised lotteries.

As for patent medicines, it is questionable if any good beyond wealth for the purveyors and security for new periodicals came out of advertising for the vast number of fake nostrums that promised to grow hair or cure any and all of the ills known to humankind. The claims went unchallenged until federal government agencies were empowered to demand truth in advertising. A few newspapers acted independently to ban the worst of the medical quackery. A major effort at proscribing such advertising followed a decision by *The Ladies' Home Journal* in 1892 to print no more medical advertising of any kind. The *Journal's* editor, Edward W. Bok, took to printing chemical analyses of some of the more widely advertised preparations. A shocked public learned that many of the cures were laced with alcohol, cocaine, or morphine. Hundreds of thousands of mothers had been quieting their teething babies with a widely advertised soothing syrup containing morphine. The Federal Food and Drugs Act, passed in 1906, was a remedy for the quack ads.

Brand Names

There are people who can remember when few goods came pre-wrapped. Pickles and soap flakes came out of barrels. The druggist decanted soft-drink syrup and perfume from large bottles. Brand names, if they existed at all, hardly mattered until massive national advertising campaigns made household words of such products as Gold Medal flour, Pillsbury flour, Kellogg's cornflakes, American Tobacco, Diamond matches, Borden and Carnation condensed milk, Campbell Soup, Heinz 57 foods, Quaker Oats, Wrigley's gum, Proctor and Gamble soap, and Kodak film.[37] When Campbell Soup paid for its first large scale ad campaign, the company secretary reportedly said to the treasurer, "Well, we've kissed that money goodbye!"[38]

The National Biscuit Company, which began to advertise in 1898, created a small revolution in food packaging by emphasizing through advertising the cleanliness, freshness, and convenience of crackers wrapped in wax paper inside a cardboard box. In a short time, the campaign led to the removal of the familiar grocery store cracker barrel, around which, according to American lore, small town folks would gather. Open barrels and bins were replaced by cans and cardboard. Grocers stopped scooping unlabeled butter from tubs. Soap was papered and branded with a colored label. Even farm families rode to town for wrapped and sealed food. Magazines did well by all this.

Philadelphia dry goods merchant John Wanamaker advertised fixed prices for his buttons and linens at a time when storekeepers charged whatever they thought a customer would pay. He hired John Powers, the first notable copywriter, to write the ads. As business doubled, other merchants took notice.

More Advertising Tools

Outdoor advertising prospered. Rows of cards above the windows of streetcars, buses, and subway trains fixed the attention of riders. No industrial city could be free of billboards, nor does evidence appear that any city wanted to. The first electrical sign went up in 1891 along Broadway, soon known as *The Great White Way* when the flashing lights of the huge Times Square advertising signs became a symbol not only of New York, but of America itself. Neon tubes came along in 1923 to display messages in colored lights.

The advertising industry readily adapted to the new behavioral science of psychology early in the twentieth century. Making salesmanship scientific had great appeal and no lack of success when the art of selling combined with psychology and statistics as *marketing research*.

The number of advertisers expanded as the nation grew. So did the volume of advertising and total ad budgets. Between 1939 and 1956, the number of national advertisers tripled and the number of brands they sold through ads nearly quadrupled.

Advertising introduced both the memorable slogan, such as Kodak's "You press the button. We do the rest," and the radio jingle, which followed the tradition of advertising

rhymes that had appeared in English periodicals a century earlier.

Radio Advertising

Radio became an advertising medium in 1922. That alone led to an explosive growth in the radio industry, but the idea of broadcasting commercials took a little selling. Broadcasters worried about how the government, which licensed them, would feel about what Herbert Hoover, then Secretary of Commerce, referred to as being "drowned in advertising chatter."[39] Broadcasters and advertisers also worried about ads that went out over the airwaves (or "ether") without anyone having any idea about who was getting the message and what effect it was having, or whether anyone at all was paying attention. A comforting answer came when a commercial for Mineralava cosmetics offered a free photo of actress Marion Davies, who had spoken about "How I Make Up for the Movies." Hundreds of requests poured in from listeners.

Albert Lasker, an important figure in the advertising industry during the first half of the twentieth century, led his agency, Lord & Thomas, heavily into radio. His agency was responsible for many of the early radio shows including the most popular of all, *Amos 'n' Andy*. The 1920s saw the start of the rapid growth of radio as a means of *free* home entertainment, the only *cost*—after the initial purchase of a radio set—being having to hear such advertising as the jingle. To a population suffering the economic effects of the Depression, that was no cost at all. Prices were not mentioned in radio ads until 1932. Catchy tunes like "Pepsi Cola hits the spot, twelve full ounces, that's a lot..." spun around in people's heads as often as any song on the "Hit Parade." Jingles even appeared in outdoor advertisements, such as the famous Burma Shave signs that motorists read, line after line, as they sped along the American highways.

Televising Advertising

Jingles typified an effort to be creative, to make an ad something more than the notification that goods were for sale. Advertisers recognized, before most of the rest of society did, that the public is likely to remember something enjoyable. That helps to explain why people who have seen the same commercial twenty times sit entranced to watch it for the twenty-first time. It is also why a child who runs off when the program is on will come running back for the commercial. More thought, energy, effort, and cold cash go into television commercials today than into television programs.

Setting Standards

Within the advertising industry itself, frequent efforts were made to establish ethical standards. In the late nineteenth century, John E. Powers, who became publisher of *The Nation*, campaigned to improve advertising copy. He said, "A good bargain in advertising, i.e., a low rate, is always of less account than to say the right things to the right people in an acceptable way."[40]

The Agate Club, formed in Chicago in 1894, brought advertising industry people together to consider common concerns. Similar clubs were put together in other cities, leading eventually to national and international organizations. New York State was the first to pass a law to block dishonest advertising.

Critics of advertising have argued that it has made society materialistic and greedy, despoiling life by equating happiness with the ownership of *things*, leaving people permanently dissatisfied with what they have and always wanting more. Researchers estimate that the average American sees or hears an ad every three minutes that he or she is awake, 500 advertisements a day.

An unintended consequence of unrestricted advertising has been the unpleasant message overload that we feel when advertisers seek to convince us that we must own or do what we know is not in our best interests, or that we really need what we have hitherto been unaware of. It has been argued that ads that rain on us in print and broadcasting have led us foolishly to deplete the money we might have otherwise saved for old age, and that has led to the old-age insurance of Social Security and pension funds.[41]

If all commentators on this subject can agree about anything, it is that advertising is a tool of communication whose impact on society cannot be ignored, not when advertisers in all media in the United States alone spend upwards of $100 billion dollars a year.

Solving Postal Problems

Postage rates between England and the colonies were high, limiting communication. Colonists rightly regarded them as another form of taxation, avoided paying them whenever they could, and included postal charges in their rallying cry, "No taxation without representation." What followed was revolution and a new nation.

In colonial days, the timeliness of news often depended upon the speed of ocean-going ships. Editors of the first newspapers in North America had to wait an average of two months for news from England. The fastest ships were packet boats, designed to carry mail, that might also carry a few passengers and light cargo. Because roads were few and overland routes were difficult to traverse, it was not unusual for news of one colony to arrive at another by way of a London newspaper and a ship from England.

During this period, newspapers that were located in towns with regular delivery of news by mail, especially from abroad, had higher reputations than newspapers without such direct access to mailed news. The average newspaper was a meager thing by today's standards. The front page carried news from Europe about politics and wars, copied from newspapers arriving from England. The remaining news columns were filled with items copied from other colonial newspapers, plus the contents of some letters that readers had received and offered to the editor for reprinting, and perhaps an item or two of gossip along with any genuine local news. If that were lacking, poetry and, where possible, advertising filled the space. As pre-Revolutionary War politics heated up, the published letters became increasingly political, signed by a pseudonym from Roman politics, like Cato, Cicero, or Brutus.

Benjamin Franklin, a printer and publisher, was a postmaster as well, a position he used to introduce changes that produced the first surplus in the colonial postal service. He established a simple accounting system for postmasters, investigated abuses by post riders, shortened routes where he could, eliminated mail transport by ferry where possible, established charges for newspapers where they had been carried free, and did whatever else he could to put the postal system on a paying basis. The Crown dismissed him for his revolutionary activities in 1774. A year later the Continental Congress asked Franklin to set up a separate postal system, the best way to get word to colonists who wanted independence. America's first important scientist, first important inventor, first important literary figure, founder of the first circulating library, first hospital, and first volunteer fire company, founder of the academy that became the University of Pennsylvania, and an architect of the American political system, Ben Franklin was also the first postmaster general of the United States. George Washington is reputed to have said, concerning the first U.S. ambassador to France, "We haven't heard from Benjamin Franklin in Paris this year. We should write him a letter."

Postmasters and Publishers

The mail service was set up to carry letters, not newspapers. The law had no provision for sending newspapers by mail, so no rates had been fixed. A postmaster could charge whatever he wanted for adding newspapers. Even a postmaster had to depend on the riders who actually delivered the mail. Publishers were unable to collect from distant subscribers or even to learn when to

stop mailing newspapers because a subscriber died or moved away. There were postal riders who, for delivering the newspapers, demanded exorbitant rates from subscribers and pocketed the money. Riders earned no government salary. Their income came from what recipients would pay for letters and newspapers, a system that continued well after the postage stamp required the sender to pay for letters. Not until 1863 did Congress vote pay for postal carriers and no charge for city delivery. Until then, those who did not want to pay for their mail asked the postmaster to hold it at the post office. If senders paid for their letters, the price covered only delivery to a post office, not to someone's home.

Franklin's policies eliminated most of these problems, provided for the free exchange of newspapers among editors, and assigned postmasters to collect newspaper subscription fees. By these policies, the American colonial post office moved ahead of the postal policies in England.

A publisher might get his newspapers delivered if he offered a bribe, but a better plan presented itself. Why not become a postmaster? Publishers pulled strings to be appointed postmasters, a position that presented a sure way to get their newspapers delivered and incidentally make life difficult for rival publishers. Some postmaster-publishers were mailing their own newspapers without postage. Others used the office to put rival publishers out of business.[42]

Among the advantages for publishers in becoming postmasters was franking their own mail; that is, sending it free under their signature. Postal law did not specifically address the matter of franking newspapers, but it did permit postmasters to frank their business mail, which they often interpreted liberally as including correspondence relating to their newspapers and indeed the newspapers themselves. They also received news dispatches before their rivals did. Appointment as postmaster also handed publishers the opportunity to collect fees, although small towns did not provide enough postal revenue to afford full salary for its postmaster, and it conferred the status of being a representative of the government.

Conversely, whatever government was in power encouraged the postmasters they appointed to start newspapers. And why not? The postmastership was most likely a political plum, so the government knew where the postmaster's sympathies lay. The postal service managed the news both by impeding the delivery of out-of-favor publications and by giving postal advantages to publications that the authorities wished to promote. Postmasters used their offices to increase the circulation of their own and their party's newspapers.

Politicized relationships continued after the United States came into being. Presidents appointed postmasters general of their own political party, and these men in turn appointed publishers of the same party to local postmasterships, all part of the great political game of scratch-my-back-and-I'll-scratch-yours.

Postal Services for Newspapers

The two institutions, press and post, grew hand-in-hand, each stimulating and shaping the other. Policies set up then still have effect today. In 1820, for example, the postmaster general told local postmasters to encourage subscribers to take local publications instead of distant city newspapers. That led editors to increase the amount of local news, a commodity that the distant big city newspapers could not match. Until this change, most country newspapers mimicked the city press in focusing on national, international, and state capitol news, ignoring local events. To this day, local news remains a staple of all newspapers, especially those in smaller communities.

The post office provided many services for the press: fast transport of news dispatches, newspaper delivery, the selling of subscriptions by the letter carriers, cheap postal rates, free delivery within a county, free exchange of newspapers among editors, and even exchange arrangements with foreign publishers. The free exchange of newspapers among editors was especially helpful in the first half of the nine-

teenth century. Congress ended the franking benefit to newspapers in 1875, but cheap second-class mailing rates continue.

Before the creation of such news services as the Associated Press the exchange of newspapers was the only regular means of moving information great distances as well as to the nooks and crannies of the country served by small newspapers. Nonlocal news being the staple of most newspapers, and many newspapers being quite partisan, their editors looked for news stories and commentaries, particularly from Washington, that supported their party's cause. At the same time, the Washington and New York partisan press clipped pieces from the country press that supported their views. As the Associated Press grew in the later half of the nineteenth century, this practice diminished.

Transporting the Mail

How long it took news to be disseminated in the late eighteenth century may be judged by the length of time it took for the Declaration of Independence to be published by newspapers in various cities. Approved on July 4, 1776, in Philadelphia, it was printed in a Philadelphia newspaper four days later. It took five days to appear in a Baltimore newspaper, six days for New York, 11 days to a Hartford newspaper, 14 days to Boston, 18 days to Watertown, Massachusetts. The text of the Declaration no doubt reached some of these cities a few days earlier, but the editors waited until their next scheduled issues to publish it.

The battle of New Orleans was fought six weeks after the signing of the treaty that ended the War of 1812. While it had no effect on the peace treaty, the battle of New Orleans considerably enhanced the reputation of General Andrew Jackson. One can only speculate on how the engine of history might have veered if the news of the peace treaty had arrived immediately.

The means of conveyance obviously limited newspaper circulation because newspapers added weight to the postman's load. Where roads were available, four-wheel stagewagons or coaches carried the mail. Postal couriers accepted the added weight of newspapers only unwillingly, so they piled up at loading points. Sometimes bags of newspapers were dropped off at a stage office to make room for a passenger plus baggage. As for magazines, postmasters had the authority to exclude them from delivery if facilities were inadequate.

Editors and readers pressed for more coaches, a vehicle that came into general use after 1785, when Congress encouraged the post office to extend its service as fast as possible. The building of post roads through the wilderness brought the stagecoaches that brought the newspapers. The first post roads ran along a north-south axis, paralleling the eastern coast. Then, post roads were stretched from the east coast cities to cities being built in the west. Further growth came with post roads directly connecting the cities and towns of the west. Where post road building lagged, newspapers were scarce.

Senator John Calhoun in 1817 exhorted Congress to "bind the republic together with a perfect system of roads and canals... It is thus that a citizen of the West will read the news of Boston still moist from the press. The mail and the press are the nerves of the body politic."[43]

> The account of the beginnings and development of the American postal service must always be read like a romance. No one can learn of the lone footman or postrider following the trails through the wilderness, across the mountain and plains, of the "pony express," or the Overland Mails to the far-flung settlements without feeling the thrill of the pioneer spirit, and a lasting respect for the men and women of those trying times.[44]

The famed western Pony Express, which lasted only 18 months, carried condensed digests of news in both directions. Because of costs ranging from $1 to $5 per half ounce, few personal letters were sent. Instead, business correspondence and news dispatches filled the rider's pouch. Only one Pony Express rider was killed on duty, although a few were seriously wounded. An advertisement in newspapers for riders read:

> WANTED: YOUNG, SKINNY, WIRY
> FELLOWS NOT OVER 18.
> MUST BE EXPERT RIDERS
> WILLING TO RISK DEATH DAILY.
> ORPHANS PREFERRED.
> WAGES $25.00 PER WEEK.

A year after the Civil War started, the telegraph spanned the continent and the Pony Express vanished. The telegraph replaced it as the conduit of time-sensitive mail between the interior and San Francisco for those willing to pay the heavy charges. "Intelligence" could now cross from California to Missouri and points east in minutes. Letters from loved ones, however, still took weeks to travel from coast to coast via Nicaragua or Panama and by stage.

As for newspapers and magazines, the westward expansion of the railroad solved most of the problems of irregular and unsure news dissemination. Trains could carry large quantities of bulky publications with considerable speed.

Speculators thrived on early information. The messenger who arrived first with news that led to a rise or fall in cotton prices promised large profits for his quick-witted employer. When the post office failed to deliver the information in an advantageous way, private express companies came forward. These companies, as competitive with the public mails as Federal Express is today, were an important factor in information delivery until the telegraph arrived. Along with these services were news expresses put together by groups of publishers to gather and transmit news dispatches. During the U.S. war with Mexico, several major northeastern dailies shared the costs of horseback riders, fast boats, railroads, and telegraph lines to beat the U.S. mail.

International Agreement

If postal regulations within each nation were confusing, the problem was compounded and compounded again between countries. Each nation had its own set of rules, its own rate and weight scales, even its own suspicions of mail from other nations, although cooperation between nations was generally willing.

> A letter to England (from the U.S.) cost twenty-four cents if it weighed not more than one-half ounce and forty-eight cents between one-half ounce and one ounce. To Greece it cost fifty-seven cents if it was under one-half ounce and went by a British ship via Southampton. The whole fee could then also be prepaid. If, however, the letter went by American ship to Bremen and thence overland, the sender could prepay twenty cents to the U.S. Post Office and the rest would be collected from the receiver. The total would add up to more than fifty-seven cents if the letter weighed more than a quarter of an ounce.[45]

Nations signed bilateral postal treaties. Strong nations tried to become transit points not only for the postage income, but for the potential of exerting political pressure, since a nation whose mail was handled by another in transit was placed in a dependent position. All nations, strong or weak, welcomed the transit fees.

At an international meeting in Berne, Switzerland in 1874, the Universal Postal Union was born. There would be a single rate for foreign mail, each nation would keep the money from its sale of stamps, but would deliver foreign mail free, nations could no longer act arbitrarily, and disputes would be settled by arbitration. As a result of the treaty, rates dropped, service improved, and mail handling stopped being part of international scheming for power. The International Bureau of the UPU was housed in Berne, where it remains.

Like the postage stamp, the international postal agreement became part of the mass communication revolution. The Universal Postal Union also gave the world a lesson in how nations benefit when they act in concert for a peaceful goal.

Photography

Photography is the most visible and perhaps the most dominant element of the present Information Age. Less than two centuries old, it has become so much a part of life that it may be difficult to imagine our society without it.

Ancient Roots

Its technology has ancient roots. Imagine a sunny street in an old city. Imagine a house with a dark room. Imagine a tiny hole in the wall facing the street. People walk past the hole. If you sit inside the room and look at the wall opposite the hole, you might see an image of those people upside down. Because the world is full of dark rooms with holes in the walls, this phenomenon has been known for centuries. Aristotle mentioned it in the fourth century B.C. The Arab scholar Alhazen described it at some length in the eleventh century. Later, so did Leonardo da Vinci. The start of photography was the *camera obscura*, from the Latin *camera (room)* and *obscura (dark)*.

During the sixteenth century in Italy, the camera obscura—still a room—aided drafting and painting. To brighten and sharpen the image, artists placed a lens over the pinhole. To preserve the image, they traced it on a sheet of paper.

The problem with a room in a house is that you can see only what is opposite the

Figure 3.3   Egyptians used shears to cut silhouettes. People were always drawn in profile.

Figure 3.4 The camera obscura was the first means of recording an image exactly. The user traced it on paper.

room. If the room were portable, you could take it to any location. By the seventeenth century, portable rooms were built, usually a kind of tent. When the users—mostly painters and landscape architects—figured out that they did not actually have to stand inside the room to get their image, the camera obscura shrank to the size of a box carried in the arms, the predecessor of our own cameras.[46] Each had a peephole, a lens, and sometimes a mirror, plus a pane of glass on which a thin sheet of paper could rest for tracing an image.

An even smaller portable device, the *camera lucida*, consisted of a glass prism suspended by a brass rod over a piece of paper. Looking through the prism, the artist could trace an image of a scene or a face on the paper. The tracing still required a lot of handwork but, aside from the impressions of artists, no other way existed to reproduce an image.

The Chemical Basis of Photography

Chemical discoveries eventually provided the way to satisfy the deep wish to capture reality as it existed, drawn not with an ordinary pencil but with what came to be called the "pencil of nature." For thousands of years, people saw that colors can change outdoors. Vegetation turns green. A shirt's color fades in the sunshine. It had been known that certain salts of silver darkened

outdoors. The reason for this, some believed, had to do with the air itself or with the heat of the sun. They were mistaken. It was neither air nor heat. The reason for the change was light. A German scientist, Johann Schulze, noticed that a bottle filled with a certain silver compound turned violet black on the side exposed to sunshine. To test his theory that light, not heat, was responsible for the change, he cut the shape of some letters out of a piece of dark paper. Schulze covered a bottle of the silver compound with the paper and put it in the sunlight. None of the silver showed except the parts with the cut-out letters. In a little while the blackened image of the cut out letters appeared in the silver.

Thomas Wedgewood, whose family manufactured the famous pottery, managed to make some photographic contact prints by placing a leaf from a tree on glass against chemically treated paper, which he then exposed to light. To show the photographs to visitors he was compelled to resort to such stratagems as displaying them only for brief moments by dim candlelight. Even this procedure could be used for just a limited time before the whole picture turned black.

In 1827, exactly one century after Schulze's publication of his discovery, and following a decade of experimenting with various chemicals, a French inventor, Joseph Niépce, used a camera obscura to produce the world's first true photograph, the courtyard outside his window. It was etched on a coated pewter plate. His exposure time was eight hours, so in the photograph the sun seemed to be shining on both sides of a rooftop.

Daguerre and Talbot

On a trip to Paris, Niépce met Louis Daguerre, a painter and theatrical producer, who was also trying to capture a camera image. They eventually became partners. After Niépce's death, Daguerre went on to improve the process, and in 1837 he produced a photograph of surprising quality, a still life with tones of light and shadow. The photo, on a copper plate coated with silver, was exposed to iodine fumes, creating a layer of light sensitive silver iodide. Daguerre named his result after himself, a *daguerreotype*. The exposed plate was the final picture. There was no negative.

While Daguerre was experimenting in France, amateur English scientist William Fox Talbot, frustrated by the difficulties of drawing with the camera lucida, achieved some success in taking contact photographs by laying such objects as a leaf, a feather, and a piece of lace directly on sheets of translucent paper that had been treated with silver chloride. This method created a negative image, the dark and light areas reversed. The translucent paper allowed Fox Talbot to make any number of contact positives, something that Daguerre could not do. Fox Talbot was soon taking pictures of buildings, a choice of subject dictated by the need for a great deal of light. Only after years of chemical and optical improvements in photography, was he able to take pictures of people, whom he posed stiffly with orders not to move because his pictures required long exposure.

Both Daguerre, the French artist, and Fox Talbot, the wealthy English botanist, had been working independently and were unknown to each other, yet they were producing similar pictures with similar chemicals and equipment. One difference was that the quality of Daguerre's work was far superior. Another was that Fox Talbot could make duplicate positive images from his negatives.

The problem of the image darkening each time it was viewed in a lighted room was solved in 1839 by treating the exposed, developed image with sodium thiosulfate (still used today, commonly called *hypo*) followed by washing with water. Its discoverer, Sir John Herschel, a well-known English scientist and a friend of Fox Talbot, also devised the words *photography* to replace Fox Talbot's phrase *photogenic drawing*, and *positive* and *negative* to replace the terms *reversed copy* and *re-reversed copy*.

Improvements spread quickly to the growing numbers of amateur photographers. In the year 1847, it was estimated that half a million photographic plates were used in Paris alone. As smaller cameras were built, the size of photographic plates

Figure 3.5   A "photogenic drawing" of a leaf by William Fox Talbot in 1839. Translucent paper allowed copies to be made. (Courtesy International Museum of Photography at George Eastman House.)

shrank. New chemicals made the plates more light sensitive, thereby reducing exposure time. A portrait lens designed by Josef Petzval in Austria cut the time needed to hold still for a pose to about 30 seconds. One of the earliest American experimenters was the artist Samuel Morse, who would soon become famous for a different means of communication, the telegraph.

Photographs could be taken not only outdoors in the sunlight, but inside in the newly created portrait studios that opened everywhere. The photographers, known as *daguerreotypists*, did a brisk trade and they took business away from painters.

By the 1850s, the cost of having a photograph taken had dropped enough to make it available to the common man. Family pictures were popular, especially pictures of children, partly because of their high mortality rate. Many children died of epidemics like measles that today are usually under control. One advertising line was: "Secure the shadow 'ere the substance fade." Photographers in the mid-nineteenth century advertised their readiness to take pictures of the dead in their coffins.

Anyone who knows what the worth of family affection is among the lower classes, and who has seen the array of little portraits stuck over a labourer's fireplace…the boy that has 'gone to Canada', the 'girl out at service', the little one with the golden hair that sleeps under the daisies, the old grandfather in the country—will perhaps feel with me that…the sixpenny photograph is doing more for the poor than all the philanthropists in the world.[47]

Wet-Plate Photography

Frederick Archer's introduction in 1851 of the wet-plate photographic process replaced both the daguerreotype and Fox Talbot's "talbotype." It provided greater sensitivity and a shorter exposure time than anything previously available. It made possible multiple prints from one plate, unavailable with daguerreotype. On the other hand, the process proved complicated and untidy. Photographs had to be exposed on a *wet plate* and developed immediately or the emulsion would dry and the picture would not appear. Chemicals had to be applied in fairly rapid succession in darkness.

That meant that a photographer on the road carried a darkroom along. To take a picture by the wet-plate process, the photographer coated a glass plate with collodion, a clear, thick, sticky liquid that had found an application as a surgical dressing. Next, the plate was coated with a layer of light sensitive silver iodide. The plate was then inserted immediately into a camera so a photograph could be taken. After exposure, the glass plate, still wet, was developed, fixed, and washed on the spot.

Photographing the World

Realizing that they had in their hands a new way to record history, travelers could hardly wait to haul their heavy cameras and darkroom equipment to distant corners of the world. In 1854, an album of photographs of ancient Egyptian monuments was published, the first time that people could own such images. Combined in sheets and bound in books, these were actual photographs. The printing of photos on regular book pages along with text would

Figure 3.6
Wet-plate photographers carried their darkrooms wherever they went because chemicals had to be applied quickly.

have to wait until the art of photoengraving advanced sufficiently toward the end of the nineteenth century, after which newspapers and magazines blossomed with photographs. In the meantime, the public could view photographs sewn together with printed pages at the book bindery. Travel photographs were featured in popular *lantern slide* shows.

It was still a complicated, awkward, and messy business. Photographers needed wagons to haul around hundreds of pounds of bottled chemicals, plus the glass plates, dishes, measures, funnels, and a water pail, to say nothing of the heavy camera, lenses, and tripod.[48]

They traveled in an age of colonization, warfare in distant climes, and curiosity in the home country about national adventures abroad. Roger Fenton traveled with fellow Englishman James Robertson and a darkroom in a covered wagon to the Crimean War in 1855. Felice Beato, an Italian, and Robertson recorded the aftermath of an uprising against the British in India. Beato went to China to take pictures of the Opium Wars, then on to Japan, newly opened to the outside world and of great fascination to outsiders. In 1858, the first aerial photograph was taken from a hot air balloon.

For the first time in history, people safe at home saw a little of what went on in a war. They would soon see much more in the grim pictures of the aftermath of battles in the American Civil War. A well-known New York portrait photographer, Mathew Brady, hired other photographers to join him at some risk to their lives traveling to the battlefields with their clumsy, clattering wagons housing their wet-plate gear. By the end of the Civil War, they had taken more than seven thousand photographs of battlefields and encampments, soldiers living and soldiers dead, officers and men, weapons and equipment. Their photographs revealed war stripped of its glory—a brutal, wearying misery, no matter how noble its purpose. Brady himself nearly died in the battle of Bull Run. Other photographers followed Brady's lead to record the scars of battle.

After the war, a number of photographers headed West to continue what in only a few years had become a tradition of visual documentary. Lugging 300 to 400 pounds of wet-plate equipment and chemicals on the backs of mules, they left to posterity a permanent record of the American Indian, of great vistas without a trace of human habitation, of the coming of the railroads, of the miners, the settlers, and the cowboys. William Henry Jackson's photographs taken in 1871 helped in the political effort to establish Yellowstone as the first national park. This may have been the first time that photography influenced social change. It would not be the last.

Figure 3.7
Photographers provided a kind of journalism. Felice Beato took pictures of the British and French invasions of China during the Opium Wars, 1860.

The Muckrakers' Photos

Journalists began to recognize photography as a means not only to present information, but to stir emotion. Jacob Riis, a Danish immigrant hired as a New York City police reporter, was determined to reveal the humanity of the poor that the better-off ignored. Riis used both words and pictures to expose conditions in the slums. He was one of the first to recognize that photographs could help to bring about social change. Riis went about his personal mission even when his primitive flash equipment panicked a roomful of sleepers or actually set fire to a house. Once he set himself on fire with his flash powder, a recent invention that for the first time permitted photographs to be taken of what had hitherto been concealed by darkness. The flashbulb would not be invented until 1925, but flash powder sitting on a pan could light up a room. Sometimes it did so in more ways than one!

Riis' books, *How the Other Half Lives* and *Children of the Poor*, became an important part of the effort known as *muckraking*, dredging up awful conditions for the public gaze. The insult of being called *muckrakers* was a muddied badge that the reformers wore proudly.

Among Riis' successors, sociologist Lewis Hine recorded the miserable lives of immigrants who were pouring out of Europe into Ellis Island. From there they went to the fetid homes and the sweatshops where they barely eked out enough money to put bread on the table. In 1908, Hine was hired as an investigator by the National Child Labor Committee. Hine said, "I wanted to show the things that had to be corrected." He focused especially on children sent to work in food processing plants, factories, and mines. He uncovered them at every turn. His photos appeared in magazines, books, slide shows for lectures, and traveling exhibits. Their publication was instrumental in passing child labor laws that took the children out of the mines and factories, and into schools.[49]

Riis and Hine were among the early social documentary photographers. During the Depression of the 1930s, Dorothea Lange, Walker Evans, and Ben Shahn carried on that tradition. From the wellspring of feeling for the downtrodden and anger at social injustice, sprang the social documentary motion picture, notably in Great Britain and the United States, but increasingly a rewarding expression throughout the world.

Photoengraving

Some documentary photographs found their way into picture magazines. The most outstanding of these magazines, *Life*, was first published in 1936, but the picture press itself started much earlier. In fact, it is just about as old as photography itself. The weekly *Illustrated London News* began to publish in 1842 with wood engravings, usually carved from artists' sketches on a wooden block. Few newspapers could reproduce images.

Picture engravers were closer to woodworkers than to modern photo engravers. In the early years, they carved drawings and daguerreotype photographs as wood engravings. Daguerreotypes, as already noted, were single images. Real publication of photographs would not be possible without the advancement of a technology that could take an ordinary photograph and convert it into a picture with *halftones*, or gray tones that held ink and could be printed on the same page as type. Photoengraving started in England, but results were poor until 1878 when Frederick Ives at Cornell University created a halftone process that broke a photograph into tiny dots that could pick up ink, giving the appearance of continuous tones from light to dark. The half-tone brought words and pictures together, leading to one of the great advances in the history of mass communication: photojournalism.

Photographs could now be printed, but they would not become common in newspapers until the quality of newsprint—the paper itself—improved toward the end of the nineteenth century. However, photographs could be seen in the pages of weekly journals and magazines. The first newspaper

Figure 3.8 Sociologist Lewis Hine took pictures of children denied the chance to go to school, forced to work from morning to night. Here they are shelling peas.

photograph, entitled *Shanty-Town*, appeared in the New York *Daily Graphic* on March 4, 1880. By the end of the century, photographs were regularly printed in newspapers and magazines.

Innovations continued as technology opened opportunities for science photography. Wilhelm Roentgen discovered X-rays in 1895. X-ray photos followed a year later.

The Copier

Although it reached the public in the middle of the twentieth century, the office copier belongs to this list of informational innovations, one more tool of communication that provides what Daniel J. Boorstin has called "the repeatability of experience," which is a significant element in democratizing society.[50]

Ancient Greeks experimented with static electricity by rubbing amber with silk to attract bits of hair. Systematic observations began in the nineteenth century with the chemical generation of electricity. By the twentieth century, scientists had extended their research to include the properties of light in what is known as *photoconductivity*. Related research was being done in television.

Trained as both a physicist and a patent attorney, Chester Carlson continued the trail of experiments with the specific goal of finding a better means than carbon paper to copy documents. Working mostly in the kitchen of his Queens, New York, apartment during the Depression with the assistance of a German refugee scientist, he produced his first fixed image after three years of experimenting. He called his invention *xerography*, which is Greek for *dry writing*. His breakthrough combined India ink, a handkerchief, wax paper, a light bulb, sulfur, mossy powder, a microscope glass slide, and a small metal plate. Carlson took his invention to one major corporation after another, but each showed what he termed "enthusiastic lack of interest." The

Figure 3.9
Inventor Chester Carlson examines a prototype of the Xerox copier. He worked on xerography for 15 years before selling a copier. (Courtesy Xerox Corporation.)

small company that eventually manufactured the Xerox sold its first model in 1950, a copier that used plain paper. The success of the Xerox 914 (referring to copies up to 9 x 14 inches) was sensational. Within six years, 65,000 copiers had been sold. Today, some 20 companies worldwide sell more than $50 billion of copiers and supplies annually.

The laser printer, the facsimile machine, and the light pen, which transmits information along a beam of light, depend upon some of the same principles of photoelectricity.

Looking Ahead

By the end of the nineteenth century, photography had changed from a few curious experiments to a significant means for recording events. Pictures appeared in newspapers and magazines. Photography as art was starting to reach the public. Photographs of loved ones were placed atop tables and in purses and pockets. Scientists in several fields were using cameras to uncover mysteries.

An important new step was about to be taken, perhaps the most important of all to most people. It would be the ownership of an inexpensive, easy-to-use camera. As the twentieth century dawned, ordinary people could take pleasure in holding cameras in their own hands.

Figure 3.10   *Harper's Weekly* engraving, 1870, of a portrait studio. Wood or metal engravings were needed until the halftone process was invented. (Courtesy State Historical Society of Wisconsin.)

Current News

The telegraph changed the way that information moved through society. Previously limited to a minuscule bit of news at the distance a human voice could shout, the speed of a fast horse, or the flash of a mirror in the sun, complex messages carried by wire traveled thousands of miles in less time than a horse could be saddled. The telegraph was a new *scientific* communications medium, although the most learned minds of the early nineteenth century did not fully understand just what electricity was or how it worked. The telegraph, the first practical use of electricity, uncoupled communication from transportation. To communicate, it was no longer necessary to carry the message.

Newspapers Change

The dot-and-dash reports humming on the wire went a long way toward removing the impediment of distance as a factor in determining what news is. As a result of this invention, newspapers would never be the same. Driven from the news columns by economic factors, opinions would take refuge on the editorial page. With information available on a national scale, weather forecasts took on a value that *The Farmer's Almanac* never provided. In the ability to inform its customers, the small town paper would draw closer to the big city press. In our own day, the communication satellite has done for television some of what the telegraph did for the newspaper, and the shakeout has not been completed.

The telegraph jolted the national economy. Before the log poles were erected parallel to the single railroad tracks that spanned most of the nation, a train had to wait on a siding, its engineer unsure of when the "8:45" would actually pass by. When the telegraph communicated that information, more trains could run. That brought more goods, lowered freight costs, and spurred business. Industry now could receive sales orders from far-flung field offices and maintain contact with them on a daily basis.

This new technology also altered the way news was gathered and distributed. Unlike the horse-based transportation it replaced, the train carried as many newspapers, magazines, catalogs, and books as readers wanted. The telegraph became the heart of a new institution, the news gathering cooperative, that helped to foster a change in just what news was and how it was delivered to mass audiences in the penny press that emerged during the nineteenth century.[51] The telegraph helped shift the emphasis in newspapers from passionate opinion to dispassionate reports of events, gave small town newspapers a better chance to compete against large dailies, freed these small newspapers from dependence upon the big city newspapers, and altered the way news stories were written. For small town newspapers, the ability to get the same news as big city rivals was stimulating and pointed to cooperative news.[52] In the growth and strengthening of smaller newspapers, the telegraph gave a clear example of how the diffusion of a tool of communication created more information producers, because it was no longer necessary to read a large city newspaper to acquire fresh news from beyond the community.

Rumor even had it that Butch Cassidy and the Sundance Kid fled to South America around the turn of the century because the telegraph made their business of robbery too risky.

Ancient Signals

The word *telegraph* comes from the Greek, meaning *to write at a distance*. Efforts of people to communicate over distance without physical transportation of the information go back at least to Homer's *Iliad*, when beacon fires heralded the coming of ships. Athenians used signal fires to warn of a Spartan attack. Roman fires warned of pirate ships. Julius Caesar followed a Persian practice of stationing soldiers with leather lungs on platforms to shout messages back and forth. The Romans and later the Moors used the heliograph, a mirror of gleaming metal that flashed in the sunlight. In the sixteenth century, beacon fires gave the English fleet the message that the Spanish Armada was nearing. American Indians sent smoke signals. Incas had a system of messengers each of whom ran about a mile at top speed to the next messenger; this relay system enabled a message to travel at the rate of about 150 miles per day across the Inca kingdom. No one figured out how to beat the Inca system until the nineteenth century.

The problem with all these devices was that they were limited to the simplest kind of prearranged message, such as "The enemy is coming." More complicated ways of signaling or more complex devices were needed to pass more information from point to point. The semaphore, a visual telegraph, depended upon the positioning of pairs of torches or flags to represent an assortment of messages or individual letters. In the nineteenth century, information passed with surprising swiftness between French cities connected by semaphore towers. A line-of-sight system was planned from Maine all the way to New Orleans.

The First Telegraphs

Two Englishmen, Charles Wheatstone and William Cooke, built a working telegraph that was installed on the Great Western Railway in England in 1843, but the greatest fame and credit has gone to Samuel F.B. Morse. While a student at Yale, Morse learned about the properties of electricity. His interest in an electrical telegraph began in 1832 aboard ship. Morse was returning to America following three years in Europe trying to make a living as an artist. During a dinner conversation with other passengers about electromagnetism, Morse realized that electrical current could be used as the basis for a telegraph. He remarked to other passengers, "I see no reason why intelligence might not be instantaneously transmitted by electricity to any distance."[53]

The world was certainly ready, and particularly the United States, whose endless

Figure 3.11   An experimental telegraph made from a picture frame, some clock wheels, and bits of metal and wood.

hills and plains were soon to be stitched together by the threads of railroad tracks.

Even before he secured a position as a professor of art in a New York university, Morse began his experiments, assisted by Alfred Vail, who is sometimes identified as the true inventor of telegraphic hardware.

In 1838, Morse sent a message down two miles of wire in New Jersey, then repeated his feat in Philadelphia and again in Washington, D.C. before President Martin Van Buren, his cabinet and a congressional committee. Several of the dignitaries showed interest, but others expressed doubt and ridicule, to Morse's frustration because he asked the government to finance a test line between Baltimore and Washington. Five more years were to pass before Morse received any of the government support he desperately wanted.

Morse's contraption was odd enough to be laughed at. His original receiving equipment consisted of a pen attached to one end of a pivoted arm, with a magnet pulling at a piece of iron attached to the arm. A windup clockwork motor drew a paper tape under the pen, which marked the tape according to the current flowing through the electromagnet. Morse and Vail continued to improve the device. Eventually, Vail invented a system that used a click key at the transmitter, and a receiver that indented a pattern of dots and dashes on a moving paper tape. Because the instrument made enough noise so the operator could hear the message, the paper tape was abandoned.

"What Hath God Wrought?"

In 1843, Congress appropriated $30,000 for an experimental line between Baltimore and Washington. When the Whig convention, meeting in Baltimore the following year, chose its presidential candidate, Vail carried the information by train to the end of the telegraph wire at Annapolis Junction and sent it on by key to Morse at the other terminal in the Capitol. Astonished Washington residents learned of the party's nominee an hour before reporters on the train arrived to confirm the news. It was the first public demonstration of the telegraph, and the first electrically transmitted news dispatch. Although the newspapers in Washington and Baltimore paid scant attention at first, they quickly came around when a nominee for vice president used the telegraph to decline the nomination. The carrier pigeon had met its match.

The line to Baltimore was completed on May 24, 1844. A formal message was sent to garner some publicity for the new invention, a quotation from the book of Numbers: "What hath God wrought?" Morse, who was deeply pious, held a mystical belief that God had chosen him to improve communication on Earth.

Morse and his backers were disappointed when Congress chose not to buy the patent rights. Development of the telegraph in the United States, unlike most of the rest of the world, would be private. As a result, great fortunes would be made. However, Vail would die in poverty. Not so Morse, although he had lean years as he tried to secure government financing.

New companies quickly formed to go into the business of telegraphy. Their ex-tension of the telegraph lines was haphazard, disconnected. By the end of 1847, lines had reached Cincinnati, Louisville, and St. Louis. Until the wires were connected, a message from the East Coast required six days of travel by special messenger, steamboat, and coach express to reach St. Louis. The completion of the line to San Francisco in October 1861 put the overland Pony Express between St. Joseph, Missouri, and San Francisco out of business almost overnight, for it could do no better between "St. Joe" and Sacramento, California than an eight-day trip in summer, ten days in winter.

Western Union Takes the Lead

Competition among telegraph companies was fierce. By the start of the Civil War, six companies, each dominating a region of the United States, formed a cartel to crush smaller rivals. The war proved ruinous for companies whose lines ran north to south. After the war three companies remained, and in 1866 one of them, Western Union, bought out its two rivals to become the first of America's business monopolies.

Both the Blue and Gray armies used the telegraph lines extensively, but the South was hampered by a lack of wire and supplies. In Grant's final campaign, wires radiated from his headquarters to every salient point, enabling him to coordinate troop movements across a wide front.[54]

News of the assassination of Abraham Lincoln was transmitted instantaneously by telegraph across the nation, but lacking a cable, the news took 12 days to cross the Atlantic.

Telegraph wires and railroad tracks spread across the face of the nation in symbiotic harmony, each benefiting the other. The railroad provided business for the humming wires, enough business to cut telegraph costs. The telegraph provided the vital information on which rail transportation depended, the nerve trail alongside the railroad spine. With long stretches of single track, engineers had little warning of a train highballing in the opposite direction. Collisions were a constant threat until the telegraph permitted a dependable switching control system. The paired growth of telegraph and railroad aided another means of communication, the mail system, which needed dependable transportation. U.S. stamps went on sale in 1847, three years after Morse's company began stringing wire. That was also the year the first practical printing telegraph was put to work, its advocates promising that the device would eliminate operator errors. One message, "See the judge at once and get excused. I cannot send a man in your place," was delivered as, "See the judge at once and get executed. I can send a man in your place."[55]

With information now moving from city to city at lightning speed, prices of goods became more uniform, a function of national supply and demand instead of local conditions. Thanks to both the railroad and the telegraph, prices declined.

In Europe, a cable laid under the English Channel tied England to France in 1851. Others soon were in operation connecting England to Ireland, and Denmark to Sweden. Then Europe and Africa were linked by a cable across the Mediterranean Sea. In 1866, after several failures, the first transatlantic cable was laid between England and Canada by the *Great Eastern*, which was five times the size of any other ship afloat, the world's largest ship.[56] Cables reached Australia in 1902 and Shanghai, China, in 1906. Now, especially for trade and politics, the world's most powerful nations linked themselves in a web of instant information. The web would not eliminate misunderstandings or wars no matter how much it was thickened by additional strands, but it could be said that these first under-the-sea cables created a sea change in how peoples dealt with each other.

Its Role in Transmitting News

The telegraph found other uses besides sending business information. Its ability to transmit news dispatches transformed the entire newspaper industry. The first quarter of the nineteenth century had found newspapers—and the *mass* communication

they represented—limited in content and distribution. News reports were hard to come by. Newspapers were often published by printers, who gathered their own news, then filled their columns with stories copied from newspapers printed by other publishers.

News gathering from distant points was time consuming, linked as it was to the slow modes of transportation. Like any message, first the news had to be reduced to writing. Then, the written report had to be put on a steamer, carriage, horse, or train, carried on foot, or, more likely, a combination of these to get to the printing house. News from the European continent or from the interior of the United States could be weeks old before it was set in type.

With the telegraph the time that news from New York took to be published in New Orleans dropped from more than ten days to one day. A *New York Herald* writer said space itself seemed to have been "annihilated." Not only did metropolitan newspapers present news more quickly, but the smaller, rural newspapers for the first time could bring national news to their readers before the city papers arrived in the mail. Big city editors did not stand up and cheer for the level playing field the telegraph provided. The manager of the London *Times* wished that it had never been invented.[57]

> When telegraph news became widely available, cities in the interior of the country could compete on the same footing with eastern cities. Equal access to news encouraged the growth of dozens of new provincial dailies.[58]

Changes in newsgathering soon followed. Before the telegraph, small-scale, temporary cooperative arrangements were put together to take advantage of specific transportation systems, such as horse expresses between two major cities or small boats that met arriving ships and then sped information to port. Or carrier pigeons winged past seagulls to carry the latest cotton prices.

Most national and international news had reached publishers by mail through the postage-free exchange of newspapers among editors. With the coming of the telegraph some stories were wired from the field to a local newspaper. Then, this newspaper was exchanged by mail with others, enabling editors in towns not yet served by telegraph to print the information.

Information itself was changed by the technology. Telegraph companies charged by the word, as much as 50 cents for 10 words between New York and Boston, so news writing was sharply truncated. Two years after Morse invented his telegraph, the New York Tribune began a column of telegraph bulletins. Competitive newspapers at times chose to share a single correspondent. Speed of newsgathering became more important, but to cut growing costs, speed was achieved at the sacrifice of story detail. To economize, reporters attempted to shorten their stories by coding news dispatches. This produced expert coders and decoders, but it also produced blunders, and led to retaliatory tactics by the telegraph companies, such as counting every three letters as one word. Editors told correspondents to summarize the news on the wire and send the details by mail.

> Insofar as the invention and spread of the telegraph provided the crucial catalyst and means for regular cooperative news gathering, it supplied the technological underpinning of the modern press; that is, it transformed the newspaper from a personal journal and party organ into primarily a disseminator of news.[59]

Sent by the clicking keys, reports of events became standardized, less opinionated, and of more interest to the broader political spectrum of readers. News stories arrived quicker and won a broader array of readers, but lost some of their bite as they rid themselves of their bile. It was the beginning of the efforts by news wire services to produce objective reporting. The new mass dailies, the penny press, now sold not just opinions and essays, but reliable, relatively uncolored facts upon which readers could base decisions.

News Agencies

Charles Havas began a European news service headquartered in Paris in 1833 using the mails and carrier pigeons. His correspondents in other capitals scoured local newspapers for items that Havas offered the French press. To remain solvent, he swapped subscriptions to his news service for advertising space in newspapers. One of Havas's employees, a German, Bernard Wolff, formed a competing agency. So did another former German employee of Havas, Paul Reuter, who had developed an interest in telegraphy from its inception. Reuter realized that a gap existed between national telegraph lines built by Germany and France. He sensed the opportunity for a news transmitting service across the gap. Reuter filled the gap in 1849 with carrier pigeons. When a telegraph connection was completed, Reuter moved to England, where, after some years of disappointment, he was able to organize a news and commercial information service by telegraph, carrier pigeon, and rail. This laid the foundation of one of the world's great news agencies, Reuters. In 1869, the three agencies, now based in France, Germany, and England, rather than compete sharply, divided world news coverage among themselves, a cartel that survived until the rise of the Third Reich.

After World War II the Havas agency, a supporter of the Vichy government, collapsed. Agence France Presse, the present French news service, arose from the wreckage. The Wolff Agency thrived until it, too, collapsed along with the Third Reich. Of the three, Reuter alone survived.[60]

The Mexican War of 1846-48 increased the American public's appetite for news. At the outbreak of the war, a mere 130 miles of wire existed, reaching only as far south as Richmond, Virginia. A combination of the Pony Express and the infant telegraph system regularly beat the government mails between New Orleans and New York. This express system was so efficient that President James Polk learned of the American victory at Vera Cruz from the publisher of the *Baltimore Sun.*

With the penny press spreading newspaper sales to a huge new customer base never before attracted to newspapers, the demand for news added urgency to the spread of the wires. The telegraph made possible cooperative news gathering on a regular basis, but the relationship between the established newspapers and the telegraph companies was often stormy. In 1848, motivated by the telegraph's speed in sending news, and only four years after its invention, six fiercely competitive New York dailies formed what was to become the Associated Press.[61] In addition to the telegraph, they also used carrier pigeons. Bird seed was cheaper than paying by the word.

Serving a growing clientele with a variety of political viewpoints, the Associated Press sought to keep its customers contented by writing in a manner that would not show a bias. A neutral, dispassionate view of events was something new in American journalism, but the AP's effort to be impartial continued. Eventually, *objectivity* set the tone for most news reporting. So did the replacement of the old, chronological storytelling manner of reporting by the newer inverted pyramid style, in which the most important facts are presented first, followed by other facts in descending order of importance. It is not fully clear whether this change was due to the unreliability of telegraph lines, which could fail in the midst of a transmission, or a continuation of a writing style introduced by Abraham Lincoln's no nonsense Secretary of War Edwin Stanton, who censored telegraph dispatches.[62] The style survived the Civil War and continues today.

In relaying the news, time was no longer a measure of distance. By uncoupling information from transportation, the telegraph changed the way information was formulated, and it changed the way people conceived of and used that information. The telegraph also fostered changes in society through new ways of doing business and through new businesses. For the masses, the telegraph served as a catalyst in the formation of the first true mass communication medium in history—the penny press.

In a historical sense, the computer is no more than an instantaneous telegraph with a prodigious memory, and all the communications inventions in between have simply been elaborations on the telegraph's original work.[63]

Changes in Service

Telegraph technology changed step by step. Thomas Edison invented a duplex device so messages could flow in opposite directions at the same time along a single wire. He followed this with a quadruplex device so two messages could flow one way while two others came the opposite way, all at the same time. He invented the phonograph while trying to improve the telegraph. In the same way, Alexander Graham Bell invented the telephone.

As the business grew it became obvious that the slowest part of message transmission was the Western Union boy on a bicycle who pedaled around town delivering telegrams. Direct private lines called *tielines* were installed between businesses and Western Union offices. The teleprinter was put into service for newspapers, business, and government, so typing skill was all that was needed to send messages that were printed out on a strip of paper one half-inch wide.

A few years later came the teletype, a keyboard printer that could print news stories on fanfold sheets of paper at the rate of 10 characters per second. Today, wire service computer printers send reams of news electronically for storage in newspaper computers, entirely eliminating paper. Telequote and Quotron machines on brokers' desks give instant access to stock market prices. E-mail, fax machines, and telephones give the telegraph more than enough competition, but it has not become an anachronism. After 150 years, the telegraph, not yet a museum piece, remains a convenient way to transfer funds. At one time, it was the means by which the armed forces announced a death. Today, it is likely to carry Mother's Day greetings or a singing birthday message.

Even if its best days are behind it, the telegraph's place in history is assured. When it was new, Henry David Thoreau, no advocate of industrial progress, wrote, "We are in great haste to construct a magnetic telegraph from Maine to Texas, but Maine and Texas, it may be, have nothing important to communicate." As it turned out, Maine and Texas had much to say to one another, and so did everyone else. Trade in perishable food could be undertaken with more certainty when communication ascertained market demand. The telegraph also evened out the wide variation in the prices of goods from city to city and brought about standard time zones. The telegraph united the United States.

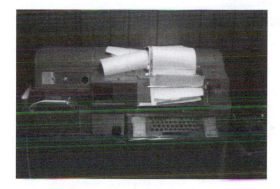

Figure 3.12   A Western Union teletype, 1959. Newspapers used them to supply stories to wire services directly or by paper tape. (Courtesy Pavek Museum.)

Voices on a Wire

Before the invention of the telephone, people could not talk to anyone they could not see. To communicate with a friend, a visit or a letter were the appropriate choices, although for the elderly, the ill, and the handicapped, visiting was not always possible. As for letters, it was estimated that the average person wrote only 17 letters a year.

Intruder and Rescuer

To summon the fire department, someone had to gallop on a horse or run on foot. No one called a doctor or a hospital or the police department. Business communication was by letter, messenger, or personal visit. Living alone posed a special danger, particularly in a rural area. And mines, uncertain places at the best of times, allowed no easy way to communicate with the surface when something went wrong below. Construction upward was also restricted by a lack of communication. Skyscrapers waited for the telephone.

In sum, life was narrower without the telephone, slower and more limited, which was not always a bad state of affairs although it could be lonesome, especially for the large rural segment of the population. For staid middle-class Victorian house-

holds, the telephone might be an intrusion into an orderly home, but for the farmer's wife the telephone could be a godsend.[64]

Some subscribers regarded the telephone as a status symbol not to be shared by the lower classes, objecting to any widening of access to the Bell system by such devices as coin-operated public telephones or telephone directories available to the general public. By expanding the limits of who may speak uninvited to whom, the telephone threatened the Victorian class structure.

Both rescuer and invader, the telephone has always performed a dual role. It both keeps others at bay and connects to them in its controlled way.

Alexander Graham Bell did not change all this by himself. Like other communication technologies, the telephone was not a new idea of a single person. If a couple of kids can tie a string between two tin cans and roughly understand each other, adults can do it better. *Lovers' telephones* using boxes or cans connected by a taut wire, could carry the sound of a voice 100 yards, the length of a football field.

To sell its service, the Bell System had to convince people that they needed a telephone for business. Doctors and business owners also acquired telephones at home. With the decision to expand into the general residential market, Bell advertised widely to create an image of the telephone's efficiency, emergency aid, and sociability. The modern slogan, "Reach out and touch someone," had its antecedents in "Call the folks now!," "Friendship's path often follows the trail of the telephone wire," and "No girl wants to be a wallflower." The telephone would alter courtship patterns and lift hopes for romance.

In Washington, the inventor of some equipment for the telegraph, Elisha Gray, went to the Patent Office to file a caveat for a telephone, a warning that he had an invention well under way and had the right to be notified if anyone else asked for a patent on the same device. Gray's caveat said he had invented "the art of transmitting vocal sounds or conversations telegraphically through an electric current." The date was February 14, 1876, St. Valentine's Day. By coincidence, that was the same day a patent application for an "improvement in Telegraphy" was filed by an attorney for Bell, a 29-year-old Scottish-born professor of vocal physiology at Boston University who ran a school to train teachers of the deaf. Bell's application described what was then Bell's yet unsuccessful method of transmitting sounds.[65] Both Gray, a 41-year-old inventor with many electrical patents, and Bell had been working separately on a "harmonic telegraph," using different tones or frequencies for sending several telegraph messages at the same time over the same wire. Bell won the lengthy court battles that followed, and that have followed so many communication inventions. It became the Bell Telephone Company, not the Gray Company.

"Mr. Watson, come here. I want you."

For a telegraph message, the current flows and is broken, again and again. To transmit a voice, a continuous current must be modified. Bell, assisted by young Thomas Watson, eventually was able to verify an old idea he had that he could transmit the

Figure 3.13   Bell's first telephone was both a transmitter and a receiver.

human voice "telegraphically" by wire if he could vary an electrical current exactly as air pressure varies when words are spoken. Bell, the teacher of speech, knew that the density of air varies with the movement of sound through it. His goal was to build a device that would make current vary. Bell, whose mother and his soon-to-be wife were deaf, modeled the telephone after the human ear.

On March 10, 1876, Bell said to his assistant from an adjoining room, "Mr. Watson, come here. I want you." And the telephone was born.

In 1876, Philadelphia held an exposition to commemorate the centennial of the signing of the Declaration of Independence. Bell exhibited his telephone there, but he was ignored until one visitor, Dom Pedro II, the emperor of Brazil, walked by, and recognized Bell as a teacher of the deaf who had given a lecture in Boston that Dom Pedro attended. Bell demonstrated his device to an astonished Dom Pedro, who reportedly exclaimed, "My

God, it talks!" His excitement made Bell's "toy"—as some dismissed it—a sensation of the exposition.[66]

Several inventors and scientists came up with improvements, and so did Bell and his assistant, Watson. The original box telephone with a megaphone used for both speaking and listening was replaced by a hand telephone with a separate transmitter and receiver, so the user did not have to wag his head between speaking and listening. A bell-shaped mouthpiece concentrated the voice, and a metal disk replaced the skin diaphragm. Copper wire replaced iron wire, so the user no longer had to shout quite so loudly.

Traveling to England on his honeymoon, Bell took along some telephone apparatus. A pair of telephones that he presented to Queen Victoria were strung between the apartments of the Princess of Wales and her children's nursery. As in the United States, Bell's demonstrations of a device that carried human voices was enjoyable, but embarrassing to grown men who were invited to step up to speak into it, because this was regarded as just a plaything, not something for a grown man to be associated with, certainly not a means of communication. Yet, in London, Bell made this prophecy:

> It is conceivable that cables of telephone wires could be laid under ground or suspended overhead, communicating by branch wires with private dwellings, country houses, shops, manufacturers, etc., uniting them through the main cable with a central office where the wires could be connected as desired, establishing direct communication between any two places in the city. Not only so, but I believe that in the future, wires will unite the head offices of the Telephone Company in different cities, and a man in one part of the country may communicate by word of mouth with another in a distant place.[67]

Sir William Preece, chief engineer of the British Post Office, responded with less enthusiasm. He told a committee of the House of Commons:

> I fancy the descriptions we get of its use in America are a little exaggerated, though there are conditions in America which necessitate the use of such instruments more than here. Here we have a superabundance of messengers, errand boys, and things of that kind.[68]

The Scottish physicist James Clerk Maxwell, whose theory of invisible waves eventually led to the invention of radio, dismissed Bell's apparatus, remarking that it could have been "put together by an amateur."[69] Bell offered to sell his invention to Western Union and was turned down.

The telephone business in each city was local when telegraph wires spanned the continent, but it was obvious that voice communication by wire could bypass skilled telegraph operators. The much bigger telegraph company, with thousands of miles of telegraph wire already strung along poles, soon emerged as a competitor, based on Elisha Gray's pending patent and a carbon granule microphone transmitter developed by Thomas Edison, which produced much better sound than anything Bell devised. Lessees of Bell telephones, tired of shouting to be heard, clamored for a transmitter as good as Edison's. Bell would probably have been driven out of business if Emile Berliner, who also improved phonograph equipment, had not developed a sensitive transmitter.[70] Eventually, the newly formed National Bell Telephone Company sued Western Union and, in an historic agreement, Western Union agreed to get out of the telephone business.

By 1878, New Haven, Connecticut, became the first city to have a commercial telephone exchange, with a switchboard of eight lines and 21 telephones. Within two years of the awarding of Bell's patent, some 10,000 Bell telephones were in use. A research and development unit was created, the forerunner of the Bell Laboratories, from which would come many of the developments in communication technology, including information theory, motion picture sound, transistors, laser beams, optical fibers, the communications satellite, and advances in computers and television.

Can the Lower Classes Use It?

An early telephone advertisement tried to explain how the telephone worked:

> "Oh! no, the Telephone wires are not hollow; the voice is transmitted by waves of electricity. Telephones are rented only to persons of good breeding and refinement. A householder becomes morally responsible for its proper use by all members of his family. There is nothing to be feared from your conversation being overheard. Our subscribers are too well bred to listen to other people's business."[71]

At first, there were no phone numbers or directories, only a list of subscribers, usually grouped by what they sold or their professions. When the list of subscribers grew unwieldy, books were issued with telephone numbers. Callers complained about having to look up a number rather than telling the telephone operator whom they wanted.

The notion of the telephone as a public utility was still years in the distance when a Washington, D.C., hotel proprietor had to go to court to prevent the local telephone company from shutting off his service because he allowed guests to use the phone in the lobby. In Leicester, England, telephone officials rebuked a subscriber for calling the fire brigade, noting that the fire was not on his property. An appeal to the postmaster-general brought the ruling that it was acceptable to use a telephone in the event of fires and riots.

Less than 10 years after the telephone was invented, the American Telephone and Telegraph Company was chartered for the purpose of connecting every city and town in the United States, Canada, and Mexico, and by cable with the rest of the world. Theodore Vail, a distant relative of Alfred Vail, Morse's assistant in inventing the telegraph, rose in office to lead AT&T from a small company to a communications giant. Vail brought standardization to the telephone industry from accounting procedures to the shape of the black telephone in every home. He saw to it that AT&T bought up every small telephone company it could. As AT&T spread its shadow, its single standard fell across the land. That would not change until a government-mandated breakup and technology introduced diversity.

The Telephone As an Early Radio

In a foreshadowing of radio entertainment, the telephone found employment in several European nations as a transmitter of live musical performances. Wealthy patrons paid to listen to operatic, theatrical, and concert performances picked up by microphones in theaters and fed along telephone wires to earphones. In her sitting room, Queen Victoria could hear the opera coming from Covent Garden or the Royal Theater in Drury Lane. In London, wealthy hospital patients could receive piped-in plays and sermons. A few homes also bought the service. In Paris, the Theatrophone Company set up coin operated headsets at holiday resorts. Similar entertainments were soon available in several American cities. Opportunities were also offered to listen to telephonic church services and to political speeches. A Canadian tavern owner was permitted to put a microphone next to the judge presiding over a much publicized murder trial. A wire carried the testimony to the tavern where patrons could listen in on one of twenty earphones at 25 cents an hour.

The most innovative use of the telephone as a vehicle for mass communication was the Telefon Hirmondo in Budapest, Hungary, designed by a Hungarian engineer who had worked for Thomas Edison. From 1893 until radio broadcasting replaced it, this service gave *a daily schedule* of programs to thousands of subscribers, who tuned in by picking up an earphone. This wired radio could also be heard in such public places as hotels, hospitals, restaurants, and dentists' waiting rooms. The daily fare offered news reports of various kinds, music, a calendar of events around Budapest, a children's concert on Thursday evenings, and even commercials tucked in here and there, a full generation before it was tried in radio broadcasting.[72] Although articles were published widely about Telefon Hirmondo, the concept failed to spread much beyond Budapest with the curious exception of a brief venture in Newark, New Jersey, which went out of business in a few months.

What was significant about Telefon Hirmondo was that, using the available technology of the wired telephone, it was able, however barely, to tap into a latent public desire for information and entertainment on a regular basis piped into their homes and public places. Meeting that dormant desire fully would have to wait until other technology permitted wireless telegraphy to become broadcasting.

Telephone Operators

In the phone instrument, engineers designed an earpiece that would be the basis of early loudspeakers. They were solving many other problems arising from the growing popularity of point-to-point communication. Heavy demand on a central switchboard by calls handled manually was eased when companies using several telephones added a private switchboard called a *Private Branch Exchange*, or *PBX*. Many are still in use. Large modern companies have now switched to a *local area network* or *LAN* to link their telephone systems or computers, but the principle has not changed.

The first telephone operators, in a carryover from the telegraph system, were teenage boys. However, after complaints of rowdiness crackled over the lines, New England Bell and the New York Telephone Company managers got the idea of employing young ladies. There was still some question about whether it was decent for a young woman to take employment outside the home, because it jeopardized her chance for marriage, but the chance to escape the family each day and to earn money of her own to spend as she pleased was a much greater lure, even though the pay packet was light and the early headsets weighed more than six pounds. A wake-up service for customers requesting it was among the duties of these *hello girls*, whose indeterminate social status approximated

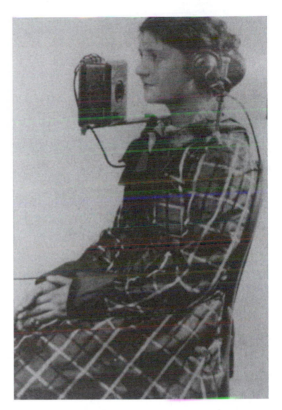

Figure 3.14   The early headsets worn by telephone operators could weigh more than six pounds.

that of domestic servants. A contemporary observer recalled:

> Before the great switchboard the girls seem like weavers at some gigantic loom, the numerous cords crossing and recrossing as if in the execution of some wondrous fabric. Indeed, a wondrous fabric of speech is here woven into the record of each day.[73]

Young women by now were also taking jobs as store clerks, where they had to come into contact with the general public. Nursing had only recently become a respectable profession, thanks to stories about Florence Nightingale and Clara Barton.

The central switchboard solved the immediate early problem of having to connect every telephone with every other telephone, but the central switchboard required telephone operators, who were not always attentive and might listen in. Kansas City undertaker Almon Strowger, who convinced himself that another undertaker had bribed a telephone operator to tell callers that Strowger's line was busy, invented what became the dial telephone and the automatic telephone exchange. They were first put into operation in LaPorte, Indiana, in 1892.

By the time the original Bell patents expired in 1893, more than a quarter million telephones were hooked up in the United States, a little less than four phones per 1,000 persons. By 1900, despite the population increase, there were nearly 18 telephones per 1,000 Americans. In many towns, the first telephone was a public phone in the railroad depot or drug store.

In some of the better establishments, a clerk would place the call, collect the money, and direct the caller to a booth. In such elegant places as modern hotels, booths might have silk-curtained windows and be mistaken for the equally elegant elevator, another recent invention. In many countries today, governments operate such systems minus the silk curtains.

William Gray constructed the first coin deposit telephone in 1888. It went into a Hartford, Connecticut, bank. Early automatic pay phone booths had different methods for allowing their use. There were few ways to get a coin back if the call was not completed. There was even a booth that locked the caller inside until a coin was deposited to unlock the door, but that concept was short-lived.

Figure 3.15   Typical in the 1880s, as many as 250 wires on a telephone pole, bowed by ice in the winter.

Into the Twentieth Century

Before the turn of the century, few long distance calls were made. Distortion over long distance was alleviated by M.I. Pupin's invention in 1900 of the loading coil, Lee de Forest's invention in 1906 of the three-element vacuum tube, and H.D. Arnold's vacuum tube amplifier in 1914. The vacuum tube was replaced in 1947 by the transistor, an invention out of the Bell Telephone Laboratories. A few decades later, transistors became part of microchips.

The wireless telephone, after successful tests in 1915, began service as an aid to the U.S. Navy during World War I. American entry into World War I created a sudden and massive need to improve communication. Washington, D.C., was no longer a sleepy backwater city. For a short time in 1918, the U.S. government took control of all telephone service. Expansion of telephone service continued unabated. Data Phone business, by which regular phone circuits can transmit computer data at high speed, began in 1958.

Despite doubts that people would pay $75 for a three-minute phone call, regular radiotelephony service between the two great financial centers, New York and London, started in 1927 during the financial boom years. The service was so popular that more circuits were needed.[74] Radiotelephony was quickly extended to the other major cities of Europe, and between Europe and Buenos Aires. At the same time, cables snaked across mountain ranges and ocean floors. The first transatlantic telephone cable was laid in 1956. The Pacific Link fiber optic cable went into service between California and Japan in 1989. The size of a garden hose, it could carry 40,000 phone calls at a time compared to less than 1,000 for the two copper cables then in service. Today, communication satellites also carry thousands of calls. The clarity of overseas calls has improved so markedly that users frequently say the other party "sounds next door." There is no way to tell if the call is bouncing off a satellite transponder or traveling across the floor of an ocean.

In addition to sending voices along a wire, telephone lines sent printed words and pictures. Printing via wire was originally known as the *printing telegraph*, then as the *teletypewriter*, then as the *teletype* as improvements were made. Its primary use has been the sending of news by wire services like the Associated Press and Reuter. The technology is similar to that of a telegraph, except that instead of dots and dashes, electrical impulses represent letters, numbers, and symbols.

The telephone company set up a *teletypewriter exchange service*, or *TWX* for short, sometimes known as telex or twix. Subscribers, who have teletype machines in their offices, were listed in a separate directory. Although telex is being replaced by newer technologies like facsimile and electronic mail, telex networks still exist around the world. In some countries, they remain the surest way to get a message through, which is the point, after all. One way or another, the world had come to rely on Mr. Bell's "toy."

Signals in the Air

Imagine typical users of radio over the span of nearly a century. In 1905, the Marconi operator at a shore station picks up dots and dashes from a ship out at sea. A decade later the hobbyist strains to hear, over a hand-built "crystal-and-catswhisker" set, the call letters of a distant station. Two decades later the family gathers in the evening around the console in the parlor in the midst of the Depression, staring at the orange glow of the dial as they listen to Jack Benny go down to his vault. (It never did seem as funny on television.) More years pass, and the same family is standing close to the shortwave radio in the kitchen, trying to understand a crackling voice talking of war. A generation later, a motorist catches news on the hour while racing down the new Interstate. Today, a jogger withdraws from the world around her by tuning into country music on a Walkman.

These represent different ways of receiving a radio signal. Each formed part of the social revolution that radio created.

> The effects of radio are quite independent of its programming. To those who have never studied media, this fact is quite as baffling as literacy is to natives, who say, "Why do you write? Can't you remember?"[75]

The history of radio went through two distinct periods of social use, point-to-point communication and broadcasting. Point-to-point communication began as wireless telegraphy and became wireless telephony. Each period led into the next. Each had its own technology, purpose, economic underpinning, sound. Wireless telegraphy, like the telegraph, was all dots and dashes, with messages going from one point to another. Wireless telephony, like the telephone, was voices, with messages from one point to another. Their primary usage was and is business communication, such as ship-to-shore. Broadcasting, whose purpose is information and entertainment, carries voices, music, and all other sounds, going from one point to many points.

Some of Radio's Societal Effects

In every country, broadcasting has exerted a push-pull on its citizens, both a centripetal and a centrifugal force. The centripetal force, uniting the nation, results from a conscious effort to exert government leadership, spread national culture, and share information. The use of a common language and a national accent in place of regional dialects also tends to hold a people together. On the other hand, radio pulls people apart not only by offering a variety of stations but by doing what every medium does that displaces direct with mediated communication. The announcer's conversational tone regards the audience as one person and speaks to each person alone in his or her private world. The announcer sometimes creates an aura of intimate conversation, ignoring the truth that it is one-way mediated communication, not conversation at all. Listeners don't seem to care.

As a source of information, radio has been universally powerful, although in many nations today radio remains strictly under government control. Unlike the United States, where the government is forbidden by law to broadcast to its own citizens (stations voluntarily broadcast presidential addresses), many governments use broadcasts precisely for the purpose of communicating with their own citizenry. However, the United States, along with a number of other nations, beams radio propaganda beyond its borders. The Voice of America broadcasts in dozens of languages. Radio Liberty, Radio Free Europe, and Radio Marti targeted, respectively, the former Soviet Union, its East European satellites, and Cuba.

Origins of Radio

In the early part of the nineteenth century, the period of great discoveries about the nature of electricity, English scientist Michael Faraday and American scientist Joseph Henry published reports of their inquiries into the connection between electricity and magnetism. Telegraph engineers, as they labored to solve problems, added information. A Scottish physicist, James Clerk Maxwell, went beyond what was known about electromagnetism with a far reaching theory of invisible waves. Although he did not try to prove his theory of electromagnetic fields, others did. In 1887, a German physicist, Heinrich Hertz, supported Maxwell's theory through experiments that sent electrical current through the air in the form of waves. Even before Hertz reported his findings, Thomas Edison had briefly experimented with "leakage" that spread out in all directions from telegraph wires and magnetized iron located some distance away. He tried to harness these electrical "leaks" as a means of wireless communication from a moving train, but failed to produce more than a random jumble of signals.

In France, Édouard Branly designed a *coherer*, a glass tube filled with iron filings. An electric current sent through the air caused the filings to pack together, or cohere, around metal rods at the ends of the tube. This completed a circuit so that electricity passed through the glass tube. English physicist Oliver Lodge improved the coherer by figuring out how to tune the transmitter and receiver to the same frequency. In 1894, Lodge went further with a demonstration that sent a Morse code message through the air more than half the length of a football field, but the coherer was still a crude device incapable of recognizing anything but short and long bursts of energy.[76]

Marconi

Maxwell, Hertz, Branly, and Lodge were scientists, not businessmen, but experiments began in several countries to make something practical out of the published experiments. Guglielmo Marconi, son of a well-to-do Italian landowner and his Irish wife, a member of the Jameson Whiskey family, would prove to be a very sharp businessman as he followed Hertz's trail. The teenaged Marconi was entranced with the idea that radio experiments might be taken out of the lab and into a money-making business. By good luck, Auguste Righi, a well-known physics professor, was a neighbor to the Marconis, and agreed to offer guidance to the boy.[77]

Studying and experimenting on the family estate, Marconi began by repeating Hertz's transmission of a few yards. In 1894, the same year that Lodge gave his demonstration, Marconi was able to open and close a relay to send a current through a coherer to sound a buzzer 30 feet away. Moving outdoors, he figured that he could increase the range by elevating the signal. After constructing an antenna, Marconi was able to receive the buzzer's sound more than two miles away on the other side of a hill. According to the tale, one day by accident he left part of his antenna on the ground while he held part in the air. To Marconi's surprise, the signal was greatly improved. Marconi continued to design new antennae by trial and error. He was soon able to send Morse Code dots and dashes for miles across the hills around his home.

It was an era when instantaneous communications were limited by where telegraph and telephone wires ran, when ships at sea had no way to receive information from the outside world and no way to signal for help if they were in distress. Marconi's mother realized the business possibilities in being able to send telegraph messages without wires, especially ship-to-ship and ship-to-shore. She applied to the Italian Ministry of Posts and Telegraphs, which turned the invention down. They saw no value in it.

Annie Jameson Marconi now turned to her wealthy and politically well-connected relatives. She and her son traveled with his equipment to England, where Marconi gave a demonstration across nine miles for telephone and telegraph officials of the British Post Office. This time, demonstrating wireless to the nation with the world's greatest navy, he found interest for a new communication system with ships at sea. The British official who had sneered at Alexander Graham Bell's telephone, William Preece, now chief engineer of the British Post Office, tried to buy out Marconi's invention on behalf of his government, but the young inventor, backed by his Jameson relatives and some solid patents, refused. Instead, in 1897 they incorporated the Wireless Telegraph and Signal Co., Ltd. and started selling radio equipment to the British army and navy. For commercial shippers, the company provided not only equipment but radio operators aboard ships and at shore stations. Marconi had taken wireless communication out of the laboratory into the world of commerce.

In 1901, Marconi and his assistants reported that they had transmitted the three dots of the Morse Code letter "S" faintly across the Atlantic Ocean from Cornwall, England to Newfoundland in Canada. Not everyone believed him, but the press ate it up.[78] Shortly thereafter, he formed an American subsidiary, the Marconi Wireless Telegraph Company of America. It would eventually become the Radio Corporation of America. One year later, without question, Marconi was able to transmit messages across the ocean.

Competition

The company tried to monopolize wireless telegraphy by ordering its coastal stations and ship operators to refuse communication with any non-Marconi operators except in emergencies, a business maneuver that raised international awareness of the power inherent in wireless communications and the dangers presented by a wireless monopoly. Germany, equipping its navy with its own system, became so incensed over the Marconi company's sharp practices that it summoned the Great Powers to a conference in Berlin in 1903, out of which came the world's first international agreement on radio. Still, it was not until 1908 that international coastal stations were opened to all transmissions.

Other inventors and scientists, seeing the potential for making a fortune, busily developed their own systems and applied for patents whenever they designed an improved piece of equipment. In addition to the Germans, inventions were coming from, among others, Oliver Lodge in England, and Reginald Fessenden, Lee de Forest, John Stone, and E. Howard Armstrong in the United States. Over the years, they

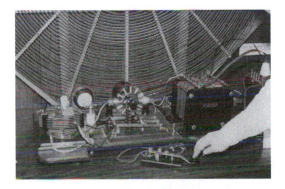

Figure 3.16 A spark transmitter, 1912. Radios using Morse Code signaled between ships and shore stations. (Courtesy Pavek Museum.)

battled each other in the marketplace and in the courts, exhausting their time, money, and energy.

In 1904, radio went into battle. In the Russo-Japanese war, both sides used wireless equipment, but not of equal quality and apparently not with equal competence. Wireless telegraphy may have helped the Japanese navy to sink most of the imperial Russian fleet. The Japanese navy was equipped with wireless. The Russian fleet apparently had shut down its radio transmission before the battle. Russia's "great white fleet," having sailed halfway around the world, was approaching its destination when the Japanese fleet, alerted by radio, sprang a trap.[79] At the battle of Tsushima Strait, the Japanese sunk nearly the entire Russian fleet, suffering almost no casualties itself, perhaps the most one-sided naval victory in history. Effectively, the war was over.

The navies of the world's major powers were equipping their fleets and shore facilities with wireless telegraphy. In the United States, radio's military possibilities expanded in 1911 with the first air-to-ground transmission. During World War I, airplanes equipped with radio were used as artillery spotters, signaling in Morse Code. The Navy had been interested in wireless communication from the beginning for obvious reasons, but some U.S. Navy ship commanders were not keen to embrace radio technology because it weakened the absolute control that a ship's captain commands at sea.

The Titanic

After radio operators on two stricken merchant ships managed to save the lives of their shipmates, Congress in 1910 passed a law requiring most passenger ships to carry radio equipment, but the law did not require operators to be on duty around the clock. Two years later, the "unsinkable" ocean liner *Titanic* on its maiden voyage hit an iceberg and went down with 1,522 passengers and crew. (Marconi himself was booked for the voyage, but other plans forced him to cancel.)[80] The radio operator on a ship only nineteen miles away, close

enough to rescue everyone, had shut down and gone to bed. The disaster led Congress to modify the 1910 law to require tighter controls aboard ships. A few weeks later it passed the Radio Act of 1912, giving priority to distress signals and requiring that a radio station be licensed before it could transmit. However, the Commerce Department could not refuse to issue a license if the applicant passed a competency exam. This early attempt to bring some order to wireless led to chaos a dozen years later, for no one dreamed of the explosive growth that commercial broadcasting would bring to radio. The battle would go on until Congress passed the Radio Act of 1927.

The Radio Act of 1912 did not limit the number of amateur broadcasters. In 1913, there were 322 licenses for amateur stations. In 1917, there were 13,581 plus thousands of amateurs who broadcast without a license. Far more amateurs broadcast than commercial operators. They used spark transmitters to send Morse Code.

Meanwhile, other nations put radio firmly under government control, along with telegraph and telephone services. Only the United States among major nations would permit the development of all three means of communication as private enterprises subject only to a minimum of government regulation.

Voice

If the main commercial use of radio around the time of World War I was to assist shipping, the business of radio was largely the business of manufacturing wireless equipment for ships, shore stations, and military communication, and leasing communication services to the shipping industry and the government.

During this period, a number of scientists set about the task of breaking the voice free of the telephone cables that held it. John Ambrose Fleming was curious about the so-called "Edison effect" that Thomas Edison had discovered in his efforts to improve telegraph transmission. Twenty years after Edison reported it, Fleming decided to pick up the trail, designing a two-element vacuum tube or *diode*, a wire filament and a metal plate housed in a little glass bulb. When the filament was heated, an electric current, alternating between a positive and negative charge, flowed into the filament, but only a stream of negative electrons flowed from the filament to the plate. This was the first *electronic* device. The alternating current of a radio wave turned into direct current that a receiving unit could detect. The *Fleming valve* allowed speech carried on radio waves to be heard, or *detected*, in earphones.

American inventor Lee De Forest added a third element between the filament and the plate, a piece of wire bent into a zigzag grid to catch as many electrons as possible as they flowed from the filament to the plate. His *audion* tube not only detected radio waves, but regulated the flow of electrons and amplified them. The volume of sound could now be controlled. Another American inventor, E. Howard Armstrong, figured out a way for the audion tube to function as an oscillator to *transmit* radio waves as well as receive them.

As patent applications flew with every discovery, the race was on to be the first to send speech through the air. Reginald Fessenden, a native Canadian who had once worked in Thomas Edison's laboratory, was convinced that Marconi's intermittent transmission could be replaced by a continuous wave transmitter and receiver bringing speech and music through the air. Fessenden won the race with a high frequency alternator that he designed in collaboration with a Swedish immigrant, E.F.W. Alexanderson, a General Electric engineer. The huge alternator, looking like a power plant generator, threw signals across continents and oceans much better than Marconi's spark transmitters.

From his laboratory at Brant Rock, Massachusetts, Fessenden was the first to publicly send a human voice over a radio frequency. It was on Christmas Eve in 1906. Except for some reporters and a few amateurs, his audience could not have consisted of more than a few amazed Marconi operators on duty at their posts on ships and at shore stations. Fessenden had informed them a few days earlier by radio-

telegraph messages, but still it must have startled them to hear a voice at Christmas reciting a biblical passage. Fessenden also sang, played the violin, and broadcast phonograph music.

This was *broadcasting*, a word that described what a farmer did when he threw handfuls of seed across the ground. Soon the word *wireless* was replaced by *radio*, based on the idea that rays of electromagnetic waves were being spread out from a transmitter. In 1908, De Forest went to the top of the Eiffel Tower in Paris, where he broadcast opera music that was faintly heard 550 miles away. From a transmitter in Virginia, AT&T sent a wireless telephone signal in 1915 that was simultaneously picked up in both Paris and Pearl Harbor.

De Forest decided to use wireless telephony to deliver music and speech into people's homes. He told a *New York Times* reporter, "I look forward to the day when opera may be brought into every home. Someday the news and even advertising will be sent out over the wireless telephone."[81] In 1915, long before commercial broadcasting began, De Forest broadcast music and an occasional news or sports report, and he manufactured equipment to tune to these broadcasts. He used his broadcasts to advertise his equipment.

Hobbyists Tune In

Sending signals was one problem, listening was another. At first, the only way to detect incoming radio signals was the coherer, a laboratory device of no use to people who wanted to hear sounds. The vacuum tube was an improvement, but it was not for the average person's purse. One vacuum tube easily cost a week's wages.

After German scientist Ferdinand Braun discovered that certain crystals transmitted electricity in one direction only, inventors fashioned a new type of radio receiver, sometimes known as a *crystal-and-catwhisker detector*. A crystal of quartz or galena, by admitting electricity in only one direction, could detect radio waves in the air if the crystal was touched with a fine wire at a certain spot. Hobbyists captured the incoming signal with a tuning coil made from copper wire wrapped around a cylindrical Quaker Oats box, then fed into earphones. Thousands of *catwhisker* receivers were built by radio amateurs who found them easy to make and cheap.

A disadvantage was that the weak crystal detectors could not amplify radio signals. Hobbyists pressed their earphones tightly to their heads, straining to catch distant radio stations. Their pleasure did not come from radio programs, for programs scarcely existed until the 1920s, but from picking up the call letters from a distant city. Hobbyists formed clubs that met by wireless. Most members were teenage boys and young men. U.S. Navy and commercial operators trying to transmit on the same wavelength complained that they could not get messages through because children hogged the ether and would not make way. Their pleas to the government to ban amateurs were stoutly resisted by the hobbyists.

The first radio stations were rooms full of electric devices connected by wires running helter-skelter. They could transmit voice and music, but the sound fidelity left plenty to be desired. Boosting the signal awaited the development of amplifiers, which were based on still other inventions, especially the feedback circuit invented in

1912 by Armstrong while he was a Columbia University graduate student. He redesigned the audion tube so it took the current of electrons that flowed from the plate and sent it back around into the zigzag grid. Round and round went the signal thousands of times a second, gathering strength each time. The feedback circuit brought distant signals booming into the earphones. The spark transmitter that Marconi used and the alternator designed by Fessenden and Alexanderson were instantly fit for a museum. When radio sets with vacuum tubes went on sale, as radio listening changed from a hobby to a means of entertainment, the crystal set was just as outdated.

What of radio existed around the end of World War I?

1. Ship-to-ship and ship-to-shore radiotelegraph and radiotelephone communication, which was both a business and military matter.
2. Manufacturing equipment for this communication.
3. Spark transmitters for amateur stations.
4. Simple receivers, often homemade, for hobbyists to tune into distant signals.
5. Tinkering by a few inventors and engineers.

The early radio receivers were not friendly. They were large, clunky, temperamental metal boxes with lots of knobs, tubes, wires, and a large messy, smelly battery filled with acid, not unlike the storage battery in an automobile. The place for a radio set was in the basement or in the garage, for it was not fit to bring into the parlor and placed on a rug or a table. Until the dangerous batteries were replaced by radio sets that could be plugged into 110-volt AC current available in the wall in the late 1920s, the radio belonged in the garage. Receivers were expensive and tricky to operate, with as many as four separate tuning stages that had to be matched to bring a faint signal into earphones, and even then they would not hold an incoming signal for long because the signal wandered from one frequency to another.

Figure 3.17   A crystal-and-catwhisker radio, 1922. A tiny wire was touched to the "sweet spot" on a galena crystal to bring in a station. (Courtesy Pavek Museum.)

With earphones, only one person could listen at a time. The first loudspeakers were little more than earphones fixed at the small end of a horn. There were no programs to listen to.

Radio was not part of the daily life of the average person. It may be that most people had never heard of it. Who could imagine that a vast market existed for radio? Radio receivers, a junky looking conglomeration of wires and metal, were not for ordinary people in their homes, even though by then the phonograph had been tamed to look like furniture and the piano had been a piece of furniture for centuries. It took vision to see past what the radio was, and to imagine what it might become.

When the United States entered World War I in 1917, the Navy took over the wireless industry along with the telegraph, telephone, and ocean cable systems. Because the Navy sometimes wanted to send messages to several ships at once without the risk of a reply, which might give away a ship's position, someone came up with the word *broadcast* to describe a message that went to several receivers without requiring a response. It was a quiet start to perhaps the most significant factor of twentieth century media, the explosive growth of one-way communication.

Movies Are Born

Steven Spielberg called them "the most powerful weapon in the world." All over the world, the movies have left a lot of people with the sense that others enjoy better lives than they do, and that awareness has created in the minds of many a sure and sometimes terrible resolve to improve their own lives, no matter what it takes to do so.

Motion pictures, the photography of movement, are the most important cultural phenomenon of this century, an invention arguably exceeding the atom bomb in their political impact and certainly in their cultural impact. If the world were deprived of the motion picture, life for most of us would be less knowledgeable and less pleasant.

The American press is read only where English is read; the American radio is heard only where English is comprehended; but the American movie is an international carrier which triumphs over differences in age or language, nationality or custom. Even the Sumatran native who cannot spell is able to grasp the meaning of pictures which move, and he can love, hate, or identify himself with those who appear in them...[82]

Movies As a Communication Medium

A few matters about motion picture history stand out:

- As with most tools of communication, no one person invented the motion picture. Motion picture technology evolved in a series of small steps. Thomas Edison is often credited as its inventor, but he had less to do with its invention than some others.

- No indication has been found that anyone involved in its early growth had any concept of how important it would become—a means of story telling that would entertain, enthrall, and influence billions of people around the world.

- The public played an important part in what the movies became, for the movies are both an art and an industry. By ticket purchases, the public influenced the course of their growth.

- Like all media, motion pictures have substituted for direct contact with other people. The time that is spent watching a film is time away from other pursuits, including direct activities with family and friends.

- Films are information, a component of our information age.

- As the years have gone by, more and more people are *making* movies at every level. Production and distribution are decentralized as never before. The motion picture today not only contributes to the world trend toward democracy by its content, but by the fact that the making of movies exists in many hands.
- Motion pictures have been a force for knocking down barriers among races, religions, and nationalities. They help to turn our focus from local and parochial matters to broader perspectives.
- Motion pictures cannot be considered in isolation. Their impact on society has been far too great.

No cultural force of such power can settle in without opposition. Almost from the onset, motion picture makers had their enemies. Middle class reformers, who attacked working class drinking, went after the nickelodeon. Representatives of the clergy managed to close some movie theaters.[83] A variety of city, state, and national censorship boards took root. Today's rating system is Hollywood's self-censorship in a constant hope of keeping outside censors away.

How Movies Began

Motion picture technology has three roots that go back for centuries. The *chemistry* of film has its roots in still photography. The other two roots are *projection*, which had its origin in the magic lantern, and *stills in motion*, which began as toys that depended on what is called *persistence of vision*. Here, because it takes the eye and the brain a fraction of a second to lose an image, a series of still pictures presented in quick succession will appear as a single moving image.

Railroad baron Leland Stanford, ex-governor of California and founder of Stanford University, wanted to settle a bet with a friend on whether a trotting horse lifted all four hooves off the ground at the same time. He hired professional photographer Eadweard Muybridge, who, after several trials, set a row of twenty-four cameras along a racetrack. Strings that would trip the camera shutters stretched across the track. The result in 1878 was a series of stills that, flipped in rapid succession, displayed the horse in motion. (Stanford won his bet; all four feet were off the ground.)

Muybridge continued his experiments by photographing the movements of a variety of animals. Exhibiting his work in Paris in 1881 he met a physician, Etienne Jules Marey, who was doing research in such animal locomotion as the flapping of a bird's wings. That meeting led Marey to take an important step forward in the invention of motion pictures. Instead of using a lot of cameras, as Muybridge had done, Marey built a single camera that could rap-

Figure 3.18
Photographer Eadweard Muybridge discovered that putting the successive photos in a pack and riffling them produced the effect of constant motion. (Courtesy International Museum of Photography at George Eastman House.)

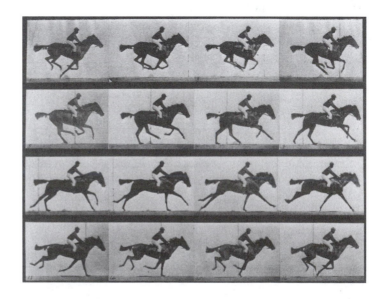

idly shoot a series of pictures on a single plate and did not require strings, which would have interfered with the fluttering wings.

Edison Orders an Invention

Soon inventors in several countries were solving the mechanical difficulties standing in the way of motion pictures. Among them were William Friese-Greene in England and the brothers Louis and Auguste Lumière in France. In the United States, Thomas Edison assigned assistant W.K.L. Dickson to build a motion picture system, based on the French *photographic revolver*, built by Marey.

Edison originally thought of motion pictures as just something to accompany the sound in his phonograph parlors. Working in Edison's laboratory in New Jersey, with strips of celluloid film manufactured by George Eastman for his Kodak still camera, Dickson in the years 1891 and 1892 invented the Kinetograph camera and the motor-driven Kinetoscope, which ran 50 feet of film in about 30 seconds. Sprockets guided the film's perforated edges past the lens with a controlled, intermittent movement like the ticking second hand of a watch. Here was the peep show, one viewer at a time.

Dickson erected a studio building that could be turned to take advantage of light from the sun coming through a roof opening. He began making movies, mostly trained animal acts, circus entertainers, and the like, each giving a brief performance in the studio. Workers referred to the studio building as the "Black Maria," because with its tar-paper covering it vaguely bore the shape of a police paddy wagon with that nickname.

In a short time, Kinetoscopes were being shipped around the country as fast as they reached the end of Edison's assembly line. They went into Kinetoscope parlors modeled after Edison's successful phonograph parlors, with the difference that admission was not free. Customers paid 25 cents upon entering, which gave them tickets allowing them to peep into five machines. Start the electric motor, gaze into the peep hole, and

there was magic! The viewer stared into a box to see the frames of film flicker by.

Motion Picture Projection

Yet, it was still not motion picture *projection*. That would come soon enough, but not at first in the United States. The inventive Dickson also built the Mutoscope peephole machine, with a series of cards that were flipped by a handle, an advantage to boys who could slow the action to a standstill when Little Egypt performed her hootchy-kootch dance. Dickson made the Mutoscope different enough from his early Kinetoscope to get around Edison's patent. Mutoscopes can occasionally still be found in old-fashioned penny arcades.

In France, the Lumière brothers, Louis and Auguste, owners of a photographic products manufacturing business, saw a Kinetoscope on display in Paris and set about to improve it. This they did with their Cinematographe, a combined camera, film printer, and projector. Substituting a hand crank for Edison's electric motor, the Lumières reduced the machine's weight so they could carry it to any location where they wanted to film. Edison's bulky Kinetograph required performers to appear in the studio. Where Edison's films gave the view of a stage, the Lumière films were like a view through a window. In addition, the Lumières were able to *project* their films onto a screen for an audience, whereas Edison's Kinetoscope accommodated only one viewer at a time.

Their first film, of workers leaving their factory, shot in March 1895 was shown at a special exhibit. On December 28, 1895, the Lumières projected the first motion pictures before a *paying* audience in the basement of a Paris cafe. For one franc apiece, the audience saw a twenty-minute program consisting of ten films, accompanied by a piano and some commentary by the Lumière's father. The only other sound was the astonished gasps of the audience.[84] In no time at all, long lines formed outside the cafe to see the show. The *movies* were born!

One excited Parisian newspaper exulted, "With this new invention, death will no longer be absolute, final. The people we have seen on the screen will be with us, moving and alive after their deaths."[85] Two months later, projected films were shown in London. Two months after that, they appeared in New York.

Projected Movies Come to America

Their audiences were drawn not primarily from the wealthy or the middle class, but mostly from the multitudes of the poor. Music halls, which normally presented vaudeville, were frequented mostly by the middle classes, but not all members of the middle class went to theatrical amusement of any kind. A strong sense of what is referred to as *middle class morality,* based on religious beliefs and on scruples set during the age of Queen Victoria kept many Americans out of all theaters.

Poor people could not afford the price of admission to vaudeville shows, which were a succession of actors, singers, dancers, jugglers, and trained dogs. For entertainment in the evening, the poor, except for a special occasion, could afford not much more than to go for walks.

By the turn of the century, moving pictures had survived their infancy and outgrown their "novelty" stage. They were no longer a plaything or a cheap novelty to be seen once and abandoned…Moving pictures had not yet assembled their own audience, but they were beginning to draw on every other kind of entertainment audience, accelerating the promiscuous mixing of disparate social groupings that would come to characterize commercial amusements in the early twentieth century.[86]

Vaudeville hall, Kinetoscope, and phonograph parlor owners foresaw that customers who so eagerly parted with their hard earned coins to look at moving pictures in a box might even more willingly spend those coins if the pictures were projected against a large screen. Lecturers who illustrated their talks with slides realized that moving pictures could be a big attraction. One way or another these entrepreneurs acquired projectors, buying them or assembling copies. In the cities, they converted stores, restaurants, and dance-halls to look like vaudeville houses, or they cordoned off a section of a parlor or penny arcade and placed wooden chairs in front of a screen, which might be no more than a white wall or a bed sheet. At county fairs a tent would do. The Warner brothers borrowed chairs from a funeral parlor nearby. When the chairs were needed for a funeral, movie patrons stood.

Projectors broke down to the accompaniment of hoots and whistles from the ticketed audience, but a bigger problem was the poor quality of films. Audiences soon tired of scratchy prints of dancers and amateur boxers.

The Earliest Films

The history of motion pictures began with real life. The first known slide into fiction arrived before the turn of the century, a pretense by a Frenchman, Francis Doublier. He combined a series of actuality shots—soldiers, a battleship, France's Palace of Justice, and a tall, gray-haired man—and called it a film of the Dreyfus case, the famous political and military scandal that rocked France. And for $1.98 worth of materials two Vitagraph photographers at the height of the Spanish American War created a cardboard version of the battle of Santiago Bay. Using threads, they pulled ships through water one inch deep past the camera as pinches of gunpowder went off and a volunteer blew in cigarette smoke from just out of camera range.

The very first Lumière and Edison films were actualities, scenes from real life: people in a park, workers leaving a factory, a man playing a fiddle, a baby being fed, a parade. In time, audiences tired of this. Motion pictures might have ended as just another novelty. What made the difference was fiction. The documentary would come to be respected more than it would be watched. Producer Samuel Goldwyn is supposed to have said, "If you've got a message, send it by Western Union." It is little wonder that Hollywood came to be known as *the dream factory.*

Notes

1. Alvin Toffler, *The Third Wave* (New York: William Morrow, 1980), 135.

2. R.M. Hartwell, "The Consequences of the Industrial Revolution in England for the Poor," in *The Long Debate on Poverty* (Published by The Institute of Economic Affairs. Printed: Old Woking, Surrey by Unwin Bros. Ltd., 1972), 10

3. Rhodes Boyson, "Industrialisation and the Life of the Lancashire Factory Worker," in *The Long Debate on Poverty*. op. cit., 80.

4. Peter N. Stearns, *The Industrial Revolution in World History* (Boulder: Westview Press, 1993), 143.

5. Stearns, 59.

6. Stearns, 42.

7. Letter dated 26 December 1795. In Mary-Lou Jennings and Charles Madge, eds., *Pandæmonium: 1660-1886.* (New York: The Free Press, 1985), 164.

8. Susan C. Karant-Nunn, "From Adventurers to Drones: The Saxon Silver Miners as an Early Proletariat," in Thomas Safley and Leonard Rosenband, eds., *The Workplace before the Factory: Artisans and Proletarians, 1500-1800* (Ithaca: Cornell University Press, 1993), 85.

9. Stearns, 3.

10. Boyson, 79.

11. Leslie Clarkson, *Death, Disease and Famine in Pre-industrial England* (Dublin: Gill and Macmillan, 1975), 1.

12. Clarkson, 14.

13. Clarkson, 174.

14. Letter published in 1796. In Jennings, 107.

15. Friedrich Engels, *The Condition of the Working Class in England*, trans. and edited by W.O. Henderson and W.H. Chaloner (Oxford: Oxford University Press, 1958), 24.

16. Christopher Clark, "Social Structure and Manufacturing before the Factory: Rural New England 1750-1830," in Safley and Rosenband, 17, 20.

17. Alexis de Tocqueville, *Journeys to England and Wales*, in Will and Ariel Durant, *The Age of Napoleon* (New York: Simon & Schuster, 1939), 344.

18. For a discussion of this point, see Gianni Vattimo, The Transparent Society, trans. David Webb. (Baltimore: The Johns Hopkins University Press, 1992) 4 ff. He writes, "...the mass media play a decisive role in the birth of a postmodern society...These means—newspapers, radio, television, what is now called telematics—have been decisive in bringing about the dissolution of centralized perspectives, of what the French philosopher Jean-Francis Lyotard calls the 'grand narratives'. This view of the effect of the mass media seems to be the very contrary of that taken by the philosopher Theodor Adorno." Adorno and Max Horkheimer "predicted that radio (and later TV) would produce a general homogenization of society...Instead, what actually happened, in spite of the efforts of the monopolies and major centers of capital, was that radio, television and newspapers became elements in a general explosion and proliferation of *Weltanschauungen*, of world views."

19. Kenneth A. Lockridge, "Literacy in Early America 1650-1800," in *Literacy and Social Development in the West: A Reader*, ed. Harvey J. Graff (Cambridge: Cambridge University Press, 1981), 183.

20. Eisenstein, *The Printing Revolution in Early Modern Europe*, 259.

21. For a full discussion of the role that printing played in the French Revolution, see Robert Darnton and Daniel Roche, eds., *Revolution in Print: The Press in France 1775-1800* (Berkeley: University of California Press, 1989).

22. Peckham, *Beyond the Tragic Vision* (New York: George Braziller, 1962), 25-7.

23. Lucien Febvre and Henri-Jean Martin, *The Coming of the Book: The Impact of Printing, 1450-1800*, trans. David Gerard (London: Verso Editions, 1984), 39-40.

24. Smith, "Technology and Control: the interactive dimensions of journalism," in *Mass Communication and Society*. James Curran, et. al., eds. (London: Edward Arnold, Ltd., 1977), 176.

25. Febvre and Martin, 210-11.

26. Alvin W. Gouldner, *The Dialectic of Ideology and Technology* (Oxford University Press, 1976), 92.

27. Michael Schudson, *Discovering the News* (New York: Basic Books, Inc., 1978), 19.

28. Theodore Glasser, "The Role of the Press and the Value of Journalism," *Focus*, University of Minnesota (Fall 1988), 8.

29. John Milton, *Aereopagitica*

30. Schudson, 46.

31. Anthony Smith, "Media Globalism in the Age of Consumer Sovereignty," *World Media*, Gannett Center Journal, 4:4 (Fall, 1990), 6-7.

32. Margery W. Davies, "Women Clerical Workers and the Typewriter: the Writing Machine," in Cheris Kramarae, *Technology and Women's Voices: Keeping in Touch* (New York: Routledge & Kegan Paul, 1988), 29.

33. Marshall McLuhan, *Understanding Media: The Extensions of Man* (New York: McGraw-Hill Book Co., 1964), 259.

34 Daniel J. Boorstin, *The Americans: The Democratic Experience* (New York: Random House, 1973) 145.
35 James R. Beniger, *The Control Revolution* (Cambridge, Mass.: Harvard University Press, 1986) 18.
36 McLuhan, 230.
37 Beniger, 269, 274.
38 Beniger, 277.
39 Edgar E. Willis and Henry B. Aldridge, *Television, Cable, and Radio* (Englewood Cliffs: Prentice-Hall, 1992) 128.
40 Frank Presbrey, *The History and Development of Advertising* (Garden City, N.Y.: Doubleday, Doran, 1929) 306.
41 W.F. Ogborn and M.F. Nimkoff, *Sociology* (Houghton-Mifflin, 1950) 546.
42 Carl H. Scheele, *A Short History of the Mail Service*. Smithsonian Institution Press, 1970.
43 Richard K. Craille, ed., *Speeches of John C. Calhoun* (New York, 1864), 190.
44 Joseph Stewart, in Alvin F. Harlow, *Old Post Bags* (New York: D. Appleton, 1938), xvi.
45 Zilliacus, 14-15.
46 G. Tansey and Horst de la Croix, *Art Through the Ages* (New York: Harcourt Brace Jovanovich, 1986).
47 *MacMillan Magazine*, September 1871, quoted in Gus Macdonald, *Camera: A Victorian Eyewitness* (London: Bastford, 1979), 5.
48 Boorstin, 398.
49 Richard Hofstadter, *The Progressive Movement, 1900-1915* (New York: Simon & Schuster, 1963).
50 Boorstin, 371.
51 Edward Cornish, "The Coming of an Information Society," *The Futurist*, (April 1981): 14.
52 Edwin Emery and Michael Emery, *The Press and America*, 5th ed. (Englewood Cliffs: Prentice-Hall, 1984), 164.
53 George P. Oslin, *The Story of Telecommunications* (Macon, GA: Mercer University Press, 1992), 16.
54 Oslin, 127.
55 Oslin, 71.
56 Beniger, 253.
57 Francis Williams, *Transmitting World News*. UNESCO, 1953: 19.
58 Sloan, William, James Stovall and James Startt, *The Media in America* (Worthington, OH: Publishing Horizons, 1989), 204.
59 Daniel J. Czitrom, *Media and the American Mind* (Chapel Hill, NC: University of North Carolina Press, 1982), 18.
60 In the United States, it is known as Reuters, not Reuter, due to the erroneous title of a popular Hollywood movie, *The Man From Reuters*. Life sometimes imitates art.
61 Oslin, 161.
62 David T.Z. Mindich, *Edwin M. Stanton, the Inverted Pyramid, and Information Control*. University of South Carolina Journalism Monograph, 1993, 24.
63 Carolyn Marvin, *When Old Technologies Were New* (Oxford: Oxford University Press, 1988), 3.
64 John Brooks, *Telephone: The First Hundred Years* (New York: Harper & Row, 1976), 94.
65 Oslin, 217.
66 Oslin, 220.
67 Marion May Dilts, *The Telephone in a Changing World* (New York: Longman's Green, 1941), 10.
68 Dilts, 11.
69 George Basalla, *The Evolution of Technology* (Cambridge: Cambridge University Press, 1988), 98.
70 Oslin, 227.
71 Dilts, 15.
72 Beniger, 285.
73 Sylvester Baxter, "The Telephone Girl," *The Outlook*, 26 May 1906, 235.
74 Oslin, 281.
75 McLuhan, 305.
76 Stephen N. Raymer, "Fessenden Revisted," Pavek Museum of Broadcasting *Newsletter*, vol. 4.4, (1993), 5.
77 Susan J. Douglas, *Inventing American Broadcasting, 1899-1922* (Baltimore: The Johns Hopkins University Press, 1987), 15.
78 Douglas, 56-58.
79 *The Russo-Japanese War* (Tokyo: Sekai-Bunkei Publishing Co., 1971), 30.
80 Douglas, 228.
81 *New York Times*, 14 February 1909, 1.
82 Rosten, *Hollywood, the Movie Colony and the Movie Makers* (New York: Harcourt Brace & Co., 1941), 7-12.
83 Miriam Hansen, *Babel and Babylon: Spectatorship in American Silent Film* (Cambridge: Harvard University Press, 1991), 63.
84 Harry M. Geldud, *The Birth of the Talkies: From Edison to Jolson* (Bloomington: Indiana University Press, 1975), 28.
85 David Shipman, *The Story of Cinema* (Englewood Cliffs: Prentice-Hall, 1982) 18.
86 David Nasaw, *Going Out: The Rise and Fall of Public Amusements* (New York: Basic Books, 1993), 152-53.

4

The Fourth Revolution Entertainment

Public Recreation

The good old days never were that good, except for a lucky few. To lift the veil of nostalgia from what actually existed reveals not only a harsh and uncertain life for most, but a public morality not much different from our own except in degree of permissiveness. The penny presses of the American Victorian era filled their pages with scandal. The working class had cheap, bawdy entertainment in vaudeville houses and the even more raucous concert saloons. The sinful pleasures of the wealthy sometimes revealed themselves as they do today, but otherwise the rich publicly showed their mettle by attending operas, plays, balls, and private dinners, again just as they do today.

The Industrial Revolution in nineteenth century America shifted population from villages and towns to cities, where paid work was to be found. Miserable as they often were, non-farm wages rose during the last quarter of the century while the cost of living actually declined. Average working hours dropped slightly. It was not unusual for workers to have Saturday afternoon off as well as all day Sunday. The idea of sum-

mer vacations was taking hold beyond the families of the rich.

The poverty of the teeming masses in slums and tenements has been well documented. Less has been said about public recreation. For those crowded into the dwellings lining the mean streets of cities, going out anywhere made life endurable. Early in this century, electric lamps lit all night on street corners and multi-colored lights illuminating stores and cafes brightened and helped make safe the streets that had been kept in shadow by dim gas lighting. The pleasure of an evening stroll, no longer much in evidence in American middle and upper class neighborhoods, can still be seen in poorer sections of our cities and especially in Third World cities, where life lacks the amenities of the average American home, and where escape from the humdrum, overcrowding, or loneliness can be found only beyond the front door.

The lighting of the lights signaled that the workday was over and the time for play at hand...

Electrification made going out at night not only safer and more exciting but easier and cheaper than ever before. The dynamos and generators that lit the street lamps also powered the trolleys that tied together the city and its neighborhoods....

On downtown streets, something new called *department stores* were built.

> In connecting the city's business and residential districts, the electric streetcars fostered the growth—and the transformation—of "downtown" into a central shopping and entertainment district.[1]

For centuries, local fairs and religious festivals had brought people together for shared amusements. Now national expositions and a series of world's fairs, starting in the United States with the Centennial Exhibition in Philadelphia in 1876, enjoyed a thriving business. They began as centers of information about the new world of industry, but soon became primarily places of recreation. Parks were constructed for the recently introduced game of baseball and for such amusement centers as New York's Coney Island, just a nickel subway ride away on the BMT for millions of New Yorkers.

Money from the Poor

The early income from projected films did not come from music halls, although throughout the country these theaters catering to middle and some upper class patrons began alternating their vaudeville acts with films. Money was drawn from the pockets of the poor in the cities, many of whom lived in crowded slums and worked in unheated, badly lit, unventilated, and often dangerous factories, long hours for meager wages. Or they worked at home doing subcontracted piecework for even meaner wages.

The poor certainly had little money to spend on entertainment, let alone dress up to go to a theater. But if you earned a dollar a day, you might be willing on a Saturday night to spend a nickel or two amid blazing lights and cheerful crowds. A penny could go into a machine testing your skill or your strength. You could listen to a penny's worth of phonograph music. You could put a penny in to crank a Mutoscope and see motion pictures or, better yet, sit in a room with your friends and neighbors for a nickel to share the experience of watching a program of movies projected against a wall. In *Not So Long Ago*, Lloyd Morris wrote:

> In the slums of the great Eastern and Middle Western cities there were herded vast immigrant populations. Largely unfamiliar with the English language, they could not read the newspapers, magazines or books. But the living pictures communicated their meanings directly and eloquently. To enjoy them, no command of a new language was essential. They made illiteracy, and ignorance of American customs, seem less shameful; they broke down a painful sense of isolation and ostracism. Dwellers in tenements, workers in sweatshops, could escape the drabness of their environment for a little while, at a price within their means. In the penny arcades, moving pictures took deep root, both as an agency for information and as a cheap form of entertainment for the masses. In the small rural communities to which they were taken by traveling showmen, they met equally responsive audiences. A broad popular foundation was being laid for a major industry, as well as a social instrument of incalculable power.[2]

As the Industrial Revolution gained strength, it gave rise not only to mass information, but to mass entertainment. Thanks to assembly lines and new technology, people could afford to buy cameras to take pictures of each other and their annual vacations. They put Victrolas in their parlors. They bought novels and magazines. In the new century, they went each week to the picture show. A few went from nickelodeon to nickelodeon. An entertainment industry grew to feed a discovered public hunger for packaged pleasure, the world's fourth information revolution.

Entertaining Newspapers

It is easier to take the measure of the newspaper as a medium for conveying information if we recognize that it has not been around forever, and that it continues to evolve. Great grandpa would hardly recognize this morning's Chronicle. Anyone who deplores the loss of newspaper readers to television ought to consider that newspapers were themselves deplored at one time for a similar reason. In 1910, sociologist Max Weber asked:

> What is the effect of newspapers on the kind of reading habits of modern man? On this all kinds of theories have been constructed. There was also the argument that the book is being replaced by the newspaper.[3]

Not all newspaper readers and certainly not all television viewers have deep concern about reports of events significant to our lives, those reports sometimes identified as "real news." The newspaper shares with television an audience segment not much given to "real news." These newspaper readers barely glance at the front page lead headline before turning their attention to entertainment, their exclusive interest, which is happily met by pages full of comic strips, horoscopes, puzzles, Dear Abby, and, if one places professional and intercollegiate sports properly in the category of entertainment, the scores. Add the television logs, the movie listings, the grocery coupons, and the insert section with the sales at the mall. For this readership, the newspaper is a bargain, delivered at the doorstep. As for the "real news" itself, serious matters in most local newspapers are placed alongside generous helpings of gossip, scandal, and police blotter extract. Local newspapers would not survive on a total diet of serious news. The public, wanting entertainment, drove the content then, as now.

Adding Color

By the late nineteenth century, spots of color appeared now and again amid the black-and-white columns of newsprint.

That staple of the modern newspaper, the Sunday funnies, was added when improvements in color printing led William Randolph Hearst to bring out a comic strip supplement in 1896. Color comics began when it was decided to add yellow ink regularly to an outlandish skirt worn by a little boy in one strip, *Hogan's Alley*. The immediate popularity of this addition led to the character becoming known as *The Yellow Kid*. More than that, the kind of sensational news featured in newspapers owned by Hearst and Pulitzer was pinned with the appellation, *yellow journalism*. The unpleasant, insulting phrase stuck long after the comic strip stopped running. As for color comics themselves, in time all the Sunday comics were printed in a variety of bold colors. Comic books followed on the magazine racks.

Pulitzer's New York *World* at two cents, built a daily circulation of 1.5 million, the nation's first mass circulation newspaper. Unlike most newspapers of its day, the *World* was politically and socially liberal. It was filled with spicy news reports (headlines like "Little Lotta's Lovers" and "Baptized in Blood"[4]), sports coverage, and circulation-raising stunts such as sending reporter "Nellie Bly" (her real name was Elizabeth Cochrane) into an insane asylum as a patient to expose its awful conditions, and in 1889 sending her around the world by ship, train, horse, and sampan to beat fictional Phineas Fogg's trip *Around the World in Eighty Days*. Nearly a million readers entered a contest to guess how long it would take her. Nellie Bly did it in 72 days.

The sensational *tabloid* (a word derived from a small, easy to swallow dose of medicine) appeared in London in the early years of the twentieth century, its news for the common man packaged in a format that could be read comfortably on a streetcar. Tabloids, like the New York *Daily News*, took advantage of the city's switch from horse-drawn buses to electrified trolleys and subways. Strap-hangers were able to read a newspaper held in one hand. To accommodate them on the jouncing ride, publishers shrank broadsheets to tabloid size, made headlines and body type larger, and added more pictures. News stories, too, were more entertaining and, in some cases, more sensational. *Tabloid* defined both the size and the content of newspapers. It still does.

Magazines for the Fragmented Public

The magazine has set the pace for the VCR, postwar radio, and cable television in what it has done for its users: it has given them, more precisely than in the past, what they have wanted. And by doing this, it has fragmented them. A handful of general interest magazines still reach millions of readers, but thousands of specialty magazines each reach just thousands of readers; for example, the trade magazine *Pizza and Pasta* and the consumer magazine *Living With Teenagers*. The corner VCR shop also fragments its customers when it rents just what is wanted on Saturday night to a customer who once went to the now shuttered downtown Bijou, which offered no choice of fare at all. Radio stations and cable television channels offer more and more choices.

All in all, information receivers use more media, but they share fewer media experiences with people they know. The *global village* looks more like the Tower of Babel. Among regularly scheduled mass media, none are so fragmented as magazines.

English and Colonial Beginnings

In early eighteenth century England, the magazine was born out of the newspaper, just as the first newspapers were born a century earlier out of the newsletter and the pamphlet. The outspoken publisher of the first weekly periodical, *The Review* was, at the time of publication, either still inside or just out of Newgate prison. He was Daniel Defoe, not yet the author of *Robinson Crusoe. The Review* was soon followed by *The Tatler* and *The Spectator*, filled with brilliant essays that are still read today.

Modeled after those in England, the first American magazines, published by Benjamin Franklin and rival Philadelphia printer Andrew Bradford, appeared in 1741. Most of these early magazines lasted for just a few issues due to insufficient funds to survive a start-up period, inadequate distribution facilities, and poor printing equipment. Unlike newspapers, no postal service provisions were made for magazines, which not only meant higher costs, but in some instances left them undelivered because of cargo regarded as more important.

At least one desperate Massachusetts publisher repeatedly offered to accept subscription payment in wood, cheese, pork, corn, or other produce.

> The editor requests all those who are indebted to him for Newspapers and Magazines, to make payment. —Butter will be received for small sums, if brought within a few days.[5]

Part of the problem that magazine publishers faced lay in a paucity of advertising and a consequent heavy dependence upon circulation receipts. Another problem was the price of an annual subscription. It would have cost a farm laborer four or five days pay during the years before the American Revolution, and more afterward. Magazines were not for the poor.

> The American newspaper was a workman, sweaty, busy, and shirt-sleeved; the American magazine was a gentleman, serious, sentimental, and sedate.[6]

Early American magazines, issued weekly, monthly, or quarterly, were about the size of *The Reader's Digest* today, consisting of about 64 pages usually printed on a stiff, rough, rag-based paper in the size of type found today in classified ads. The few illustrations they contained were likely to be woodcuts, although the wealthier magazines afforded an occasional steel or copper engraving, especially if the publisher was himself an engraver. A single engraving plate might have cost a publisher as much as the entire literary content of an issue. Although the American magazines imitated their European, particularly their British counterparts, the New World lacked many elements necessary to put out a magazine of quality, notably competent artists and dependable presses. As a result, what went out of the publisher's door was often crudely fashioned.

Plagiarism Was Common

Also lacking was much original writing. An early American magazine owed more to the editor's scissors than to anyone's pen. Appropriated were the entire contents of pamphlets, segments of books, newspaper articles, verse, essays, and fiction lifted from other magazines, especially English magazines. Plagiarism was not only common and legal two centuries ago, but was expected, for reprinting was a way to spread information. The most significant essays and literature of the era sooner or later found their way into the pages of American magazines. Through much of its history, the magazine brought literature to readers who could not afford the expense of books. In fact, book publishers hesitated to publish an author who had not already won public recognition through magazines. The material was not copyrighted and, in most cases, was not credited to the original source. By the nineteenth century, however, periodicals were printing the works of writers, known as *magazinists*, who wrote primarily for this medium.

The expansion of the new United States in the early nineteenth century was matched by an expansion in the number of American periodicals of all kinds. At the time the penny press was introduced, there were general monthly magazines, literary weeklies, quarterly reviews, special magazines for women, religious periodicals, and magazines that focused on a particular region of the country. Many of the Sunday newspapers were not really Sunday editions of daily newspapers, but were basically separate magazines. The Sunday supplements of modern big city dailies, notably those of *The New York Times*, continue that tradition.

The first magazine with a mass market was also the first magazine to use woodcut illustrations extensively. *The Penny Magazine* of the Society for the Diffusion of Useful Knowledge was published in England from 1832 to 1845. It was written for artisans and laborers who were literate, and its goal was to improve their minds and behavior.

Of the women's magazines, the most famous, *Godey's Lady's Book*, was published in the United States by a man, Louis A. Godey, whose attitude toward women was one of gallantry untouched by the beginnings of a movement toward equality for what was then referred to as *the fair sex*. Its editor for 41 years was Sara Jocelyn Hale. Its circulation reached 150,000, extraordinary for the period. The *Lady's Book*'s mixture of short stories, poems, articles, and advice on important topics was scrupulously edited to avoid the slightest appearance of indelicacy. Nevertheless, its pages, as pure as the driven snow, afforded women with literary talent the opportunity to be published. Among them was Harriet Beecher Stowe, who would later write *Uncle Tom's Cabin*. Male contributors included Emerson, Longfellow, Holmes, Hawthorne, and Poe, a stellar list of American writers. Eventually, the *Lady's Book* fell behind others in popularity, was absorbed by another magazine which itself was merged into a third magazine, *Argosy*. This pattern of failures and mergers became an all too familiar part of the history of the American magazine.

By 1900, at least 50 national magazines boasted circulations above 100,000, ranging from relatively costly quality monthly periodicals like *Century* and *Harper's*, addressed to a well-educated readership, to low-cost weeklies filled with sentimental romance fiction and, thanks to new technology, lots of pictures.

The Nickel Magazines

Publisher Frank Munsey increased the circulation of his popular-taste magazines by selling them for less than their production costs, as little as five or ten cents a copy, making his profits from increased advertising rates. In so doing, he tapped an even larger market of readers that had largely been ignored.

Low-priced magazines changed the focus of publishers. Originally, their primary attention had been on editorial copy. With substantial advertising support coming in, the focus did not shift so much as it widened to include specific consumer groups. Profit in the face of rising production costs came from high volume, especially among readers who fit a certain profile appealing to advertisers.

There were even instances in the twentieth century where a magazine purged its circulation list of older subscribers because it was assumed they spent less on what was advertised. The pleasure of reading some magazines was to be rationed.

How curious it was that this medium that, of all media, best defined the meaning of communication choice, denied choice to anyone.

THE NOVEL

In the eighteenth century, a new literary form emerged in England and spread to Europe and the United States. The novel, a product of middle-class sensibilities and morality, put fictional characters through a complex of events within a recognizable social setting. The key element in an English novel was the gain or loss of social status, a topic that preyed on the minds of the middle class readers. From its beginnings until the twentieth century, the novel was typically dominated by class consciousness. Themes that raised social problems or personal foibles resonated with readers.

Popular fiction writers like Charles Dickens serialized their novels in weekly newspapers and magazines before they appeared between hard covers. To keep the readers buying magazines, writers ended chapters on a note of suspense. At home, families read these serialized novels aloud as a form of entertainment.

Along the way came the discovery of a public appetite for novels that were easy to read, did not tax the brain, and were filled with action, adventure, and romance. Characters, absolutely evil or purely good, were similar from book to book. Outcomes were predictable. The very predictability of the stories was one of their most desired features. Purists may sniff at what they term *trash*, but it certainly sells.

Continuous web papermaking machines and large cylinder presses plus lower quality paper allowed weekly newspapers in the 1840s to print novels cheaply, first by serializing them and then by printing entire novels in newspaper format. The printing technology and new binding methods, with cloth covers in place of leather, also reduced the prices of hard-cover books. These changes put books into the hands of people who otherwise could not afford them.

In 1875, the *dime novel* was born in a Chicago publishing house, Donnelley, Lloyd & Co. Other publishers quickly followed. Printed on rough paper with a brightly illustrated cover, dime novels were soon being turned out at the rate of one a day, and obviously were snapped up just as fast. Longer novels sold for 15 to 20 cents, but plenty were available for 10 cents. The novels were issued with the imprint of a *series* or *library* just like the paperback westerns, detective stories, and romance novels of today, which are direct descendants of the dime novel.

As usual, technologies changed. Tastes did not.

Entertainment on a Plate

Every nation, every tribe has made its own music. Their melodies, their songs, the musical instruments they have fashioned lie at the very root of their culture. That the music comes from the soul of the people has mattered more than brilliant performance. Friends, family, and neighbors entertain one another oblivious to ragged singing and uncertain fingering.

Today, the technology that brings the genius of Mozart and the latest pop song pouring into our ears has deformed the universal characteristic of playing the music that we make ourselves. Unlike the time of our great grandparents, the custom of singing or reading to one another is more the exception than the rule. Why try to harmonize when the Supremes do it so much better and we can hear them with such clarity? We do not pause to consider that an unintended consequence of listening to Barbra Streisand instead of our sister is the loss of a bit of family closeness. A century ago someone remarked:

> The home wears a vanishing aspect. Public amusements increase in splendor and frequency, but private joys grow rare and difficult, and even the capacity for them seems to be withering.[7]

Even so, few among us would choose that way of life when we have available music of a quality beyond imagining a century ago. Admittedly, the old-fashioned pleasures have not been totally abandoned. Battered pianos and guitars are still around. The karaoke and the electronic keyboard are plugged in at parties.

Along with its sister invention, the telephone, the phonograph—for the first time since humans began to speak—extended the sound of the voice beyond the distance someone could shout. Now there could be preserved not only a famous person's thoughts as written, but the flavor of personality in the style and nuance of speech. Voices and actions important in the history of the twentieth century were captured on disk and tape. Recorded sound is, of course, also what we hear at the movies and in television news reports.

More than a century ago the phonograph, in McLuhan's phrase, broke down the walls of the music hall.[8] The phonograph was the first means to bring nonprint professional entertainment into the home, an entertainment machine that, like the piano, was destined to be encased as a piece of furniture to civilize it for the parlor. A generation later another entertainment machine, the radio, would follow it there, also disguised as furniture. Another generation would introduce still another, the television set. These machines of steel, plastic, and glass bring into the home entertainment created somewhere else. When stereo reached a peak of popularity, people who could afford the most expensive pieces preferred their equipment to look like the machines they were. Less expensive stereo systems were combined as furniture items.

The Start of Recorded Music

In 1807, an Englishman, Thomas Young, picked up sound vibrations with a stylus that traced their amplitude on a smoke-blackened cylinder. A Frenchman, Leon Scott, went one step further in 1857 with a *phonautograph* that captured vocal sounds with the same type of stylus apparatus. French poet and inventor Charles Cros designed, but did not build, a voice-reproducing device. Cros envisioned a machine that would reproduce conversation visibly so the deaf could *read* it. In the same year, 1877, that Cros, too poor to afford a patent, left his idea in a two-page document in a sealed envelope at the Académie des Sciences in Paris, an American, Thomas Edison, actually built a machine.[9] It is of at least passing interest that the two inventors, Cros and Edison, designed a voice *recording* machine one year after two other inventors, Alexander Graham Bell and Elisha Gray, designed (and patented on the same day) a voice *transmitting* machine.

Edison, interested in speeding up the rate of information transfer of telegraph messages, got the idea for recording sound as he listened to the irregular whine of a telegraph disk revolving at high speed.[10] He was using an apparatus he had invented for recording dots and dashes, which included a revolving disk on which he put a piece of paper covered with paraffin wax. One day he noticed that when the disk revolved at a certain speed it sounded a musical note. As an experiment, he put a fresh piece of paper in the machine and as it was going through, he shouted, "Whooooo." When he sent the paper back through, he faintly heard his own voice. Edison himself described what happened next:

> I had built a toy which included a funnel (and a diaphragm)... A string... was connected to a little cardboard figure of a man sawing wood. When someone sang "Mary had a little lamb" into the funnel, the little man started sawing. I thus reached the conclusion that if I could find a way of recording the movements of the diaphragm I could make the recorder reproduce the original movements imparted to the diaphragm by the person singing, and thus reproduce the human voice.[11]

Edison kept at it. His first test was of the words, "Mary had a little lamb. Its fleece was white as snow." Those are the first words ever recorded.

Nothing Ever Like It

Edison improved the phonograph and gave some demonstrations but, recognizing the commercial limitations of tinfoil recording with its scratching and hissing that made the recording all but inaudible, he set it aside to work on another invention, the electric light, which he invented two years later.[12] In granting Edison a patent in 1877 for a speaking machine, the U.S. Patent Office found no previous evidence of anything resembling his invention, an unusual situation in patent history.

The development of hard wax-covered cylinders rekindled Edison's interest a decade later. After studying the market, he concluded that a talking machine could aid dictation. It could record books for the blind. There could be coin-in-the-slot phonographs.[13] He imagined a talking doll, toys, and music boxes. The phonograph could preserve the last words of dying family members. Also, people who did not own one of Alexander Graham Bell's new telephones could record a message in their own voice, then take it to a telephone transmitting station. More presciently, he foresaw it as a record keeper, a preserver of speech, and as a source of music, although, growing deaf, the inventor did not at first think the public would be much interested in recorded *music*.

By this time, Alexander Graham Bell and his associates had produced a better talking machine, which they called the Graphophone. The competition was intense as Edison during 1887 and 1888 took out 33 patents for improvements to his phonograph.[14]

Edison also created a new type of microphone to change air vibration into electrical vibration. A cylinder phonograph converted the vibrations into scratches as a permanent record, but at this point the phonograph was a technology in search of something commercially worthwhile to do.

The next year, 1878, two stenographers to the Supreme Court agreed that the phonograph could be used as a dictating tool. They got a license from Edison to sell the gadget in Maryland and the District of Columbia. However, its limitation of a half minute of scratchy sound rendered it useless as a business tool. Lecturers who took phonographs on lyceum circuits were equally disappointed once the novelty wore off for audiences. The stenographers named their new company the Columbia Phonograph Company. It would eventually mutate into CBS, the Columbia Broadcasting System.

Something more exciting awaited the phonograph as the centenary of the French Revolution was celebrated in Paris with a great exhibition. Gustav Eiffel's tower symbolized progress and technology. Edison crossed the Atlantic with his best inventions, including the electric light and the telephone, to which he had contributed a great deal. For the phonograph, he set up listening booths. It caused a sensation:

> The public queued eagerly at the listening booths. The phonographs stood on tables, with an attendant to change the cylinders, and rubber tubes with earpieces led to listening booths around each table. People awaiting their turn looked in astonishment at listeners' faces, unable to explain the rapt expressions and sudden outbursts of mirth.[15]

Phonograph Parlors

The first significant cash rewards came from nickel-in-the-slot and penny-in-the-slot *automatic phonograph parlors* that sprang up in stores all over the nation. That set in motion the first demand for phonograph recordings. Marching band music was the most popular. Patrons also parted with their nickels to hear singers, whistlers, instrument soloists, and talking records, including dialect humor. The first phonograph parlors, well lit and decorated with potted palms and rugs on the floor, invited passersby with free admission. The current selections were listed. Entire families or young women need suffer no embarrassment by entering a phonograph parlor. Couples shared listening tubes.

Having found a use, development of the technology proceeded. Tinfoil produced poor sound. Bell and his associates developed wax-coated cylinders that gave better sound, although still a long way from the *high fidelity* today's audiophile has come to expect. Bell also added a speed governor to the machine, so that the cylinder turned at a constant speed regardless of the cranking speed. Listening tubes gave way to horns, with those for lecture halls measuring several feet in diameter at the mouth. Edison provided hundreds of improvements, patenting everything as he and his assistants introduced them and, as usual, ready to sue over any infringements.[16]

Bell's American Graphophone Company prospered in the home market with a simple cylinder phonograph that sold for $10. At the turn of the century, Edison was selling a cylinder player for the home at about $20, but his biggest market remained the phonograph parlor, Columbia advertised machines for home recording with the slogan, "That Baby's Voice in a Columbia Record." Like audio tape and video tape today, the home recording feature proved attractive, but not nearly so much as the chance to play recordings of popular professional performers. The practice of listening to canned music in preference to home-made had begun.

Emile Berliner, who had invented a microphone and contributed to Bell's telephone apparatus, added three innovations. For a better recording medium, he substituted a coating of fat for wax, side-to-side tracking instead of up and down "hill and dale" tracking, and the most important, recording on a disk instead of a cylinder. But the flat zinc disk that he produced was not to be sold to the public. Rather it was used like a waffle iron, as a master to stamp out records in flat circles. Easy to manufacture, records would be sold cheap. Berliner, the immigrant son of a German, Jewish Talmudic scholar, had found a way to make Edison's brilliant invention available to everyone.

The Phonograph as Furniture

To improve his screechy hand-cranked machine, Berliner took it to the New Jersey machine shop of Eldridge Johnson, who became so fascinated with it that he got into the business himself, founding the Victor Talking Machine Company. Johnson described how he got into the business:

> During the model-making days of the business one of the very early types of talking machines was brought to the shop for alterations. The little instrument was badly designed. It sounded much like a partially-educated parrot with a sore throat and a cold in the head, but the little wheezy instrument caught my attention and held it fast and hard. I became interested in it as I have never been interested before in anything.[17]

Figure 4.1   A Victor phonograph manufactured early in the twentieth century. (Courtesy Pavek Museum.)

Years of legal battles ensued over patent infringements. Johnson won in the courts. He had already drastically improved the sound performance of the machine. Now his company began to build the mechanism into a cabinet. From its introduction in 1906, the Victrola made sound recording less of a novelty and more of an instrument of social use. By this time, someone got the idea of putting music on both sides of the record.

In London, a shabby artist turned up at the Gramophone company office. It seems he had painted a picture of his terrier, *Nipper*, listening to an Edison company machine, but nobody would buy the picture. The artist, Francis Barraud, actually painted Nipper from a photograph; the dog had died four years earlier. Barraud offered the picture to the Gramophone Company. The office manager liked it, so a deal was struck. The artist painted out the Edison cylinder phonograph and painted in a flat-record Gramophone machine. The result is "His Master's Voice," probably the most reproduced advertising picture of all time. The artist earned a decent living painting copies of his original picture. A brass monument was erected to the dog in the town

where he died without ever having listened to a recording.

Dancing and Jazz

About the time of the first World War, the recordings, especially from Victor and Columbia, helped to create a new social phenomenon, the dance craze. It was the day of the one-step, the turkey trot, and the tango. It was also the start of jazz. At the same time, a little concern was felt about the accelerated pace of national and cultural development.[18] For some people, things were changing much too fast.

Meanwhile, Edison kept manufacturing and selling cylinders by the millions until the Depression of the 1930s. Yielding to popular demand, his company turned out flat records as well. For the most part, he stayed away from opera and the classics. Edison sold what he called *cracker barrel music* for the enjoyment of common folks. Yet, his recordings boasted superior quality, thanks in part to the plastic his cylinders were made of and thanks in part to his diamond-tip styluses, which were better than the metal tip and wooden tip styluses used on disks. Volume from speakers was controlled physically by a handle that pushed a cotton ball into the throat of a speaker or by closing the doors in front of the speaker. Despite having become deaf, Edison continued his interest in talking machines until shortly before he died at 84.

The highly profitable recorded music industry attracted a lot of competitors in Europe and America. The Pathé brothers, Charles and Emile, made a fortune manufacturing phonographs and records, but they are more famous for their contributions to cinematography. Gianni Bettini of Italy and Henri Lioret of France manufactured both the machines and the recordings. Lioret built them inside dolls just as Edison had envisioned and long before the first little girl would hug a *Chatty Cathy*. Imaginations soared to novelties beyond talking dolls, whose success awaited the microchip, and coin-operated phonographs, forerunner of the jukebox. Inexpensive toy phonographs enjoyed a spate of popularity.

Phonographs were hidden in fake cameras, stacks of books, lamp shades, hat boxes, and even a Buddha with a phonograph concealed in his belly, all hiding the machine.

The *Graphophone*, the *Ronephone*, and the *Ediphone* were early dictating machines. The *Phonopostal* produced recordings for mailing like postcards. The *Pathégraphe* was an audio-visual device for learning foreign languages. The *Tempophon* and the *Peter Pan Clock* were talking clocks, an obvious predecessor of the radio alarm clock. Augustus Stroh, a German living in London, attached a phonograph diaphragm and horn to a violin in place of its wooden case to produce what people called a *phonofiddle*, a turn-of-the-century version of the amplified electric guitar.

High Fidelity

By 1920, vacuum tubes were amplifying voices in public address systems and were beginning to find applications in the recorded sound industry. The application of electronics to the sound system transformed sound technology from a mechanical scratchiness to high fidelity. Electrical engineers at AT&T's Bell Labs and General Electric turned their attention to the design of microphone and loudspeaker, recording and playback stylus, pre-amp, and amplifier. Where the feeble force of a stylus moved a diaphragm that made the sound, now the stylus movement created a feeble current that was amplified clearly and cleanly. A strong current moved the diaphragm in the loudspeaker so the master's voice could be reproduced loudly enough to damage Nipper's hearing. Stereo, developed by Bell Labs in 1933, was demonstrated to the public in 1940 through the soundtrack of Walt Disney's *Fantasia*.

The "Automatic Phonograph Parlor" was reborn with the jukebox in the 1930s. By 1940, a quarter of a million neon-lit jukeboxes were in bars and restaurants. People were still willing to pay a nickel to hear a tune, but recorded music was taking on a new role where it was less the center of attention. The jukebox song was a drinking

Figure 4.2   A 1934 Wurlitzer jukebox offered ten selections. (Courtesy Pavek Museum.)

companion, a background to conversation, and the rhythm for a dance.

Muzak's soothing tones accompanied us while shopping, riding elevators, and working. It has been appreciated, ignored, or derided by people who felt trapped and forced to listen. Muzak staff members rearranged popular songs to eliminate any passages that might attract attention, leaving only a neutral, pastel environment that is more soothing than silence, which can be perceived as hostile and threatening. Cows reportedly gave more milk and chickens laid more eggs when soothed by music. And, of course, credit cards danced out of wallets.

Although we no longer hear our own music as often as we did, the music is of our own choosing. For hundreds of years, humankind dreamed of capturing and then releasing, the human voice, but no technical means of doing so existed. It was not until the nineteenth century that the dream came true. No longer would the direction of music be limited to the choices of wealthy patrons of the arts. By buying the records it fancied, the mass public would decide the direction that music took. Without the phonograph record, jazz would not have sent its notes across America and then around the world. Nor would swing, nor rock 'n' roll, nor country, nor rap. The phonograph brought democracy to music. It is the real meaning of going gold or platinum.

Portable Recording

People have grown painfully aware of fellow citizens who insist on sharing their musical tastes with passersby by carrying boom boxes or playing car stereos at volumes considerably louder than personal listening requires. By doing so, the radio owner commits an aggression, an errant knight with noise as his (seemingly always "his") weapon. The owner is identified not by heraldry, but by choice of music. His intent is not simply a challenge, for this particular music lover while irritating the unappreciative invites a friendly response from those who share his musical tastes.

Unheard music in someone else's Walkman may also annoy us if we want communication with the listener who prefers the music to communion with anyone, including us. We have all seen someone jogging, walking, or skating down the street while shutting out the world with a Walkman.

Figure 4.3   A jogger listening to recorded music is now a familiar sight.

Is the user of the Walkman more considerate than the master of the "monster box"? Each moves in a portable acoustical bubble, and while the effect of the miniaturized unit is less political than the box (certainly an important distinction), each of the users displays some attempted mastery of his or her own movable turf.[19]

Moving down the street the earphoned individual hears none of our community of sound. There isn't the slightest need to interact with anyone as long as the portable tape recorder is there.

The video world abhors face-to-face interaction. It asks only to interact with the machine. Just walk down Main Street. Look at the numbers of people with earphones listening to their own music, oblivious to the world about them. The proliferation of the Sony Walkman and similar sound devices is strikingly symbolic. Look at the faces. They are blank. With earphones on, the individual closes out all outside stimuli. He is his own captive audience.[20]

The Story of Audiotape

The two technologies that are most commonly used to record sound—the phonograph and audiotape—have similar fundamental characteristics of recording and reproducing sound. The way each has been developed for consumer use, however, gives them markedly different appeal for the home user. Phonograph records and CDs have been marketed only as a storehouse of sound. Audiotape's recording capabilities, plus the portability of its recording apparatus, have rendered it a much more versatile tool.

The story of audiotape began in 1888 when Oberlin Smith published a theory that information could be stored by magnetizing iron particles. He noted that when a magnet was moved under iron filings scattered across a piece of paper, the filings rearranged themselves into arcs. Smith held that the same result would occur with even smaller particles, and that if there were some way to fix the particles firmly, the magnetic impulses that were put into them could be extracted.

Ten years later, a Danish inventor, Valdemar Poulsen, figured out how to extract that stored magnetic information using steel wire wound on a brass drum. Poulsen thought of his Telegraphone as a voice recording device to be used in a telephone answering machine or an office dictation device, and for recording and playing back music in the home. The Telegraphone won the Grand Prix at the Paris Exposition of 1900, but Poulsen's company, lacking the funds that would open the door to entertainment, eventually went broke.

Little in magnetic recording happened until 1928, when a German, Fritz Pfleumer, built a successful prototype of a tape recorder. The chemical firm I.G. Farben's BASF division manufactured plastic-base audiotape. It still does.

Germans Move Ahead

By the end of World War II, Magnetophon audio tape recorders delivered better sound quality than many phonograph records. Adolf Hitler's speeches recorded on audio tape, distributed on high-quality phone lines, and played over radio stations in different parts of Germany confused Allied short-wave listeners who could not figure out how the Fuehrer could get around so fast. Later, as they heard music with excellent fidelity from the Berlin Philharmonic and other orchestras in the middle of the night, they realized that the Germans had moved far ahead in sound recording.[21]

On the Allied side of the war, steel bands and steel wire were the available magnetic recording media. Editing of steel bands had to be accomplished with a soldering torch. Steel wire used in the field could be tied in a square knot and heated with the tip of a lighted cigarette to fuse the ends. By 1943, portable wire recorders were in the hands of radio journalists, but their audio quality left a lot to be desired

G.I.s pushing into Germany found radio stations equipped with something that apparently no one on the Allied side had been aware of, recorders using magnetic tape instead of steel. The audio quality was far better. Editing was as simple as a snip by a pair of scissors and the slapping on of a bit of adhesive tape.

U.S. Army Major John Mullin, a Signal Corps engineer who discovered a Magnetophon at a Frankfurt radio station, brought audiotape recording to the United States. Singer Bing Crosby, who didn't like to do live broadcasts, asked Mullin to tape Crosby's radio shows for later playback. Mullin would later become one of the engineers who invented videotape recording as a means of storing and time-shifting television programs. Both audiotape and videotape changed broadcasting. It would never be the same again.

A Tool for Journalists

Radio journalists loved audiotape. It expanded what they could put into their news reports. Listeners could now hear what reporters heard—the sounds of everything from artillery to crickets, from politicians to babies. The portable recorder and microphone went wherever the reporter went.

Recorded music was on phonograph records, but the superior sound of audio tape changed that. What began in radio stations soon spread to the home. People who could afford it wanted their own tape players and music libraries on tape. At first, the players were all reel-to-reel, but a consumer market

Figure 4.4   One of the two Magnetophon recorders that Mullin brought to the United States. (Courtesy Pavek Museum.)

existed for portable record players that would be as convenient as portable radios. The endless loop cartridge player, first 4-channel, later 8-channel, met the demand. Tape unwinding from the center of a coil moved past the audio heads to the outside of the coil. The much simpler cassette soon took over the market.

The Sony Walkman, the first widely used personal stereo, appeared in 1981, a lightweight, portable, battery operated device with a headphone. The portable product line has expanded to encompass not only cassette tape players but radios, compact disc players, and even television. By creating a private space, an acoustic environment that shuts out the sounds and even the sights around them, the users reject interpersonal communication and appear at times to risk safety.[22] About 100 million personal stereos have been sold.

Meanwhile, audiotaped books have been available for years on loan like library books through organizations for the blind. A market for car drivers has been tapped with a range of abridged books on tape sold through video stores, groceries, gas stations, and stop-and-shops.

New Formats

By the mid-1990s, several digital formats of audiotape and compact disks competed for public favor.

DAT, or *digital audio tape*, could copy compact discs without losing audio quality. This prospect angered and frightened the music industry, which feared wholesale piracy of recordings. Music industry spokesmen lobbied in Washington for federal legislation to force Japanese manufacturers of digital audio tape players to modify these machines to prevent illegal copying. The manufacturers resisted; the copying feature was, after all, one reason why people bought such machines. A royalty arrangement was negotiated instead.

Digital compact cassettes (DCC) and the *Minidisc (MD)* were later additions to the range of hardware/software audio equipment. The DCC player took both analog and digital cassettes and could be hooked to a television set to display the words of the songs. The Minidisc player had the advantage of recording and erasing signals. As for which system provided the best fidelity, each had its proponents. Obviously, not all these new formats could survive.

If the personal Walkman and its clones seem to be the antithesis of *mass* communication, they are not, for the hallmark of mass communication exists in the one-way transferal of information from a distant source to the audience. The jogger, alone on a rural road, listening over headphones, is part of a mass.

Broadcasting

World War I was over. The U.S. Navy still controlled radio, its means for point-to-point communication. But civilian radio amateurs were interested in something else. From the Navy had come the word *broadcasting*. The amateurs pressured the government to abandon its restrictions on radio and force the Navy to return stations to private ownership. Thousands of amateurs had answered the country's call to use their skills as radio operators for the Army and the Navy. Now, they wanted to start new stations, and many were eager to use the new continuous wave technology to broadcast voice and music.

Among those experimenting with radio was Frank Conrad, a Westinghouse Corporation engineer who had manufactured portable equipment for the Signal Corps. From the garage of his home in Pittsburgh, he spoke to other amateurs and broadcast music by placing his microphone next to a Victrola. Conrad asked for postcards from anyone who could hear him. To his surprise, listeners wrote in to request tunes. So many wrote, in fact, that Conrad tried to oblige by transmitting the broadcasts according to a schedule. He added sports scores and some singing and instrument playing by his children. A Pittsburgh news-

went on the air with the call letters KDKA on November 2, 1920. The date was chosen so that the first broadcast could be of the returns of the Harding-Cox presidential election. A few thousand people tuned in.

By 1923, broadcasting had an audience of more than two million people served by more than 500 stations. A half-million sets in 1923 were followed by two million in 1925. By 1926, one house in six had a radio.

Isolating Listeners

Listeners were also eagerly buying into the separation from others that a home with a radio afforded. Appreciative writers of letters to radio stations and magazine articles spoke of the pleasure of sitting in comfort at home alone or just with a family member to hear a concert or a talk.[23] When loudspeakers replaced earphones the social structure of radio took another step by making listening to distant information and entertainment as normal and natural as family conversation around the dinner table. A writer in 1923 was delighted:

> How easy it is to close the eyes and imagine the other listeners in little back rooms, in kitchens, dining-rooms, sitting-rooms, attics; in garages, offices, cabins, engine-rooms, bungalows, cottages, mansions, hotels, apartments; one here, two there, a little company around a table away off yonder...[24]

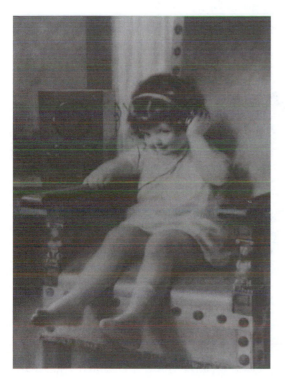

Figure 4.5 "The Bedtime Story," an RCA publicity photo, 1922, for a one-tube radio without a loudspeaker or an amplifier. (Courtesy Pavek Museum.)

paper printed a story about his concerts and his audience swelled. A record store owner agreed to lend him some phonograph records in return for mentioning the name of the store on the air. The owner soon discovered that the records Conrad played were in more demand than any others. In a few other places, experimental broadcasts were going out, but in Pittsburgh something unique happened. After Horne's Department Store advertised wireless sets for sale so people could listen to Conrad's broadcasts, his employer, Westinghouse, decided to manufacture inexpensive radio receivers. A major corporation had finally recognized that a market existed beyond point-to-point transmission.

To win customers, Westinghouse followed Conrad's lead by providing a regular program schedule. It also erected a transmitter at the Westinghouse factory, which

Corporations now saw radio as a money spinner, but no one controlled all the inventions needed. General Electric, Westinghouse, RCA, and the American Telephone Company battled each other for the rights to broadcast, to manufacture radio sets, and to manufacture broadcasting and signaling equipment. Compromise came in cross-licensing agreements for companies to use each other's patents.

In most countries of the world, where radio was strictly controlled and the only stations allowed were government stations, development was orderly and sensible, but rigid. That was not the situation in the United States, where radio stations popped up like mushrooms.

Figure 4.6
An ad by one of the hundreds of manufacturers of radio sets during the 1920s. (Courtesy Pavek Museum.)

High school students formed radio clubs around their own stations. University engineering departments built experimental stations and professors lectured on them. Preachers set up transmitters; evangelist Aimee Semple McPherson had a loyal, even fanatic following. A newspaper publisher might create a station to attract subscribers by reading aloud stories from each day's edition. A department store owner hoped that a farmer who heard a broadcast might buy a shirt the next time he came to town. The shirts were not advertised. Nothing was.

Figure 4.7   A Holmes-Jordan radio with three tuning stages, 1925. Three types of batteries were needed, including a lead acid car-type battery. Acid burns in carpets were common. (Courtesy Pavek Museum.)

Most of the stations were low powered "coffee pots" with little range. No one could have dreamed that the curiosity of wireless and vacuum tubes in the corner, leading over the years to AM, FM, and TV licenses, one day would be worth more than the entire department store or newspaper.

The Radio Act of 1927

In the years following World War I, all stations shared the same frequency, with a second frequency for crop and weather reports, a workable arrangement for ships, where sender and receiver talk only for a short time, say what they have to say, and then go silent. A broadcast station, however, might never be silent. As radio stations drowned each other out by 1922, it became plain that something better was needed. The government made more frequencies available, but new stations appeared even faster. The frustrating babble worsened as some broadcasters increased their power output, others shifted to new frequencies or new transmitters, and poor equipment sent signals wandering.

The government responded to pleas from radio station owners for regulation by calling four conferences, but these were stormy affairs, with station owners wanting to limit competition, small stations distrustful of the large corporation stations, radio amateurs opposing any limits on their freedom, and not everyone quite sure how to finance the radio industry. Reluctantly, the government and industry inched toward regulation, but with the intention of expanding broadcasting, not limiting or censoring it, as one might expect when government seeks to regulate. Finally, Congress passed the Radio Act of 1927, broadening it in the Communication Act of 1934, which was the basic broadcasting law until it was modified by the Telecommunication Reform Act of 1996. Yet its basic principles continue.

At its heart is the belief that the airwaves belong to the public. Licenses are granted only to qualified persons who agree to operate in the public interest, and the government has the power to regulate broadcasting, but the role of censor is forbidden, at least in theory. However, the power to issue licenses—through the Federal Communications Commission since 1934—is, in effect, the power to determine who will get a loud voice, and accusations have persisted that government authority has been used to this purpose.[25]

Commercials

As for who would pay for all this radio broadcasting, by the mid-1920s the answer came loud and clear. AT&T, in the business of renting its equipment to people who want to communicate with other people, saw the radio studio as a kind of telephone booth. In 1922, its New York station, WEAF, was made available for what it called *toll broadcasting*, an experiment in letting any member of the public use its station like a telephone booth to make a telephone call to everyone at once. AT&T sold blocks of time to advertisers, starting with a real estate company, the Queensboro Corporation, which paid $50 for ten minutes to tell listeners about the joys of living in the apartments they offered for sale in the Long Island countryside. That $50 investment brought in $127,000 in orders.[26] Advertising on radio was born.

Commercials began carefully. Telephone company officials were afraid that the government might get angry about using a radio station, which depended on a government license, to sell a product. They worried at first that toothpaste might be too intimate a product to advertise. Prices were not mentioned. Many listeners were offended by the entire idea of using radio to sell goods, and there was talk of passing a law to prohibit commercials. No other country permitted them. AT&T held fast. Soon other advertisers signed up. Despite objections by AT&T that it had exclusive rights to offer this service, other radio stations, sniffing dollars, jumped in. Across the country, a trickle of advertisers became a flood. Radio now had the answer to the question of where the money would come from.

> As a medium for those who hoped to control mass behavior, radio offered numerous advantages over print media. Like graphics but unlike the printed word, radio could influence illiterates (6 percent of U.S. adults in 1920) and preliterate children, so that Ipana toothpaste, for example, could make its radio pitch for "the one in the red and yellow tube." Unlike newspaper and magazine ads, radio commercials could not be skipped over—they interrupted desired programming and could follow listeners from room to room...Not only could one listen to radio while engaged in other activities, including reading, one could continue to listen long after becoming too tired to do anything else—so that broadcasting promised (or threatened) to fill every waking moment of the day.[27]

While AT&T saw radio broadcasting as a kind of one-way telephone service, RCA (Radio Corporation of America), General Electric, and Westinghouse saw broadcasting as a service to create public demand for the radio sets that they manufactured. Put another way, AT&T and Western Electric, known as the *telephone group*, concentrated on the senders of messages, later called *sponsors*. The other companies, known as the *radio group*, concentrated on the receivers of messages, the audience. What finally emerged was a combination of the two approaches, one leading to commercials, the other to programming. What we hear and see on radio and television today is the result.

Broadcasting Policy in Other Countries

Broadcasting in America followed competitive market principles to capture the largest possible audience. Educational broadcasting, there from the beginning, continued to be a poor relative of commercial broadcasting, dependent on donations to survive at all. By 1939, it had been all but squeezed out by commercial interests. Britain, on the other hand, established the government-run British Broadcasting Corporation, which programmed what those who were in charge believed listeners needed to hear and should hear. It was—and still is—financially supported by annual license fees on television sets. Starting in the mid-1950s, the BBC permitted an independent commercial service, ITV, to operate under strict regulation. Many nations followed the British model.

Besides commercials and license fees, a third method evolved for supporting a national broadcasting system: direct government funding. In authoritarian nations, radio and television stations got funds from direct grants, which kept the broadcasters firmly attached to the purse strings in the hands of the government leaders.

Networks

At first, each U.S. radio station transmitted only its own programs, but the advantages of broadcasting the same program over several stations were obvious by 1922. Networking would provide cheaper operating costs for broadcasters, give advertisers a larger audience, offer better programs to listeners who lived far from large cities, and limit effective competition. A broadcast speech by the president of the United States demanded the largest possible audience. In 1922, telephone company engineers experimented with hooking up stations to

transmit the same program. This led at first to informal temporary networks, but in 1926 RCA created two permanent networks, the *Red*, which today is NBC radio, and the *Blue*, which eventually became ABC. A year later, the CBS network was put together. The Mutual Broadcasting System, started in 1934, became a national network, and regional networks were formed in New England, the Midwest, and the Far West.

The biggest advantage of networks was a higher quality of programs than any station could manage. Money from commercials broadcast nationwide paid for the writers, actors, musicians, announcers, journalists, producers, engineers, and others who put together the dramas, comedies, variety shows, children's shows, and news programs that made the radio in the parlor the favorite place for the family to gather in the evening. In the 1920s, advertisers identified their products in the names of the programs themselves, garnering extra publicity when newspaper logs listed such programs as "The Eveready Hour" advertising batteries, and "The A&P Gypsies" advertising the grocery chain.

In the home, radio sets were powered by batteries until 1926. It was inevitable that radios would also go into cars. A battery eliminator for cars was developed in 1930. Cars and radio have been together ever since. Car owners who could afford it had custom-made AC-powered radio sets installed.[28]

Technology had brought radios into the parlor. Commercials provided an economic base. Networks added a programming base. The Federal Radio Commission, later the Federal Communications Commission, added controls. One more element would be supplied for the start of the *golden age* of radio, spanning approximately 1930 to 1950, when millions of people decided to stay home instead of going out. It would be called the *Depression*.

Owning Cameras

Tens of millions of us all over the world own cameras, and with them, we create memories. Changing technology has consistently enabled more of us to afford to participate in the making and acquiring of photographs of better and better quality. From the time of its invention, photography was more than a means of information. It was a source of deep personal pleasure.

Technical Improvements

It had also become a medium for artistic expression. Alfred Stieglitz and Edward Steichen built reputations rivaling painters who used brush and palette. Henri Cartier-Bresson, Ansel Adams, and Edward Weston followed them. Stieglitz led a movement named the *Photo Secession* devoted to the idea of photography as an art form and a means of personal expression. He exhibited photographs in his New York gallery and founded *Camera Work*, a magazine for fine photographic art. More than anyone, he saw photography as a form of art and he raised it to a new level.

The stereo camera, its lenses spaced as far apart as human eyes, produced the stereograph, a picture pair that, viewed through a stereoscope, gave a three-dimensional view. Old stereoscopes and pictures can still be found in antique shops. The stereo-scope's vistas of faraway places, so real that you could imagine yourself at the pyramids or the Taj Mahal, provided pleasure, information, and escape for decades.

From the beginning, photographers fretted about the length of time it took to expose a picture. At first, people could not be captured on film at all. When exposure time shortened, the subjects had to hold still, the number of seconds decreasing as the technology improved. Because the early cameras lacked shutters, the photographer simply took the lens cap off for the number of seconds required to expose the plate. As film improved, inventors formulated better ideas for exposing the film for shorter and shorter time periods. The demand for stop-action pictures pushed the inventors of optical and mechanical equipment and photochemistry to bring to the marketplace such new products as the focal plane shutter, located between the lens and the film.

As long as glass plates served as the recording medium base, cameras would remain bulky. The wet-plate process gave way by 1878 to a gelatin silver bromide dry-plate process that provided even greater sensitivity. It freed the photographer from carrying a darkroom wherever he went. Cameras small enough to hold in the hand removed the requirement of a

Figure 4.8
Three U.S. soldiers during the Korean War. Photos like this do much to shape attitudes toward distant events. (Courtesy U.S. Army.)

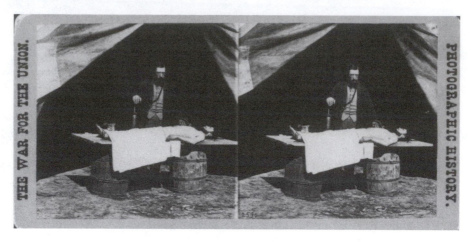

Figure 4.9   A stereograph gives a three-dimensional view. A Union Army surgeon with a soldier's body. (Courtesy State Historical Society of Wisconsin.)

tripod. But the glass plates themselves had limitations. They were heavy and fragile. They required special chemicals and special handling. These difficulties led to a search for a substitute material, something lightweight, but flexible enough to be rolled around a spool, yet tough and transparent. Inventors turned to nitrocellulose, the source of collodion, an important chemical in glass plate photography. Simply put, they threw away the glass and, as a film base, kept a version of the sticky stuff that stuck to the glass.

The Kodak

George Eastman marketed rolls of light-sensitive celluloid—*film*—similar to the kind that we buy today. The word *film* now joined the buzz about photography. Eastman put the new film in a basic camera which he called a *Kodak*. The name had no meaning. Eastman chose the five-letter word because it sounded simple and wasn't easy to imitate.

By the end of the nineteenth century, some 50 different types of cameras were manufactured. The Kodak offered camera owners simplicity, reducing the usual ten or more operations needed for an exposure to just three: pull the cord, turn the key, press the button.

Taking a series of pictures without reloading, the first Kodak cameras featured a fixed focus lens with one speed and a fixed aperture. Owners returned the camera to the company with the film still in it. The camera was mailed back to them reloaded and ready to go, accompanied by the packet of pictures snapped by the owner. The price for a typical Kodak model was $25 including a roll of 100 pictures, plus $10 for developing and mounting the exposed pictures and putting in a fresh roll. Eastman's slogan was, "You Press the Button, We Do the Rest." The photographer did not need to understand any chemistry. For the first time, anyone could take a picture. Millions soon did. Camera clubs sprang up everywhere.

The hobby of photography, not just the price of a single photograph, was becoming more affordable for average people, although $25 was still a lot of money in those days. Eastman would soon manufacture models that brought the price down as low as one dollar. Eastman said his cameras brought photography "within the reach of every human being who desires to preserve a record of what he sees." When Eastman's Brownie camera sold for $1 with a six-exposure roll of film that cost 15 cents, photography was truly available for "the man in the street." Eastman had

Figure 4.10 The Brownie was built for children, but adults liked its price and simplicity. (Courtesy International Museum of Photography at George Eastman House.)

designed the Brownie for children, but adults used it, too. Pictures that could be taken easily came to be known by the way that hunters described shooting a rifle from the hip without aiming: *a snapshot*.

More Improvements

By the turn of the century, experiments were being done with color film and color filters. Eastman-Kodak's Kodachrome color film was invented in 1935. The year 1947 brought another major invention, Edwin Land's Polaroid camera process that allowed quick film development and printing inside the camera. The back of the camera carried separate negative and positive film rolls. The act of pulling the film out of the camera sent it between two rollers that broke small pods of developing gel, spreading them evenly across the film surface. One minute later the positive print was ready to be peeled away. The *instant print* process was available in color by 1963, followed in 1972 by the Polaroid SX-70, which combined the negative and positive materials in a single unit, thanks to fourteen separate coatings.

From Japan came the point-and-shoot, automatic-everything camera. The focus adjusted instantly to whatever was in front of the lens. Like so many inventions, the camera itself grew more complicated in order to make its operation more simple. Back in the days of the daguerreotype and wet-plate photography, the camera was little more than a box with a lens, but getting pictures took training, practice, and skill. By contrast, the Japanese cameras were crammed with microcircuitry and intricate mechanical and optical parts, but anyone could press a button. Eastman's old advertising slogan, "You Press the Button, We Do the Rest," could hardly be truer for the automated single-lens reflex camera controlled by computer chips and infrared sensors.

The filmless camera arrived in the early 1980s. The Sony Mavica CCD camera recorded images onto a small digital disc that, without chemical processing, could be transmitted over ordinary telephone lines or by satellite. Another device, the photo CD player, used photographs encoded digitally on compact discs. The photographs could be displayed in color on a home television set, accompanied by any functions the owner wished to add, such as pans and zooms, skip selection, audio narration or music, text, and graphics.

Kodak and Japanese camera and film manufacturers joined to introduce the Advanced Photo System in 1996. Moving even more *buttons* inside, it featured drop-in, no-threading film canisters. Users could choose standard or wide framing for each shot, and on the back of a print could identify the date, location, and subject. The film conveyed the instructions to the processing equipment to compensate for poor lighting.

Pictures that Lie

Digital imaging converted images into dots that could be moved or removed. Electronic changes eliminated any evidence of tampering. Customers came to the shops of expert digital imagers with beloved old photographs that had seen better days. The experts scanned the photos into a computer, cleaned up the damaged areas, and reproduced them as photographs. Other requests have included taking unidentified people out of a photograph; adding missing relatives to a family reunion; bringing grand-

Figure 4.11   In 1996, Kodak introduced cameras for the Advanced Photo System that carried instructions to photo finishing equipment. (Reprinted with permission from Eastman Kodak Company.)

mother, mother, and daughter together for a three-generation portrait, closing gaps in a photograph of relatives to make the scene cozier, or eliminating braces on teeth before the orthodontist could. A divorced woman popped her ex-husband's image out of a family portrait. And a boy named Brian got a poster of himself perched atop a movie marquee advertising the Monty Python movie, *The Life of Brian*.

The old adage that the camera never lies can have few remaining adherents. Modern photography can certainly lie. In the 1920s, a few newspaper editors combined pictures into *composographs*, which brought images of people from different photographs together in close proximity. The pictures were outright fakes, visual lies. Publishers justified using them because they sold newspapers. At times, these distortions had political value. Enough voters were deceived during the McCarthy era of the 1950s to defeat liberal Senator Millard Tydings for re-election after he was shown standing beside Communist leader Earl Browder, an event that never happened.

But the old manipulation of still pictures was crude compared with digital imaging. Computer software for digital retouching shifted the pyramids at Giza to improve the

Figure 4.12   Photojournalism can convey powerful emotions, but the strongest pictures bring a public outcry such as attended this picture of the execution of Ruth Judd. The photographer strapped a tiny camera to his ankle.

framing of a *National Geographic* cover in 1982. An expert explained:

> With the new technology we can enhance colors or change them, eliminate details, add or delete figures, alter the composition and lighting effects, combine any number of images, and literally move mountains, or at least the Eiffel Tower, as one magazine did to improve a cover design. *TV Guide* didn't even stop at decapitation—it placed Oprah Winfrey's head on Ann Margaret's body![29]

Holograms

Work continued on practical, affordable holography, a two-dimensional photographic system that produces three-dimensional photographs using laser beams. A

Figure 4.13 About 1960 Wisconsin Senator Alexander Wiley sent out this composograph of three separate pictures as a Christmas card. (Courtesy State Historical Society of Wisconsin.)

message to a spaceship. If, one day, motion holography can be delivered to the home as television pictures, there is little doubt about its acceptance. To view a video hologram would be more like looking through a window at the street outside than like watching TV.

From its beginnings, photography has given people information, entertainment, and aesthetic pleasure.

As a tool of journalism, photographs delivered information that words alone could not. The eyes of starving African children with flies hovering about helped launch cargo planes. The pained eyes of brutalized Bosnian women shook Western nations into action. The eyes of baby harp seals just before the fur hunter's club crashed down led to a halt to the slaughter. As a tool of medicine, photography has helped to improve our health. As a tool of science, it has transformed what is unknown to what is known.

At the same time, we have derived enjoyment from still pictures in mass media, notably magazines, and from motion pictures. And if the first expensive tool of communication we purchase is not our own camera, it will likely be the second or third. Photography also enables us to share memories over a family photo album or pause alone for a reflective moment in a busy day with a photo in a wallet. The command "Smile!" carries a lot of meaning.

hologram can appear to extend deep into the wall on which the picture is hanging or it can seem to extend outward into a room so viewers carefully walk around what is not actually there. Holograms have a number of scientific uses. They can also be found on magazine covers and on museum walls. The first of the *Star Wars* films contained a hologram appearance by "Princess Leia," the heroine, who delivered a "mailed"

Movies Tell Stories

Movie audiences loved stories. France's George Méliès, who had run a magic show, produced the first openly fiction films. Modern audiences enjoy *A Trip to the Moon*, as a whimsical introduction to the history of space flight. Méliès was among the first to stretch the film from less than one minute to an entire reel of 10 to 15 minutes length.

Nickelodeons

Exhibitors strung a few of these brief films together in random fashion as a program. In this way the nickelodeon began, its name reflecting the price of admission. The first nickelodeon opened in Pittsburgh in 1904. Within a year, 2,500 were operating, selling 200,000 tickets a day by 1907. Nick-

Figure 4.14   A movie theatre about 1920 advertising its spectacle. (Courtesy State Historical Society of Wisconsin.)

elodeons popped up in every corner of the land, gaudy and brightly lit, sometimes with a barker out front aided by a loud phonograph to fill up the house.

The nickel theaters attracted shoppers with tired feet, office workers on their lunch hour, unaccompanied women for whom a movie theater was a safe and generally respectable place to go. Victorian middle class morality limited entertainment for women. For them, the cinema had a particular appeal.

> More than any other entertainment form, the cinema opened up a space—a social space as well as a perceptual experiential horizon—in women's lives... Married women would drop into a movie theater on their way home from a shopping trip, a pleasure indulged in just as much by women of the more affluent classes. School-girls fill the theaters during much of the afternoon, before returning to the folds of familial discipline. And young working women would find in the cinema an hour of

diversion after work, as well as an opportunity to meet men.[30]

Nickelodeons brought in packs of "smudgy urchins,"[31] couples looking for a dark place for their dates, and entire working class families including their squalling babies. The cinema brought affordable entertainment to the poor, who had neither the disposable income nor the time for other paid amusements, but only the *white* poor, for *blacks* were usually barred from nickelodeons.

> Most of the early comedies borrowed their characters, if not their plots, from vaudeville skits. As in vaudeville, ethnic and racial parodies were prevalent, with dim-witted Irish servants blowing themselves up trying to light the stove or taking off their clothes when asked to serve the salad "undressed"; unscrupulous Jewish merchants in full beards and long black coats cheating their customers, and blacks behaving like children—cakewalking, grin-

ning, shooting craps, stealing chickens, and eating watermelon...[32]

Customers sometimes packed in from morning to night, one show after another, seven days a week. They streamed out of one nickelodeon into another, beguiled by the barkers, the flashing lights, and the colorful posters outside until their endurance or their pockets were drained. Between shows, the nickelodeon owners sent their relatives up and down the aisle selling snacks and soda pop. In some theaters, the attendants squirted the air with a solution to mask the foul air, which did nothing about the pestilential germs that city inspectors worried about. To keep up with demand for new movies, exhibitors changed the bill daily, or even twice a day.

> The nickels rattled down like hailstones as workingmen and their families crowded into the lobbies, overflowed in long patient lines on the street. Inside the program lasted from twenty minutes to an hour: a brief melodrama or chase; a comedy; a news picture or travel picture; a glimpse of dancers or acrobats. Between films the projectionist inserted "hand-colored" slides of popular songs, the pianist pounded out the melodies, and the whole audience sang... "Waltz Me Around Again, Willie."...Far too often, in the middle of a picture, the projectionist inserted a slide reading, "One Minute, Please!" This indicated a break in the film, or trouble with the machine. Everyone began stamping in unison. If the necessary repair required a little time, there were slides advertising the stores of local tradesmen, and announcing future programs. The audience, impatient for a renewal of illusion, whistled and shouted. Youngsters carrying trays piled with peanuts, candy, popcorn and soda-pop rushed up and down the aisles, crying their wares. Presently the machine resumed its sputtering, and the screen came alive again. There was a ripple of applause, a fluttering sigh of contentment. Then silence, broken by the crackling of peanut shells and popcorn, the whimpering of a frightened child. In the fetid darkness, tired men and women forgot the hardships of poverty. For this was happiness. This was the Promised Land.[33]

A writer of the times observed:

> Opposite the barren school yard was the arcaded entrance to the Nickelodeon, finished in white stucco, with the ticket seller throned in a chariot drawn by an elephant trimmed with red, white and blue lights... Here were groups of working girls—now happy "summer girls"—because they had left the grime, ugliness, and dejection of their factories behind them, and were freshened and revived by doing what they liked to do.[34]

Fear of Revolutionary Ideas

The wealthy classes did not frequent the nickelodeons, but from their ranks came expressions of worry that uneducated workingmen and women were being fed revolutionary ideas. Suggestions were made that the content of the nickelodeons be regulated, censored, or even suppressed. Some of these suggestions came from saloon owners who were losing customers, managers of vaudeville houses, and ministers who saw their congregations sharply diminished. In time, the nickelodeons would indeed be put out of business, but only by better quality theaters and better shows.

> As long as there was no alternative to the nickel theaters, customers were content to squeeze themselves into darkened, airless storefronts to watch 15- to twenty-minute shows with seven- or eight-minute features.[35]

After about a decade, as the appeal of motion pictures expanded beyond the poorer classes to be enthusiastically embraced by middle-class Americans, the nickelodeons, the store fronts, the backs of the arcades, and the circus tents gave way to theaters built for movie watching, and later to a considerably grander architecture, movie *palaces*. In summertime, the blessings of air conditioning drew in patrons.

As feature films took hold, it became obvious that nickelodeons and small movie theaters could no longer depend upon income from a rapid turnover of audiences who came for a string of short films. The audiences liked the longer feature films.

The solution was much larger theaters that could seat audiences of many hundreds or even several thousand. The first movie palace, the Strand Theater on Broadway, opened its doors in 1914 and was an immediate success. It could seat almost 3,000 patrons at a time. Once again, the public decided the direction that a medium of communication would take. Within two years, approximately 21,000 newly built or extensively remodeled theaters were completed. Downtown in large cities, the more ornate motion picture showplaces featured orchestra pits, pipe organs, and plaster Byzantine architecture. They were designed to attract middle class patrons who were beginning to go to motion pictures, but would not enter dingy, crowded nickelodeons.

Film exchanges, instead of *selling* films to exhibitors, *rented* them. In time, as the industry matured, distribution centers and chain owners would dominate the mom-and-pop beginnings of film exhibition. Movie theater chains with hundreds of outlets either contracted with studios or had the same corporate ownership, guaranteeing both a steady supply of product and dependable distribution. Warner Bros. films opened in a Warner Bros. theater in every large city, Paramount films at a Paramount, MGM films at a Loew's theater.

A Market for Simple Stories

The movie-going public had enough problems of their own. They liked escape into fantasy. Reality in the form of actuality film was not what they entered the darkened theater to see. Eventually, the public would express its preference for color and sound, for these added even more pleasure to an evening of going out to the movies. And always, the actors.

> Never in history has the public been so avid for information about mortals who earn a living by posturing... The sheer magnitude of this adoration invites awe. Each day millions of men, women, and children sit in the windowless temples of the screen to commune with their vicarious friends and lovers.[36]

In 1903, director-photographer Edwin Porter made *The Great Train Robbery*, the first memorable story film and the first to utilize film editing to establish relationships. In eight minutes, bandits hold up a mail train, a posse is formed, they chase after the bandits, a shoot-out follows, and the bandits are wiped out. For the first time, too, the camera moved with the action, indoors and out. Excited audiences lined up to get in and demanded more. Moviemakers listened.

Figure 4.15
The Great Train Robbery introduces cutting to advance the narrative. Film makers discovered that audiences loved stories. (Courtesy State Historical Society of Wisconsin.)

A lot of ticket buyers were poor and had little formal education. Many immigrants were illiterate in the English language. Reasonably, they wanted to see what they could understand. The burlesque tradition, particularly pratfall comedy, filled the bill nicely. So did simple stories of adventure and romance that everyone could enjoy. Literates in the audience read the subtitles to those sitting nearby. People willingly plunked down their hard-earned coins for visual comedy and stories.

Audiences sometimes wanted more than excitement and romance. They wanted a chance to laugh. *Fred Ott's Sneeze* (1893), an early Edison film for the Kinetoscopes, began a long tradition of film comedy. Under the guiding hand of Mack Sennett, slapstick grew from its limited roots in burlesque to an art form. The Keystone Kops' nonsensical appearance and incompetence allowed people to laugh at a social institution that was anything but humorous. For immigrants from many countries, regarding the policeman as a figure of fun must have been strange indeed.

In the slapstick comedies, danger was constant and hairbreadth escapes were common, but no one died and no one was even seriously hurt. Settings were realistic, but the realism was exaggerated to absurdity by fast-motion film, ridiculous props, split-second timing, and incongruous film cutting. When the screen comic hero's automobile missed the oncoming locomotive by inches, the audience suspended belief and laughed. Sennett, the director, was followed by silent film actors who took the comic art to yet greater heights. Harold Lloyd, Buster Keaton, and, above the rest, Charlie Chaplin blended slapstick with pathos. His meld of mirth, romance, and sadness created one of the classic characters of any age and culture, the little tramp, in such films as *The Kid*, *The Gold Rush*, and *City Lights*.

The Actors

As usual, the customers had something to say about what they were paying to see. Audiences showed by their ticket purchases an attachment for certain actors and actresses. The result was Hollywood's creation of a star system early in the history of the motion picture. Moviegoers, it turned out, identified with the characters looming so large on the screen.

The first screen actors were people who appeared in front of the camera only because they were not busy working behind it. Wives, friends, visitors took a turn. When stage actors began arriving at the new movie studios to look for work, they were given acting jobs, but not the publicity they expected, because studio owners were

Figure 4.16
Immigrants loved seeing the Keystone Kops. Where many of them came from, policemen were nothing to laugh at. (Courtesy State Historical Society of Wisconsin.)

afraid this would lead to demands for better pay. This situation soon changed. Theater owners reported to producers that audiences looked forward to seeing familiar faces. Word raced through town that the actor or actress who had appeared in such-and-such a role could be seen again at the Bijou in a new motion picture. That meant ticket sales.

In 1914, Charlie Chaplin was being paid $125 a week. By 1915, he was getting $10,000 a week plus $150,000 for signing the contract. By 1916, Mary Pickford was getting $10,000 a week plus half the profits of her pictures. For the business they brought in, they were worth every penny. In the darkened movie houses, the fans could feel close to the famous actors who looked out at them in close-ups. For at least a short time, the moviegoer could displace whatever existed in his or her life with mediated pleasure. That experience has never gone out of our lives.

Moviegoers wanted formula films that did not vary much from one comedy to the next, one cowboy western to the next. Most of all, they wanted happy endings. The popular melodrama easily made the transition from stage to screen. The hero dashed up at the last minute to save the tied-down heroine from the oncoming train, then turned to thrash the villain. Film cuts kept the pacing and mood, and fades kept the story line from scene to scene. It was certainly better than raising and lowering a stage curtain. Real locomotives and spinning circular lumber saws enhanced the sense of reality better than the cardboard imitations of the stage. The melodrama and outdoor filming were clearly made for each other.

Adolph Zukor spent $35,000 to bring to the United States in 1912 a film made in France, Sarah Bernhardt's portrayal of Queen Elizabeth. He charged $1 a ticket, an unheard of price, and rented a major theater. Zukor, who created Paramount Pictures, has been called the *father* of the feature film. He once said, "The public is never wrong."

Assembly Line Production

The melodrama evolved into the romantic drama with *The Birth of a Nation* (1915), a feature film nearly three hours long. Director D.W. Griffith's manipulation of long, medium, and close-up shots, pacing, and optical effects, plus his choice of locations and his attention to actors' movements set new standards for the motion picture. He insisted on close-ups of actors despite protests from studio executives that audiences wanted to see the actors from head to toe and would not accept "half an actor." Starting with *The Birth of a Nation* film would have a visual language that the public would understand, a language to which it would respond. Although a silent film, *The Birth of a Nation* had the accompaniment of live music, anything from a 70-piece symphony orchestra to a single piano playing a musical score written for the film.

> The new possibilities of the movie camera (especially in the early days before sound) tempted movie makers to exploit the peculiar capacity of the movie screen to depict what could not have been physically represented on the stage. The first great box-office success...was D.W. Griffith's *Birth of a Nation*, which attracted millions by its expansive battle scenes, its torrential action, and its close-ups of the faces of leering villains and of dead soldiers. This was the first movie ever shown in the White House. After seeing it, President Wilson is said to have remarked, "It is like writing history with lightning."[37]

The Birth of a Nation was also a racially biased movie, portraying blacks in cartoonish ways as vicious and inferior, while holding up as noble the white-sheeted Ku Klux Klan. It created considerable public anger, including protest marches and complaints by prominent citizens, but this only increased its popularity at the box office. It was probably the first "must see" film. As for black movie patrons, their feelings were of little concern because they were not welcome in movie theaters. They were, in the South, either barred outright or directed to balconies reserved for them, and in the

Figure 4.17
The Birth of a Nation electrified audiences because of its techniques, but also caused riots because of its bigotry. (Courtesy State Historical Society of Wisconsin.)

North unceremoniously escorted by ushers to seats in the balcony or near the side walls.[38]

Motion Pictures in Other Countries

Sooner or later every large nation in the world and many small nations fashioned their own cinema. Along with a national airline, the possession of a film industry became a point of national pride.

While American motion picture production was shifting to Hollywood and surrounding communities in Southern California, other nations constructed their own film industries. Germany and Denmark each claim the first motion picture studio. World War I gave a boost to Hollywood because almost all the European studios shut down. Among the wartime shortages was cellulose, the film base, also used to make explosives. Lacking their own, Europeans began to import American films. After the war, their national production resumed.

France, the early leader, fell behind in building a strong postwar film industry, but led experiments into unusual forms of expression, notably the avant-garde movement in film as well as in poetry, painting, and music. Avant-garde art looked at the world in new, symbolic ways. Expressions

of art that had a shock value were prized, "decadent" or not. After World War II, a new tradition swept a revived French motion picture industry. Called *New Wave*, it rebelled against accepted morality and normal codes of behavior. With it grew the *auteur* tradition, which saw movies as the product of a single mind, that of the director, rather than as a collaboration of the talents of writers, actors, and dozens of others.

In Russia after the Bolshevik revolution of 1917, a Soviet film industry and the world's first film school fostered Marxist ideology. Recognizing the political power of mass communication, Lenin said, "The cinema for us is the most important of the arts." To build support, so-called *agitprop* trains fanned out across the countryside carrying propaganda lauding communist ideals. The film industry was led by such brilliant directors as Sergei Eisenstein whose theory of montage—the relationship of one scene to another—has influenced many film makers. His *Battleship Potemkin* has been called the most important film ever made because it showed the broad possibilities of film editing based on rhythm and the connecting of visual images. Meanwhile, radio sent the communist message across the vast reaches of the new Soviet Union. In rural areas where few radios existed, loudspeakers went up on poles in village squares.

In Germany, a sturdy film industry grew in the fifteen years following World War I, with films that were more psychological than the lightweight American product. They explored darker visions of the soul, reflecting the despair of a once proud nation bitter and defeated, when a barrelful of money bought one loaf of bread. It was said that the low point of the nation was the high point of its silent film. Here the techniques of the moving camera expanded. When the Nazis took power, some of Germany's greatest directors, actors, and technicians escaped to Hollywood. The Nazi takeover transformed German cinema into a propaganda arm of the state. After World War II, a revived German film industry emphasized strong and unusual dramatic themes.

In Britain, a social documentary tradition grew during the Depression and World War II that identified a host of problems confronting their society and suggested governmental solutions. The British were also able to enjoy a good laugh at themselves. A string of postwar British films like *Passport to Pimlico* and *Tight Little Island* tapped a vein of gentle self-mocking humor. They drew appreciative audiences in the United States and the British Commonwealth. The *Monty Python* brand of humor evolved from earlier examples of dry British wit.

Italy after World War II originated a school of *neorealism*, the exact opposite of Hollywood glitter. Films like *Open City*, *Shoeshine*, and *The Bicycle Thief* had the gritty look of documentary as they chronicled the bleak lives of poor people in distress.

Japan's film industry sparkled because of its directors. Akira Kurosawa is the director best known to Western audiences. His *Rashomon* (1950), a costumed drama set in Japan's long feudal era, is a classic that someone will mention in ordinary conversation to make the point that people who go through the same experience may have different memories of it. In the *Rashomon* story, a husband, a wife, and the bandit who

attacks them in the woods later recall what happened. Each version flatters the speaker at the expense of the other two. A woodcutter who happened to be in the forest relates a more objective, presumably accurate tale of the event, which makes all three participants look bad. Critics list *Rashomon* among the great films of all time.

India and China have also developed notable film industries. India produces more films than Hollywood. From China in recent years have come award-winning films that combine epic action with considerable emotional sensitivity.

The Coming of Sound

Silent movie theaters were anything but silent. The audience kept up a cheerful racket. Slides carried the message, "Please Do Not Stamp. The Floor May Cave In." Some movie palaces boasted orchestras, organs, or sound effects machines like the Noiseograph, the Dramagraph, and the Soundograph, whose keyboards sent out glass crashing and horses galloping. Professional actors interpreted the dialogue behind the screen:

> The systematic use of…live performers during motion picture presentations began at least as early as 1897…and during the first decade of the century a number of professional actors companies were founded to provide such services to theaters on a regular basis….In fact, then, the "silent film" is a myth. It never existed. Furthermore, the term was rarely used prior to 1926—only afterwards.[39]

The only real interest in sound films materialized from Warner Bros., when it was nearly bankrupt and desperate. although Harry M. Warner reportedly asked, "Who the hell wants to hear actors talk?" As it turned out, the public did. Using Vitaphone, a system that synchronized phonograph disc recordings with a film projector, Warners in 1926 presented some sound shorts and a silent film, *Don Juan*, to which the studio added a music score, plus the clash of swords for a duel, but made no effort to lip-sync words. A year later, Warner Bros. tried again with a silent fea-

Figure 4.18   The Vitaphone camera that photographed *The Jazz Singer*, 1927, was encased in a soundproof booth without air conditioning.

ture film that had music accompaniment and four singing or talking sequences. *The Jazz Singer* starred Al Jolson, who belted out "Mammy" and, in the second reel, uttered those prophetic words, "Wait a minute! Wait a minute, I tell ya! You ain't heard nothin' yet."

Hollywood executives wanted to leave well enough alone and stay with silent film.

> (Most producers) were annoyed with Warner for rocking the industrial boat. Box office was down slightly and competition from the new sound entertainment of radio seemed one possible cause, but it was by no means certain that the addition of recorded sound to movies would bring larger audiences into the theaters.[40]

Actually, ticket sales rose sharply and soon *talkies* were pouring out of the Hollywood studios. In 1929, *Broadway Melody* won the Academy Award for best picture.

Most studios and stars, notably Chaplin, preferred the silent screen with the dialogue printed on cards that appeared after the words were spoken, but the public again, by their ticket purchases, forced the switch to sound. In so doing, the public determined the direction that films would take. Lines at the box offices swept aside the argument that sound was for lowbrows

while the more sensitive, intelligent audiences wanted silent films. Hollywood executives should have known better because talkies followed right behind broadcasting, which was spreading as fast as people could afford to buy radio sets.

The Coming of Color

At first, a few films were hand painted, frame by frame, clearly an impractical solution. In another process, scenes were tinted; segments of black-and-white film were simply dipped into dye so scenes showing a lot of sky might be blue, scenes of a burning building might be tinted red. An improved method chemically toned the darker areas and shadows, leaving the highlighted areas clear. These attempts strove to heighten the mood of the film rather than to add realism.

The first patent for a color process was issued in 1897, shortly after movies began. Several optical color processes used colored filters or dyes, with less than spectacular quality. Only Technicolor, invented by Herbert Kalmus, was successful, emerging in 1922 as a two-tone process, but changing over the years to a much better three-tone process. The complicated method involved not only printing images on special film with layers of emulsion, but shooting with special camera lenses that split the light beam, sending the split images through different colored filters. Technicolor gradually took over Hollywood films, although most of its establishment did not seem to care about it one way or the other.

> The improvement in the Technicolor system was unquestionably the most important technical advance of the decade (of the 1930s), but was regarded with almost total indifference by most people in the industry.[41]

The public did care and, as usual, prevailed. Long lines for *Gone With the Wind* in 1939 should have convinced any doubters that the public loved romantic stories in lush Technicolor.

During the 1980s, when old black-and-white films were colorized for television,

Figure 4.19
Crowds greeting the opening of *The Jazz Singer* convinced the film industry that sound was here to stay. (Courtesy State Historical Society of Wisconsin.)

the establishment did come out firmly, this time against color, arguing that computer-generated colors ruined the directors' original visions. Once again, the public seemed to prefer color. Once again, the public prevailed. To colorize a black-and-white film, technicians using computer graphics software choose a color for each *field* in a *frame*. For example, the technician might assign light blue for a woman's dress or a man's shirt, neither knowing or worrying about what the original colors really were.

The Stars and Their Films

The first movie fan magazine, *Photoplay*, appeared in 1910. When *Motion Picture Story* a year later asked readers to choose their favorite film stories, many of them responded with questions about their favorite actors and actresses.

The star system was one of several ways in which the public determined the direction that movies would take. The love affair between movie fans and the objects of their adoration on the silver screen deepened with the passing decades as the movie studios and actors themselves turned out to be expert at churning out publicity. The star system reached its zenith when the big studios themselves reached their peaks in the 1930s, '40s, and '50s. Decade after decade the top actors and actresses became household names: John Barrymore, Greta

Garbo, Jeanette MacDonald, James Cagney, Gary Cooper, Katherine Hepburn, Cary Grant, John Wayne, Bob Hope, Bing Crosby, Humphrey Bogart, Ingrid Bergman, Danny Kaye, Judy Garland, Fred Astaire, Marilyn Monroe, Errol Flynn, Bette Davis, Paul Newman, Elizabeth Taylor, Frank Sinatra, Sophia Loren, Henry Fonda, Audrey Hepburn, Marlon Brando, Goldie Hawn, Mel Gibson, Madonna, Clint Eastwood, Arnold Schwarzenegger, Sean Connery, Harrison Ford, and Julia Roberts. Their names alone on a theater marquee were guaranteed to sell tickets.

The musicals from the 1930s onward were Hollywood at its brightest. If audiences loved fantasies mixed with glitter, the "dream factories" were only too happy to turn them out on the production lines. Several studios produced musicals, but none with such success as MGM, which had a stable of gifted performers under contract. That the plots were usually absurd and always predictable only added to their charm. The audiences wanted to escape into a singing, dancing, Technicolor fantasy, and the studios gave them what they wanted.

If any type of Hollywood movie was even better known around the world than the musical, it was the western. Ever since *The Great Train Robbery* put movies firmly on the track of narrative fiction, Hollywood produced "horse operas" and created the myth of the lone cowboy doing what was right, no matter what the odds. Westerns could be turned out cheaply and quickly, with familiar plots, pedestrian dialogue, heroes in white hats, villains in black hats, and Indians who said little more than "How!" and were shot off their horses on cue, perpetuating the stereotype. Generations of little boys, dreaming of becoming cowboys, attacked the Indians.

As for historical epics, to put it simply, audiences loved them. Ticket buyers filled the theaters at premium prices for a big budget film with the biggest stars, the most lavish costumes, the grandest sets, and a cast of thousands.

Action adventures are just as much a staple today as they were in the silent days when immigrant populations could enjoy films without knowing the language. They require neither much thought nor language competence. Karate movies from Hong Kong play well to English-speaking audiences and Sylvester Stallone movies play well to Chinese-speaking audiences. It may be unfortunate that violence travels well, but it does.

Censorship

From the start of the fiction film, the forces of order saw the potential for disorder and moved to contain it. The history of the motion picture, not only in the United States but in most of the world, could be told in terms of the continuum from control through moderate freedom, then extensive freedom, to total abandonment of control, a condition arguably not yet reached.

Censorship of movies began in 1909 with the establishment in New York of the National Board of Censorship of Motion Pictures, created by members of the industry itself. In 1922, the industry set up what became known as the Hays Office, named for its first president, Will Hays, to protect audiences from the indecent and violent. A Production Code Administration enforced a code of acceptable on-screen behavior, but these guidelines were softened over the years as moviemakers challenged the limits. Fundamentalist Protestant and Catholic leaders, arguing that Hollywood's

self-censorship code was too weak and that Hays himself was nothing more than an employee of the industry, led an attack that went on for decades.

The focus on sex and violence was soon expanded to include political views. Barred were disputes between labor and management, government or police corruption, and injustice. Motion pictures were considered an improper vehicle for political controversy. Films that failed to meet strict standards were blacklisted and boycotted. A number of states and cities set up censorship boards to examine movies, but the standards varied from one board to another. The Kansas board, for example, banned scenes of smoking or drinking and limited kissing scenes to a few seconds.

A series of United States Supreme Court decisions from the 1950s to the 1970s on the constitutionality of state laws about obscenity gave moviemakers more leeway. The import of foreign films and the rise of television also influenced an ending to censorship restrictions. Still pressured from all sides, the motion picture industry decided that instead of a single standard for what should be seen and heard in the films, there should be audience controls based on age. In 1968, modeled on a system used in Britain, a self-censorship code was adopted that we know today by the G, PG, R, and X designations.

Political Issues

During the Depression, when economic misery stalked the land, the public expressed its preference for light comedy and adventure films that gave them escape from their dreary lives. For the most part, audiences stayed away from sad and serious films, so the Hollywood motion picture industry turned out few of them. The quarter that paid for an average cinema admission could have bought a pound of beef, a gallon and a half of gasoline, or enough postage stamps to mail eight letters with a penny left over for a postcard. By 1939 an average of 85 million movie tickets were sold each week.

During World War II, Hollywood aided the war effort with patriotic films. After the war, a few producers summoned up their courage and, for the first time, the Hollywood film industry tackled social issues like racism and anti-Semitism with such films as *Home of the Brave* (1949), *Pinky* (1949), and *Gentleman's Agreement* (1947). *The Lost Weekend* (1945) dealt with alcoholism, *Brute Force* (1947) with prison brutality, and *The Snake Pit* (1948) with horrid conditions in insane asylums.

However, the Cold War that closely followed World War II brought with it a "Red Scare." Deep political divisions emerged in Hollywood. Actors, writers, and directors suspected of Communist leanings were blacklisted and denied work. Following hearings by the House Un-American Activities Committee, a few went to jail. Frightened studios put a temporary end to films that advocated social change. Escapism was more popular and less trouble.

It took years, but eventually this pain went away, though its scars persist to this day. Social problems reappeared in movies, which were gradually becoming more frank than ever. At one time, such themes as hostile race relations, homosexuality, police brutality, and political corruption lay beyond the pale. No longer. Spike Lee won critical applause and lines at the box office with motion pictures like *Do the Right Thing* (1988), which examine, with no holds barred, black-white race relations. Today, nothing lies beyond the boundaries of what moviemakers will examine. Movies compete nationally and internationally for the audience's dollars, marks, and yen with explicit sex and considerable violence. The audience obviously is willing to pay to see all this and more, and the audience, as usual, gets what it is willing to pay for.

The Drive-In

Downtown movie palaces and neighborhood theaters shut down as television reached across the land in the postwar generation and middle class people in cities migrated outward to the suburbs, but one kind of movie theater thrived. In an era of suburban outdoor living, of gardening, boating, and barbecuing, the drive-in theater was a natural. The movie stars competed with the stars in the sky. By 1958, nearly one theater in every three was a drive-in, even though they had to close for half the year in the northern states. More families had automobiles, gas was cheap, and so was an evening at the drive-in, with free admission for kids, and no problem with bringing your own sandwiches, even the whole dinner. You could talk. Instead of sharing a theater with strangers, you had a family outing or an evening with friends, not unlike an evening with the television of the period, except that the movies were better, or scarier, the screen was bigger, plenty of acting or spectacle or singing and dancing filled the screen, the image was certainly a lot clearer than on a round, gray television tube, and the commercials, if any, appeared between the movies.

You didn't have to dress up or pay for parking or a baby sitter, no small consideration in the baby-boom postwar years, the same considerations that lead people to stay at home now to watch a rented videotape. The drive-in's snack bar did a brisk business. Some drive-ins provided playgrounds, laundromats, and even picnic spots and miniature golf courses. All provided a hangout for teens away from their parents. It was also the favored "make out" place.

The double feature was usual, the triple feature not unknown. No "B" picture was so bad that it could not be found at some drive-in. Rising real estate values along with better choices on television eventually shut down the "ozoner." Teenagers found their escape from the family at the new shopping center multiplex. The rest of the family would do their eating, talking, and baby minding in front of the VCR.

Enter Television

Studio executives in the 1940s and '50s at first tried to ignore television as just a fad, denying the new medium access to its actors, directors, scripts, studios, and film libraries. Little by little, television chipped away at each of these barriers. None stand today. With their heavy overhead and expensive talent on contract, the big studios were losing millions of dollars. To protect themselves, they cut their staffs, ended

Figure 4.20
The postwar popularity of drive-in theaters foreshadowed the growth of videotape rentals. They shared many of the same advantages. (Courtesy National Archives.)

contracts with their stars and other high priced talent, and began renting out their studio facilities to television production companies. This weakness allowed independent producers to step in, make smaller films, take artistic chances with new approaches to subject matter, and distribute their films to theaters that were no longer in the tight grip of the major studios. Some of the films tested the limits that censors would allow. A fresh breeze was blowing through studios whose practices had become stiff and stale.

Despite fears about the new medium, television certainly has not killed the motion picture, nor has it killed the motion picture theater although there have been changes. Gone are most of the ornate downtown picture palaces, the mom-and-pop single neighborhood theaters, and the suburban drive-ins, replaced by the more efficient, unadorned multi-room cinema complexes in shopping malls, where they share parking spaces with supermarkets and clothing shops. Here and there the landscape is being dotted by mega-multiplexes with 15 to 20 screens and a lobby reminiscent of the old movie palaces in an effort to make going to the movies a more enjoyable experience than simply watching a movie. Some of these mega-multiplexes offer IMAX screens six stories high and some even provide love seats that may blur the distinction between home and public recreation.

Marshall McLuhan once observed that each new medium uses as its content the medium it displaces. With the arrival of television, moviegoers stayed home to watch their favorites on their television screens instead of going out to the neighborhood theater, but the content of much of television and almost all of rented videotape is movies. To put it accurately, only the delivery media have changed. Taste is less receptive to change.

The Distribution Schedule

It is a mistake to think of motion pictures as an industry that begins with production and ends with distribution to motion picture theaters. Considered that way, the old medium certainly suffered with the advance of the new medium, television, just as the television industry suffered with the popularity of the even newer medium, videotape. Seen purely from the production standpoint, however, the motion picture medium has expanded. Around the world, more motion pictures are being made, both on film and on videotape, than ever before, and they are being distributed through an increasing number of outlets to an increasing number of viewers.

We "go to the movies" in different ways, using new hardware for the Hollywood software we love to watch. Nowadays we may travel no further than our comfortable living room sofa, fortifying ourselves with a bowlful of freshly microwaved popcorn before we tune in or pop in a promising flick.

In the *software* distribution pattern of the 1990s, a feature motion picture usually starts its life in first-run mall theaters. From there the more popular films go to cheaper second-run discount theaters. A few months after their introduction, while the public still remembers the newspaper ads and reviews, films reach the videotape stores for sales and rental, and cable pay-per-view. After that come HBO, Cinemax, and other premium cable channels. Next, network television. Several years after they are first issued, the films are syndicated to local television stations and free cable channel *superstations*. Along the way there is an extensive network of foreign distribution and such specialty outlets as airlines.

Four new technologies may further change motion picture delivery. *Direct broadcast satellites*, or *DBS*, beam films and other television programming directly into homes from a single source, eliminating the need for either local television stations or local cable companies. Second, *high definition television*, or *HDTV*, displays pictures and sound of a quality available only in first-run movie theaters. Third, *fiber optics* may bring cable-to-home transmission of videotapes from a library of tapes as large as the stock of a video store. That would eliminate the present fetch-and-return rental system. Fourth, movie-length *compact disks* may supplant videotape with digital quality pictures and sound. All four technologies are at present either on the way or already here.

Making Movies Cheaply

Home movies have been around at least since 1923, when the Cine-Kodak film camera and the Kodascope projector went on sale. This, too, forms part of the story of motion pictures. Today, in homes far from Hollywood, more *movies* are being made than ever before as a result of the availability of the easy-to-use, moderately priced video camcorder, a combined television camera and tape recorder, introduced in 1984. Millions are sold each year. Proud mothers take home videos of their two-year-old son's birthday party, and fathers videotape their daughter's wedding with enough pans and zooms to make a sailor seasick. Then they present (or inflict) the results to guests as after-dinner entertainment.

The technology that supported motion picture production during the decades of the golden age of Hollywood required enormous sums of money. Although that helped to concentrate, in just a few hands, the ability to make films (and still does in the rarefied world of high budget film making), more recent technology is pushing in the opposite direction—outward to many hands. Production and distribution of motion pictures both on film and, now, on videotape is broader than ever.

While big budget movies are still being turned out, so are movies of quite good quality that are shot on a shoestring. Computer-based technology is bringing within reach of the average income the editing processes of *desktop video* with special effects, such as morphing, that only recently were limited to machines costing hundreds of thousands of dollars. Production facilities to shoot and edit video motion pictures are going into schools, offices, and businesses that once would not have considered doing such a thing as making a movie.[42]

It is possible to find someone who has never read a book or a magazine or a newspaper. It would be much harder to find someone who has never seen a film. All generations have stayed home to watch movies instead of visiting relatives and friends or going to dances, sports events, club meetings, or bowling alleys, activities that television to some extent displaces. Most movie theater tickets today are sold to young people going on dates or spending an evening out with friends, glad for the chance to leave the house where the older generation is settling in to watch their movies on television screens. As happened so many times, new mass communication technologies have had a significant impact on the lives of ordinary people.

Notes

1   David Nasaw, *Going Out: The Rise and Fall of Public Amusements* (New York: Basic Books, 1993), 8-9.

2   Lloyd Morris, *Not So Long Ago* (New York: Random House, 1949), 29.

3   Speech to the German Sociological Association, 1910, in Hanno Hardt, *Social Theories of the Press: Early German and American Perspectives* (Beverly Hills: Sage Publications, 1979).

4   Edwin Emery and Michael Emery, *The Press and America: An Interpretative History of the Mass Media*, fifth ed. (Englewood Cliffs: Prentice-Hall, 1984), 259.

5   *Worcester Magazine*, III, 181 (first week, July 1787).

6   Carl Bode, "Popular Magazines," in Norman Cantor and Michael Werthman, *The History of Popular Culture* (New York: Macmillan, 1968), 485.

7   Marshall McLuhan, *Understanding Media: The Extensions of Man* (New York: McGraw-Hill Book Co., 1964), 283.

8   Harry M. Geldud, *The Birth of the Talkies: From Edison to Jolson* (Bloomington: Indiana University Press, 1975), 5.

9   Dyer, Frank and Thomas Martin, *Edison, His Life and Inventions* (New York: Harper & Bros., 1929), 206-07.

10 Daniel Marty, *An Illustrated History of Phonographs* (New York: Dorset Press, 1981), 18.

11 George P. Oslin, *The Story of Telecommunications* (Macon, GA: Mercer University Press, 1992), 227.

12 Marty, 55.

13 Geldud, 13.

14 Marty, 71.

15 Marty, 22.

16 B.L. Aldridge, *The Victor Talking Machine Company* (Camden, NJ: RCA Sales Corp., 1964), 118.

17 Carolyn Marvin, *When Old Technologies Were New* (New York: Oxford University Press, 1988), 203.

18 Victor "Red Seal" records and performances by Enrico Caruso and other European opera stars gave American record buyers a taste of European culture that was generally unavailable except to the wealthy.

19 Gary Gumpert, *Talking Tombstones and Other Tales of the Media Age* (New York: Oxford University Press, 1987), 91.

20 Richard Hollander, *Video Democracy* (Mt. Airy, MD: Lomond Publications, 1985), 132.

21 J.M. Fenster, "How Bing Crosby Brought You Audiotape," *Invention and Technology* (Fall 1994): 58.

22 Rebecca Ann Lind, "You Can Take It With You: Uses and Gratifications of the Personal Stereo." Unpublished M.A. thesis, University of Minnesota, 1989: 1.

23 Susan J. Douglas, *Inventing American Broadcasting, 1899-1922* (Baltimore: The Johns Hopkins University Press, 1987), 308.

24 Orange E. McMeans, "The Great Audience Invincible," *Scribner's Magazine*, April 1923, 411.

25 Ithiel de Sola Pool, *Technologies of Freedom* (Cambridge: Harvard University Press, 1983), 122.

26 Erik Barnouw, *The Sponsor* (New York: Oxford University Press, 1978), 16.

27 R. Beniger, *The Control Revolution* (Cambridge: Harvard University Press, 1986), 367.

28 Oslin, 283.

29 Arthur Goldsmith, "Reinventing the Image," *Popular Photography*, 97:3 (March 1990): 49.

30 Miriam Hansen, *Babel and Babylon: Spectatorship in American Silent Film* (Cambridge: Harvard University Press, 1991), 117.

31 Barton Currie, "The Nickel Madness," *Harper's Weekly*, 24 August 1907, 1247.

32 Nasaw, 167.

33 Morris, 34-35.

34 Simon Patten, *Product and Climax* (New York: B.W. Huebsch, 1909), 18-19.

35 Nasaw, 186.

36 Leo Rosten, *Hollywood, the Movie Colony and the Movie Makers.* (Harcourt Brace & Co., 1941), 7-12.

37 Daniel J. Boorstin, *The Image, or What Happened to the American Dream* (New York: Atheneum, 1961), 127-128.

38 Nasaw, 236-37.

39 Raymond Fielding, "The Technological Antecedents of the Coming of Sound: An Introduction," in E.W. Cameron (ed), *Sound and the Cinema* (New York: Redgrave Publishing Co., 1980), 5.

40 Ellis, Jack C., *A History of Film*, 2nd ed. (Englewood Cliffs: Prentice-Hall, 1985), 152.

41 David Shipman, *The Story of Cinema* (Englewood Cliffs: Prentice-Hall, 1982), 389.

42 See, for example, David Biedny, "Movie Magic," *MacUser*, August 1993, 92ff.

5

The Fifth Revolution

The Toolshed Home

The Communication Toolshed

Electricity had hardly emerged from the laboratories when the realization dawned that here was a way to move information without locomotion. At first, what was transmitted were dots and dashes that combined into words, and they did not flow directly into our homes. The next step, the telephone, brought even better communication without transportation—the communication of sound—yet this audible communication was generally limited to information, not the complete range of desirable communication, which must include entertainment. Entertainment by sound first arrived at the home the way printed matter carrying information did, in physical form. It was the phonograph record. Roughly about the same time, as both information and entertainment, the published photograph arrived. They joined printing in the form of the book, the magazine, the newspaper, and home delivery mail in the steady process of making the home a communication toolshed.

Next, although it was a tremendous advance in so many other ways, the motion picture took a small step back in requiring people to leave their homes for the infor-

mation and, especially, for the entertainment. Radio, which had its "golden age" at the same time as the movies, came directly into our homes. The age was anything but golden for most people, for it brought the Depression and World War II. Until the United States tooled up for war, the nation had mass unemployment, bread lines, soup kitchens, padlocked factories and stores, and families evicted from their homes, their furniture carried out to the street. For people with little money, radio programs were a godsend, free entertainment. The years with radio, followed after 1948 by commercial television, saw homes increasingly functioning like places where people used communication more than they did anything else.

What Makes a House a Home?

The uncomplaining companions who could wake us up and put us to sleep, radio and television, followed us from room to room, kept us company no matter what else we did, and were there for us when we were too tired to think. Radio even stayed

138

with us when we went outside for a drive, a walk, or a jog. Cable TV pumped its many selections into the home as it was inexorably changed into a communication toolshed, the place that functions for storing and using tools of communication more than for any other purpose.

The computer and the modem that reached the Internet, the communications satellite dish, E-mail, facsimile, and the humble answering machine all contributed to furnishing the toolshed with the appurtenances to make dwelling there a more attractive proposition than the unconnected home. Newspapers were tossed on the doorstep, magazines were stuffed in the mailbox along with catalogs, and books sat on shelves. If a home lacked even a few of these tools or if the tools were out of date, its occupants, pitied by friends, planned to catch up. The tools of communication, not "a heap o' livin'"[1] were what really made a house a home in the second half of the twentieth century.

Two or three generations ago, new homes were built with front porches, a natural place to sit and swing, to sip iced tea, to chat, and to greet the neighbors. Times changed. One generation ago the *conversation pit* was advertised as an arrangement of living room furniture to form a nook for a desirable activity, conversation. Times again changed. Here is a more recent newspaper ad for furniture, under the heading "State-of-the-art surroundings for your state-of-the-art home theater":

> Audio and video technology let you capture the superb sound and picture quality of a real theater performance at home. Our Berkline reclining chairs, sofas and loveseats are light years ahead of real theater seats. They're spacious, soft and can put you in exactly the most comfortable reclining position. (Yet they're quick to adjust when the movie has you on the edge of your seat.) Built-in drawers hold video tapes, books or magazines and a pull-down table and drink holder holds your popcorn and pop. And Berkline's Touchmotion Wallaway mechanism permits smooth, effortless reclining at the touch of a button while furniture can stand just 3 inches from the wall. [2]

No reference to conversation can be found in the ad, only communion with various media. Television had become the true reality, the desired reality. Who has not telephoned or visited a friend, even after a long separation, to find the television set on and no desire by the host to turn it off? The visitor feels like an intruder who has interrupted what really matters. What television station or network has not been besieged by furious telephone calls when a news bulletin interrupts a soap opera?

Here is another ad, this one from Radio Shack:

> Jim just had to have a new stereo system... Dolby Pro Logic® Surround Sound, Great Speakers... the whole nine yards. So I made him a deal. If he gets his new stereo, then I get my new 486 PC with Windows, a CD-ROM, great software...The whole nine yards![3]

Contacts Decrease

The average American family spends more and more time and money on home entertainment.[4] As we weave our communication cocoon around us, physical contact with others decreases, replaced by a more sedentary way of life. News stories about multiple cable channels resonate with anticipation, for Oz lies at the end of the 500-channel yellow brick road. We consumers look forward to ever more wonderful means of technology to bring content into our homes that will pleasure our senses. We can be entertained without being entertaining.

The proportion of Americans who say they socialize with neighbors more than once a year has declined. Memberships in organizations fell sharply after television entered the home, and so did participation in civic associations and volunteer work. The number of bowlers increased by 10%, but membership in bowling leagues dropped 40% between 1980 and 1993.[5]

When friends invite friends over to watch television, the communion is with the screen. The whisper heard up and down every street when someone breaks the silence is, "Ssh! I'm listening (watching, reading)." The result is a growing isolation from close, attentive interaction with other people. In extreme examples, it is not difficult to ascertain a spreading social impairment.

> The technologies now available for the home give us many more options in choosing our lifestyles, but each exacts a price. There is a monetary price for hardware, software, and electricity, and there is also a sacrifice of interpersonal contact. Think, for a moment, of the number of communication technologies you may have in your home that eliminate the need for face-to-face interaction, or perhaps any contact with other people. Telephone answering machines, electronic security devices, home shopping services, and computerized electronic mail are only a few of today's possible alternatives to engaging in interpersonal communication.[6]

If the enticements of life can be found within the home, there seems little reason to seek diversion outside, including visiting friends or family members so often. There seems less reason to take time even for idle thought when diversions come so nicely packaged. All we need each evening are the tools of communication, electronic or printed. In the communication toolshed home, we ponder the vital question, "What's on tonight?"

> In earlier times, to see a performance was to become part of a visible audience. At a concert, in a church, at a ball game or a political rally, the audience was half the fun. What and whom you saw in the audience was at least as interesting as and often humanly more important than what you saw on the stage.[7]

Extending the Toolshed Home

Personal media extend the toolshed home beyond the outer walls. The difference between a living room stereo system and a Walkman has less to do with the difference between sitting and jogging than with bringing the toolshed to the great outdoors. Great-grandma's pride, the handsome veneered Victrola in the parlor, in great-granddaughter's version, shrinks to a couple of ounces of plastic wrapped over

the ears plus a few ounces more fixed to a belt. The same thing happened to the incredible shrinking radio, no longer Grandpa's 12-tube Philco permanently rooted in the parlor, and to the roaming cellphone, which first went from the home to the car and now accompanies the person, guaranteeing that someone is "at home." Like using other personal media, talking over the phone means that the wearer is less tuned to the immediate environment.

> …The same logic applies to the replacement of vaudeville by the movies and now of movies by the VCR. The new "virtual reality" helmets that we will soon don to be entertained in total isolation are merely the latest extension of this trend.[8]

The French architect Le Corbusier described the modern home as a "machine for living." Everything that plugs into or sticks out of the wall forms part of the machine, but we must distinguish between the non-communication devices and those that bring us communication. The former, such as clothes washers, bread toasters, and hot water pipes, keep us more comfortable and presumably make us happier inside the machine home. The communication devices carry us mentally outside the machine. It is a distinction with a difference.

In place of human intimacy, emotional bonds have grown with the fantasy worlds of the media. Fictional characters on soap operas receive gifts upon the "birth" of a baby. Disturbed fans stalk actresses, sometimes with dreadful consequences. Violence on the screen is permission for imitative violence in the street. Screen sex suffuses thought. The phenomenon is not totally new. The death of a Dickens character during the weekly serialization of his novels evoked floods of tears during the nineteenth century, but the reaction has reached unprecedented levels in the television age.

At its most functional, the toolshed home can be dysfunctional indeed. Jerzy Kosinski offered an interesting flight of fancy in his character Chance the Gardener, the protagonist of Being There,[9] who has known few people in a blank lifetime, but manages well enough by constructing a fictional social reality from endless hours of television. Chance gets along day by day, but he does not understand. He has been socialized not by human contact, but by television.[10] He is an exaggeration, but perhaps not by much. It used to be said of some people that they "lived through books." It can certainly be said of others today that they "live through television." Life, more than occasionally, imitates art.

> Each of us likes to think of himself as being rational and autonomous. Our ideas seem to be peculiarly our own. It is hard for us to realize how little of our information comes from direct experience with the physical environment, and how much of it comes, only indirectly, from other people and the mass media. Our complex communication systems enable us to overcome the time and space limitations that confined our ancestors, but they leave us with a greater dependence on others for shaping our ideas about how things are in the world. While becoming aware of places and events far from the direct experience of our daily lives, we have given up much of our capacity to confirm what we think we know.[11]

Problems with Heavy Media Usage

"What did you watch?" is a frequently asked question. "How much of your day was spent watching?" is not asked. In the pre-television days, time spent watching moving images on a screen was typically confined for children to Saturday mornings and for their parents to one evening a week at the movies. When a suggestion is offered to limit viewing, a predictable response is, "I didn't buy my TV set to turn it off." For parents concerned about overuse of computer games, a program called "Time Out" can be set to control the daily hours a child—identified by a password—is allowed to spend at the screen. A programmable timer called "TV allowance" limits television watching. "No" means "No," at least when the electronic device says so.

Heavy use of media leads to conditions we often associate with unhappiness, such as a lack of emotional and physical contact with others, an increased amount of solitary behavior, reduced physical activity, overeating, an indulgence in snack foods, and dependence upon non-human stimuli. In a word, alienation.

Youthful dependence upon television, Nintendo-type computer games, and recorded music delivered either through radio or CD has become a national scandal. Children ages 4 to 6 were asked in a survey, "Which do you like better, TV or your daddy?" "TV," said 54%.[12]

And from a study of television viewing:

> One subject was reading a book as the TV came on. As soon as she looked up, her brain waves slowed significantly. Within thirty seconds, she was in a predominantly alpha state—relaxed, passive, unfocused.[13]

More on the alpha state trance:

> Grazing is the well-known activity of sitting in front of the TV in an alpha trance, eyes wide open, with information, good or bad, flowing in. The networks used to point with pride to the fact that viewers who tuned in at 7 P.M. were most likely to watch the entire evening without bothering to change the channel.[14]

The convergence of the tools of mass communication in the home—the toolshed home—and in the toolshed office seems to accelerate each passing year with a rapidity that shows no sign of diminishing. Like the universe itself, the ever expanding information industry continues to create new forms as it widens, inventing new information and entertainment products, for which the public's appetite appears insatiable. Where once a conversation pit was pointed out with pride to visitors, homes boast multi-media centers chock-full of communication gear: computer, television, radio, telephone, fax, answering machine, videocassette recorder, and more. As active members of the Information Age, we like being tuned in to media.

We will not, of course, give up our modern tools of communication. The television set will stay where it is. When, in one of those publicized surrenders of television watching for a few weeks, people were asked what it felt like to live day after day without TV, one honest participant bleakly concluded that it was like "a death in the family."[15] He said this in a television documentary. It is worth noting that Don Quixote went mad reading books. We learned this, of course, in reading a book.

The world's fifth information revolution takes place in the communication tool-sheds we call home.

Home Mail Delivery

We ought to think of the postal service the way we think of radio or television. Each is an organic combination of machines and human beings that brings information and entertainment to our homes. To function, each has required international agreements, national standards, and some level of government supervision. Each depends on communication technologies, the least obvious being the postal service's dependence on paper.

Above all, each has had an impact on humankind beyond calculation. If the world had never known any one of these methods of communication, our daily lives would be much different and, arguably, inferior. Differences exist, to be sure, such as the personal, point-to-point communication that only the postal service now provides, and the physical reality of the machine in the living room, which only radio and television provide, or the beginnings of postal service in the dawn of history compared to this century's broadcast industry.

If the postal service is government run, why so is broadcasting in most countries. If most of radio and television in the United States is commercial and competitive, why so are Federal Express and United Parcel Service. The biggest stretch of imagination may be in thinking of the friendly uniformed letter carrier with a sack on the shoulder and mail in hand in terms of a *device*, but obviously the carrier is only the most visible tip of a huge international communications aggregation.

An even closer analogy than broadcasting can be drawn between the postal service and the telephone, the telegraph, or the communication satellite. Today, with telephones, radio, television, and automobiles available in every corner of the United States, it may be difficult to imagine how isolated farmers and rural residents were a century ago. Almost their only links to the outside world trickled in from letters and newspapers that arrived in the mail.

Free Home Delivery

Before the American Civil War, city residents walked to the nearest post office to pick up or mail letters and parcels. In 1863, the assistant postmaster in Cleveland, Joseph Briggs, conceived the idea of free home delivery because he "was appalled at the sight of anxious wives, children, and relatives waiting in long lines at the local post office for letters from soldiers off fighting the Civil War."[16] An immediate success, the service quickly spread through cities of the North. By 1890, 454 American cities and towns had free home delivery. Also in the postman's bag were newspapers and magazines, thanks to the 1879 Postal Act, which lowered their mailing costs. From 1885 until World War I, this second class matter was carried for one penny a pound.

Free rural delivery began in 1896. For farmers, the nearest post office might have been a day's travel away. Consequently, mail pickup was delayed for days or weeks until it could be part of a journey to town for groceries and hardware. The post office itself was likely to be located in the general store.

> When a weekly trip to the village post office was the farmer's only way of receiving mail, it was pointless for him to subscribe to a daily newspaper and periodically receive an armful of stale news. Then his needs were best served by the country weeklies.[17]

Figure 5.1
Rural mail boxes lined up beside a Minnesota road.

The Post Office eased this isolation with Rural Free Delivery (RFD) starting in 1896 as an experiment in West Virginia. The new service was so welcome that after a few months one farmer commented that it would take away part of his life to give it up. However, RFD did not come without the social cost of displacement that has accompanied so many tools of communication. The farmer could now communicate with the world, but at the price of reducing some of the old face-to-face contacts that were part of the trip to town to pick up the mail.

Rural Free Delivery added further impetus to expand the American network of roads and bridges. The horse-drawn postal wagon gave way to the automobile. The tunnel-shaped rural letter box with its red flag went up on fences and posts along every dirt road in place of lard buckets and soap boxes. Circulation of daily newspapers skyrocketed.

There were no Indians to fight along the rural routes and no Pony Express riders to race across the prairies. Mostly there were only muddy country roads and eager farmers, cranks, politicians, and fourth-class postmasters to provide what drama there was.

And yet the establishment of the farmers' free delivery service was not without its epic proportions. More money was spent, more men employed, and more paperwork done to lay out the rural delivery system than to establish any single extension of the postal service.[18]

Parcels, Catalogs, and Junk Mail

These efforts were followed by parcel post, started in 1913, a politically explosive issue that brought the federal government into competition with private express services. Parcel post was a huge boon to farm families in providing a variety of useful products and material comforts by mail order, but it did not achieve a promised goal of helping farmers to ship their produce to market, "farm-to-table" through the mails. Instead, coupled with catalogs, parcel post doomed the businesses of many country storekeepers. Once again, a new tool of communication displaced something worth keeping. Like Rural Free Delivery, parcel post was a form of mediated communication that exerted a centrifugal force that pulled people living in the country away from part of their local community. The general store, which once thrived, survives mostly as a part of American folklore.

A more enduring means of mass communication by post has been direct ("junk") mail, which enables advertisers and others with a message to reach the public in their homes at rates below the cost of ordinary first class mail. Mailings can be huge, for the fat catalogs mailed to millions of households by Montgomery Ward and by Sears and Roebuck were a principal means of shopping, thanks to Rural Free Delivery. The 540-page catalog mailed out by Montgomery Ward in 1887 listed 24,000 items for sale. Unhappy local merchants put pressure on their newspapers to fight the "Mail Order Trust" by refusing their newspaper ads.

> The triumph of mail order, and its new literature, brought visions of new ways of living which were a triumph of a larger over a smaller community. It was a victory of the market over the marketplace. And it spelled the defeat of the salesman by advertising. In a word, it was a defeat of the seen, the nearby, the familiar by the everywhere community.[19]

Figure 5.3   A modern Post Office optical character reader automatically identifies the numbers in a ZIP code.

Changes

With the passing years, the amount of mail per household grew and so did the number of households. Mail trains and even some buses were equipped as rolling post offices; clerks sorted as they traveled. But dependence on railroads to move mail steadily declined and dependence on airplanes increased. The first experimental mail flights

Figure 5.2   Air mail pick up and delivery in 1944. The mail container rests on the ground between two poles.

began in 1911, with permanent service in 1918. Charles Lindbergh, an airmail pilot who flew between Springfield, Illinois, and St. Louis, took time out in 1927 to fly solo across the Atlantic.

Mail was metered after 1920. ZIP (Zoning Improvement Plan) codes were introduced in 1963 and ZIP-plus-4 and bar codes in 1983, the year that federal government subsidies ended. In 1970, the Postal Reform Act made the U.S. Postal Service an independent establishment and the cabinet post of Postmaster General was abolished. The postal emblem changed from a post rider to the nation's symbol, the eagle. A variety of computerized machines, including automatic optical character address readers, replaced handling done by a postal employee standing in front of a sorting bin or a row of gray sacks. Coin-operated stamp vending machines and office metering machines became familiar sights. In 1988, a government brochure, "Understanding AIDS," was sent to 107 million addresses. In 1990, approximately the same number of census forms were mailed. By 1996, close to 600 million pieces of mail were handled daily.

Despite all the newer means of communication, nothing matched the sheer volume that traveled by mail.

New Uses for Phones

The telephone has become the hallmark of the modern world. In 1995, seven million American families had additional telephone lines installed in their homes for personal calls, business calls, fax transmissions in and out, e-mail in and out, and time spent on the Internet. A telecommunications analyst predicted that by the year 2000 half of the 97 million households in the United States would have two or more phone lines.[20]

By the early 1970s, computers and their terminals were swapping information over telephone cables. In subsequent decades transmissions of electronic mail, images on the World Wide Web, bit-mapped facsimile images, and reams of data from on-line databases vastly increased the traffic, but were manageable with such improvements as fiber optics and better memory chips.

Thousands of inventions have improved the telephone system, among them the co-axial cable, the means to transmit computer data, the introduction in 1963 of the Touch Tone, the conversion from analog to digital signals to improve clarity, microwave, satellite communication, and fiber optics. The Pacific Link fiber optic cable, laid in 1989, could carry 40,000 phone calls at a time. Integrated Services Digital Network (ISDN), a technology of the '90s, converted analog to digital signals for more efficient transmission of telephone calls, fax, computer, and video. In a variation from the highway metaphor, someone described the modern telephone system as an entire farm irrigation system, compared to the "garden hose" of a single telephone line.

Telephone Company Reorganizations

A utility so central to the functioning of a nation could not escape government attention. Whereas telephone systems in most nations are as controlled as highway systems, AT&T grew as a private enterprise regulated with a light touch. Its virtual national monopoly, established when it bought up smaller telephone companies, was shaken in 1968 by the FCC's Carterphone Decision, which for the first time allowed equipment not manufactured by AT&T's Western Electric subsidiary to tie into the telephone network. Two years later, the FCC's MCI Decision set up competition in the long distance market. An antitrust suit ended with the breakup in 1983 of AT&T into seven regional operating companies, plus AT&T as a long distance carrier now in competition with other carriers.

The consent decree that broke the Bell system into the national AT&T and regional *Baby Bells* was followed in 1991 by permission for these regional telephone companies to offer informational services

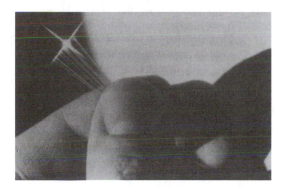

Figure 5.4   Fiber optic wires as thin as human hairs carry large amounts of data digitally in the form of light pulses.

Figure 5.5   Fiber optic lines in a telecommunications center.

over their own lines. MCI, GTE, and Sprint joined the mix of telephone companies competing to provide service. Because of their economic strength, telephone companies organized to transmit specialized news, sports, and stock market reports, electronic Yellow Pages, and a variety of information and services.

The Telecommunication Reform Act of 1996 led national telephone companies and the seven regional companies to compete for much of each other's businesses and to compete with cable companies for the delivery of information and entertainment into homes. The Baby Bells, with their experience and facilities, held joint venture and merger talks with such information providers as cable companies, movie studios, and newspaper chains. Copper telephone lines were being pulled up so fiber optic lines could be laid along trunk lines and into homes.

The telephone companies were shifting from a primary reliance on *POTS (Plain Old Telephone Service)*, once universally visible in the AT&T-supplied black telephone. For decades, the policy was that if you wanted telephone service you took what the telephone company offered, and you had better not try to fool around with or add anything to Bell equipment. The only permissible telephones were those that the company provided. According to one story told years ago, a housewife was refused permission to put a crocheted cover around her telephone directory.

Cellular Phones

After World War II, mobile telephone service began commercially. Phone calls made within a radius of 50 miles of an antenna could be placed through an operator; callers spoke by depressing a button on the handset, like a CB (citizen's band) radio.[21] In addition, people bought Walkie-Talkies for communication over short distances. A generation later came cellular automobile telephones hooked by electronic transmission to *cells*, low-powered receiver-transmitters scattered throughout cities, connected to the telephone system through switching centers. For people who must drive, portable

fax machines connected to acoustic couplers can now dial into the cellular telephone network from automobiles.

When mobile satellite service is realized, a portable phone call could be placed between any two spots on earth; the technology is reported to be already in place, awaiting only international regulatory agreements.[22] The ultimate goal is to allow any two people anywhere on Earth with pocket phones to talk to one another with the clarity that will attend digital communication.

The convenience of cellular telephones led to a rush of sales that was diminished, but by no means stopped by rumors, started in 1993, that the emitted radio waves from cellular phone antennas held alongside the ear for long periods were causing brain cancer.

Pagers, another personal communication device, developed by Motorola, used a radio network to download written information. Pagers received and stored as many as 15 written messages of 120 alphanumeric characters each. Parents gave them as a birthday present to a teenage daughter or son as a means of keeping in touch. The teenagers use them as a link to friends. Some owners gave out their beeper number in order to keep home numbers private.

Pocket Phones

The newest type of personal phone service, known as PCS (personal communication service) is digital, using frequencies auctioned off in 1995 by the Federal Communications Commission. Because it is digital, voice quality is superior to the mostly analog cellular transmission. The PCS telephone itself is small enough to fit into a shirt pocket.

All mobile telephones are an extension of the toolshed home. A telephone call is directed toward a phone at a fixed location where, the caller hopes, a specific person will be present. A daughter phoning her mother, for example, is actually calling her mother's telephone in the expectation that her mother will be nearby. The cellular telephone, or *cellphone*, introduced in 1983, took a step toward letting the daughter reach her mother more directly.

The pocket phones come within inches of Dick Tracy's wrist radio, life imitating art. In 1996 a combination telephone-computer that fit into a pocket was sending and receiving faxes and e-mail, and hooked into the Internet.

Pocket phone calls have been received or initiated not only in such expected places as the middle of a traffic jam or the edge of a swimming pool, but in such unlikely places as restaurant tables, public rest rooms, public buses, even while a teenage owner is skateboarding down the street. Backpacks have rung in the middle of class. Some schools ban them and also ban beepers because they are not only disruptive, but they are a favorite tool of drug dealers. The pocket phone has quickly gone from novelty to necessity. Except by Superman fans, few tears were shed for the passing of the telephone booth.

The New Picturephones

In 1924, the Bell Laboratories in New Jersey, one of the nation's best communication research facilities, transmitted pictures over telephone wires. Despite public excitement when a prototype of the *Picturephone* was introduced at the 1964 World's Fair, the fuzzy pictures were a commercial failure. The *Picturephone* was exhibited in Disneyland and world's fairs, but did not catch on with the public because of high operating costs, poor pictures, and some real doubts about who would want to see or be seen by someone on the telephone. There were wry comments about mothers telephoning their daughters and clucking in disapproval of the disheveled state of the daughter's hair and apartment.

A generation later, with improved technology and a new name—*video teleconferencing*—the picture telephone returned with every prospect of success. The size and price of equipment had shrunk, and high speed data lines that once cost as much as $1,000 an hour were trimmed to close in on the cost of a long distance call. With lower costs and the success of business teleconferencing, the renamed videophone appeared to be making a comeback.

Successes in early marketing tests have been reported, with the marketing aimed not at business users, but at families and lovers separated by distances. The advantage of face-to-face communication between distant cities without the need to travel could not be denied.[23]

A Variety of Uses

Companies with products to sell or surveys to take use 800 and 900 numbers to do so. *Telemarketing*, the organized selling by telephone, has grown into a large if annoying business. There is also a general awareness of the mini-industry of chat and "adult" lines for which per-minute fees are levied. As for the 800 numbers, they became so popular that no room was left. AT&T added a new bank: 888.

In a world of electronic gadgetry, the humble answering machine tends to be overlooked, yet it is among the most empowering of communication devices. Its most obvious use is to free the telephone owner from the need to remain at home to receive messages. The answering machine also gives a measure of protection against the annoyance of the telemarketing solicitor, the overly insistent acquaintance or relative, and the obscene caller. An improvement on the answering machine, *EVM* or *electronic voice messaging*, is the voice mail system operated by the local telephone company, a corporation, or an outside business service. Features include allowing a caller to leave a recorded message for someone who is on the phone at the time.

Local telephone companies offer other new features to customers. A kind of telephone peephole, *Caller ID* guards the customer's privacy by identifying the caller's phone number or, alternatively, by identifying the caller as someone who chooses not to reveal his number. Peripheral computerized attachments add the caller's name, address, and any facts to a database. A person answering the phone can immediately greet the caller by name. To discourage persistent or obscene callers, incoming calls can be automatically logged.

Call forwarding, call waiting, and custom ringing, each available for a few dollars a month, are other options. Telephone owners can also decide whether to attach a fax or a computer modem on the line or acquire a separate line.

To cite other examples of new telephone usage, a caller could by telephone acquire a diet plan based on information punched onto Touchtone telephone buttons. The *Chicago Reader* was among newspapers that offered a wide variety of telephone-based services, such as classified personals and classified apartment listings, information about where musical bands are playing, with snippets of band music pouring out of the telephone earpiece; movie information including dialogue from the previews of coming attractions, and restaurant listings with the option of being transferred to a restaurant to learn the specials of the day and to make reservations. All the caller needed was a Touchtone phone.

Further out, Japanese and British researchers were working on automatic translation telephones: two people speaking different languages to each other and the phone doing the translating. Despite test demonstrations, a workable system seemed years off. More progress has been reported with print. CompuServe offered a worldwide forum that automatically translated, with a fair number of mistakes, written on-line messages in English, French, and German. A Japanese software pro-gram, also with mistakes, automatically translated text files between English and Japanese. Much more accurate and less expensive Japanese text file programs required some human intervention, such as choosing among meanings for words with the same Japanese *hiragana* spellings.

Reach Out Without Touching

The telephone has become a way to do business, to arrange a meeting or break a date, to express anger, to reveal secrets, to apologize, to whisper sweet nothings, or just to pass the time with someone who has nothing else to do either. It extends conversation to unseen people, but at a cost to the deeper interaction of face-to-face communication. On the other hand, some people appreciate the instrument's ability to maintain contacts without personal meetings. Plainly, the telephone allowed you to talk to Aunt Ethel, whom you cannot visit just now, but if you talk to Aunt Ethel over the phone, you do not *have* to visit.

The telephone slogan, "Reach out and touch someone," has not lost its appeal, although it involves no touching at all. "Keep in touch" means "write or telephone." As the new millennium nears, mediated communication remains more popular than ever. It is not touching.

"Free" Entertainment

Americans at home were glued to their radios in the 1930s and '40s as the networks poured out a daily stream of programs from the morning soaps through the children's after school adventure programs, to the dinner time news analysts, and on to the prime time dramas, comedies, quiz shows, and specials. During the Depression years, with 15 million Americans out of work, this "free" entertainment was all that many people could afford. Radio sets could be bought for as little as $15. On every night of the week, there were favorite radio shows that listeners eagerly awaited. Radio had found a social role. Like the Victrola, the radio by now looked like a piece of furniture, with simpler tuning, less static, and no battery. The new radio plugged into the wall, the parlor wall.

Announcers were chosen for their lack of regional accents. The broadcasting industry didn't plan it that way, but by emphasizing a standard American speech pattern, radio helped the national effort to bring all Americans together, a function heretofore largely relegated to the schools. Radio and the movies heated the fire under what was called the *American melting pot*. Yet, not everyone agreed that the network system was a totally wonderful arrangement, for to a certain extent the network system, dominated by NBC and CBS, limited the ability of local stations to develop their own quality programming. Network programs, targeted to national audiences, tended to ignore regional and local culture and issues.

The American Federation of Musicians certainly did not want recorded music, and James Petrillo's union had become a powerful force in the broadcast industry.[24] Most of radio was live, with few recordings, which were called *electrical transcriptions*. Radio did not turn extensively to recorded music until the disk jockey craze in the mid-1950s. Until the early 1950s, sound was recorded on phonograph records, and because recording equipment was bulky, it seldom left the studio. Audiotape would change all that and break down the walls of the radio newsroom.

Political Broadcasts

President Franklin Roosevelt, opposed by most newspaper publishers, bypassed them by using radio to bring his policies directly before the voters. His unprecedented four terms were evidence of his success and, not incidentally, the efficacy of a microphone in the possession of a masterful orator who understood the intimate nature of radio. Secretary of Labor Frances Perkins recalled:

> As he talked his head would nod and his hands would move in simple, natural, comfortable gestures. His face would smile and light up as though he were actually sitting on the front porch or in the parlor with them.[25]

When the war clouds gathered and burst over Europe and Asia first, and then over America, radio brought the voices of European leaders into American homes. Adolf Hitler's stridency and Winston Churchill's

eloquence flowed through the patterned cloths covering the speakers of the consoles in the parlors and the table models in the kitchens of America's homes. Radio had found a political role. Hitler recognized the force of oral communication in *Mein Kampf*:

> I know that one is able to win people far more by the spoken than the written word. The greatest changes in the world have never been brought about by the goose quill. The power which set sliding the great avalanches of a political and religious nature was from the beginning of time, the magic force of the spoken word.

Cultural Influence

With everything from Sunday morning church services to symphony orchestras and "Your Hit Parade," radio also played a strong cultural role in American society. During the "golden age" of radio, approximately the decades of the 1930s and 1940s, programs were available for almost every taste, from the cerebral *Information Please* to the clownish *It Pays to be Ignorant*. There were soap operas in the morning, adventure shows for kids just before the supper hour, and a prime time schedule of sitcoms, dramas, and variety shows. Just as movie stars became household names, so did Eddie Cantor, Jack Benny, Fred Allen, and, after World War II, Arthur Godfrey. The programming structure and fixed schedule of half-hour and one-hour blocks was similar to today's network television scheduling, not like today's loose radio programming.

A demonstration of the emotional power of broadcasting came on the evening of October 30, 1938, when Orson Welles' Mercury Theater presented H.G. Wells' novel *War of the Worlds* in a manner that convinced many of the estimated audience of six million that Martians had invaded the earth and were slaughtering everyone with death rays; a few listeners ran into the streets screaming that the world was coming to an end. In the same year, the CBS World News Roundup made radio a serious news medium.

Improving the Sound

E. Howard Armstrong, who invented the feedback circuit and other improvements to the radio signal, invented FM radio in 1933. The president of RCA, David Sarnoff, recognized its potential but saw FM as a hindrance to RCA's development of television. Sarnoff managed to block the diffusion of FM radio until years after the end of World War II. Frustrated by this and other setbacks, Armstrong committed suicide.

Audio engineers, who labored successfully to improve the quality of sound in broadcasting and recorded music, shook up the industry that built the home receivers. It was no longer enough to buy something that delivered a dependable sound. An important segment of the public became *audiophiles* who compared equipment specifications for tuners, turntables, preamps, and loudspeakers placed in exactly the right spots in the family living room.

The decades of the 1950s and 1960s saw a diffusion of technology that included FM, stereophonic transmission, high fidelity audio tape and records, tape cassettes that permitted automation, and the invention of the transistor, which not only improved the reliability of radio station equipment, but more importantly led to the vast new market of listeners to portable and automobile radios.

Radio Reinvents Itself

With the rapid spread of television, radio broadcasting seemed on a one-way road to ruin. Station and network assets fled eagerly to the new medium, taking staff, talent, and energy with it. In the home, the old Philco console was moved out of the parlor to make way for the RCA round-screen 7-inch television set. Yet, radio survived. Today there are far more radio stations than at the start of television broadcasting. By 1992, with 11,338 radio stations and 576 million radios in use—5.6 radio sets for every household on average—and radios in 19 of every 20 cars in the United States alone, on average Americans listen to the radio 3 hours 20 minutes a day.[26]

Radio programming in the TV age sounded more personal than it did before television, as local stations loosened the rigid program scheduling that networks once dominated. Realizing that the valuable evening hours, *prime time*, was lost to television, radio stations focused on *drive time*, the morning and afternoon hours when most listeners were on their way to and from work.

Underlying the new television-era radio programming was the concept of *narrowcasting* and technological advances. Each station, instead of reaching for the greatest possible audience by trying to program for everyone, sought *niche* markets by identifying themselves with a unique *sound* that would distinguish them from their competitors. That sound derived not only from the type of music they played, but from the patter of the disk jockeys, the items chosen for the newscasts, and the types of commercials. A station that advertised pimple ointment for teenagers would not be likely to advertise false teeth cleansers, play classical music, or employ solemn announcers. Merchants used radio to channel the youth culture into a youth market.

Record sales soared as musical tastes sharply splintered radio stations in large cities, seeking audiences based on generational, ethnic, or regional distinctions. Twirling the dial brought in rock and roll, jazz, MOR (middle-of-the-road), country western, mariachi, rhythm and blues, classical, big band, and on and on. Some urban stations became all-news or all-talk.

The radio networks, losing audiences to their own television networks, abandoned most programming except news. Joining a shift to narrowcasting, ABC Radio divided itself in the 1970s into four information networks, later into seven. CBS, NBC, and Mutual also split up like amoebae, each with its own life.

The '90s saw a new kind of network via syndication, an explosion of political talk led by the bombastic, conservative Rush Limbaugh. Striving for market share or giving expression to their own prejudices, some stations brought in talk show hosts who tested the edges of what could be said on the air. Howard Stern's gutter language earned him a national following and even support as a candidate for governor of New York.

Citizen's Band

The FCC, in response to pressure from ham radio operators, set aside frequencies for a citizen's radio service. The CBers, who operate on the citizen's band, at their peak numbered in the millions. Most famous of all CB operators were truck drivers who revealed to other drivers that "Smokies" were parked behind a billboard waiting to pounce on the unwary. A lot of CB rigs are gathering dust today, replaced by cellphones.

Besides CB bands, a number of other services use radio frequencies. Among them are police and fire communications, air control, radio astronomy, mobile operator-assisted telephone service (now largely supplanted by cellular telephone), and beeper paging systems. Cordless telephones are actually transmitter-receiver stations that tie into telephone lines.

In remote corners of America, radio has found a more personal role. In some of the hills and hollows, beside woods and lakes, listeners depend on radio not only for entertainment, but for the personal information that telephones convey in cities. Owners of the radio stations respond by offering a free message exchange. The Jones family informs the Smith family of the time they'll arrive. The pastor announces the topic of next Sunday's sermon. Mention is made of a pot luck dinner. Everyone tunes in, for the radio is the community link.

Looking in Radio's Crystal Ball

Another change catching attention is AM stereo radio.[28] The future promises more diversity in radio just as in other tools of communication, a continuing chopping up of the audience. Direct broadcast satellites are creating a number of national radio stations that send signals directly to home or car.[27] In the mid-'90s, approximately two million cable radio subscribers each paid about $10 a month for their choice of all-music or all-talk formats. Satellite-fed *digital audio broadcasting (DAB)*, which may in future replace AM and FM with CD-quality sound, would sharply increase the number of radio stations because less bandwidth and less power is needed for digital transmission while keeping all the quality of the sound source.[29] Distance would no longer imply static and loss of quality. The signal could also be fed through cable lines.

Except for satellite feeds, the networks, and shortwave broadcasts, radio is local. The appearance of radio channels on the World Wide Web promises to change that. Because Web sites do not require F.C.C approval and occupy no space in the electromagnetic spectrum, the number of stations is potentially unlimited except by commercial considerations.

The Benefits of Broadcasting

For many people, a radio voice or music was the first sound heard in the morning, the last at night. Radio accompanied the day's activities: drive, jog, work, eat, study, play. For those listeners who preferred the constant din of broadcasting to quiet reflection, radio could short-circuit any thinking at all. Lee DeForest, self-styled "father of radio," was proud of his "child":

> Radio has kept the wanderer home at nights, it has brightened the gloom of separation and shortened the long hours of loneliness. It is a comforting companion to the shut-in; it soothes the pain of the suffering. It brings counsel to the housewife, information to the farmer, entertainment and gaiety to the young. On silent wings it flies to the forgotten corners where mails are uncertain and few, where the cheer of kindly voices comes only through the head-phones, where music is never heard...[30]

Enthralled with its inanimate friend, radio, the public has grown less likely to socialize with neighbors while at the same time finding out more about the world in which we live. Like so much else, radio has been both servant and our master. In 1932, when radio broadcasting was barely a dozen years old, a list was compiled of no less than 150 effects on society of wireless communication. Here are a few of them:[31]

1. Homogeneity of people increased because of like stimuli.

2. Regional differences in culture become less pronounced.

3. The penetration of the musical and artistic city culture into villages and country.

4. Distinctions between social classes and economic groups lessened.

5. Illiterates find a new world opened to them.

6. Standardization of diction and discouragement of dialects.

7. Aids in correct pronunciation, especially foreign words.

8. Another agency for recreation and entertainment.

9. The enjoyment of music popularized greatly.

10. Entertainment of invalids, blind, partly deaf, frontiersmen, etc.

11. Interest in sports increased, it is generally admitted.

12. Entertainment on trains, ships, and automobiles.

13. Broadcasting has aided adult education.

14. Health movement encouraged through broadcast of health talks.

15. Broadcasting has been used to further some reform movements.

16. Wider education of farmers on agricultural methods.

17. Discouragement, it is said, of preachers of lesser abilities.

Pictures in the Parlor

The average American television set is on for 7 hours 45 minutes a day. City streets are deserted each evening. Drive along any avenue in the United States or any other industrialized nation and you will see the bluish glow from television sets in darkened rooms of house after house. How mass communication separates people has never been more obvious.

Probably more than school, church, community, and maybe even family, television has become a national educator and standard setter, even though no responsible person either inside or outside the television industry ever said this is a desirable state of affairs. The telegraph, telephone, motion picture, radio, and the post office each radically changed the way we get information and entertainment. In short, much of the way we live. Television has

gone further than all of these in affecting how we spend our hours and our money, how we relate to others, and what we talk about and think about. In our toolshed homes, television is the most visible tool.

As an oral version of a written culture, television is positioned to deliver both oral and written cultures. As an oral culture, it has the advantage of reaching audiences who prefer to hear and see activity passively instead of the more active experience of reading. It can also call upon the breadth of written culture, with its infinite resources.

It is short-sighted and pointless to criticize television because it is not print, yet that is the gist of many of the complaints. Marshall McLuhan regarded the movies, radio, and television as classrooms without walls.[32]

Literate man is not only numb and vague in the presence of film or photo, but he intensifies his ineptness by a defensive arrogance and condescension to "pop kulch" and "mass entertainment." It was in this spirit of bulldog opacity that the scholastic philosophers failed to meet the challenge of the printed book in the sixteenth century. [33]

Time Spent Watching

According to Nielsen Media Research, the average adult man watches television 3 hours 44 minutes a day and the average woman 4 hours 25 minutes a day. Mothers use it as a babysitter. The average American preschool child watches more than 27 hours of television weekly. [34] For the elderly it can be life, as a visit to any nursing home attests. Teens watch an average of 2 hours 43 minutes of television daily. By 18, the average American child will have spent about 25,000 hours doing this. [35]

Has any society been held in thrall by a single passive activity for nearly one half of its waking life? Has any technological instrument every exerted such immense influence over how we think and act? Many view television as a fatal attraction, a sort of cultural death wish. It stands accused of weakening our social institutions, driving up our crime rate, attenuating our attention spans distorting our perceptions of reality and illusion, eroding our regional distinctions in speech and dress, usurping the games of childhood, encouraging illiteracy, pregnancy and even obesity in adolescents and reducing all it touches—politics, education, economics, religion—to 525 lines of phosphor-dot frivolousness. [36]

Time alone is evidence that broadcasting affects lives. Four hours is, after all, one sixth of a day; if extended over years, it represents a substantial portion of a lifetime spent in front of the tube. Subtract the hours spent sleeping, and the percentages shoot up. Subtract the hours spent sleeping or working, and the percentage of time with television reaches astonishing, alarming heights. Never in human history has there been what seems to be mass hypnotism on such a scale. Even the circuses of ancient Rome and the medieval Crusades did not compare.

Television is cheap and readily available. It requires little energy, intelligence, or education to enjoy it. For one or another of these reasons, it is most popular with the poor, the uneducated, children, and the elderly. Someone said that society's most powerless received television as a consolation prize. [37]

A color television set sat in 98% of all American homes in the 1990s. More homes have TV sets than bathtubs or telephones, and far more homes than are on newspaper delivery routes. For a dedicated few, small TVs are plugged into car cigarette lighters and strapped onto wrists. Even smaller TVs fit into wraparound eyeglasses, projecting an image floating about ten feet in front of your nose.

Television is different because it encompasses all forms of discourse. No one goes to a movie to find out about government policy or the latest scientific advances. No one buys a record to find out the baseball scores or the weather or the latest murder. No one turns on radio anymore for soap operas or a presidential address (if a television set is at hand). But everyone goes to television for all these things and more, which is why television resonates so powerfully throughout the culture. [38]

Research has shown that many people, although they have favorite programs, watch television as a form of relaxation, no matter what is on. It has been said that if nothing else were available, viewers would watch test patterns! As a result, network executive Paul Klein proposed the *L.O.P.—Least Objectionable Program*—policy, by which programmers would develop not what viewers wanted to watch, but what they least objected to, based on the assumption that many viewers scan the offerings until they find something they can tolerate. Viewers do not watch programs. They watch television.

The Scientific Roots of Television

Television means *seeing at a distance*. Its roots reach back at least to 1817, when Swedish scientist Jon Berzelius discovered that selenium, a sulfur-like chemical element that is a byproduct of copper refining, conducted electricity, depending upon how much light shone upon it. In 1873, an Irish telegraph operator, Joseph May, by exposing a selenium resistor to light, sent a signal across the ocean on the Atlantic telegraph cable. Two years later, American engineer Philip Carey proposed a means of television using a camera containing an array of selenium cells, each wired to a light bulb in a matching array in a receiver. All this happened before Marconi sent the first radio signal, even before Alexander Graham Bell patented his telephone.

In 1842, on a different track, Scottish inventor Alexander Bain demonstrated a device with brushes that made an electrical contact as they passed over raised metal letters, sending a current over a wire to another set of brushes that recorded an impression of those metal letters on sensitized paper. Five years later, the Italian Abbé Caselli managed to send drawings from Amiens to Paris by wire. The result was crude, but visible. *Seeing at a distance* now meant *seeing by electricity*. English, Italian, German, French, Russian, and American inventors improved the means of transmitting a picture from one place to another. Their efforts led to such inventions as modern wirephoto transmission, fax machines, and to the flashing lights that spelled out news headlines on New York's Times Square.

On still another track, English scientist Michael Faraday in 1830 sent an electric current through a vacuum in a glass bottle. Improving on this experiment, Sir William Crookes in 1878 built a bottle that sent rays of electrons from its *cathode*, or negative terminal, to its *anode*, or positive terminal. Another Englishman, Sir J.J. Thomson shifted the direction of the stream of electrons with a magnet. A German scientist, Karl Braun, in 1897 added a fluorescent coating to the inner face of the Crookes tube so it glowed when struck by the cathode rays. The television set in the home today uses a cathode ray tube with magnetic deflection that paints the television picture on the face of the tube.

German science student Paul Nipkow may have been the first to scan a scene optically point by point fast enough to reach the human eye's persistence of vision, the basis of television. In 1884, he transmitted a still picture in an experiment using a rotating disk with a spiral of holes that broke the image into segments of varying light intensity that struck a selenium plate and as a result could be transmitted with varying electrical current. Another rotating disk with spiral holes reconstructed the image. Here was the start of true television. It was, however, mechanical not electronic scanning, a blind alley that some inventors followed until the 1930s. Technical problems were overcome, one by one, at a time when the excitement of communication inventions was in the air: the typewriter, the telephone, the motion picture, the phonograph, radio, all developed to a usable level within a few years of each other. Rapid strides were being made at the same time in photography and printing. Television's day was still a few years off, but only a few.

Electronic Television

Efforts to perfect a mechanical system based upon the Nipkow disk continued, especially in England by John Logie Baird. His results were so poor that there was no chance of commercial success, although he stubbornly continued to try to improve mechanical systems almost until World War II. Alternating between mechanical and electronic systems, the British Broadcasting Corporation started the world's first regular television service in 1936. Very soon after, German engineers began a limited electronic television service. By this time, experiments in the United States were well along.

By 1907 a Russian scientist, Boris Rosing, had designed an electronic system of wireless transmission using a cathode ray tube. Because of the turmoil in the years leading up to the Russian Revolution, Rosing, who disappeared during the revolution, was unable to develop television beyond the laboratory, but two young men familiar with his work continued along the path. Vladimir Zworykin had been Rosing's assistant. Philo Farnsworth, an Idaho teenager, never came within a continent of Rosing, but read about his work in a popular science magazine. And unknown to Rosing in Russia, an English scientist, A.A. Campbell Swinton, was following the same electronic path, which started still other scientists to work on television in their laboratories.

When he was still a high school student, Farnsworth described his idea of electronic television to his chemistry teacher. Encouraged, he began experimenting. By the time he was 19, supported by some California investors, Farnsworth acquired the first of many patents and was able to demonstrate a crude *image dissector*, the heart of his electronic system. The sensitivity of the image remained rough compared with the device that Zworykin, who came as an immigrant to the United States, was constructing at Westinghouse. In 1923, he gave a television demonstration using a camera tube to transmit a still image to the face of a cathode ray tube. The invention of television is often dated from Zworykin's 1923 demonstration. Steady improvement resulted in the first commercially practical television *pick-up* tube, Zworykin's *iconoscope*. Zworykin went to a fellow Russian immigrant, RCA's David Sarnoff, and convinced him of the potential of electronic television. Sarnoff pulled together a research team from Westinghouse, General Electric, and RCA under Zworykin to develop a commercial television system. As was true with radio, no one company held all the important patents; cross-licensing agreements were needed to combine the best inventions into a single system.

In 1925, an American inventor, Charles Francis Jenkins, sent the image of moving windmills to a receiver five miles away, the first transmission of a moving object. AT&T, the telephone company, was also experimenting. In 1926, a Bell Telephone Labs team under Herbert Ives was sending a motion picture around the lab. AT&T was

Figure 5.6   Felix the Cat was used in experimental telecasts.

able to transmit a black-and-white still photo from Washington to New York in 1927 and color photos in 1929 of a bunch of red roses, a green and red watermelon, and the red, white and blue American flag. But these were images of poor quality, done by mechanical scanning that depended upon hundreds of wires connected to the face of the receiving tube, not unlike a huge plate of spaghetti. Nevertheless, any color television was a leap forward. AT&T also developed the coaxial cable and microwave transmission, both essential to modern television.

From England Baird transmitted a barely discernible still picture across the Atlantic Ocean in 1928, the year that an experimental General Electric station in Schenectady, New York, started telecasting programs three times a week, mostly to engineers with mechanical scanners. NBC, the radio network owned by RCA, had its own experimental television station in New York. It eventually became WNBC-TV. CBS also had an experimental station in New York, which is now WCBS-TV. Throughout the 1930s and 1940s at these and other research stations, engineers improved the television signals and the receivers. The number of scanning lines, which determine picture detail, grew from 120 to the present 525. There was no question that the future belonged to electronic television. Mechanical television, with its moving parts, was a blind alley.

The Public Is Introduced to Television

At first, it wasn't clear where the market for television lay. Movies were shown in theaters, so perhaps television would replace film there. Dr. Allen DuMont thought the future lay with television in the home. His DuMont Laboratories began selling the first all-electronic television sets to the public in 1938. Columnist E.B. White wrote:

> I believe television is going to be the test of the modern world and that in this new opportunity to see beyond the range of our vision, we shall discover either a new and unbearable disturbance of the general peace, or a saving radiance in the sky. We shall stand or fall by television—of that I am quite sure.[39]

Far-sighted radio industry leaders, with David Sarnoff in the lead, recognized the potential popularity of adding pictures to radio broadcasting. The general American public first saw television in 1939 at the RCA Pavilion in the New York World's Fair, whose theme was "The World of Tomorrow":

> Each day, from a primitive studio at Radio City, RCA beams to the fairgrounds a vintage cartoon ("Donald's Cousin Gus") or a travelogue ("Jasper National Park, Washington - Shrine of Patriotism") or a culinary lesson (usually a simple salad), since the heat in the studio is almost enough to roast a cook... Yet to many among the millions of fairgoers who come to gape (at the New York World's Fair in 1939), the video image that lingers longest isn't anything on the screen; it is the sight of the set itself. A clunky, all-wooden set housing a glass rectangle exactly five inches high. A miniature looking glass.[40]

NBC and CBS each received a license to begin commercial broadcasting from their experimental stations in New York City. Among the difficulties they confronted in these pre-air conditioning days were hot lights that raised studio temperatures well past 100 degrees. Sweating delegates to the 1940 Republican convention in Philadelphia asked that the NBC telecast be turned off. No delegate to a modern convention would dream of making such a request, when conventions are organized for maximum television coverage. Another difficulty was convincing the public to buy television sets, big, bulky pieces of furniture with small screens that presented poor black-and-white pictures when they had anything to show at all. A set cost nearly as much as a new car. NBC and CBS created a limited program schedule for the New York area, but aside from television executives and engineers who had sets placed free in their homes, plus a small number of rich people who, Depression or not, seemed oblivious to the price, there was no home market. In the years before World War II, television sets went mostly into bars as a way to attract patrons who wanted to see baseball and football games.

The Federal Communications Commission had hardly begun to issue television licenses when war intervened, freezing television development, just as World War I had frozen radio development. Research and production were needed for the war effort, creating radar systems and other electronic devices. During World War II, only six experimental stations broadcast programs occasionally to no more than 10,000 sets in the country. However, newspapers and magazines carried stories about television's promise. When the war ended the pent-up demand for TV was ready to explode. Broadcasters wanted licenses, manufacturers wanted to build TV sets and broadcasting equipment, and the public wanted to be entertained by pictures in their parlors. Commercial television was making such an impression that factory production of sets went from 6,000 in 1946 to 1,160,000 in 1948. The number of sets in use rose from 5,000 in 1946 to nearly one million in 1948 to almost 10 million in 1950, typically with 7-inch or 10-inch round screens.

The Fight Over Standards

A battle between RCA and CBS over color standards kept television in a monochrome world. Because of the decision to restrict station allocations to the VHF (very-high frequency) band, channels 2 to 13, bitter and extended quarrels arose for licenses. It seemed that everyone wanted these scarce and valuable licenses, especially radio station owners and newspaper publishers. Unable to resolve the problems of who would get the limited space in the VHF spectrum, and aware that it had not allowed enough separation to prevent interference, the FCC halted the licensing of television stations. It reworked the national television spectrum allocation plan to provide for more local television stations in U.S. communities. The freeze on new stations was to last from 1948 to 1952, but television technology did not wait. By 1951, coaxial cables and microwave signals sent network programs coast to coast. The FCC also opened up the UHF (ultra-high frequency) band, channels 14 to 69, to answer the demand of applicants who wanted their own television stations; it assigned channels to more than

1,200 communities. Color television standards were finally agreed upon in 1953. By 1954, more than 350 stations, VHF and UHF, were on the air.

VHF channels proved to be a financial bonanza from the start. British media baron Lord Thomson once said: "A license to broadcast is a license to print money." UHF stations fared less well because most of the early television sets lacked UHF dials. Even after the FCC in 1964 required television set manufacturers to add UHF dials, they did not require the precisely tuned click dials used for VHF stations. Viewers avoided the UHF stations, advertisers would not spend money where there was no audience, and networks had little wish to affiliate where few viewers or advertisers went, which meant that UHF stations could not get network programs. Not until the coming of cable did many UHF stations operate profitably.

The FCC decided to let television develop according to pre-war standards, unlike European countries, which waited until better standards came along in the postwar years. The result has been that the American television standard, called *NTSC* (for the National Television System Committee that developed it), is not quite as good as the European *PAL* and *SECAM* systems of 625 lines. Japan, Canada, and the other nations of the western hemisphere adopted the American NTSC system of a picture made up of 525 lines that are refreshed 60 times a second, interlacing the even-numbered lines and the odd-numbered lines alternately, 30 *frames* per second. European nations were divided between two other systems, each with more lines and better picture quality than the American system. France's SECAM system was chosen by the Soviet Union, China, and the nations of Eastern Europe. Germany's PAL system was chosen by Britain and most countries of western Europe. Other countries of the world selected one of the three systems for cultural and political reasons or because of a compatible electric grid. A former British colony might select the PAL system because of the ready availability of British programs.

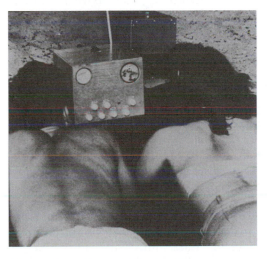

Figure 5.7   Portable TV set, 1948, had a 3½-inch screen.

HDTV

In the '90s, a new system emerged, *high definition television*. HDTV presented a cinema screen-like 16×9 width-to-height ratio instead of the standard television 4×3 ratio, plus at least twice the number of scanning lines of NTSC pictures, and therefore at least twice the sharpness. Both the pictures, carrying at least ten times as much color information, and the compact disc-quality sound, encoded for transmission by digital sampling, had much more clarity than existing television.

In addition to home delivery of television programs, another possibility for HDTV may be as a replacement to film distribution. Movies arrive in theaters the way they have for decades, as cans of film carted from place to place. Instead, visionaries imagined a theater without film or tape. An HDTV signal would be sent by satellite in scrambled form to theaters where audiences are waiting; in short, a superior version of HBO for theaters. This would permit the distribution of motion pictures with small potential audiences in each city but a sizable, cumulative audience.

A reasonable question might be: why bother with theaters? Why not just make tapes available for viewing at home on VCRs? Experience has shown that going out to a movie, seeing it on a large screen while surrounded by other people, is a social event that sitting at home does not equal. However, the comforts of the toolshed home have repeatedly outweighed such considerations for most people.

The Commercial Basis

Television developed as a private business in the United States, unlike most other countries, a legacy from the mid-nineteenth century when the Congress refused the opportunity to take over Morse's young telegraph service. Bell's telephone grew as a private venture, and about twenty years after that, so did Marconi's point-to-point wireless radio service. After another quarter century, privately owned, government regulated wireless radio had expanded into broadcasting, whereas in other countries the government owned and managed all these services.

Pressure from educators led to the assignment of a relatively few, poorly funded educational radio stations and, later, television stations. Dissatisfaction over this state of affairs led to many painful adjustments and no end of legal and political wrangling to reach the present situation in the United States of a non-profit, partly government-funded public television network, the Public Broadcasting System, plus two public radio networks, National Public Radio and Public Radio International.

Programming

In the 1920s, neighbors gathered around the first radio on the block. As television sets were sold across the nation during the late 1940s and '50s, people without sets would crowd into a neighbor's home or stand in front of radio shop window displays to watch the antics of Milton Berle and Sid Caesar, or the glum-faced Ed Sullivan introducing bright young talent, including Dean Martin and Jerry Lewis, the Beatles, and Elvis Presley, plus any number of folk singers and trained dog acts. Part of the excitement for viewers was that the entertainment was live, happening right then out in Hollywood or New York while the whole country watched! Vaudeville, killed by the movies, was reborn on a grand stage.

In time, television and movies would go together like ham and eggs, but not at first. Major studios saw television as a threat to the motion picture industry, not as an additional distribution channel. Indeed, considering the financial links between the studios and the theater chains, television *was* a threat. Those links weakened in a 1948 U.S. Supreme Court decision, *U.S. v. Paramount,* breaking the vertically integrated structure of the studios and the movie theaters.

It was only a matter of time before the networks, hungry for material to fill their available hours and cash rich, would get movies to show their rapidly expanding audiences. Among the first to arrive were B-grade westerns, the cheaply made horse operas that kids watched on Saturday mornings. Cowboy actors Gene Autry and Hopalong Cassidy, who owned the television rights to their dozens of films, made considerable fortunes. Walt Disney signed a deal with ABC to start a weekly one-hour series in 1954. One by one the other studios opened their film libraries. After movies became available in sufficient numbers and after videotape revolutionized television production, the live dramas that were the centerpiece of the so-called Golden Age of Television of the 1950s yielded to programs that could be shot anywhere, edited, and kept on a shelf.

Settings and Plots

Formula Hollywood Western movies on television were followed by made-for-television western series that kept the same formula of good guys and bad guys shooting it out in the frontier town. Unlike the best of the Hollywood studio westerns, the characters lacked depth and the plots were cookie-cutter. Viewers eventually tired of western settings, but not of two-dimensional adventures. Out went the cowboys of *Bonanza.* In came the secret agents of *Mission Impossible* and *I Spy,* a series that made history when a black actor, Bill Cosby, was chosen to play one of the two heroes. Private eyes, cops, and doctors followed one another on the tube.

The basic plots did not change much, but character changes reflected and sometimes led social attitudes. For example, the serious and pure old-time cowboys were replaced by world-weary private detectives with personality flaws. The lone hero became the leading member of a team that included a black or a woman, sometimes both. If a black cop was not a member of the team that went after the villains, the growling, middle-aged superior would be black. Steven Bochco's *Hill Street Blues,* peppered with the gritty realism of the South Bronx and a variety of social concerns, provided a television-watching home for liberals during the Reagan era. Its rich characterization and seamless flow back and forth among several plot lines set a style for a number of shows that followed it, notably

L.A. Law, which Bochco also produced, and the hospital drama, *ER.* Social issues were again featured.

Other changes saw kidding between the heroes become a staple of dialogue, and the villains' crimes become more violent and more sex-related. The decade in which an adventure show was made could be guessed with reasonable accuracy by its sex and violence content. As early as the 1960s, the National Association for Better Broadcasting estimated that the average child was likely, between the ages of 5 and 15, to see more than 13,000 people destroyed violently, identifying not only guns but fire, rape, poison, acid, spiders, snakes, crocodiles, pitchforks, knives, time bombs, live steam, poison gas, hypodermic needles, and an assortment of blunt instruments. That the powerful images of violence have affected both children and adults and have pushed some disturbed teenagers and adults into mimicking the violent acts should by now be beyond dispute. Yet, for a significant segment of society, including large numbers of children and teenagers, the powerful images of television still provide a moral compass, sometimes the dominant moral compass.

Fred Friendly wryly commented, "Commercial television makes so much money doing its worst, it can't afford to do its best." Under the Telecommunication Reform Act of 1996, television manufacturers were installing a *v-chip* in each set so parents could block out violent and sexual programs. Networks, cable channels, and independent producers, faced with government and public pressure, reluctantly agreed to come up with a rating system that would be the *software* for the v-chip.

Soap Operas

Soap operas, the popular afternoon melodrama series that were staples of radio for decades, moved effortlessly from radio into television. Radio had its *Stella Dallas, Ma Perkins,* and *The Guiding Light.* Television carried on with *All My Children, Days of Our Lives,* and—no surprise—*The Guiding Light.* Except for newscasts, they have been the most enduring of all broadcast fare, while even the most popular adventure shows, dramas, and situation comedies exhausted themselves after several years. Soap operas keep bubbling. Although their primary audience is housewives, their appeal extends to the work place, retirement homes, and college campuses. Over the decades, social messages were introduced, but the biggest change is in the amount of sex both talked about and shown. Soaps have come a long way from radio's *The Romance of Helen Trent*, when the announcer daily asked the audience whether a woman over the age of 35 could still find romance.

With huge, faithful audiences, the plots have required little change from formulas that worked so well on both radio and television. With ensemble casts, each soap opera carries several plots along simultaneously from day to day. Unlike nearly all movies and ordinary dramatic programs, a soap opera offers no happy ending followed by a fade-out. If one painful romantic problem seems to be resolved, others are not, and the "nice" characters do not always get their hearts' desires. The real message has always been: stay tuned.

Soaps proved such a television draw that they moved into evening prime time as well, with long-running shows like *Dallas*, *Dynasty*, and *Knots Landing*, which had strong appeal to working class audiences; *thirty-something* and *L.A. Law*, which attracted the upscale "yuppies"; and *Beverly Hills 90210*, which appealed to teenagers. Prime-time soap operas like *Dallas* traveled well to foreign countries, where they were in competition with Mexican and Brazilian *telenovellas*, soap operas that usually ran for several months.

The Sitcoms

The half-hour prime-time radio comedy show moved to television as the half-hour situation comedy. Each week stock characters bumbled predictably through new dilemmas to the audience's delight. Beginning with *The Honeymooners* and *I Love Lucy*, and going to *The Beverly Hillbillies* in the 1960s, *The Mary Tyler Moore Show, M*A*S*H*, and *Happy Days* in the 1970s,

Cheers and *Roseanne* in the 1980s, the sitcoms went on to *Friends*, *Seinfeld*, and *Married With Children* in the 1990s. The most noticeable change of the passing decades is the celebration of sexuality and crude behavior.

The situation comedy has proven to be an ideal vehicle for social issues. The protective balloon of escape entertainment was punctured by *All in the Family* in the 1970s. The central character was made a figure of fun for his empty expressions of bigotry toward anyone unlike himself. *All in the Family*, unabashedly liberal, was willing to raise contemporary issues like abortion and homosexuality. Other sitcoms followed in opening up controversial subjects that once were ignored by broadcasting.

What Is for Children?

Children's programs changed considerably. Radio had offered 15-minute adventure programs weekdays before the supper hour and Saturday morning programs like *Let's Pretend*, which encouraged imagination and the reading of books. Television replaced these at first with live programming such as *Howdy Doody* and *Kukla, Fran and Ollie*, and filmed adventures like *The Lone Ranger* and *Lassie*, but over the years these gave way to animated cartoons in half-hour blocks on weekday afternoons and particularly Saturday mornings, where one cheaply made cartoon adventure followed another. Some of these were shameless advertisements for toys. Advertisers filled the air with other commercials for sugared cereals, candy, and toys of dubious quality. The general level of programming for children became a national scandal. Reformers besieged Congress and the Federal Communications Commission. On PBS, *Sesame Street* and *Mr. Rogers' Neighborhood* offered a reason for pride.

An effort to mandate a Family Viewing Hour, the first hour of prime time, failed to survive a court challenge. Despite broadcasters' promises to retain it voluntarily, with programs like *The Waltons* and *The Brady Bunch*, the Family Viewing Hour gradually dissolved into standard evening fare.

Edward R. Murrow once said:

This instrument can teach. It can illuminate. Yes, and it can even inspire. But it can do so only to the extent that humans are determined to use it to those ends. Otherwise, it is merely wires and lights in a box.[41]

At this writing, the highest ratings in the history of the Public Broadcasting System were earned by the eleven-hour documentary series, *The Civil War*, presented in one-hour and two-hour prime time blocks, a combination of old photographs and commentary by historians. Yet, to all but a relative handful of producers, television was still wires and lights in a box. Neil Postman put it this way:

Television does not extend or amplify literate culture. It attacks it. If television is a continuation of anything, it is of a tradition begun by the telegraph and photograph in the mid-nineteenth century, not by the printing press in the fifteenth.[42]

Talk Shows and "Infotainment"

Because they produced high ratings, the television industry stood its ground against criticism of violence and sex. One or the other could be found in abundance on any day of the week somewhere on the schedule. Violence was a staple of the popular genre called "infotainment." *Hard Copy* and *America's Most Wanted* had the look of news programming and counted former television journalists among its staff members. Many viewers could not tell the difference, for it was not always clear, especially when a ratings month seduced local television station newsrooms to forget that they were supposed to be holding the ethical high ground.

Heavy criticism was leveled against afternoon talk shows because of frequently lurid sex content. Hosts introduced guests to discuss a topic, often deviant behavior, the stranger the better. Guests openly discussed matters that, a few years before, many people did not know even existed, let alone were fit for exposure to millions of viewers who apparently sat at home in rapt attention shaking their heads in amazement. A studio audience asked questions and gave opinions. Viewers were sometimes invited to telephone more questions and opinions to add to the stew. Hosts such as Donahue, Geraldo, and Oprah became household names; in fact, a single first name was enough to identify them instantly to the public. The daily procession of tabloid topics led to an angry reaction, with demands in Congress that television should clean its skirts.

Dozens of other types of programs filled the air, from Sunday morning church services to televangelists badgering the public for donations, from political interviews to travelogues, plus prime-time specials on every conceivable subject, including the annual Emmy awards for the best in television. Sooner or later, somewhere on the dial, something was available for everyone. Considering television's enormous appetite for programming, it was a feat simply to fill all the available hours. One television executive put it this way: "Hell, there isn't even enough mediocrity to go around."

Paying for Programming

The principal ways to pay for broadcasting are:

1. Government allocations. Totalitarian governments prefer this method, which makes broadcasting a department of government, and its employees dependent upon those in power.

2. Viewer and listener license fees. This method supported the B.B.C., Japan's NHK, and Scandinavian state broadcast organizations, among others. Critics regard this user fee as a regressive tax, penalizing poor people, who are charged as much as the rich, but supporters consider it the best way to fund broadcasting.

3. Advertising. The American system is criticized for its materialism, for pushing people to buy what they do not need, for its blatant selling to children, and for injecting commercials inappropriately into the middle of programs and news reports. However, it has proven durable and popular. Most of the nations that once rejected broadcast advertising have accepted it either on state television channels or on separate commercial channels.

Advertisers remained convinced of the efficacy of spending tens or even hundreds of thousands of dollars for a few seconds of commercial time. Many viewers enjoy watching a favorite commercial so often that they can recite every word. Like popular songs and children's favorite movies, some commercials seem never to grow stale. Children in particular enjoy watching commercials.

> The child is right in not regarding commercials as interruptions. For the only time anyone smiles on TV is in commercials. The rest of life, in news broadcasts and soap operas, is presented as so horrible that the only way to get through life is to buy this product: then you'll smile. Aesop never wrote a clearer fable.[43]

The Decline of Broadcasting

As cable choices expanded, the audience for the Big Three American networks shrank from more than 90 percent of the total television audience to about 60 percent. It did not totally wither, but the decline sent a shock through the networks, which never considered that their cumulative audiences could go *down*. Each network was taken over by a larger corporation: CBS by Westinghouse, NBC by General Electric, and ABC by Disney. They reduced their news staffs and reached out for other media businesses. The old captive audience was gone because of the new communication technologies. The American commercial networks battled over a thinning share of the total audience.

European public television networks, complacent and overstaffed, suffered far worse than America's big three networks. Wracked by commercial competition, cable, satellite, and videotape rentals, Italy's triple-headed RAI, Spain's RTVE, and Germany's ARD and ZDF faced financial ruin.[44] State-run Asian television networks were also hurting as viewer choices increased. In France, Russia, Eastern Europe, and Mexico, among other nations, state owned stations were being sold to private interests.

Meanwhile, the Federal Communications Commission approved *low power television (LPTV)* technology for limited-area service. Approximately half the stations were in remote rural areas not well served by existing television stations. More than one-third appealed to such special and varied audiences as tourists, students, Hispanics, and children. Many urban LPTVs concentrated on either religion or shopping.

In two generations, television broadcasting had been born as a lusty baby, had for decades exceeded every prediction about its health, and, as the end of the century approached, showed definite signs of middle age. It was not ready by any means to lie down and curl up its toes, but it was looking nervously at its numerous offspring, the variety of cable channels, direct broadcast satellite services, packaged entertainment on tape and CD, and the potential of Internet video. To no one's surprise, the kids looked just like Dad.

Tragedy in the Parlor

A Minneapolis television station took note of viewer complaints that television news did not reflect "my world."[45] The viewers were correct. As they were constituted, television newscasts not only did not, but could not, reflect a viewer's world for at least three reasons. First, an average viewer's world was normal, consisting of driving to work and shopping safely, passing the day uneventfully, enjoying dinner amid kitchen aromas, and sleeping peacefully. In contrast, television news reported the out-of-the-ordinary. While people avoided accidents and violence in their own lives, television news showed pictures of it. Walter Cronkite once remarked that the cat stuck in the tree was news, not the hundreds of cats safely on the ground. Television news cameras were aimed at the "cats in the trees." News had become one more televised spectator sport. Viewers watched arrests, fires, weeping victims, ecstatic sweepstakes winners, and politicians. Life itself had become a spectacle, not something to participate in, but to watch.

Second, television newscasts, as a part of broadcasting, sought the widest possible audiences, which required a dispersal of focus; the wider the spread, the less that anyone's "world" could be attended to.

Third, the centrifugal effect of all media, including television news, took people away from their world.

The narrower audience focus of the growing numbers of neighborhood cable newscasts and newscasts from specialty channels such as the Christian Broadcasting Network and MTV were more likely to please their audiences in this regard. The trade-off of gaining greater focus on the viewer's world at the expense of giving up part of the audience does not thrill television stations.

By their choice of news coverage, television journalists help to determine what in town and what in the world demands our attention. The phenomenon is known as *agenda setting*. For example, the famines in Ethiopia and Somalia were widely reported in heart scalding pictures of stick thin men, women, and children, flies buzzing about their eyes. Reaching American viewers in their comfortable homes the stories led to a massive outpouring of aid and, in fact, military intervention in Somalia. Yet, in nearby Sudan, people were also starving in an equally brutal civil war at the same time, but because the Sudanese government sharply restricted journalists, few television pictures reached viewers, and there was no outpouring of help. Similar misery in Mozambique and Angola went largely unphotographed and unreported, and consequently largely unaided.

What many people know of what is happening outside their community, they know only through television news. And, if it is not *shown*, instead of just *told*, in a newscast it may as well not have happened.

> As the places of public assembly continued to diminish, and people began to divide their time almost exclusively between home and work, television news would become for many the most important link to the larger world.[46]

Radio News

News by broadcast began not long after broadcasting itself began. Newscasts in most countries reflected government supervision of broadcasting. In the United States, radio stations reported local news as part of their commercial presentations. Travel lecturer Lowell Thomas, whose reports brought Lawrence of Arabia to public attention, began the first American network radio newscasts in 1930 for NBC. Trouble soon emerged as newspapers, frustrated by radio's economic gains while they sustained losses during the Depression, forced the Associated Press and other wire news agencies to deny regular service to stations and networks.

Unwilling to accept the meager diet of news that the newspapers offered as a compromise, radio broadcasters developed their own information channels. The "Press-Radio War" ended in 1935 with a newspaper rout. CBS and NBC continued to build strong news departments with staff and stringers across the United States and in Europe.

Radio's advantage in immediacy was offset by its lack of depth, a limitation imposed by the nature of the broadcast medium, whose goal is to keep the attention of a large audience. A newspaper editor may let a story run for many paragraphs, knowing that an uninterested reader can move on to the next story merely by shifting his gaze. A radio listener must wait for one news item to run its course before hearing the next.

Instead of simply describing an event, audio technology allowed radio to bring an audience of millions to the event itself, everything from sports to political conventions. Baseball, football, boxing, and horse racing broadcasts enthralled millions of fans.

The most famous of radio reporters, Edward R. Murrow, used the medium brilliantly during the German aerial bombardment of London in World War II. Night after night from the rooftop above his studio, Murrow's microphone picked up the sounds of anti-aircraft fire as Murrow painted word pictures of the bombing. Across the Atlantic in a nation still at peace, listeners eagerly awaited his CBS Radio reports, which helped to shift American sentiment from the isolationist wish to avoid war to a feeling of wanting to come to the aid of the beleaguered English populace.

At the same time that newsreel and documentary cameras were poking into the far corners of the world, radio reporters were generally confined to studio sound booths. This state of affairs would not change until radio reporters during World War II got their hands on the new portable wire recorders. Tape recorders, a German invention, were not available in the United States until after the war.

Two Roots of Television News

News on television grew from two roots, newsreels and radio newscasts. In its earliest days, television separated the two. Television newsreels, like the newsreels in movie theaters, dealt with such lightweight material as fashion shows and the appearances of movie stars at a benefit. The newsreels suffered the logistical problems of getting a heavy 35 mm camera, the kind used to shoot Hollywood feature films, and all the gear that went with it, to the scene of an event, bringing the film to a processing lab, and then distributing it either to movie houses or television stations. As a result, events were more likely to be covered if they were conveniently located and if timeliness was not important.

The other root, radio news, lacked visual interest. What was the point of watching the bald spot on top of a man's head as he hunched over a microphone to read a script?[47] Yet, early television newscasts of-

fered no more visual treat than that. It was just a radio newscast with a camera.

Modern newscasts developed step-by-step from those inauspicious beginnings. The "talking heads" and the fluffy pictures came together slowly over the years, as imaginative producers devised ways to enliven and illustrate newscasts using still pictures, maps, charts, and rear projection to position the pictures over the shoulder of the newscaster. Newscasters became aware of the camera, and eventually read from cue cards, then prompters. Images appeared first on cards and slides, later in electronic storage. Sets replaced bare tables. On the set, the newscaster was eventually joined by live shots to reporters at remote locations. The newsreels were melded into the radio-style newscasts. *Double chaining* mixed audio and video to tell a story, adding a separate sound track to film scenes. In the field, television networks opened news bureaus in distant countries, and television stations opened bureaus in nearby suburbs and towns. Network newscasts were improved by newsfilm feeds *upstream* from affiliate stations using the same telephone lines that brought them network programs *downstream*. Bulky Hollywood studio 35-millimeter film cameras were replaced by 16-millimeter film cameras, which gave way to video cameras and videotape.

Starting in 1963 network and local newscasts expanded from 15 to 30 minutes each, and changed from black and white to color. *ENG*, or *electronic news gathering*, arrived when CBS-TV News sent a video camera and a tape recorder to cover President Richard Nixon's trip to Moscow. For the television news audience, ENG meant more pictures at the scene of news events, more coverage of late breaking news, and reports of events as they were happening, frequently the now familiar combination of a reporter live at the scene plus videotape of earlier activities.

Based on videotape, ENG did away with the time consuming process of developing film. A few years later, able to combine video cameras with portable transmitting equipment that used microwave links, photographers no longer had to drive back to the station with their pictures, thereby saving even more time and permitting much more latitude in what news stories could be covered. In the 1980s, ENG was supplanted by *satellite news gathering (SNG)* which allowed reporters to send pictures and live reports back from remote corners of the nation and the world instantly and often cheaply.

As a result of the new technology, television stations depended less upon networks for news coverage outside their areas. New linkages developed among stations that did not share the same network affiliation, but were connected either because of station ownership or because the stations had decided to join together to exchange video stories. Much as the telegraph encouraged the formation of the Associated Press a century earlier, communication satellites, lightweight cameras, and videotape recorders encouraged the formation of satellite news gathering organizations, such as CONUS and Worldwide Television News (WTN), which fed news stories to member stations.[48]

News staffs put together not only several daily newscasts, but interview programs, documentaries, and specials. Political conventions designed their schedules to catch the prime time audience. Election coverage became a victim of its own efficiency and popularity as a cry arose across the nation that the reporting and projection of results in eastern states affected the outcome in western states. By combining journalism with computer technology and statistical probability, television news had the potential to distort a presidential election.

Kennedy Assassination Coverage

When television news began, the best radio reporters wanted no part of it. Edward R. Murrow, whose *Harvest of Shame* shocked a complacent America, commented in 1958, "Television's indifference outshines Nero and his fiddle, or Chamberlain and his umbrella."[49] Newspaper reporters and still photographers pulled camera cords out of wall sockets, refused to attend "press" conferences if television cameras were al-

lowed, and made obscene gestures during important camera shots. Critics who sniffed at the newscasts did not reckon with their growing popularity as television antennas sprouted from every roof.

Attitudes changed on November 22, 1963, the day of the assassination of John F. Kennedy. The murder of the President under mysterious circumstances, followed by the murder of his alleged assailant, both shown as they happened, led not to angry citizens taking to the streets, but to a citizenry glued to television sets to watch the drama that unfolded over more than three days. All programming, all commercials, and all other news vanished. Television news pictures hypnotized viewers as night and day the unfolding events were told and shown over and over. Researchers reported that, with the aid of television:

> People who on Friday exhibited emotional reactions that usually precede collective disorder appeared to have acquired after the funeral a more realistic appraisal of the assassination's implications for the future of the country.[50]

Far better than printed reports could later relate, television news showed the strength and continuity of the American government in the orderly transition of power. It helped pull the nation together with unforgettable images of the violent events in Dallas and the funeral in Washington. During the nation's deep grief, television news had its most shining hour. At one point, more than nine out of every ten Americans were watching. The world watched, too, as the news and pictures went by satellite to 600 million viewers in 23 countries.[51]

The Civil Rights Movement

The capacity of television news to generate emotion surfaced frequently during the coverage of the Civil Rights movement in the South. Nowhere was its impact more clearly demonstrated.

> Coverage rose with the lunch counter sit-ins, the Freedom Rides into the Deep South, and other highly visible demonstrations demanding change. When Birmingham Police

Commissioner "Bull" Connor used fire hoses and dogs on civil rights marchers in 1963, television news carried pictures of blacks being knocked off their feet by the water jets and being attacked by dogs to a shocked and morally outraged nation. At least, in the North. Many stations in the South downplayed the unfolding drama, perhaps limiting coverage to a short segment called "News of Our Colored Folk."[52]

Viewers were caught up by the live coverage of the integration of Little Rock Central High School under the protection of National Guard troops, the lunch counter sit-ins, the bombing of Martin Luther King's home and a Birmingham church, the Freedom Rides carrying cameramen among others on the buses heading south, the entry of James Meredith into the University of Mississippi, Selma, Alabama, deputies swinging clubs and pointing cattle prods, and children in their Sunday-best clothes marching off to be arrested. These and dozens of other video images filled with violence shocked a nation that had placidly accepted the status quo of segregation. Scenes of mob hatred toward black children entering all-white schools following the federal desegregation mandate stirred the American conscience. So did the scenes of civil rights marchers in Birmingham being scattered by police dogs and high pressure fire hoses. Martin Luther King knowingly organized demonstrations to gain maximum television coverage, and found an unwitting ally in the brutal Birmingham Police Commissioner, Eugene ("Bull") Connor.

Most historians, political scientists, and journalists agreed that without the television cameras to show Police Commissioner "Bull" Connor and his police dogs in Birmingham, without the sight of Sheriff Jim Clark and his posse using cattle prods and clubs on blacks in Selma, there would have been no Civil Rights Act in 1964, no Voting Rights Act in 1965. The leaders of the movement became masterful at manipulating television, conscious of the way certain images could be used to move the electorate. Martin Luther King specifically chose Selma as the place to kick off his voting rights campaign because he knew Sheriff

Clark could be counted on to lose control at the sight of marching blacks, with an audience of millions watching.[53]

Civil rights advocate Allard Lowenstein said it took police dogs in Birmingham to sell civil rights to Des Moines. President Kennedy said the televised attacks on women and children made him "sick."[54] National support, partly energized by all those gripping televised images, led to passage of the Civil Rights Act.

These events had all occurred in the South, yet many television stations in the southern states sharply limited what their viewers saw of the Civil Rights movement. The anger that drove to passage of the Civil Rights Act may have puzzled some southern viewers.

The same television cameras that elicited sympathy for the plight of blacks in the South showed very different images and created sharply different emotions when they reported the riots that flared in the urban ghettos of California and the North, starting with Watts in 1965, followed by riots in Chicago, Cleveland, Newark, Detroit, and Washington, D.C. Now television showed blacks not as victims of violence, but as its instigators. Instead of "We shall overcome" viewers heard "Burn, baby, burn." The response was white fear, a lessening of sympathy for black hardship, and an increased flight of the white middle class and its tax base from cities to safer suburbs. Just as segregationist whites in the South had blamed television camera crews for inciting trouble by their presence, so were those crews now being blamed for worsening the urban riots by their presence. Television news was also faulted for displaying only the surface events, but failing to examine their underlying causes.

Anti-War Demonstrations

Anti-government, anti-war demonstrations outside the Democratic convention in Chicago in 1968 led to a confrontation that has been described as a riot by police out of control, beating innocent spectators. The film of the events on the street, played and replayed on the networks, totally overshadowed what was happening inside the convention hall and created such an uproar that the Hubert Humphrey campaign for president was never able to recover. Chicago's Mayor Richard Daley, in the center of events, issued a complaint that has often been heard, even from television reporters themselves when their reports have been shoehorned into tight newscasts.

> Regardless of how objective radio or TV news editors wish to be, they cannot make a fair presentation, a fair evaluation of an important and complex issue in two or three minutes... Where's the action? This is becoming nearly an obsession with some news editors.[55]

"The Living Room War"

Vietnam was "the living room war,"[56] when for the first time in history those who lived far from the scenes of conflict could see the face of war in color, in moving images with sound. Television brought the reality of war evening after evening into American living rooms, to the kitchen tables at dinner time, at bedside as citizens woke in the morning or tried to drowse off at night. Most of the scenes were not ugly, but rather of routine military activity. Still, bringing them almost every night for years to the family living room must have raised questions in many families about the need for American troops fighting a war so far away. The purpose it served became less and less clear. As the war dragged on, pictures landed a harder emotional punch. Seeing fresh young American faces arriving in Vietnam and rows of body bags awaiting the return trip was clear evidence to viewers at home that the Vietnam War was not a John Wayne movie. Images of pathetic villagers caught in the midst of carnage, their huts set ablaze, gave impetus to the anti-war movement.

Reporters, sound technicians, and cameramen lugging 16 millimeter sound-and-picture film cameras on shoulder braces were permitted to travel wherever in South Vietnam a military unit was willing to take

them. They joined platoons penetrating overgrown, dangerous trails, helicopters strafing the treetops or rescuing the wounded, and bombers on runs that made the jungle explode. Day after day the film flowed out of Saigon and the battle zones. Night after night it appeared on the network evening news, and so did the pictures of rising anti-war unrest on streets of American cities.

The television coverage polarized the public. Many viewers who strongly supported the war found in the television pictures even more reason for their support, but those who strongly opposed it were being joined by members of that large majority of Americans with fairly neutral opinions. Opponents in growing numbers took to the streets and to the airwaves demanding an end of American military involvement there. Gradually national sentiment shifted against the Vietnam War. Television coverage was credited—or blamed, depending on one's point of view—with forcing the war to its end without the victory that Americans had come to expect of their wars.

The bitter experience raised the question of whether in the television age any democracy with full freedom of the press would be able to fight a protracted war, especially against an enemy that restricted the television that its people would be allowed to see. Military leaders learned all too well the lesson of television coverage of Vietnam. In the British war with Argentina in the Falklands and in subsequent U.S. mini-conflicts in Grenada and Panama, journalists' access to combat and combatants was restricted. During the Gulf War, control was so extensive that television news seemed at times to be an extension of the military effort. At its conclusion, the theater commander, General H. Norman Schwarzkopf, with mordant humor, thanked the journalists whom he had misled into reporting that American marines were planning a seaborne invasion, so that Iraqi guns remained pointed seaward when the real invasion came across the desert. Television newscasts made Schwarzkopf a popular hero, and the public, grateful that

American lives had been spared, responded gleefully to the news that he had put one over on the journalists.

The best reporting of the brief Gulf War came from Peter Arnett of CNN, who remained in Baghdad. Technology by 1991 had advanced so far from the days of the Vietnam War that it was common for a network to switch live from a military headquarters in Saudi Arabia to Tel Aviv to Washington D.C. to Amman, Jordan. It all appeared so effortless. The viewing public was transfixed by the technology of smart bombs and the television news technology that showed them, but did not show the bodies piling up. It played out like a video game.

Not Newspaper Journalism

Television news was not another version of newspaper journalism, and could not be measured by a newspaper yardstick. It did not match the detail of printed news. On the other hand, newspapers did not equal the ability of television to generate emotion, which translated to involving viewers at a deeper level than newspapers normally could. The capacity to present pictures and sound that impelled viewers to respond was demonstrated in the coverage of many stories.

Among them were the Watergate story, which was investigated by two or three national newspapers, but changed the nation after television began reporting what the newspapers were uncovering and how government officials were reacting. President Nixon might have survived the investigations of the *Washington Post* and the *New York Times* if the television networks, which broke little new ground themselves, had not picked up the story and broadcast it to tens of millions of living rooms.

The race to the moon owed much to television news reports and documentaries for engendering the excitement that supported the expensive space program. Perhaps one billion viewers in a worldwide hookup saw live pictures of Neil Armstrong and "Buzz" Aldrin walking on the face of the moon.

The problems of the environment got a share of television news attention, adding to the movements to heal the earth.

> (CBS newscaster Walter) Cronkite's interest in the environment... almost certainly helped create the climate for passage of the environmental legislation of the seventies... By what they ignored as well as what they emphasized, the editors of network news not only helped to shape the national agenda but also to color the average citizen's notions of reality.[57]

Sometimes a Global Village

Marshall McLuhan's "global village" metaphor came to life when television presented an event of interest and importance that transcended national boundaries, languages, and cultures. Live coverage could attract an audience that could only be guessed at, at times upwards of half a billion souls. The Olympics were such an event. So was the state funeral of an assassinated leader of world stature, such as a John Kennedy, Anwar Sadat, or Indira Gandhi. Here was communication technology in full strength, creating what Daniel Dayan and Elihu Katz called *a civil religion*.[58] Major media events interrupted routine as people took a holiday to gather in front of a television set. Depending upon the event, watching television can capture some of the aura of attending church. If the family gathers to watch, the living room radiates a family warmth it normally lacks. For a short time, the television set unites the family that it usually divides.

> The reverent tones of the ceremony, the dress and demeanor of those gathered in front of the set, the sense of communion with the mass of viewers, are all reminiscent of holy days.[59]

The public responded positively to interesting newscasts that were relatively cheap to produce, so broadcasters added more of them, from local newscasts at dawn with items of particular appeal to farmers through network and local "cut-in" news during the breakfast programs, local newscasts at noon, afternoon, and early evening blocks of network and local news lasting up to three hours, and finally to news at bedtime.

In 1980, Ted Turner, a cable channel entrepreneur, added a 24-hour Cable News Network, and two years later a second network, CNN Headline News, of 30-minute newscasts around the clock. CNN also spread its services worldwide, so people in other countries who had never heard of the older established ABC, CBS, and NBC became faithful viewers of CNN. The BBC and others added world news services. In 1995, ABC and NBC announced plans for competing 24-hour news channels. *Surfing* across the cable channels with a *clicker* also brought the viewer a financial news network, sports news, news breaks in channels heavily devoted to movies, and even news reports prepared for music video watchers.

> Television marched into America's living rooms and took over for 50 years. First it transformed childhood into Howdy Doody time, adolescence into puberty rites with Elvis Presley and the Beatles, and politics into news bites on the networks. Television took us to Little Rock, Arkansas, and Birmingham, Alabama, blessing the civil rights movement for two decades. It cast infamy on Orval Faubus and Bull Connor and beatified Martin Luther King, contributing heavily to the passage of new laws against discrimination. For three decades television

exalted feminism and other forms of sexual liberation. TV took us to Dallas and made John F. Kennedy into a national icon. It took us to the moon. It awakened us to the horrors of war in Vietnam. It made a few hundred corpses on Beijing's Tiananmen Square loom larger in the American mind than the many millions of deaths that occurred under the rule of Chairman Mao Tse-tung.

Television heavily determined which books and magazines we read, which cultural figures ascended to celebrity and wealth, and which politicians prospered or collapsed. It pilloried Joseph McCarthy, Lyndon Johnson, and Richard Nixon. It made Ronald Reagan the most popular president of the era.[60]

From our armchairs, the Gulf War was a diverting, bloodless exercise in technology, a video game that others played while we were permitted to cheer at the play and the ascending score. How primitive the Vietnam War, the world's first "living room war," was by comparison, with its images of faces full of pain, its dead, and its dying. Historians considering the gains and losses of television's ability to cover the Vietnam War may look back and conclude that the television coverage was more significant than who won or lost that war. If this notion is startling, it may not seem so in another decade or two.

Wiring the Toolshed

It was beyond imagining at the beginning that these wires hanging from electric poles and fence posts could harm the television broadcasting industry. Cable was originally planned just to improve television reception, and originally broadcasters welcomed it as such. Yet, by 1996, about two-thirds of the homes in the United States were hooked to a multi-channel cable or had direct broadcast satellite or wireless service, and network audiences had shrunk by one-third. A cable executive compared cable television to air conditioning, "You don't need it, but once you live with it you can't live without it."[61]

Only in the early 1980s, after cable companies began distributing HBO and other new services via satellite, did cable actually begin narrowcasting, relaying a diversity of cultural services, entertainment, and information. Narrowcasting became a fact of life.

Cable was supposed to bring us together. In fact, the proliferation of channels has had the exact opposite effect as viewers select from an ever thicker menu. Television broadcasters find themselves forced to move away from the central tendencies of broadcasting to the market share philosophy of narrowcasting, segmenting the audience into more narrowly focused interests, the marketing approach that guided post-war radio programming in the United States. Cable channels have fractured along ethnic and generational lines just as radio stations did in the 1960s. Much of the nation may share such mainstream programs as the Academy Awards, the Super Bowl, the election returns, and one or two hit programs, but then viewers go their separate ways to their channels of choice. The flow is centrifugal, not centripetal. We do not all want to share the culture of a global village or to seek out common values. Nothing expresses this more clearly than the breeding of cable channels.

Two Trojan Horses

Broadcasters who welcomed the fledgling industry because it brought them additional viewers changed their tune when cable, a Trojan horse in their midst, thinned out their share of the audience and also competed for advertising dollars.

Years later cable system owners themselves would learn what it felt like to be attacked by a technology they had once welcomed. For the cable industry, the Trojan horse was the communication satellite. The satellite transponder originally was regarded as an unmitigated boon to the cable business. It indeed produced a financial bonanza by attracting huge urban audiences with a variety of cable-delivered channels, but in the 1990s it loomed as cable's competitor because of direct broadcast satellite technology, which can bypass both local stations and cable systems to deliver those same channels directly from a source transmitter to the viewer.

How Cable Began

The spectacular postwar growth of television in the United States was shadowed by the growth of cable reception, only a step behind the local television station and its network programs.

By the end of 1947, the basis had been laid for expanding *master antenna television (MATV)* to *community antenna television (CATV)*, and from CATV to what we know

as *cable TV*. Origination of programming was not part of the business of cable companies, but as the medium evolved it developed its own content. Cable grew from being merely a rebroadcast service into an industry that provided many kinds of programming services, in some places allowing viewers to perform various tasks with interactive cable services.

As a way to bring entertainment and information into the home by wire, cable can be traced back to 1893, the wired radio service of Telefon Hirmondo in Budapest, a combination of radio programming and a telephone network. The first community antenna, bringing a radio signal by wire to many outlets, may have been set up in Dundee, Michigan, in 1923. By the time of World War II, such radio systems were common in the larger cities of the United States, as well as in England and parts of continental Europe.

As for television, a year after the BBC began the first service in 1936, a wired master antenna television reception was available to some wealthy apartment dwellers in London's West End. As the service spread, apartment house owners wanted one antenna to serve all the apartments that contained TV sets, aware of the danger of allowing each tenant to climb to the roof to install a separate aerial with wires snaking across rooftops and down walls, not to speak of the ugly sight of a forest of aerials and the signal interference that could lead to tenant "antenna wars." To solve the problem, a master antenna went up on the roof. Television signals received by the antenna went directly to the TV receivers without amplification. However, as more receivers were hooked on, the shared signal weakened; amplification became necessary, one booster per station. Much of this activity took place in New York, but the next step was taken far from city pavements. Most innovations start in big cities and eventually filter down to small communities, but cable television was a country mouse that went to the city.

The industry began in 1948, shortly after the beginning of postwar commercial television in the larger cities when people in hilly rural areas wanted better reception or any reception at all. Line-of-sight signals that were not totally blocked by hills deteriorated over distance. People were frustrated that their town's location denied them the wonderful new entertainment they were reading and hearing about. Lost sales frustrated appliance dealers even more.

The first systems were isolated. While most television stations were connected to networks via microwave links, community antenna systems were not connected to anything. By simply retransmitting station signals, they brought in nothing but what the nearest local stations were broadcasting.

CATV Pioneers

Exactly where CATV began is a matter of dispute. Several entrepreneurs, unaware they were cable pioneers, tried to solve a puzzling business problem: How do you sell television sets in a town that can't pull in television programs?

John Walson, a maintenance man for the regional power company and part owner of an appliance store in Mahanoy City, Pennsylvania, sold television sets when he could. He had to talk fast because local residents could barely receive Philadelphia's three network stations off the air. Reception in their homes was poor, blocked by the surrounding hills. For demonstrations, Walson drove prospective buyers and television sets to the top of a nearby mountain where he had erected an antenna. It was an uncomfortable way to sell his goods, Walson recalled. "To prevent the embarrassment of taking people up the mountain at night, I decided to run the cable down into the store."[62] In June 1948, Walson brought the signal into town by stringing army surplus twin-lead cable from the mountaintop antenna to his store, tacking it to trees, fence posts, and the eaves of houses along the way. The power company gave him permission to hang the wire from some of their poles as well. When he was done, Walson could display working sets in his store window. The sharp television pictures right there in town caused a

sensation among residents. Crowds outside his store were so thick that the police had to clear the blocked street. The police chief became so fascinated with what was going on that he went into the CATV business himself. After Walson ran an extension to a neighbor's home and one to his own home, other neighbors begged for extension wires to their homes. Walson offered to hook up any home in Mahanoy City that bought a television set from him. At first, he refused to accept additional payments, but by the following year he was charging an installation fee of $100 plus $2 a month. By 1950, 1,500 subscribers were hooked up to his system, which he had switched from twin-lead wire to sheathed coaxial cable. He also asked for and received a franchise from town authorities.

At about the same time, in Astoria, Oregon, L.E. Parsons, a radio station operator, experimented with cable television partly, he later said, because his wife wanted "pictures with her radio." Mr. and Mrs. Parsons had seen television demonstrated at a national broadcasting convention. When Seattle's first television station went on air in 1948, Parsons was able to receive a fuzzy picture in Astoria 125 miles away by mounting an antenna on the top of the eight-story Astor Hotel, located near his own apartment. Parsons may have been motivated only by the wish to please his wife, but soon his home was packed with visitors. Excitement among Astoria residents led Parsons into the cable business. Like Walson on the other side of the nation, Parsons extended the signal to nearby homes. He received the signal on one channel and sent it out on another via coaxial cable to subscribers in the community, but Parsons took a step that Walson had not taken. He asked for and received permission from the Seattle television station to retransmit their signal. Newspaper stories about Parsons' experiment got the attention of the Federal Communications Commission, which wrote to Parsons asking for more information, but took no formal action.

Milton Jerrold Shapp got a lot of attention at an electronics convention in 1949 with his master antenna both for apartment houses and for dealers to use to demonstrate television sets. His $500 investment in materials was the start of Jerrold Electronics, a multi-million dollar cable equipment business.

In Lansford, Pennsylvania in 1950 four radio and appliance retailers led by Robert Tarlton decided to go into the cable business. Unlike previous ventures, this was planned from the start as a business whose profits would come from renting a cable service. Jerrold Electronics designed the system, leading from an 85-foot tower erected on a hill to receive signals from Philadelphia transmitters 70 miles away. High gain receiving antennas amplified the signals and retransmitted them via coaxial cable to homes in Lansford. The local power and telephone companies gave permission to string the coaxial cable on their poles for $1.50 per pole per year. Customers paid an installation charge of $100 plus $3 a month.

These efforts won national publicity in newspapers and magazines. Hundreds of would-be operators drove to Lansford to pick up ideas. Jerrold Electronics could not turn out equipment fast enough. The cable systems that these early businessmen went home to build came to be known as *community-antenna television systems (CATVs)*. They differed from the simple master antennas of apartment houses in three significant respects:

1. A "head end" booster for each channel amplified signals to serve many homes.
2. Cables traversing streets required a community right of way, which meant payment to the utilities that owned the poles. Also required was a town's permission or, better still, a franchise for exclusive rights to lay the cables.
3. It was a profit-making enterprise, with income coming from user connections.

Like the Lansford system, early CATV systems received broadcast television signals off the air and distributed them over coaxial cable to subscribers' television receivers for a monthly fee. These systems did not originate programming. They merely retransmitted the signals of television stations in nearby large cities.

Originating Programming

Martin Malarkey and his family owned several music stores in the Pottsville, Pennsylvania, area. They were trying to sell television sets that were coming off the RCA factory assembly lines, but sales around Pottsville were slow because of the dim, snowy over-the-air reception. To Pottsville, located 96 miles from the nearest television station, RCA engineers came to the rescue when they offered to help Malarkey test their television receiving equipment in the town. A few weeks after the Lansford system was in operation, Pottsville also had CATV, but something different happened in Pottsville. Malarkey owned a small television camera. In 1951, he used it to send out a live 30-minute program, in cooperation with a local radio station, of interviews with politicians and local celebrities, including the winner of the Soap Box Derby and his family. Pottsville viewers were delighted. Local origination was born. And by serving as more than a community antenna that picked up programs, "CATV" became "cable TV."

Many small communities at this time were too small to support a television station. The fact that stations cost too much to build and run added to the continuing spread of cable.

Cable's Early Growth

Cable system owners organized themselves in 1951 as the National Community Television Council, a forerunner of the National Cable Television Association, a trade group not unlike the National Association of Broadcasters. In the years to come, it would grow into a powerful lobby for the cable industry.

During the freeze on new television licenses imposed by the Federal Communications Commission between 1948 and 1952 as it struggled with policy questions, only 108 television stations were on the air. Both commercial broadcasters and the government expected the CATV phenomenon to die after the government ended the freeze, but cable continued to grow. Reception improved when better amplifiers and other devices extended the range and raised the quality of cable service.

The years following the end of the freeze saw a sharp increase in the number of television stations, which was more than matched by the spread of cable systems. These were still mostly mom-and-pop operations that gave little hint of the huge businesses that they would become inside a generation.

	1952	*1959*
Television stations	108	510
Television viewers	15 million	43 million
Cable systems	70	560
Cable subscribers	14,000	550,000

Cable systems now began penetrating areas that already received full network service by offering better reception of local signals and by importing signals from other cities. To attract customers, some cable services originated service on unused channels. A typical offering was a feed taken off a camera swiveling from a thermometer to a barometer to a clock. Another feed came from a camera focused on an AP teletype machine carrying a news service for newspapers. More enterprising cable owners added local coverage of the city council and high school basketball games.

Information programs and ads turned a cable station into a television version of the neighborhood shopper newspaper. Public access stations mandated by contract with cities, also gave cable a community appearance. Beyond this, cable companies created their own local fare. A blossoming of neighborhood cable programs, including newscasts, which would become the fastest sprouting segment of all types of newscasts during the decade of the 1990s, met the Federal Communications Commission long-standing encouragement of localism.

The FCC was committed to encouraging local broadcasting. It faced a dilemma when the presence of a cable system in a community economically inhibited the introduction of a television station. While a television station could broadcast its single signal to everyone within its radius, a cable system delivered many signals, but only to a restricted population, stringing its lines to neighborhoods with a high enough population density to deliver a profit. Should the government support sending a single channel to everyone or many channels to only part of the community? The FCC, wrestling with the policy question, was aware, too, that cable was the newer technology; to attempt to limit it to protect an older industry ran counter to basic American enterprise.

Following the old admonition that "if you can't beat 'em, join 'em," television station owners invested in cable systems, a business obviously related to their own industry. Multi-media conglomerates in time would own both television stations and cable systems as part of their communication empires.

City Franchises

Cities at first had greeted the arrival of CATV with pleasure and charged nothing or very little for a franchise. As the years went by, the cities saw how profitable the new business was, and began demanding compensation for the use of city streets. Besides asking for a percentage of the income, cities asked for channels to be reserved for public schools and for public access, plus providing equipment and staff for members of the public who wanted to present a program or make a videotape. City councils learned what other cities had acquired in contracts, information that proved useful in their own negotiations with cable companies eager to gain a city franchise. In a number of instances, the cable companies agreed to generous terms then, a few years later, went back to the bargaining table to alter them on the grounds that circumstances had changed.

As the decades passed, cable's role changed. At first, isolated CATV systems were merely retransmission systems that provided clear television pictures to communities with poor reception. The industry evolved into systems all over the nation, including its largest cities, which provided local program origination services as well as distant signal importation in addition to traditional CATV retransmission services.

Pay-TV Without Cable

Zenith's Phonevision experiment in Schenectady, New York, began pay-TV without cable. It continued in Hartford, Connecticut. Phonevision broadcast three movies daily via electronically scrambled images. When a subscriber telephoned the service to place an order, the station would activate an unscrambling device attached to the subscriber's set. Most of Phonevision's programs consisted of old movies, plus a few live or filmed special events.

One experiment, subscription television, known as *STV*, depended on subscribers paying $1 a week for regular programs plus extra billing for special programs. The STV experiment set off alarm bells in the offices of established media. Broadcasters and theater owners feared that if STV was successful, a pay television network would compete for their audiences. Theater owners worried with good cause that people would prefer to watch movies in their own homes instead of going out to the movies. The popularity of drive-in theaters should have been a clue, if one were needed, that people liked the liberated pleasures of watching movies in home comfort. Waging an aggressive campaign, opponents of the STV experiment succeeded in declaring pay television illegal in California, but by then STV, harried by ruinous delays and challenges, had been run out of business. STV's failure had a discouraging effect on pay television's development for the next ten years, but the industry's innovative managers never forgot about it.

Twin County Cable of Allentown, Pennsylvania, designed a converter that allowed both pay-per-view and regular pay cable service in 1971. As the FCC loosened cable rules in the early '70s, the groundwork for cable's next step forward was being laid.

It would put cable television firmly on one of the lanes of what someday would be called the *Information Highway*.

Videotape, a New Book

Videotape recorders are the fastest-selling domestic appliance in history. In the communication toolshed home, the movie fan can schedule the day around it. The morning newspaper's television log lists the "must see" programs, which will be taped for viewing later in the day by pre-setting the recorder. Once or twice a week, and especially on the weekend, the movie fan swings by the neighborhood video rental shop to pick up a film or two.

Advantages of the Home VCR

It is more convenient to watch a motion picture at home than to go to a movie theater. There is no need to dress up, or to get dressed at all. In fact, we can be downright sloppy without worrying about what friends will say or strangers will think. We can talk as loud as we like during the showing. We can stretch out on the sofa. We can talk to a pal on the phone or leaf through a magazine while the tape rolls. We can snack on whatever we like, no matter how crunchy. We can stop the tape to go to the kitchen or the bathroom. We can put the baby to bed and later check the crib. Stop the movie, start it, back up, don't miss a syllable, and no baby-sitter, no driving, no parking fees.

There is one thing that home viewing is not. It is not an *event*. We recognize that going to a movie theater gives us a different experience than watching at home. Being surrounded by lots of others who are sharing the moment, seeing the action on a big screen, and hearing the sound all around us adds to the sense of escapism that movies give us, a pleasure that still builds lines at the box office. Nevertheless, it is not enough on a blustery evening to drive most people out of their communication toolshed homes.

The video store dazzles us with its variety. Instead of the limited choices of new releases, we can opt for anything else, far more choices on every shelf than all the theaters in town advertise, and the big stores are stuffed with shelf after shelf of movies.

With videotape we can "time-shift" television programs so we can watch at our own convenience. Prime time is now whenever we like it. We can fast forward through commercials too, so that so-called "free" television is really free for us, and it's just too bad that our having this freedom is upsetting to the advertisers who paid to provide those programs. As a result of the appeal of this easygoing lifestyle, we as a society leave the house less often, socialize less. A pattern of alienation continues that began with our first purchase of a television set. Our pattern of life is marked by less reading of books, a drop-off in church and lecture attendance, and fewer visits to friends and family. When adult friends or relatives drop by for an evening, we can fill the hours pleasantly with a rented movie. When the friends of a son or daughter visit the house, the social activity may be Nintendo accompanied by a minimum of conversation as each participant is glued to the game on the television screen.

We can keep our own library of movies, just like books, in our bookcase. Centuries ago a book was a precious possession that only the rich could own. Now, of course, anyone can own a book. Today it is becoming almost as easy to own a movie.

A *Wall Street Journal* poll found that Americans most desired those inventions that yielded convenience and control. The VCR landed near the top of the ratings. Only the microwave oven was prized above the videocassette recorder. Interestingly, the VCR was not the most cherished device of the elderly, who preferred the automatic coffee maker, or the 18-25 group, who voted for the answering machine.[63] But the VCR always ranked among the top choices. In the United States alone, more than four billion cassette tape rentals were recorded in 1995, generating a revenue of almost $11 billion, plus nearly 700 million prerecorded cassette sales, and VCRs could be found in 85% of American homes.[64] The first videotape recorders, large monochrome-only consoles, were sold in 1956 to television stations for $50,000 each. Today, small VCRs showing far superior images in color sell for $200.

Trying to Record Television

Attempts at recording television are nearly as old as television itself. John Baird, who led Britain down the blind alley of mechanical television in the 1920s and '30s, tried without success to record a picture signal on phonograph records. American radio pioneer Lee deForest built an apparatus that included a revolving wheel and needles that etched a moving film coated with silver. It too failed. Two Englishmen, R.V.L. Hartley and H.E. Ives, finally devised a way to record a television image on film, but the quality of the *kinescope* left much to be wished for.

The explosive growth of television in the 1950s sharpened the demand for recorded programs. Until wide-band telephone or microwave links could be established for live feeds, a blurry kinescope was the only means by which a network program could be played on a local station.

The First Videotape Machines

In 1951, engineers at Bing Crosby Enterprises gave a demonstration of a black-and-white videotape recorder that used one-inch tape running at 100 inches per second. At that rate, a reel of tape three feet in diameter held about fifteen minutes of video. Ten heads recorded video, plus an eleventh head for audio and a twelfth head for a *control track* to synchronize the recording with the tape speed. With all of that, the picture had lots of problems. Crosby continued to fund the research, driven not only by a sense of its business possibilities, but his wish to record his television programs so he could play golf without being tied down to live performances.

Two years later, RCA engineers fabricated their own recorder, which turned out not only black-and-white, but color pictures. However, tape ran past the heads at 360 inches per second, which is more than 20 miles per hour. Neither machine produced pictures of adequate quality for broadcast. It was just not possible to produce a stable picture at such a high tape speed.

At the same time, a California electronics firm, Ampex, built a machine on a different principle. Instead of sending the tape racing past the recording head, Ampex engineers spun the recording head. Using rotating instead of fixed video heads as a means of reducing tape speed, they succeeded in 1956 with a recorder the size of two washing machines. Four video heads rotated at 14,400 revolutions per minute, each head recording one part of a tape that was two inches wide. One of the engineers on the project was Ray M. Dolby, who began work on audiotape just after he left high school and later grew famous for his tape noise reduction process. The breakthrough company was named after the initials of its founder, Alexander M. Poniatoff: A-M-P, plus E-X for excellence: Ampex. Another company, 3M, worked with Ampex to make high-quality recording tape. The quality of Ampex video recordings was a tremendous improvement over fuzzy kinescope images. The broadcasters who saw the first demonstration, presented at a national convention, actually jumped to their feet to cheer and applaud. The television industry responded enthusiastically. It was the start of the video age.

Delighted stations on the West Coast could now, without sacrificing picture qual-ity, delay live East Coast news and entertainment broadcasts for three hours until evening prime time, when most viewers reached their homes after work. A few years later, sports fans watched defining moments on instant replay. No long downfield football run or "Hail Mary" pass, no baseball centerfield homerun or double play, no boxing championship knockout escaped the rewind button.

By 1958, the networks were recording video in color. A machine was built that was synchronized with a television signal so a director could not only *cut* to tape, but could employ the familiar film editing techniques of the *dissolve* and *wipe* into and out of tape. These two-inch reel-to-reel Ampex and RCA machines (the size in inches refers to the width of the tape) survived for a generation before they were replaced by more compact and efficient one-inch reel-to-reel *helical scan* machines and three-quarter-inch cassette machines.

While Ampex and RCA were manufacturing two-inch, four-head video recorders, Japanese and American engineers were building the prototypes of today's helical scan video recorders. Their picture quality would remain inferior to *quad* machines for another ten years, unsuitable for the broadcast industry, but the smaller, more user-friendly helical scan machines, costing a fraction of the price of larger machines, quickly dominated the industrial and educational markets.

Electronic News Gathering

An Ampex portable two-inch recorder that could be worn as a backpack with considerable effort was used by television networks in 1968. In 1971, Sony introduced the U-matic three-quarter-inch cassette tape recorder. From now on, there would be no more physical handling of tape. It put video cameras in the hands of television news photographers in place of film cameras. It was an important step on the way to electronic news gathering. As these machines improved, television news departments switched totally from film to videotape because the tape needed no developing time, was reusable, and was more suited to the television medium than film. As the technology improved further, television news editors stopped cutting tape with razor blades and began editing electronically.

With broadcasting, educational, and industrial markets in hand, Japanese video companies turned their attention to the potentially vast home market. Hobbyists had already shown the way. With slightly modified portable reel-to-reel machines, they were taping television programs at home to play again later. Some of these self-styled *video freaks* were actually building a library of movies, heretofore unheard of for ordinary folks.

Going to the Movies at Home

Sony had considered the home market from the start. Recognizing that not only television stations, but viewers, ought to be able to time-shift programs, Sony president Akio Morita said, "People do not have to read a book when it's delivered. Why should they have to see a TV program when it's delivered?"[65] Sony introduced its half-inch Betamax machine in 1975. A year later, rival Japanese companies, led by JVC, brought out VHS (Video Home System) machines, a format incompatible with Betamax. Sony lost the competition as VHS gradually captured the home market. Videocassette recorder sales soared with the

discovery that people were eager to rent movies to watch at home.

Tape renting took off when businessman Andre Blay made a deal to buy cassette production rights to fifty 20th Century Fox movies. Blay discovered that few customers wanted to buy his tapes, but everyone wanted to rent them. Rental shops soon sprouted like corner groceries. In fact, sometimes the corner grocery itself devoted a shelf to videotapes, making it simple to stop by after work to pick up the fixings for the evening's dinner and entertainment. In time, these video shops would be joined by video supermarkets that displayed tens of thousands of titles in sections labeled *new releases, comedy, adventure, mystery, science fiction, romance, children, family, inspirational, exercise, travel, concert, foreign, classics, documentary,* and, in a separate room, *adults only.* *Music videos* and *games* got their own sections in some stores and so did *how-to's* on everything from losing weight to cooking. *Jane Fonda's Workout* was the first successful *how-to* tape. Larger cities had shops specializing in kung-fu movies, foreign films, or even home-delivery of tapes plus a bag of microwave popcorn.

CBS tried and failed in the mid-'60s with a film cartridge called *EVR.* Rival RCA had no better luck in 1973 with its *Selectavision* videotape system, using a type of motion picture hologram. RCA later introduced another *Selectavision,* this time a kind of phonograph that played discs; a needle made

Figure 5.8
Vietnamese videos line the shelves of a grocery that caters to a Vietnamese population in St. Paul, Minnesota.

Figure 5.9   A shopping cart full of children and videotapes rolls down aisles featuring thousands of titles in at least a dozen categories.

physical contact with the disc. MCA and Philips countered with *DiscoVision*, a more expensive alternative that had the advantage of a laser beam that eliminated the wear and tear on videodiscs of physical contact. It had random access, freeze frame, and the capacity to store an entire encyclopedia on a single disc. The motion picture industry considered the *videodisc* a better way to bring a movie into the home, pointing out that the videodisc had a sharper picture image, stereo sound, and a lower cost. Best of all, the motion picture industry felt, the videodisc was playback only. No record button, so no free copying.

Unfortunately for the videodisc, the public wanted to be able to record, not so much to copy rented films illegally as to record movies and television program favorites off the air while the owner was away, for later playback. Videodisc players could not do this. They did not match the flexibility of videocassette recorders for time-shifting. If tape could not quite equal laser discs for image quality, that was alright with most

people. Tape was good enough. Besides, thanks to the head start that Betamax and VHS tape players had, more movies were available in this format. The slightly lower cost of discs did not matter either because most people chose to rent their movies. To add to the problems of videodiscs, Selectavision and DiscoVision were incompatible with each other and with a third format, high density discs.

In the battle over competing disc and tape formats, VHS tapes emerged the clear winner. One by one, the other production lines shut down, although the late 1980s saw a resurgence of the laser videodisc. More threatening competition to videotape as a carrier of motion pictures came from *DVD (Digital Video Disc)*, special CD players using digital compression techniques to place a feature film on a single 4.7-inch disc.

The Near Future

For both the video and the computer industries, the future of information storage and

Figure 5.10   Videotape gets equal billing with deli and liquor at a neighborhood store.

retrieval may lie not with tape, but with such optical media as DVD, the videodisc, CD-ROM, and CD-I, which offer the advantages of high density, random access, and no physical contact between the storage medium and the pickup device. The ideal is an erasable compact disc, capable not only of recording, but of storing digital audio, still and motion digital video, animation, graphics, and text.

Video stores face competition from the communication-without-transportation delivery system of 500 or so channels promised by a cable industry that hopes to feed movies on demand through fiber optic cables. To protect themselves, the video stores are considering reinventing themselves as entertainment centers filled with interactive movies and games, and trusting that the public, particularly the young, will enjoy wandering in close proximity to one another down aisles chock-full of movie tapes.

As the videocassette industry matured, prices dropped and more features were added to the machines. VCR owners who figured out the instructions for time-shift recording could go on vacation with the expectation that the fresh two-hour tape they loaded at slow speed would fill with favorite shows. For owners confused by all the buttons, a remote control keypad let them command their machines to tape a program by punching in a code number listed beside the program in newspapers and *TV Guide*. The date, time of day, and channel number were taken care of automatically.

The simplicity, flexibility, low cost, and high quality of tape technology created new worlds of visual production. In the final decade of this century, one hundred years after motion pictures were invented, millions of users could "make a movie." Video cameras even found their way into elementary schools as a learning tool.

Spreading Worldwide

Videotape has had wide impact everywhere on earth, including remote villages, where inexpensive tapes bring information and entertainment. A truck carrying a video-tape player, a television set, and a portable generator is not an uncommon sight in many parts of the Third World. Peoples living as far from urban centers as the Kayapo of the Brazil rain forest and the Inuit of northern Canada have been introduced to video, and have themselves produced tapes to argue for political justice.

Several Third World governments actively promote videotape programs for adult education. For example, the Village Video Network in several countries provided an exchange for tapes on such subjects as farming, nutrition, and population control. International groups give some villages video cameras and training to produce their own films, which were later shown to other villages.

Visual technology seems to be everywhere. Long distance buses in India equipped with VCRs help relieve the boredom. Many Indians refuse to ride buses without video shows. It was reported that when one bus broke down for seven hours, hardly a word of complaint was heard from the stranded passengers, who happily watched a movie twice.

In electrified rural areas of the Philippines, the "betahan" does a lively business among the poor. ("Betahan" is a combination of "Betamax" and "tindahan," meaning "store.") In scenes reminiscent of the start of the nickelodeons nearly a century ago, men, women, and children pay from one to three pesos (roughly 4 to 12 cents) to sit on benches or folding chairs to watch a rented videotape. Betahan audiences are more relaxed than those in movie theaters. They gossip, eat, socialize, and throw out comments about what they are seeing. They are more like an extended family than an audience. Betahans began in villages and barangays (small communities) when a family bought a personal videotape recorder. Neighbors dropped by and began contributing to the cost of tape rental and electricity.

The Philippine government sends vans with useful agricultural tapes to farm areas. To entice people to attend, they will advertise an old film which they have brought along. Families gather to watch the advertised film, then most members slip away, leaving the family heads to watch the agricultural training tapes.

The Persian Gulf was the first Third World region to experience the video revolution. After the oil boom of the 1970s brought fortunes to many Gulf country residents, Japanese-made VCRs poured in. In Saudi Arabia, estimates put the number of television homes with VCRs in 1985 at 85 percent. Imported workers ship VCRs back to their homes in Pakistan, Egypt, Syria, and elsewhere. As prices for VCRs drop, the number of VCRs rise sharply even in the poorest countries. Just as in the more developed nations, videotapes compete with moving picture theaters. While movie *watching* has grown, formal movie *going* has suffered.

Developing countries have video clubs and traveling videotape shows. Bus drivers going to remote areas deliver a few fresh tapes and take back the old ones. Hospitals, hotels, and restaurants feature videotaped entertainment. Video movies highlight wedding receptions and birthday parties. The Malaysian minister of information commented that housewives returned from shopping with fish and vegetables under one arm, cassettes under the other.

> In most Arab countries, women generally do not go to movie theaters. Because of the rapid spread of VCRs, Arab women are among the fastest-growing group of movie watchers. After the Israeli army invaded Lebanon, the first ship to arrive at the Lebanese port of Sidon was loaded with videocassette recorders. The city had suffered heavy damage in the fighting, people were desperately in need of cement, housing materials, and other staples, but what came steaming into the port were VCRs from Japan. First things first.[66]

Here is a 1990 story from Moscow reported by the Associated Press:

> Hundreds of people clamoring to buy imported VCRs surrounded stores in a Soviet city for five days, and some even staged a hunger strike and protests demanding the chance to buy the devices…The newspaper *Sovietskaya Rossiya* described the incident in Yaroslavl as a "video uprising."…Finally,

after five days of turmoil, a happy buyer walked out of the store with the first VCR, called the local TV station and declared, "Victory! The Panasonic is in my hands!"[67]

Broadening the Video Journalist Base

Still another result of video diffusion has been a widening of video journalism capability. The anti-government riots in Thailand in 1992, during which soldiers fired directly into crowds of peaceful demonstrators, were never shown on Thai television news, but were seen in other parts of the world. Videotapes taken from American news programs, brought secretly to Bangkok, reportedly commenced to be the most popular rental item in videotape stores.

The taping of the Rodney King beating by Los Angeles police was just one example of how ordinary citizens made a difference, not only in news coverage, but in the course of events. The King tape, shot from an apartment window, played again and again on television, fueled the African-American anger behind the Los Angeles riots. The riots in their turn were taped, fueling white and Asian-American resentment. The potential for a "video vigilantism" by "visualantes" has not gone unnoticed, with its effects not only on journalism, but on law enforcement itself. Some television stations invited camera owners to contact them if they had shot tape suitable for a newscast.

Video Piracy

Hooking two VCRs together, a video pirate could make a hundred copies of a current movie. That happened in many parts of the world. Video piracy was rampant everywhere. A vast underground network fed millions of illegal copies of videotape movies throughout the world. Tapes of new films turned up in shops from Cairo to Singapore, sometimes within days of their release in first-run American movie theaters. Pirated videotape movies were even shown on television stations, whose owners argued that they could not afford the dollars charged for Western programming.

The national film industries of a number of countries have been battered both by the pirating of their own films and by the influx of cheap illegal copies of Western films. Viewers who prefer American films were watching them instead of programs approved by their governments. Indonesian officials complained that fewer people watched their newscasts because they would rather watch entertainment programs on their VCRs.

The broader questions of intellectual property and copyright protection continued to bedevil bilateral relationships between nations, nowhere more keenly than between China and the United States. Sino-American relations in the mid-'90s, which festered over such issues as the status of Taiwan, the use of prison labor, and the treatment of orphans, were not helped by American accusations that large and sophisticated Chinese factories protected by corrupt officials churned out illegal audiotapes, videotapes, CDs, and computer software with no regard for copyright. The weight given to this issue in diplomacy offered still another proof of the centrality of communication technology in modern life.

"Cultural Imperialism"

It may be expected that government officials in many countries will not be pleased that their populations have easy access to non-approved information and culturally unacceptable values, among them consumerism. Among other problems, poor people who see richness beyond their grasp can become even more dissatisfied with their own lot, and that is fuel for crime and even revolution.

Western movies are seen privately throughout much of the world where governments limit such imports in their effort to promote their own national cultures. Among these Western films, pornography is sneaked into private homes in places where the government forbids such programs. Pirated tapes of the latest movies pop up everywhere. Videotape flows across the world in a floodtide that governments and the most powerful entertainment industry corporations seem helpless to stop.

In formerly communist countries, rigid political censorship created appetites only VCRs could help satisfy. Clandestine VCR tapes hastened the end of those repressive regimes...

VCRs help make up for often inadequate Third World television schedules and poor program quality. Few individuals in such countries can afford to buy a VCR outright, but rentals, club purchases, and group viewing in bars, coffee houses, and even on buses resolve cost problems. In some cases heavy censorship encourages VCR growth—as in Saudi Arabia, where puritanical Moslem standards severely limit broadcast television. A worldwide underground market in VCRs and tapes defeats most government attempts to limit sales and rentals.[68]

The United States has been accused of practicing "cultural imperialism" by bringing American culture and American values into other countries. These nations cannot counter American movies and television programs with what they can produce themselves because they cannot afford to make movies that are as attractive as the American product. The remedy of censorship has been widely attempted, but with only limited effect. Such Western films as *Gandhi* (India), *Sadat* (Egypt), and *Missing* (Chile) were banned in the countries where their stories unfold, but nevertheless have been widely seen there on tape.

Video Production Diffusion

Future historians may conclude that nothing about this communication revolution has mattered more than that it has empowered ordinary people. Among the specific changes that videotape has made is an expansion of the producer base. Limited just a few years ago to television news photographers, video cameras have been diffused as the Kodak Brownie once was.

Television and movies stored on videotape may be deplored by educators as a waste of time and a poor substitute for books, but the fact is that the high school library is now being called "the media center."

The camcorder has joined the still camera as a means of preserving family memories.

Videotape of what the children did on vacation may one day be sent to grandparents, utilizing fiber optic pathways instead of the mail service, a possibility raised by the Federal Communications Commission in 1992 when it ruled that telephone companies may operate their lines to transmit TV programs and related services to their customers.

Today, both professionals and amateurs can produce a motion picture of technically acceptable quality at a cost that would have brought derision just a few years ago. The costs keep dropping and the quality rises, accompanied by improvements in ease of use and number of features. The phrase *desktop video* has found its way into the language next to *desktop publishing*. For a wide range of activities, software permits a microcomputer to replace much of the Hollywood bag of editing tools, even special effects. Fades, dissolves, animation, sound tracks, and optical effects are programmed in off-the-shelf computer programs. Because moving images can be turned into strings of 1s and 0s, they can be compressed, stored, decompressed, and altered *off-line* with *nonlinear editing*, catch-phrases of the digital video technology.

There seems to be no end to inventive uses for videotape. A tape of swimming fish called "Video Aquarium" and the tapes of "Ocean Waves" and "Video Fireplace" have been sold by the thousands.

There is also videotape as matchmaker, communication technology put into service for the introduction to suitable partners.

In video dating clubs, participants tell a video camera of their interests, their virtues, and the type of person they would like to meet. Their videotape is shown to prospects.

A few people who knew they would soon die left a farewell videotape instead of a farewell note for their loved ones. Someone reportedly started a "talking tombstone" business, a video display screen and audio recorder as part of a solar powered headstone.[69]

Words and pictures recorded on camcorders may replace personal letters. In high schools, the video yearbook joins the printed version. Even in some grade schools, curious little fingers push the camera buttons.

> "This is called a camcorder," she says. "Can you say cam-corder?"
>
> "Cam-corder," her pupils respond in singing unison.
>
> "Good," she says. "And what do you think 'camcorder' stands for? That's right. It's a video camera and a video recorder. Now, can you say 'battery pack'?"
>
> "Battery pack," the students sing out in fascination. Their eyes are as wide as CBS' famous optical trademark.
>
> Welcome to TV 101... At North Star Primary School in Minneapolis, where Sue Krueger is a media specialist, and at other schools in Minneapolis and St. Paul, teachers are turning students on to video at an early age.[70]

Setting New Records

The post-World War II years saw not only the television set, but the stereo system become furniture. With engineers perfecting every element of the recordings and the home equipment, people sat in their toolshed homes to listen to sounds of concert hall quality.

To accompany the new equipment, new music came along. In 1951, the Cleveland record store owner who sponsored a show by a radio disc jockey, Alan Freed, invited

him to stop by for a visit. What Freed saw was a store filled with white teenagers dancing in the aisles to rhythm 'n' blues, which was generally identified as "Negro music." That visit convinced Freed to start a new show, which he called "Moon Dog House." He called the music "rock 'n' roll." It shook up the recording industry. Critics accused Freed of corrupting a generation of teenagers. The youngsters also responded to recordings by Elvis Presley, who was originally referred to as "the white boy who sang colored." His popularity through movies and the sale of records opened the way for black singers to extend their music into a mainstream community that had been closed to them. As for the white teenagers, they may have delighted as much in a new way to get out of that comfortable home and separate themselves from their parents' generation as in the new music itself.

The power of recorded music to influence behavior became clear as early as World War I, when "Over There" and other songs helped to stir feelings of American patriotism, just as "Lili Marlene" appeared to do for German patriotism. During World War II, recorded songs such as "The White Cliffs of Dover" and "Coming in on a Wing and a Prayer" did the same.

"We Are the World" sold four million copies in six weeks. Its impact went beyond big business when the profits of $50 million in the six months following its release went to "USA for Africa," paying for an outpouring of food and medicine for regions of East Africa suffering under a terrible drought.

Emotionally effective media can breed controversy, and recorded music receives its share. Because recorded music is so tied up with home and children, people feel vulnerable and violated at hearing lyrics they regard as obscene. Allegations were made that rock 'n' roll lyrics led to drugs, sexual promiscuity, violence, teen suicide,

Figure 5.12   At Musicland, customers can stand at listening stations to sample different kinds of music before they decide to buy.

pregnancy, abusive parents, and broken homes. Rap music, part of the African-American culture, was accused of demeaning women and spreading hate against whites in general and Jews and police in particular. Suggestions were made that records be labeled dangerous, like cigarette packages.

Radio and Recording

When program producer Herbert Morrison of WLS, Chicago, traveled to Lakehurst, New Jersey in 1937 to describe the arrival of the German dirigible *Hindenberg*, an engineer went along. The recording they made as the *Hindenberg* burst into flames remains one of the most dramatic in radio history. NBC lifted a ban on recordings to play it several times over the network. A Pathé newsreel photographer was present as well; the combined sound and pictures are frequently presented in historical programs.

During radio's golden years, the American Federation of Musicians was able to enforce a ban of broadcast recordings to protect musicians' jobs. A permanent breakthrough in this ban came in 1946, when ABC brought Bing Crosby over from NBC by promising to allow him to record his programs.

With the coming of television, radio needed a new format to survive. Recorded music provided a way for radio stations not only to survive, but to thrive. The number of radio stations has doubled and redoubled

Figure 5.11   We may have more types of music available today than most people knew songs before recorded music. Retail chains like Musicland introduce people to different musical genres.

since the arrival of television. Recorded music spun by disk jockeys at local stations became the primary source of programming by the late 1950s. The joining of radio and recording made sweet music for both industries.

> The large segment of the public that had bought phonographs provided a ready market for a radio broadcasting service and gave radio broadcasters a preconditioned audience. The network of retail stores established to sell phonographs and records was available to perform the same function for radios. At first, radio broadcasting was considered to be a competitor of the record industry. In time, however, the industries developed a symbiotic relationship. Radio needed records as a source of programming, and records needed radio for sales promotion.[71]

High Fidelity

High fidelity, meaning the faithful reproduction of music, was begun in the 1930s when circuits incorporating "negative feedback" became available. A small market for quality loudspeakers had stemmed from Hollywood's interest in good movie theater acoustics dating back almost to the introduction of sound film. But during the Depression, engineers at CBS and AT&T's Bell Labs reversed the view held by major phonograph and radio manufacturers that hardly any home market existed for precise sound. In the decades that followed, James Lansing, Henry Kloss, Paul Klipsch, and Rudolph Bozak designed speakers for audiophiles, founding such famous companies as KLH, Advent, JBL, Altec Lansing, Bozak, and Klipschorn. Other inventors and engineers, many of them Japanese, perfected other components of high fidelity and stereo recording and playback from low mass pickup heads and tone arms through improved turntables, receivers, and amplifiers to Dolby noise reduction for audio tapes and the laser reading of compact discs. For those without the means or opportunity to hear world-class orchestras in major halls, let alone invite prominent performers into their homes to play, high

fidelity provided an unprecedented opportunity to enjoy music.[72]

A Hungarian-born engineer working for CBS, Peter Goldmark, came up with a replacement for the clay-and-shellac 78 rpm record with its five minutes of playing time. In 1948, his LP ("long playing") record, made of plastic, thinner, lighter, with more grooves, played with a finer needle and, at a slower 33 1/3 rpm, provided 23 minutes of music per side with better audio quality and longer wear. Goldmark further improved audio quality with sapphire-tipped needles, condenser microphones instead of ribbon mikes, and turntables without rumble. As the sound of music improved, record sales soared, matched by growth in the phonograph and audio components industry.

RCA responded to the LP with the small 45 rpm that played one song to a side. Made of cheap, unbreakable, and colored plastic, the 45s were a hit with the postwar teen generation and were a significant factor in the growth of rock 'n' roll. The "record wars" set an example of large corporations attempting to define turf through technology—a situation repeated a generation later between Sony and its rivals in the Betamax-VHS war, the HDTV war, and several others.

In the 1980s and 1990s video games cut into the music business, but music videos, notably MTV, and digital technology brought it back as people began to replace their record collections with CDs.

By this time, the large recording companies were part of media conglomerates. Their names notwithstanding, most of the largest were foreign owned. In the middle of the 1990s, CBS Records was owned by Sony. MCA was owned by another Japanese communication equipment manufacturer, Matsushita. RCA Records was a subsidiary of Bertelsmann of Germany, and PolyGram by Philips of Holland. Capitol was owned by an English-American consortium. Only Warner Music among the largest firms was totally American owned.

Innovations in consumer sound recording have had mixed results. Quadraphonic sound systems and recordings—the logical successor to stereo—never caught on. Digital audio tape (DAT), introduced in 1987, failed to catch on with the public despite its ability to record music with perfect fidelity.

The compact disc (CD) fared better. The optical pickup system of compact disc players, using a laser that read microscopic pits on records without the physical contact and accompanying wear of a stylus head, won widespread acceptance with sound superior to conventional audio cassette recordings. The CD suffered the disadvantage (from the consumer's perspective) that the home user could not record on the disc, which pleased music producers who estimated that home dubbing already drained one-fifth of their sales. However, recordable CDs were on the way. Computer CDs, used for encyclopedias, could also play music CDs. Some FM stations catered to the home dubbers who recorded on audiotape by announcing that they would play an album without interruption. As compensation for lost revenue, Congress approved a one percent tax on blank audio tapes, which was passed on to music writers, performing talent, and publishers.

Other formats had not caught on with the public by the mid '90s. The digital compact cassette (DCC) and the Mini-Disc were not compatible with anything else or with each other. The DCC was being marketed in boom boxes and as a replacement for analog tape recorders in home stereo systems.[73] The 2.5-inch Mini-Disc had the advantage lacking in the CD of being both recordable and insensitive to shocks, which pointed to use both as a portable unit and a player in cars, two extensions of the communication toolshed home.

WE STILL HAVE BOOKS

"I think I'll curl up tonight with a book" promises pleasure without contact with other people. The book exemplifies the withdrawal and isolation that accompany the adoption of many of the tools of communication. While illiterate people acquire information by direct communication with others. The reader separates from other people and cuts off all senses but sight. It could be argued that a kind of communication may exist between the reader and an author, but it is mediated in the way that a phonograph record and a film are, through distance and imaginative constructs.

Book marketing took a leap forward in 1926 when the Book-of-the-Month Club began business. Because of its success, competitors sprang up to tap a booming new market despite the Depression. Book clubs catered to occupational groups, hobbyists, and ethnic minorities.

The dime novel of the nineteenth century found an echo in the *paperback* book of the twentieth, another revolution in book buying that began just before World War II. The dime novel with its predictable plots laid out on rough paper between glossy covers remained popular, although the price crept upward. For 25 cents the paperback put a mass-produced classical work of literature, a modern novel, or non-fiction on a wide range of subjects into the hands of millions of people who seldom if ever could afford new books. In the half century since then, billions of copies have been sold, many of them reprints of hardcover books. Other novels and non-fiction see life only in this cheaply printed and glued edition with brightly colored, glazed covers in drug stores, bus depots, and supermarkets. Public libraries now feature racks of the familiar paperbacks.

Between 1950 and 1990, the number of books in print grew nearly tenfold, from 85,000 to almost 800,000. One early study found that television viewing cut into the reading of escapist fiction, but not into books or magazines with serious information.[74] Part of the change is in how books look.

As knowledge has become more plentiful and less permanent, we have witnessed the virtual disappearance of the solid old durable leather binding, replaced at first by cloth and later by paper covers. The book itself, like much of the information it holds, has become more transient…

And the paperback revolution, by making inexpensive editions available everywhere, lessens the scarcity value of the book at precisely the very moment that the increasingly rapid obsolescence of knowledge lessens its long term informational value.[75]

Continued

We Still Have Books *(continued)*

Director Steven Spielberg remarked at an Academy Award ceremony, "In our romance with technology, we've lost something: the love of books." The sentiment, even if based on a fallacy, is admirable. The audience appreciated it. In truth, books are part of the romance of communication technology. The question must arise as to how well books, an older technology, can survive against newer media. The answer seems to be that books are doing fairly well, but could certainly do better. Americans on average read only one book a year, but those Americans who do read are willing to spend more for books, the number of titles trends upwards, and the number of stores selling books has been increasing. Media conglomerates have purchased several large book publishing houses.

Books remain influential because influential people add to their store of knowledge from them and may take action from what they learn. Rachel Carson's *Silent Spring* (1962) helped form the environmental movement and led to the banning of DDT and other pesticides that killed birds and wild animals and entered the human food supply. Betty Friedan's *The Feminine Mystique* (1963) energized the feminist movement.

The book itself was the first mechanical mass medium. What is really being asked, of course, is: can books' monopoly of knowledge survive the challenge of the new languages (other media)? The answer is: no. What should be asked is: what can print do better than any other medium and is that worth doing?[76]

Some large bookstores reinvented themselves as quasi toolshed homes, with reading tables and coffee. Adding to the policy of "If you can't beat them, join them," plans were afoot to launch a cable channel to be called Booknet offering round-the-clock readings, author profiles, interviews, news of the publishing industry, and book shopping services. Novelist E. L. Doctorow, one of its founders, said, "Booknet will combine the two most powerful communications tools ever invented—the printed book and the television image."[77]

Meanwhile, the bookmobile chugged along the rural back roads of the Information Highway. Begun in 1905 and reaching a peak of 2,000 bookmobiles during the 1960s, this vestige of the automobile age has been declining in numbers due mainly to tight county budgets. That about 1,000 bookmobiles, at last count, are still there to serve readers who live far from public libraries says much about the staying power of books.

Notes

1 From the poem "Home" by Edgar A. Guest.
2 Minneapolis *Star Tribune*, 14 August 1993, sec. A3.
3 *Newsweek,* Nov. 1, 1993: 78.
4 Up 10.2% between 1985 and 1990, according to Veronis, Suhler & Assoc., *Communications Industry Forecast*, June 1991: 13.
5 Robert D. Putnam, "Bowling Alone: America's Declining Social Capital," *Journal of Democracy* (January 1995): 65-78.
6 Jarice Hanson, *Connections: Technologies of Communication* (New York: Harper Collins, 1994), 241.
7 Daniel J. Boorstin, *The Americans: The Democratic Experience* (New York: Random House, 1973), 393.
8 Putnam, op. cit.
9 Jerzy Kosinski, *Being There* (New York: Harcourt Brace Jovanovich, 1970.)
10 Ronald J. Faber and Thomas C. O'Guinn, "Expanding the View of Consumer Socialization," *Research in Consumer Behavior*, vol. 3, 1988, 58.
11 Jack M. McLeod and Steven R. Chaffee, "The Construction of Social Reality," in James T. Tedesch, ed., *The Social Influence Process* (Chicago: Aldine Atherton Publishing, 1972), 50.
12 Jack Mingo, *The Official Couch Potato Handbook: A Guide to Prolonged Television Viewing* (Santa Barbara, CA: Capra Press, 1983), 28.
13 Research by Herbert Krugman. Reported in Marshall McLuhan and Bruce Powers, *The Global Village* (New York: Oxford University Press, 1989), 63.
14 Stewart Brand, *The Media Lab* (New York: Viking, 1987), 43.
15 "A Death in the Family" was made the title of a documentary by WCCO-TV, Minneapolis, aired 3 December 1978.
16 James H. Bruns, *Mail on the Move* (Polo, IL: Transportation Trails, 1992), 89.
17 Boorstin, 135.
18 Wayne E. Fuller, *RFD, The Changing Face of Rural America* (Bloomington: Indiana University Press, 1964), 36.
19 Boorstin, 135.
20 Minneapolis *Star Tribune*, 26 December 1995, sec. A12.
21 John S. Reineke, "Cellular Telephones," in Grant, August E., and Kenton T. Wilkinson, eds., *Communication Technology Update, 1993-1994* (Austin: Technology Futures, Inc., 1993), 293.
22 Carlos R. Leos, "Mobile Satellite Service," in Grant et al, 305.
23 Kimberly Ann Vavrek, "Videophone," in Grant et al, 321-23.
24 George Seltzer, *Music Matters* (Metuchen, NJ: Scarecrow Press, 1989), 40.
25 Boorstin, 475.
26 1992 figures, Radio Advertising Bureau. *Radio Marketing & Fact Book*, 1993.
27 B. Eric Rhoads, "Looking Back at Radio's Future," *Media Studies Journal*, Columbia University (Summer 1993): 18-19.
28 Michael Wusterhausen, "AM Stereo Radio," in Grant et.al., 121.
29 P. Lane Shannon, "Digital Audio Broadcasting," in Grant et.al., 111.
30 Essay found in DeForest archives, reported in Stephen Greene, "Who Said Lee de Forest Was the 'Father of Radio'?" Unpublished paper, 1991.
31 W.F. Ogborn and M.F. Nimkoff, *Sociology* (Boston: Houghton-Mifflin, 1950), 536-40.
32 Marshall McLuhan, *Understanding Media: The Extensions of Man* (New York: McGraw-Hill Book Co., 1964), 283.
33 McLuhan, 195.
34 Brandon S. Centerwall, "Television and Violent Crime," *The Public Interest*, (Spring 1993): 61.
35 According to President Bill Clinton, *Newsweek*, 11 March 1996, 62.
36 *Newsweek,* 17 October 1988, 84.
37 Todd Gitlin, "Flat and Happy," *Wilson Quarterly* (Autumn 1993): 48.
38 Neil Postman, *Amusing Ourselves to Death: Public Discourse in the Age of Show Business* (New York: Viking, 1985.), 92.
39 E.B. White, *Harpers Magazine*, October 1938.
40 *Newsweek,* 17 October 1988, 84.
41 Address to Radio Television News Directors Association, 1 January 1952.
42 Postman, 84.
43 Edmund Carpenter, *Explorations in Communication* (Boston: Beacon Press, 1960), 165.
44 *The Economist,* 13 February 1994, 12.
45 WCCO-TV, 1994.
46 Barbara Matusow, *The Evening Stars* (New York: Ballantine Books, 1984), 126.
47 Drew Pearson, who was sponsored by a hat company, and Walter Winchell wore hats while they read their televised newscasts.
48 Peter Swearingen, "Satellite News Gathering," in Grant, et al, 251-52.
49 J. Fred MacDonald, *Blacks and White TV — Afro-Americans in Television since 1948* (Chicago: Nelson-Hall Publishers, 1983), 89.
50 William Mindak and Gerald Hursh, "Television's function on the Assassination Weekend," in *The Kennedy Assassination and the American Public*, ed. by Bradley Greenberg and Edwin Parker (Palo Alto: Stanford University Press, 1965), 141.

51 Edward Bliss, Jr., *Now the News: The History of Broadcast Journalism* (Columbia University Press, 1991), 340-41.

52 Hodding Carter III, *The Black American and the Press* (Orinda, CA: Ward Ritchie Press, 1967), 41.

53 Matusow, 99.

54 Robert J. Donovan and Ray Scherer, *Unsilent Revolution: Television News and American Public Life* (New York: Cambridge University Press, 1992), 16-17.

55 Robert MacNeil, *The People Machine* (New York: Harper & Row, 1968), 92.

56 Michael J. Arlen, *The Living Room War* (New York: Viking Press, 1969).

57 Matusow, 138, 304.

58 Daniel Dayan and Elihu Katz, *Media Events* (Cambridge: Harvard University Press, 1992), 16.

59 Ibid.

60 George Gilder, *Life After Television* (Columbus: Whittle Direct Books, 1990), 8-9.

61 Lloyd Trufelman, Cable Television Advertising Bureau.

62 "Profile: Service Electric's Walson: One of the Grandfathers, at Least, of Cable Television," *BR,* 27 May 1974, 75.

63 *The Wall Street Journal,* 19 September 1989, sec. B1.

64 Alexander & Associates, *Video Flash.*

65 James Lardner, *Fast Forward* (New York: W.W. Norton, 1987), 68.

66 Thomas L. Friedman, *From Beirut to Jerusalem* (New York: Farrar, Straus & Giroux, 1989), 33.

67 Associated Press, 8 January 1990.

68 Sydney W. Head, Christopher H. Sterling, and Lemuel B. Schofield, *Broadcasting in America: A Survey of Electronic Media,* seventh ed. (Boston: Houghton Mifflin Co., 1994), 561.

69 Gary Gumpert, *Talking Tombstones and Other Tales of the Media Age* (New York: Oxford University Press, 1987), 5.

70 Minneapolis *Star Tribune,* 6 March 1989, sec. 1E.

71 Andrew F. Inglis, *Behind the Tube* (New York: Focal Press, 1990), 19-20.

72 David Lander, "Technology Makes Music," *Invention and Technology,* 6:1 (Spring/Summer, 1990): 63.

73 Timothy J. Mellonig, "DCC and MD," in Grant, et al, 191-96.

74 Paterson, *Magazines in the Twentieth Century* (Champaign: University of Illinois Press, 1964), 54.

75 Alvin Toffler, *Future Shock* (New York: Bantam Books, 1971), 161-2.

76 Edmund Carpenter and Marshall McLuhan, *Explorations in Communication: An Anthology* (Boston: Beacon Press, 1960.)

77 Minneapolis *Star Tribune,* 24 July 1993, sec. 1E.

6

The Sixth Revolution The Highway

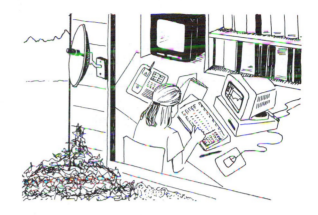

Heavy Traffic

The postmodernist thinker Mark Poster frames an interesting question, rhetorical and unanswerable:

> If I can speak directly or by electronic mail to a friend in Paris while sitting in California, if I can witness political and cultural events as they occur across the globe without leaving my home, if a database at a remote location contains my profile and informs government agencies which make decisions that affect my life without any knowledge on my part of these events, if I can shop in my home by using my TV or computer, then where am I and who am I? In these circumstances I cannot consider myself centered in my rational, autonomous subjectivity or bordered by a defined ego, but I am disrupted, subverted and dispersed across social space.[1]

At the end of a century filled with turmoil and change, we are no longer limited to where the wires run. There are clear signs that they do not run through McLuhan's "global village," for the very technologies of cable, television, and satellite that were once regarded as elements to unite society alienate us from those who are close to us even while forming links that give us unseen acquaintances who are nearer to us in their interests. However, the acquisition of knowledge is not a zero sum game. A person can be sensitive to the loss of rain forest in Brazil and still pull weeds in the back yard.

McLuhan, the brilliant prophet of the Information Age, his eye on the technological potential, figured that mass communication technology could make the human family one tribe again, but neglected to ask whether the human family *wanted* to be one tribe. Apparently that is far from what we want, which is to enlist the tools of communication in discrete ways for diverse purposes. The evidence thus far seems to be that only occasionally do we want to come together to share the same information and entertainment. Inside the global village, if that is indeed where we reside who live during the Information Age, we prefer to stay in our own electronics-filled, print-filled, picture-filled, music-filled homes, our own communication toolsheds, and go our separate ways.

Radio during its golden years, the decades of the 1930s and 1940s, acted to bring Americans together as a nation, to speak a common language with a common accent so far as possible, to share moral values, and to survive the Depression and World War II. No longer. Radio has been balkanized. So have the movies, whose tightly run studio system is a fading memory. So has television, now that cable channels have undermined the three old networks. In a word, American culture is being *niched* by the media that once pulled us toward each other. The metaphor for what is happening is "the Information Superhighway," or less grandly, "the Information Highway." There may be better metaphors to express the variety of possibilities, but we are probably stuck with this one.

The Information Highway extends communication in three important areas:

1. It provides new media and more communication options, which increase our choices, and those choices separate us from family and community.

2. It is interactive, which gives users more control of the information and entertainment being transmitted. Interactivity allows "upstream" requests for "downstream" data feeds. Interactivity also connects people who will forever remain unseen, unheard, disembodied writers to one another via e-mail and bulletin boards.

3. It makes distant connections to personal activities. More than ever before, people can work from home, learn from home, shop from home, and bring distant entertainment into the home, all of which has the potential for shaking up society much as the Industrial Revolution did, but in opposite directions. This has global implications as well as the potential to alter cities.

Perhaps it is worth noting, in passing, a comparison with the Holy Roman Empire, which was neither holy, nor Roman, nor an empire. The Information Highway, Leo Bogart has noted, is not likely to be primarily about information, nor will it be a highway.[2] As for how super it will be, Bogart withheld comment.

Choices

As any means of communication diffuses through a free and open society, greater diversity of channels, of sources, of voices, of content, and of audience follows. More producers transmit more material of greater variety to more receivers. This necessarily happens over more channels because the volume of material, the pressure of competition, and the desires and needs of the receivers cannot be accommodated by the existing channels.

> The choices are exhilarating, but also alienating. The basic principle is centrifugal: market segmentation targets those qualities that distinguish people from each other rather than emphasizing the things we have in common. It is the developed world's equivalent of the retribalization taking place in Eastern Europe, Africa, and Asia.[3]

Diffusion has meant not more people receiving the same number of choices, but ever more abundance and variety.

> We can expect that there will be a great growth of specialized intellectual subcultures. There will be operas and opera news available for opera lovers, microbiology information bases and exchanges available for microbiologists. All of these will draw some portion of people's time and attention away from the common concerns of the nation's sports, politics, heroes, and news...
> A society in which it becomes easy for every small group to indulge its tastes will have more difficulty mobilizing unity.[4]

What the nineteenth century Industrial Revolution massified, the Information Highway demassifies. Massification was a natural product of the Industrial Revolution. Demassification is just as natural a product of the post-industrial information revolution. A glance at what is happening to media industries, which are based on the various tools of communication, makes the point.

Consider, for example, recorded music. For all the centuries of recorded time, only a limited range of music was available to each society, and almost all of it performed by members of the immediate community. One century ago, when the notion was new that music could come in a package from the store, that limitation began to fall away.

Today, we have available to us in large record shops and catalogs a considerable variety of *types* of music. As for individual selections, they are as plentiful as blades of grass. If it seems obvious in the economically advantaged and politically open West that more users will lead to more music choices, the logic would not be so obvious to every society. There are places where more users mean only more units, not more variety, which represents a fundamental difference between free and controlled societies.

Or, consider motion pictures. Once a few major studios controlled the fabrication of this product. MGM, Warner Bros., Paramount, Columbia, 20th Century Fox, Universal, and a few others turned them out almost on an assembly line for distribution through fixed channels. A few other nations had even more controlled production. Today, production companies are everywhere in the world, forming, dissolving, and reforming. New communication technologies have created both new ways to make films and new distribution channels undreamed of during the heyday of the studio system. The non-U.S. market equals the U.S. market and is expected to dominate it before the decade ends.[5]

Or, consider books. When production was limited to what monks copied or what early printing methods could manage, there was relatively little variety. Well into the nineteenth century there were people who said the only books necessary to read were the Bible and the *Farmer's Almanac*. Now, in libraries and bookstores unfettered by censorship, the problem is abundance, what to keep on the crowded shelves and which of the new titles to choose from publishing houses pouring them out like dozens of sorcerer's apprentices.

Radio broadcasting became narrowcasting, as stations targeted audiences segmented along age, ethnic, educational, and cultural lines. Since World War II the total number of radio stations in the United States doubled and redoubled. Like the few large-circulation general magazines that went out of business, the three dominating radio networks, ABC, CBS, and NBC, shrank to little more than news distributors. A new technology, radio on the Internet, holds the promise of a considerable increase in the number of radio stations.

Or, consider magazines. Two generations ago American magazine racks were dominated by a few large-circulation weeklies. Now, new specialty magazines focus sharply on what readers want. It would be hard to identify any ethnic group, religion, job, hobby, or sexual preference that lacks at least one magazine, newspaper, or news letter. The specialty magazines do what radio did after television arrived, and what cable is now doing. And with specialty publications has come specialty advertising. The magazines regrouped their audiences along dimensions of culture and interests.

> Minority media of communication represent a centrifugal force in social organization through their capacity to organize differentiated speech communities and to confer national identity on groups and nationalize their interests.[6]

As for newspapers, urban afternoon dailies were clearly hurt by television, but suburban papers came along. With the aid of desktop publishing technology, so did other forms of printed information, such as newsletters. To this mix should be added electronic print, the text of news reports on the Internet.

Interactivity

Most of what is written about it has been limited to only one side of the Information Highway, the side that will carry the traffic of information and entertainment from distribution points via satellite and microwave and optic strands to the millions upon millions of people at home and work. We read less about the traffic going the other way, from the home to the distant distribution nodes, except that the optical lines will permit upstream requests for data and movies.

Interactive cable offered the tantalizing vision of people voting from their homes or participating in a twenty-first century version of the New England town meeting. American poet laureate Rita Dove imagined appearing in one classroom to talk about poetry while children in scattered classrooms watched, listened, and asked questions.[7]

> With artful programming of telecomputers, you could spend a day interacting on the screen with Henry Kissinger, Kim Basinger, or Billy Graham. Celebrities could produce and sell their own software or make themselves available for two-way personal video communication. You could take a fully interactive course in physics or computer science with the world's most exciting professors, who respond to your questions and let you move at your own learning speed. You could have a fully interactive workday without commuting to the office or run a global corporation without ever getting on a plane.
>
> You could watch your child play baseball at a high school across the country, view the Super Bowl from any point in the stadium that you choose, or soar above the basket with Michael Jordan. You could fly an airplane over the Alps or climb Mount Everest—all on a powerful high resolution display.[8]

The possibilities have not been lost on marketing specialists. It is not inconceivable that a shopper at a computer terminal could be asked to identify a product in which the shopper is interested, answer questions formulated according to the shopper's responses, and walk away with a printout of information and advice. Commercial sites on the World Wide Web are close to that now.

Separated by Communication

The chopped-up media mirror the chopped-up family. Extended families under one roof were the norm at a time when media choices were limited. Where media choices today are limited, such as in totalitarian regimes, many extended families are likely to be found. It is no accident that all totalitarian societies have glorified the traditional family while rigidly controlling the civil society.

By contrast, broken families and single occupant apartments are the products of a society full of choices. Inside the modern nuclear family home, parents and children go their separate ways to their own sources of communication. By 1993, 37% of American children aged 9-11 had their own television sets, 49% of 12-13-year-olds, and 54% of 14-15-year-olds.[9] "Individual" has become "indi-video."[10] Radios are flipped on loudly, earphones clamped firmly to young heads determined to ensure that other family members cannot encroach. Noses poke deeply into magazines and books, media that are more socially acceptable means of escaping other family members than earphones.

It is the unusual, even quaint American family that augments an evening meal with spirited conversation on significant topics. A meal with television is more like it for two-thirds of all Americans. Supermarkets cooperate by setting aside a chilly section for "TV dinners." Garrison Keillor remarked on an evening at the home of friends in Denmark:

> …suddenly I am struck by the fact that we've had an entire hour of dinner and conversation, three adults and two teenage boys, and nobody has bolted from the table to go play soccer or watch television.
>
> Civilization is what we carry on over lunch and dinner and, in America, where a family can go for weeks and never sit down in one place at one time and say 25 words or more, you sometimes wonder if conversation or stories will exist 20 years from now or if we'll just network by E-mail.[11]

Through media, our personal community has shifted from ties based on blood, marriage, and neighborhood to networks of interest groups whose members may be faceless or voiceless, or just temporarily one or the other as we speak on the phone, send E-mail, or faxed notes, or find any other convenient way to exchange messages without having to look anyone in the face. Computer chat lines and bulletin boards grow like crabgrass. Pick up a popular magazine to see how, for politicians as well as movie stars, the images filtered through mass communication become the reality we prefer. Pick up an electronic magazine on CD-ROM or visit a hot World

Wide Web site to acquire a sense of just how fast that reality shifts under our feet.

We wander among communication choices among radio stations, cable channels, and video selections, to say nothing of magazines and paperback books in every mall, drugstore, and grocery. On the front steps bloom the weeds of unwanted throwaway newspapers. The mailbox is crammed with unasked for catalogs to be discarded.

The future holds more choices. We are living in the midst of a fundamental shift in how people acquire information and entertainment, and in what they choose to acquire.

Media take us out of the here and now. Long before television, Charles Dickens saw what the postman might bring with his bagful of mail. In *Bleak House*, Mrs. Jellyby ignores her children so she can concentrate her attention on improving the lot of the people of Borrioboola-Gha on the left bank of the Niger River. Her children are dirty, the house is a mess. Mrs. Jellyby sees nothing beyond the two hundred letters she receives daily regarding conditions in Africa. And televised soap opera had not yet been invented!

Distant Connections

Increasingly, the user interacts with the machine to make distant connections, and that may work for work itself, as much of the travel is expected to be over electronic highways from places of employment to toolshed homes. In a word, *commuting*, but doing so without walking through the front door. Those homes might be located in more exciting cities than where a business has its headquarters or perhaps deep in the countryside, where the employee has yielded to the age-old desire to own a piece of land and live with nature. The population movement from the countryside into cities forced by the Industrial Age may yet be undone by the newest Information Age.

The Information Highway that runs through *cyberspace* is a road through a place literally constructed out of bits of nothing. Everything is *virtual*, not actual. Yet, these electronic vapors are as real as any concrete and steel highway and they are changing our world. The highway passes through real cities, real countries, and real continents. As riders cruise the electronic highway for their jobs, their shopping, and their fun, what will happen to the real cities? Elite citizens of the new wired world could use information technology to insulate themselves from the seething urban cores of cities.

> For centuries, cities were where diverse groups of people came together to interact. They were places of plurality and complexity. Today, the elites are detaching themselves from these physical places...The new technologies increasingly liberate them from being tied to any one place.[12]

Manuel Castells has predicted a worldwide social upheaval in which entire regions of the world, such as Africa, become irrelevant to the information society. Africa has the fewest phone lines, the lowest call-completion rate, and the highest cost for international calls in the world.

At the opposite end of the Information Highway lies Denmark, with a population of 5 million and 99% literacy. In 1995, the government announced a plan to put all government offices, hospitals, doctors, pharmacies, businesses, schools, and research institutions on-line within five years. Each Dane would be issued a numbered I.D. card. Public records would be readily available to everyone, a vision of an open, paperless society.

In the media-rich West, databases proliferated to the delight of people who had undreamed of amounts of information at their fingertips. An article in *New Scientist* asked, "Who needs libraries now that the world's information is accessible through computer networks?"[13]

The centrifugal force of mass communication pulls us away from what is close at hand, and that includes the ballot box. In the media-rich United States, with television on election day filled with imploring reminders that the polls are still open, voter turnout remains embarrassingly low. As a nation of spectators, we see elections as just one more activity to watch. More people watch national election returns on television than vote. As for local elections for mayor and for city initiatives, turnout is a matter for despair. That should come as no surprise; after all, most of us abandoned local community affairs long ago.

Small, personal bits of evidence have emerged on the Information Highway. People who wanted to adopt a baby, stymied locally, found a list of adoptable babies in other countries on the World Wide Web. They got details and a photograph at a mouse click. For anyone tired of long, cold winters, the Web was a daydreamer's delight.

Few outposts remain in the world where communication does not reach. There are tales of Burmese mountain tribesmen huddled to watch BBC television, and a guide on the Zambezi River telling others in the canoe what he saw on *The Simpsons*.[14]

The world's sixth information revolution is the highway through cyberspace.

Computer at the Wheel

At the end of World War II, computers did not exist except for one or two hand-built monsters that filled a large room in a university's department of engineering. A half-century later they are at every hand, not only the familiar micro with a TV screen on top and a keyboard in front, or the increasingly familiar laptop, but chips the size of a fingernail. They replace workers, help the handicapped, play noisy games, teach children, control machines, and on and on. It becomes harder each day to think of an area of human endeavor in which a computer is not involved. The ultimate fate of the computer seems to be to fade into the background—to be everywhere.[15] But like all tools of communication, the computer also separates us from our immediate surroundings.

> For many years computer were thought to be a centralizing force—those in the upper levels of a hierarchy could access up-to-date files on millions of people and keep an Orwellian eye on their domains. But since the advent of personal computers and distributed networks like the Internet, we now understand that the essential character of the computer is decentralizing... a threat to dictators, who have to choose between keeping their countries in the digital dark ages (and suffering dire economic consequences) or liberating a technology that might dangerously open up the entire society. But the same dynamic confounds managers everywhere, as computers and networks amplify the powers of individuals and twist the corporate organizational charts into spaghettilike tangles.[16]

Alvin Toffler called the computer

> ...a greater threat to the Second Wave family than all the abortion laws and gay rights movements and pornography in the world, for the nuclear family *needs* the mass-production system to retain its dominance.[17]

A Tool of Communication

Communication was certainly not an area originally envisioned for computation devices, yet the computer has become integral for almost every sort of personal and mass medium. At a large modern newspaper, computers assist the offset lithography process all the way from the reporter's fingertips at the keyboard to stacks of newspapers sorted and counted, awaiting the delivery trucks. Beyond mere improvement, such as aiding journalists in preparing their copy by means of word processing programs, the computer has created an upheaval in entire communication industries.

Inexpensive microcomputers and easy-to-learn desktop publishing software generates output of a quality that only a skilled printer had been producing with bulky machinery. Feeling the economic pinch of desktop publishing, printing firms have adapted to the new technology by offering printing and binding services that tie in with what desktop publishers do at home, creating camera-ready pages designed with word processing, type fonts, graphics, photo, and page layout software, plus scanners and laser printers. Writers have discovered that publishing their own magazines and books is not beyond their reach.

Through databases, journalists access published reports. But indiscriminate access to files of information can violate privacy, another change in our lives. To cite one example, after tax returns were placed in a national data bank, Internal Revenue Service staff members were caught snooping into the returns of acquaintances, relatives, and celebrities. The troublesome question of the information rich/information poor disparity has also surfaced:

> We already know that those without money have less access to quality information than those with money, and we know that a poor student is four times less likely to have used a computer than an affluent one. Will this unequal dissemination of information create a social schism as wide as that between the ignorant peasants of yore and the literate aristos who hoarded all the books?[18]

Until the 1960s there was barely any awareness that a computer could be used to store and transmit words. Its history was based on the dream of a machine to calculate mathematical problems.

> Until recently, there have been only three major developments in (the handling of information): the invention of written (or painted or carved) language, some five or six thousand years ago; that of simple arithmetic operations, using what would now be called a digital representation of numbers, about a thousand years later; and that of printing, about five hundred years ago...[19]

How It All Began

Mass communication was not a consideration during most of the history of the computer, which can be traced to the ancient abacus used across the Mediterranean civilizations, Asia, and Africa as a calculating device. Leonardo DaVinci drew a design for a computing machine, and two seventeenth century philosophers, Blaise Pascal and Gottfried Leibniz, built working models.

In the nineteenth century, a 20-year-old math student at Cambridge University,

Charles Babbage, designed an "engine" to figure tables of numbers that were needed in banking, navigation, surveying, mathematics, and the sciences. Babbage derived his notion of punch cards to feed numbers into his engine from their use in the weaving industry, where cards forced threads into complex patterns on a loom.

Decades later in the United States, Census Bureau employee Herman Hollerith invented machinery to calculate punch card data. The business he began became IBM. A half century later at the Bell Telephone Laboratories, engineer George Stibitz built the world's first electric digital calculator, a crude computer. And, at a demonstration in 1940, he hooked up a teletype keyboard machine to his computer through an ordinary telephone line connecting New Hampshire to New York; it was another first, telecommunications, the first tie-in of computers and telephone lines.

In 1952, a Univac introduced the public to a computer when it helped the CBS network forecast an Eisenhower landslide on the night of the presidential election, instead of the close results the experts expected. It was another first, a computer joining television for the communication of information to a mass audience, but the significance of the union was ignored in the excitement over the election.

Desktop Publishing

Desktop publishing was preceded by word processing, which began in 1971 as an automatic typewriter with limited editing functions designed by a Chinese immigrant to the United States, Dr. An Wang. Xerox Corporation researchers conceived of a graphics-based computer that not only could be controlled by a mouse, but also displayed typefaces on a screen and sent the displayed output to a laser printer, beginning what would become known as *WYSIWYG*: "What you see is what you get." The PostScript page description program, the Hewlett-Packard low-cost laser printer, and the introduction in 1984 of the Macintosh computer brought to the public the reality of *desktop publishing*, a term coined the following year by Paul Brainerd, developer of Pagemaker, which became the leading page layout program.

The Information Age has added archives and databases on CDs, on hard and on floppy disks, both magnetic and optical media. Nexis and Lexis are typical of more than 4,000 data bases available for retrieving data.

By themselves, computer and laser printers, the principle equipment in desktop publishing, have not created the first opportunity for people of moderate means to publish. After all, typewriters and mimeograph machines have been around for a long time. What computers and laser printers provide is egalitarian, the means to offer an attractive and sometimes professional looking product. Tens of thousands of people now do what only a relatively few people could do in the past, which is to package their writing attractively without having to turn to others for help. In a real sense, desktop publishing offers the possibility of putting the ability to disseminate information into many hands.

Primary users have been businesses that once went to commercial printers to produce in-house magazines and brochures. They are no longer dependent on a printer's schedules and promises, and are less worried about last minute changes.

Schools, government offices, clubs, and organizations of every sort turn out innumerable newspapers, newsletters, magazines, and flyers. Restaurants print menus, theaters print programs, and students hand in slick looking term papers.

In a historical sense, desktop publishing is as old as the start of printing in Europe, for Gutenberg and those who followed him a half millennium ago were printer-publishers. So was Benjamin Franklin, for that matter. Things changed with the introduction of big and costly machinery a century ago as part of the Industrial Revolution. The newest communications revolution has, in a sense, turned the clock back. Said one observer:

> What really excites me…is the idea that some monumental author whose work might otherwise be destined for obscurity will use desktop publishing to write a book or pamphlet or newspaper that will have immense impact on our culture.[20]

Even for those afflicted with writer's block, the evanescent screen may be a boon, knowing that words lack the apparent permanence of the printed page. Word processing also gives comfort to form letter writers.

> At first, for instance, there seemed to be a kind of social deception entailed in sending 50 people letters which, apart from tiny 'personalized' alterations, were identical to the point that no one could be sure whether he or she was the only recipient. We no longer think that the loss of that traditional Gutenbergian distinction is a deception, or even that it is particularly bad manners. It is simply an opportunity offered by the word processor which is ours by right if we have the technology.[21]

Desktop publishing, still a young industry, has already affected the way a lot of written matter is created and distributed. Writers, editors, publishers, librarians, and book dealers have adapted to the new technology, which holds the promise not only of fundamental changes in the way that words reach readers, but in the diversity of what is available. As in every aspect of mass communication, more producers are delivering more content on a greater variety of topics to an ever expanding audience.

MAGAZINES TARGET THEIR READERS

Despite growing competition from other media, magazines continue to be a highly desirable way for people to receive inform-ation and entertainment. A magazine industry study reported that nearly nine out of ten American adults read an average of ten copies a month. As might be expected, upscale readers consumed more magazines, but magazines—glossy, slick, packed with pictures, art, and color—were also in the hands of people with little education and even illiterates. Travelers to foreign countries leafed through the pages of a magazine to look at pictures and pick at headlines and picture captions even if they could not understand the language.

Magazines were the leading edge of the centrifugal force, the trend to demassification that separated people. The magazine industry showed the way for other media to seek targeted audiences for their printed and electronic products. Thousands of trade and specialty magazines concentrated on groups of readers who abandoned popular periodicals and daily newspapers, but hung onto subscriptions to those magazines that limited their messages to identifiable occupations, interest areas, age groups, hobbies, religions, and organizations.

Like general circulation magazines, radio was a victim of television's popularity following World War II. Radio stations responded by targeting specific audiences, as magazines do, although the local nature of radio restricts its capacity to narrow its audiences according to their interests the way that magazines can. If the new technology of radio on the Internet proves successful, the kind of narrow audience targeting that magazines accomplish may be expected. As the number of available cable television channels grows, a similar narrowing is taking place.

Circulation Leaders Offering huge viewership numbers to advertisers who had supported mass circulation magazines, television was blamed for the demise of *The Saturday Evening Post*, *Life*, *Collier's*, and *Look*, all of which had circulations of more than one million. But more focused magazines thrived. Their advertising rates were lower and their readers were more likely to respond to specific ads.

Huge circulation magazines are still being published. *Modern Maturity*, the bimonthly sponsored magazine of the American Association of Retired Persons, prints more than 20 million copies per issue. The newspaper Sunday supplement *Parade* has a total print run of 36 million.[22] Some large circulation magazines do business in separate editions. *The Reader's Digest*, founded in 1922, has dealt each year with an intricate distribution scheme because of the sheer size of its circulation. Each month the *Digest* has published some forty editions, including Braille, in eighteen languages, and delivered about 30 million copies around the world. The weekly *TV Guide* has printed close to 15 million, but does so in many separate editions.

The logistics of distribution are a major consideration of publishers of national news magazines like *Time* and *Newsweek*, as well as of national newspapers. To provide home delivery either through special carriers or the postal system on Monday with information that was written on Sunday, satellites send pages to regional printing plants, and from there magazines go by airplane and truck to local distribution points. Readers of large circulation magazines were startled when they first discovered that their names, addresses, and subscription data were imprinted on the actual magazine covers instead of on paper labels.

Magazines have also come up with different answers to the question of generating income from subscriptions versus sales at the checkout counter magazine racks. The more dependable subscriptions are usually sold at a considerable discount from rack sales, but advertisers like to reach single-copy buyers. *The New Yorker* prefers subscriptions. *Cosmopolitan* went the other way, reduced the cost at the checkout counter and raised the price of a subscription.

However, most magazines exist on quite small circulations, eking out a profit on a combination of subscription revenue and advertising targeted for that fragment of the public interested in the particular topic. Among them are the *zines*, self-published magazines that are part of the world of the alternative press. Sometimes mimeographed, hundreds of zines reach out to anyone who shares the views of the publisher/author, or

Continued

Magazines Target Their Readers *(continued)*

who is willing to be convinced. Zines exist as part of the alternative or underground press in many countries, notably in the Soviet Union and Eastern Europe as the *samizdat* that not long ago criticized the communist governments. American zines are no more respectful of American leadership. The chief difference is the freedom to publish.

The newest idea for a magazine in the mid-'90s is a different kind of zine, the electronic zine. It was probably inevitable that the Internet, which offers so many ways to connect people by interest, should offer magazines. By 1996, hundreds could be found on the World Wide Web with more being added daily. Each zine features a home page, buttons that call up articles and sometimes ad-

vertising, and links to other places on the Web network. A few zines can also be bought as CD-ROM disks, central elements in the world of multimedia.

Many of the small circulation magazines and the even smaller circulation newsletters that sprang into existence in the 1990s owe their continued existence to the tools of desktop publishing. With a microcomputer, a black-and-white scanner for photographs, a laser printer to produce camera-ready pages, and a page layout program, the smallest publishers set themselves up in business, visible reminders that advances in technology have allowed more producers to provide a wider range of communication to more consumers than ever before.

Figure 6.1
Magazine stands can offer thousands of periodicals. This is just part of the computer section.

Multimedia, a Newer Book

Molly Armstrong, a junior at Trinity University in San Antonio, Texas, took images of the heart of a chick embryo from microscope slides. She transferred them to a computer on which she created a rotating 3-D model. She offloaded the images on videotape that she presented to her microanatomy class professor as her term paper.[23]

What Is Multimedia?

Her impressive work fits one definition of multimedia, for it combines several media to produce a result. A narrower definition requires interactivity by the user who can

access such elements as graphics, animation, video, and audio through linkages that let the user click effortlessly from anyplace to anywhere.

As an example of such linkages, let us start with media history on the World Wide Web with the topic of media history. We enter the phrase "media history" into a search engine. We are rewarded with a list of choices. We click on a graphic to "The Media History Project." By hyperlinks, we click on "Connections" to "Television." From there, let us click to the "Airwaves Golden Age Media Page." Among the choices, we click to "The Shadow," which teases the reader with "Who knows what hyperlinks lurk..." Some of these connections could lead to still or moving images and to sound. If we were clicking on a CD-ROM, we might find enough text and visual information to fill an encyclopedia.

A University of Delaware professor offered this definition of what multimedia is and what it is not:

First, there must be a computer to coordinate what you see and hear, and to interact with. Second, there must be links that connect the information. Third, there must be navigational tools that let you traverse the web of connected information. Finally, since multimedia is not a spectator sport, there must be ways for you to gather, process, and communicate your own information and ideas.

If one of these components is missing, you do not have multimedia. For example, if you have no computer to provide interactivity, you have mixed media, not multimedia. If there are no links to provide a sense of structure and dimension, you have a bookshelf, not multimedia. If there are no navigational tools to let you decide the course of action, you have a movie, not multimedia. If you cannot create and contribute your own ideas, you have a television, not multimedia.[24]

CD-ROM

If videotape offers an Information Highway version of a book, so does CD-ROM. Thousands of *compact disk—read only memory* discs are being published on subjects that range the alphabet from astronomy to zoology. Carrying data on silvery disks that fit in the hand, this tool of communication contains not only reams of reading matter, but full stereo sound and both still and moving images. Databases permit users to skip back and forth almost as easily as flipping the pages of a magazine, with the difference that the page can talk.

Major CD-ROM players—Sony, Phillips, Time Warner, Toshiba—agreed on a universal format for DVD, the digital video disc that carries a full-length movie on a CD-ROM disc. DVDs will compete with videotape, which retains the advantage of recording. However, these digital disks deliver far better images than videotape's analog signal can offer plus multi-channel sound. In addition, the user can go directly to a favorite scene. At the end of the video, there is no tape to rewind.

The reinvention of books on compact discs has added to the list of CD-ROM titles. Encyclopedias and other reference books have been followed by hundreds of titles on a broad range of subjects, particularly books for children. Here is a review of one such book on a single CD-ROM disk:

You'll find it hard to believe the wealth of Quicktime movies, photos, animal sounds, stories, and well-written information The Software Toolworks has stuffed into *The San Diego Zoo Presents... The Animals!* This multimedia tour of the San Diego Zoo explores the lives and habitats of more than 200 animals, depicted in 1,300 photos and an hour of video clips. The software safari is lucidly explained in 2,500 carefully cross-referenced pages and presented in a polished package of handsome graphics.[25]

If it is difficult to regard this work as a book, despite its 2,500 pages of reading, the identification may be a little easier with *The Mayo Clinic Family Health Book—Interactive Edition*, which "contains hundreds of illustrations, video clips, and animated segments showing medical procedures and parts of the body."[26] Or consider *Aesop's Fables*, a CD-ROM in which "each fable's accompanying music is well chosen. Children can have the fables read to them or read them themselves."[27]

Books on audiotape have been available for many years to the visually impaired. In abridged form they are especially popular with drivers facing a long daily commute.

Educational disk producers were criticized for trying to outdo children's television in flash and dash. Critics contended that educational tools should not build CD-ROMs out of video clips and sound bites that attempt to out-dazzle MTV, for that simply continued the departure from literacy and logical thought.

> But while multimedia may appeal to the MTV-fueled rhythms of a hot-wired generation, some critics believe that all that hot-linking is an educational detriment. Considering the sorry state of literacy, there's real danger in even a partial abandonment of narrative forms and rigorous modes of thought associated with logical arguments; where A leads to B. Multimedia's forte is not reason, but hot emotional impact—the same ingredients that make local TV news compelling yet less filling.[28]

By 1996, thousands of CD-ROM disks were available, and more were coming to market daily. A casual skimming of a catalog offered such choices as an encyclopedia of postage stamps, an encyclopedia of the JFK assassination, maps of every street in the United States, every phone number in the United States, an enormous number of books and games, plus art and photography on everything from bikini models to classic paintings. Of more than passing interest is *Understanding McLuhan*, which carries hours of his videotaped and audiotaped lectures and reviews, plus the complete texts of *Understanding Media* and *The Gutenberg Galaxy*.

CD-ROM Zines

Blender was one of about six magazines produced in the United States on CD-ROM in 1996. *Blender* sold about 75,000 copies of each issue at about $12 per copy in record and software stores or by subscription. Like most of the other CD-ROM magazines, or *zines*, it covered pop culture and entertainment news, but it could just as easily have covered politics or economic news. What came in each CD-ROM disk was a combination of text, audio, animation, graphics, and video, all color and digital. *Blender*, published bimonthly, offered film and music reviews with audio and video samples, video interviews, articles, games, and advertising.

The publisher's slogan was, "The first wave of new media." It carried advertising that took advantage of interactive multimedia. For example, ads for Dewars scotch and Puma tennis shoes were games with clues. In the Dewars ad, someone could push a button that revealed a joke involving Dewars scotch. Push another button and you could order Dewars merchandise. Push another for cocktail recipes. An ad for Sony put someone on a motorcycle crossing the desert traveling through a story that had the feel of a foreign intrigue movie. The viewer was entertained while encountering Sony products. The user might spend half an hour wandering around in a

Figure 6.2
CD zines like *Blender* reach tens of thousands of mostly young users with a fast-paced multimedia mix. (Courtesy *Blender*.)

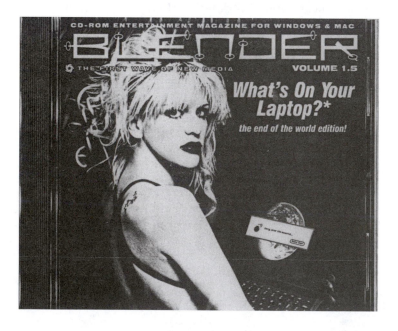

Dewars world or a Sony world. Levi's, Toyota, and Universal Pictures offered other advertising environments. Advertisers took note that this was voluntary time that the viewer chose to spend with a commercial, compared with having to sit through a broadcast commercial. Advertising agencies and large advertisers opened themselves up very quickly to CD-ROM and the World Wide Web.

As the century draws to a close, the direction that multimedia will take and the vehicles that will carry it are not fully clear, for multimedia synthesizes several emerging and competing technologies. What is abundantly clear is that multimedia is here to stay.

Cable Narrowcasting

Until the mid-1970s, cable television was mostly a means of improving signals and bringing over-the-air broadcasts to communities far from television stations. That was about to change.

Home Box Office began with a test in Wilkes-Barre, Pennslvania, in 1972 as a movie and sports pay channel. Nearby cable operators liked the idea and wanted to sign on, so HBO expanded its microwave system to include additional cable companies. The cost of relaying HBO's programs via microwave led HBO to take a chance on contracting to distribute a program via RCA's domestic communications satellite, SATCOM. That gave it a potential for national distribution. Looking for a program that would draw a large audience nationwide, HBO chose a boxing match, perhaps recalling the excitement that greeted Tele-PrompTer's experimental Key-TV pay television broadcast of the second Floyd Patterson-Ingmar Johansson heavyweight match.

On September 30, 1975, HBO broadcast the Joe Frazier-Muhammad Ali championship fight from Manila by satellite transmission. The "thrilla from Manila" cablecast, as Ali dubbed it, was such a success that Time, Inc., the parent corporation, leased a SATCOM transponder on a long-term basis to transmit HBO programs to any cable system owning, or willing to spend $150,000 for an earth station receiving dish 10 meters in diameter. This move transformed HBO from a regional to a national network distributing uncut and uninterrupted movies, special events, and live sports via satellite. By 1977, 262 cable systems were subscribing to HBO services. Technology moved quickly enough that by 1977 dishes as small as 4.5 meters, costing under $10,000, brought reception within the means of all but the smallest cable systems.

Ted Turner Moves In

Independent Atlanta broadcaster Ted Turner, observing that cable operators were buying satellite dishes to bring in HBO, put his UHF station on the same SATCOM satellite. Unlike HBO's method of charging individual subscribers for an extra channel without commercials, Turner offered, for a small per-subscriber charge, inexpensive programming with commercials to cable systems that until then were giving subscribers little more than a basic service. All subscribers to the cable service could receive the programming. His station featured movies, sports, and news around the clock. By going national, his money-losing UHF station, now called *WTBS*, became the first "superstation." Turner recalled, "HBO kicked it off, but one service really wasn't good enough to wire the country because all they really had at the time was movies. We brought baseball, basketball, and hockey."[29]

The HBO and Turner success stories did not pass unobserved. Among new channels via satellite came televangelist Pat Robertson's Christian Broadcasting Network (CBN); the Learning Channel, which took on the educational mission that the major networks ignored; Bravo, reaching a thoughtful audience with discerning films from around the world; Lifetime, programming to adult women; the Getty Oil company's Entertainment and Sports Programming Network (ESPN), focusing on adult men; MTV, whose images were primarily aimed at young males; the Disney Channel and Nickelodeon, which set new levels for children's programming. The Cable Satellite Public Affairs Network (C-SPAN) was created to distribute the proceedings of the U.S. House of Representatives to cable systems via satellite. Two more "superstations," Chicago's WGN and New York's WOR, joined the growing throng of available cable channels. Advertiser-supporter music video channels were launched, including Music Television (MTV) in 1981 and the Nashville Network in 1983. In 1985, The Discovery Channel made its debut, providing educational nonfiction programming about such topics as nature and history. HBO's use of a satellite was followed by such pay-TV movie-laden channels as Showtime, The Movie Channel, and Cinemax.

In 1980, Turner Broadcasting began distributing a nationwide news service, the Cable News Network (CNN), via satellite. Its success led to a second CNN channel of continual 30-minute newscasts. During the Gulf War of 1991, polls reported that CNN was the public's first or second choice for news.

In school classrooms, the controversial Channel One beamed newscasts containing commercials. Schools got free television monitors, videocassette recorders, even satellite dishes as an inducement to sign up. Students were exposed to newscasts prepared for them, full of stories with teen appeal and fast moving graphics. Many of the students, being exposed to commercials every day, could not understand why social critics tore their hair.

New Channels

Other specialized channels formed, with audiences being calved like ice from a glacier. By 1996, channels were in existence or planned for Spanish-speaking, African-American, and Asian audiences, plus more channels designed for children, teenagers, young adults, and the elderly. There were also either plans afoot for—or the realiza-

tion of—an all-talk channel, international news, two all-golf channels, a channel with old sports footage, two history channels, an all-food channel, plus separate channels for fitness and for wellness (exercise and health), home and garden, military matters, money matters, consumer matters, channels with shows about single people, books, fine arts, Christian music, country music, how-to-do-it advice, crime programs, westerns, war movies, horror movies, movie previews, soap operas, game shows, plus an international channel in several foreign languages, several shopping channels, a channel selling sex-related merchandise, and two channels of advertising, one for classifieds and one for infomercials.[30]

Anyone who imagines television as a unifying force in society has only to look at the cable listings in the daily newspaper. Talk show host Larry King commented, "In some ways this will be good for politicians and their media consultants because it will be easier to target niche audiences with specific messages."[31] Perhaps not all social critics were calmed by such prospects.

Some concern has been expressed in the United States about the disparity between the poor in America, who as a group watch a lot of television, and the middle class, who watch less. There are places in the world where watching TV might be envied, but in the relatively wealthy United States, the unenviable truth is that the poor watch much more advertiser-supported "free" television than do the middle class. To some extent, the difference is due to an educational differential, and to some extent it is due to the cost of other kinds of entertainment. The likelihood is that when other channel choices siphon off audience segments, the poor will be left behind, and the communication spread between the poor and the rest of the society will expand, supporting the "knowledge gap" theory, which states, "As the infusion of mass media information into a social system increases, segments of the population with higher socio-economic status tend to acquire this information at a faster rate than the lower status segments, so that the gap in the knowledge between these segments tends to increase rather than decrease."[32]

Home Shopping

The Home Shopping Network and Cable Value Network combine two activities on the top of the enjoyment list of millions of people: watching television and shopping. Its champions prefer to call it *electronic retailing* or *direct-to-home selling*, while operators stand by ready to take 800-number orders.

Shopping from the toolshed home adds a further dimension to the concept of communication without transportation. It encompasses not only the cable shopping networks, but television shopping programs, infomercials (program-length commercials), interactive television marketing, telephone database marketing, and shopping via computer modem. By the mid-1990s, total sales were in the billions of dollars and growing, with nationally famous manufacturers and retailers entering the business. Separately on the Internet, merchants by the thousands have been setting up home pages on the World Wide Web and advertising in Web zines. As electronic retailing increases, normal mail order merchandising through catalogs is expected to decline, along with many retail stores.[33] Brand names are expected to lose some of their appeal and the marketing is predicted to follow the concept of cutting the potential market into small, specialized groups. Plans have also been germinating to sell groceries and drug store sundries by interactive cable.

Communication technology that came along in the last century had made possible the mailed catalogs and the popularity of brand names that are now taken for granted. The small town general store suffered. New communication technology is now turning the wheel once again, this time at the expense of catalog mailers.

Cable Franchises

Cable industry revenues in the United States exceeded $1 billion by 1978. Two years later, revenues passed the $4 billion mark. By 1994, the total passed $23 billion from cable users plus more than $4 billion from advertisers. While many small, private cable systems remain, the cable business increasingly belongs to the multiple systems operator (MSO) which is likely to have a communications empire embracing

Figure 6.3
Shopping from home while watching television combines activities many people enjoy. Brisk business at the Home Shopping Network call centers require a lot of order takers.

broadcast stations, pay cable channels, newspapers, magazines, and even enterprises like book publishing and record producing.

Satellites sparked phenomenal growth for cable television in the late 1970s and early 1980s. Until then the cable industry had been providing millions of small town viewers with clear reception of local stations and sometimes a few stations from a nearby larger market, but it did not offer enough to metropolitan or suburban viewers to justify wiring the big cities. Satellites changed that. Cable television evolved from being mostly a retransmitter of broadcast signals to being a source of hitherto unavailable programming.

When cable moved into the cities and suburbs, cable franchising wars ensued in the rush to win major market franchises. The cities, however, proved to be harder bargainers than small towns. City councils specified requirements the cable operator had to meet, such as the number of channels, subscriber rates, and the length of time to get the system up and running. An important part of the franchise was local access programming, including channels set aside for education and civic affairs, plus public access channels so any resident could present a program or a viewpoint. A cable company that wanted to come into the city would have to offer a range of public services. In other words, cable could not be merely a vaudeville stage. It would have to be a town hall and a street corner soap box as well. To acquire franchises, cable companies promised equipment and personnel to program its public access channels.

Franchises gave cable companies exclusive monopolies in the cities where they built systems, but their monopoly positions came under attack from rival cable companies or citizen groups which argued that the franchise holders were not living up to their contracted promises. Competition seemed an obvious solution. By 1992, at least 50 cities had competing cable services, and the number is growing. The Telecommunication Reform Act of 1996 allows telephone companies to compete.

Pay Cable

Many of the program services that are not pay-TV at some level are known as *basic cable*. Beyond the basic cable are one or more tiers, or bundles, of cable channels available at higher monthly rates. Beyond these are channels with a fixed monthly charge, such as HBO. Some cable systems also offer pay-per-view (PPV) channels. When someone phones in an order for a movie or a special event advertised on a preview channel, the cable company obliges by piping the show to an addressable converter at the subscriber's home. Each subscriber has a number as unique as a telephone number.

A pay-per-view test that began in 1991 allowed Denver area viewers to order movies from a list of more than 1,000 titles fed out of a video center to a viewer's home through fiber optic lines. It created a video store in the living room without the need to return the movie. At the head end the technology was old-fashioned by the fast moving standards of this century. It depended on employees finding videotapes on shelves and punching them up on video players for the customer.

Time Warner and other American media giants invested heavily to develop new interactive and multimedia services that combined the bandwidth of fiber optic cable with the flexibility and storage of computers. Time Warner's Full Service Network video-on-demand experimental service in Orlando, Florida, used a multimedia navigation system to show viewers what options were available. Helping to solve the problem of the bandwidth demands of moving pictures were not only satellites and fiber optics, but digital video compression.

The high-powered merger negotiations of cable and telephone companies have made for exciting headlines, with their promises of 500 channels. That arbitrarily chosen number, incidentally, is misleading. A virtually infinite number of channels beckons.

Technological promises have been hedged by political issues such as whether the promised service would be available to everyone. Another question revolves around common carriage. Will all cable service entrepreneurs have access to the conduit? Will production of content be separated from its distribution? At what point does the First Amendment collide with anti-trust regulation? By the mid-1990s, telephone companies in the United States were merging with cable companies and extending their reach to entertainment production and media of various kinds, alarming observers who see danger from power shifting into a few corporate hands. The Telecommunications Reform Act of 1996 allows everyone to play in everyone else's yard: long distance, local phone service, cable service, and media production. Broadcasters can own more stations, cable companies can raise their rates, and electric power companies can offer a range of telecommunication services. Despite the fears of monopoly, it is still true that more producers are sending a greater variety of material over more channels to a larger total audience than ever.

Both basic and pay services suffer from piracy if people who do not pay for the programming tap the signal by hooking into a neighbor's feed, either wiring up special electronic devices or buying satellite dishes. The cable industry figured it was losing $500 to $700 million annually because of service theft. HBO and other pay channels responded by scrambling their feeds. In 1986, HBO began scrambling the feeds of HBO and Cinemax. Other channels quickly followed suit. The unscrambled feeds were offered to owners of backyard dishes for a fee.

Of the American homes that are able to subscribe to cable service, fewer than two out of five chose not to do so. Investors in direct broadcast satellite systems saw these homes as a potential market, which led to DBS service now offering not only regular cable fare, but an increased number of movie channels, a taste of the so-called 500-channel universe to come.

Wireless Cable

An older technology, wireless cable, also attracted some attention. Its services were identified by such initials as MDS (multipoint distribution service), MMDS (multichannel multipoint distribution service), ITFS (instruction television fixed service), and OFS (operational fixed service). Wireless cable was in a limited sense direct broadcast satellite without the satellite. Microwave towers transmitted the television picture to any home, hotel, apartment house, or business equipped with a receiving dish. Unlike a satellite whose footprint can span a nation, a microwave signal is local, limited to reaching receiving antennas within line of sight of the transmitting antenna.

Wireless cable often provided a cable-like service of up to 33 channels, usually in markets too small for cable companies to bother with. That number could increase to 300 channels with digital transmission, which would also overcome the problem of weather affecting the signal, and possibly put wireless cable into real competition with standard cable. In the mid-1990s, wireless cable was available in at least 38 countries.[34]

Also still used is satellite master antenna television (SMATV), also known as *private cable*, which was little more than a satellite dish atop an apartment house, hotel, hospital, office building, or condo building, with cables running to apartments or rooms. It is a cable system in miniature.

Fiber Optics

Optical fibers made of glass less than a hundredth of an inch in diameter present a promising technology for cable distribution. Transmitting information in the form of light, a single hair-thin strand can convey up to 16,000 phone conversations, compared to 24 for copper wire. An optical fiber can transmit 167 television channels, while a bundle of six strands the size of a telephone cord can feed out more than 1,000 video signals.

Sending a message by light is as old as the ancient Greek heliograph, a brightly polished shield flashing in the sun. Before Alexander Graham Bell pushed a voice along a wire, British physicist John Tyndall showed a light beam trapped in a stream of water. Bell himself tried to prove that light could transmit the voice with a photo phone to carry voice signals, but bad weather interfered with transmission. Norman French received a patent in 1934 for an optical telephone using solid glass rods to conduct voice signals, but the big breakthrough came from Arthur Schawlow and Charles Townes, the scientists who in 1958 invented the laser. Corning Glass Works figured out the efficient manufacture of optical fiber made of silica glass the thickness of a human hair. By the start of the 1990s, a laser with a light source the size of a grain of salt could blink one billion times a second, converting voices, pictures, and text into a string of 1s and 0s. A photo detector at the receiving end of the fiber strand reconstituted the light flashes as an electronic signal that converted back into voices, pictures, and text.

Because light travels much faster than electricity, transmission speed increased markedly. It has been estimated that the entire text of the *Encyclopedia Brittanica* and the Bible could circle the Earth over a fiber optic strand in less than two seconds.

> Theoretically optical fibers can, when tucked into a household's telephone line, deliver a virtually infinite number of channels. By wedding that awesome capability to the vast penetration of their phone lines, the Baby Bells could make both the networks and cable instantly obsolete. And when linked to a central computer bank via an interactive hookup, an optical fiber system would serve as a kind of omnipotent electronic genie. At the touch of a button, subscribers could do their shopping and banking, send messages, book theater seats, make travel arrangements, call up an old newspaper article or request a lesson in the new math.[35]

Lightweight and strong, the fibers can stand much physical abuse, but unlike copper cable, which can carry its own electrical power, fiber optics cannot function during a power outage. They blink out. Telephone companies would have to provide alternative backup power. Although the cost of creating and installing pure glass fibers has become competitive with copper for new uses, the cost of replacing existing copper wire with the new technology is a delaying factor. So is the cost of putting into a television set the unit needed to convert an optical digital signal into an electrical analog signal.

The quality of digital pictures and sound transmitted along glass fibers astonishes first-time viewers. Electrical signals sharing a copper wire begin to blend after a short trip, but not so with light transmission through glass. Also, two-way transmission poses no problems for glass, unlike copper. As production of optical fiber increased, prices fell sharply and, at the same time, the capacity of optical fiber lines to carry data soared. The capacity expanded even more when the signal was altered by the technology called *DVC, digital video compression*, which made more efficient use of existing channels.

Programming Through Optical Fibers

Because it is not always convenient to watch a film starting at 8 p.m. or 10 p.m., HBO has experimented with multiplexing the same film at staggered hours through several channels, using digital compression and fiber optics.

In addition to the possibility of a much greater range of program choices than cable now delivers, among the potentials of new technology is a marriage with high definition television to deliver wall-sized pictures of such quality that the image might hardly be distinguishable from the original. The day may come when a waterfall will look real enough to splash in.

> Japanese researchers envision golfers practicing their swings in front of three-dimensional simulations of courses... "Doctors could have world offices, not local offices. And I could go on vacation — or pick a vacation spot — by immersing myself in a different environment, stroll down the streets of Barcelona or along a Caribbean beach," says Mr. Smoot, an executive at Bell Communications Research.[36]

Coaxial cable seems to do well enough for the cable service that was originally delivered. It can also handle videotex and home shopping. What a fiber optic line into the home can do is provide hundreds of channels, plus movies on demand, which is probably how most of those channels will be used. If the public is willing to pay for the service, fiber optics switched networks or hybrid fiber-coaxial networks (fiber for the main lines, coax for the drop into homes) will replace trips to the video rental store.

The members of the plugged-in society will settle deeper into their toolshed homes, grateful for communication replacing transportation. Jeffrey Reiss, Request TV chairman, predicted, "The home would become the world's largest electronic theater. People would begin to say, 'Why do we ever have to go out?'"

Footprints on the Globe

Satellites have redefined the meaning of distance. What the telegraph began, the communication satellite completed. An Intelsat executive recalled a holiday trip:

> We were in Guaymas, Mexico, several weeks ago, riding through a small poverty-stricken area with a guy from Chicago. He was busy denigrating the area, "Who could stand to live here, you wouldn't know anything about the world, it is so squalid, etc." I was busy taking pictures of houses perhaps 25 feet square with a 1954 Chevy pickup in the driveway and a satellite dish on the roof. An area of perhaps 1,000 people, with about 50 satellite dishes!
>
> He said, "What do those dishes do, anyway?" I said, well, these people can get 130 TV channels from at least seven nations in five languages, and in addition they can get sub-carrier FM stereo. In other words, they have Quebec, Venezuela, Mexico City, all of America, BBC, and even Japan occasionally; and they get the Chicago Symphony as clearly as you do.
>
> He was stunned. Then he said, "What do they think when they see all that, and they look at this, where they live?" And I was silent, and my wife was silent, and he was silent.[37]

How might poor people react? They could demand reform in their own countries. They could revolt. They could grow even more resentful at the world's "haves." Some might steal. They could retreat into fundamentalism. Or they could risk everything in an effort to migrate into the rich countries they see on television.[38]

Geopolitical Considerations

Arthur Clarke, who originated the idea of communication satellites in geosynchronous orbit, has commented, "The communications satellite is going to spread ideas and concepts throughout the world more powerfully (than the printed medium has done)."[39] The geopolitical implications are startling. Direct broadcast satellites (DBS), which are not routed through a control point, but go directly into people's homes, have not been greeted as an unalloyed joy in Third World countries concerned with programming imported from industrialized countries. Intended to point us toward the heavens, these communication satellites instead rekindle old quarrels about cultural imperialism. DBS's potential for "coca-colonization" or even direct propaganda television broadcasts is not offset by an unwilling host nation's ability to block reception. Unlike incoming radio signals, satellite television transmission is difficult to block. Viewers receive television programs from whatever the satellite has to offer, and no government censor is likely to intrude.

By 1996, more than a dozen satellites beamed programs to Asia. Many people put up dishes, but not all governments welcomed them. Rupert Murdoch, owner of

Star-TV, declared that technologies such as satellite television "proved an unambiguous threat to totalitarian regimes everywhere," a comment that led China to restrict dish use. [40] It also declared its intention to ban Star-TV, which was enough to convince Murdoch to placate China's leaders by removing the BBC World Service from Star-TV. China limited the dishes to luxury hotels and some businesses, although an estimated one million illegal dishes were pointed where they could receive western programs.

In 1994, Iran declared home dishes illegal. Direct reception was also banned in Syria, Saudi Arabia, Lebanon, Qatar, Iraq, Vietnam, and Singapore, although the bans were not always enforced. In much of Singapore, Hong Kong, and Taiwan, the gatekeepers are the small cable operators who put dishes atop apartment blocks. Myanmar dealt with unwanted programming by a prohibitive license fee on dishes. Malaysia had restrictions similar to China's. Indonesian President Suharto even banned advertising on his own country's Palapa satellite apparently out of fear that rural people would see how much better some urbanites lived. The ban remained in effect for eight years. Indonesian viewers were later permitted to watch, but their dishes had to be pointed only at the Palapa satellite. With hesitation, Japan—of all countries—agreed to permit pointing home dishes at foreign satellites, and South Korea agreed to pointing at a Japanese satellite. Its DBS *footprint*, or reception area, spilled over into part of South Korea, which did not please that government.

Being a nation under someone else's footprint is not always considered disadvantageous. More than a dozen East European, Mideastern, and North African nations that fall under Europe's Eutelsat footprint can buy its service, whereas attempting to match the service by launching their own satellites would be prohibitively expensive even if frequencies were available.

Banning satellite reception at home does not stop transmitting abroad. The state broadcasting corporations of Singapore, Malaysia, and Iran were either broadcasting or planning to do so internationally by satellite.

A Split-Second Apart

Of all the things one can say about modern communications, the most remarkable is that people on opposite ends of the globe are a split-second apart, yet men and women are alive who were born before the first airplane flew and even before the first radio transmission. Consider, for example, how strange and how quaint the people of Japan seemed to Americans at the start of this century and how strange and fearsome Americans seemed to the Japanese. Now a young Japanese rice farmer and a middle-aged Minnesota housewife can watch the same live television broadcast of the Olympics in Europe. As far as the technology is concerned, they could even watch each other while carrying on a conversation. The day may come when newer technology will permit that conversation over telephones that do their translating.

By means of communication satellites, the Atlanta Olympic games were seen worldwide by billions of people, an astonishing feat considering that the first geosynchronous communication satellite went into orbit a little more than three decades earlier. Matching improvements in satellites have been the receiving dishes. The first terrestrial earth stations cost $10 million each and required a staff of engineers. The newest home dishes sell for a few hundred dollars and can easily be set up. Once again, we see the characteristic shared by so many mass communication tools of becoming smaller, cheaper, and easier to operate at the same time that their capabilities grow.

Changes in News Reporting Structures

Like the telegraph, communication satellites have been a catalyst for changes in news reportage. Just as the telegraph boosted the news reporting capacity of smaller and inland newspapers, the satellite has widened the reach of local television stations. The telegraph made prompt reports possible of the Mexican-American and the Civil War. It encouraged cooperative reporting arrangements from far-off locales, leading to the formation of the Associated Press and the promotion of objectivity and uniformity in writing style. The communication satellite, by making distant coverage much cheaper and more available, has led local television stations to send reporters all over the United States and to remote corners of the globe. When the Berlin Wall came down, reporters from local American stations were among those who beamed live reports across the Atlantic.

"Live via satellite" is a familiar phrase. Television networks' frequent use of satellites to transmit sports, newscasts, and individual news stories filed by reporters has been matched by local stations that exchange news items with one another through such independent networking arrangements as *Conus*. Local news directors have more choices of national and international news than ever before. A generation before, distance had to be factored into a decision to cover an event. Around the time of the Vietnam War, television stations simply did not transmit news over great distances. ABC, CBS, and NBC did so, but when AT&T charged $3,000 to rent loops and lines for a cross-country video transmission, even the networks did not act casually to arrange reception of a reporter's film from the scene of a story.

By the 1990s, video pictures were sent across the country for $75. The dropping costs of satellite transmission have made the filing of stories via satellite from reporters to their networks or stations a daily occurrence. With *ENG* (*Electronic News Gathering*) supplanted by *SNG* (*Satellite News Gathering*), local station news trucks equipped with satellite uplinks roam far from base to cover stories. A reporter can beam live reports from the scene of an event in minutes after the truck arrives.

By providing an alternative to traditional television network connections, the communication satellite has been one of the causes of fundamental alterations in the structures of television news coverage. Local station news departments that can cheaply receive remote reports no longer depend solely upon the major networks.

It has not gone unnoticed that a large city station that decided to replace a network newscast with its own version could realize millions of dollars in extra income a year. Whether network newscasts—sometimes referred to as *dinosaurs*—can survive is a much discussed question.

In addition to relaying video, audio, and written news dispatches to newspapers and broadcast stations, satellites transmit data from the Dow-Jones News Service, Nexis, Lexis, and other online services directly to readers. Satellites also beam page plates for newspapers such as *The Wall Street Journal* and *USA Today* to regional printing plants.

For the average citizen, satellites have had their most obvious impact on cable television service for entertainment. The entire cable industry relies on satellite relay of entertainment programs, a practice initiated by HBO with the Ali-Frazier boxing match.

The Beginnings

The satellite era began when the Soviet Union launched the first *Sputnik (fellow traveler)* in 1957. The United States, surprised and embarrassed, reacted with a crash space program. John Kennedy was elected partly on his promise to get America moving with more determination into outer space.

Military satellites produced significant advances in communication, but it soon became evident that the satellite was an ideal vehicle for civil communication traffic. In 1962, Congress enacted and President Kennedy signed the Communications Satellite Act, creating a privately owned corporation, COMSAT, to launch and operate a global system. It was then impossible to get a live television picture from Europe to the United States. Instead, film was flown across the Atlantic. The television networks covered the Vietnam War by shipping cans of undeveloped film by commercial air transport from Saigon via Tokyo to San Francisco, where it was developed, screened, and sent by microwave to New York for use on the evening news. With videotape and satellites, coverage of wars has become much more efficient, as, to be sure, have the wars.

Scientists recognized the communication potential of satellites as a kind of great antenna tower, but the first American communication satellite, *Echo 1,* in 1960, was little more than a silvery balloon put into orbit for a short time, a passive reflector bouncing back radio signals. Because of that silvery sheen from a coating of aluminum and because *Echo* was as big as a ten-story building, tens of millions of people saw *Echo* in its low orbit over the earth. As communications technology went, a plastic balloon wasn't much, but Americans who saw it felt heartened that they could actually witness, from their own back porches, what their country was doing in the space race, even though the Soviet Union had already sent a dog, Laika, into space equipped with machines that radioed back the beating of her heart. Two months after *Echo*'s launching, the U.S. Army's *Courier I* carried a receiver and transmitter for two-way communication. News commentators, envisioning Buck Rogers weapons in space, opined that in the Cold War, the Russians had seized the high ground early, but the Americans were counterattacking. A different analogy would serve better today, that of control of land and ocean trade routes. The most valuable trade of all is information.

Two years after *Echo* came *Telstar I,* the first commercial communications satellite. This AT&T satellite, a microwave tower in the sky, carried *transponders* (transmitters and responders), which received, amplified, and retransmitted radio signals between powerful ground stations. Launched primarily for transatlantic communication, *Telstar I* was joined a year later by *Telstar II* primarily for transpacific communication. Among Telstar I's limitations was an earth orbit of approximately once every 90 minutes, during which it would have line-of-sight with stations in both Europe and the United States for perhaps 15 minutes at a time. Huge, expensive tracking antennas had to follow the Telstars because they were in a low, nonsynchronous orbit.

Arthur Clarke, best known as a science fiction writer, in a 1945 article wrote that if a satellite was placed 22,300 miles above the Equator in an orbit around the Earth of 24 hours, it would remain stationary in relation to a fixed point on Earth. Three satellites *parked* above the Equator and spaced equidistant from one another could receive *from* and transmit *to* almost any point on the globe. Clarke wrote:

> Many may consider the solution proposed in this discussion to be too far-fetched to be taken very seriously. Such an attitude is unreasonable, as everything envisaged here is a logical extension of developments in the last ten years—in particular the perfection of the long-range rocket of which V-2 was the prototype.[41]

By the mid-'60s, Clarke's theory had been proven in the form of packages of electronics hurtling through weightless space in fixed orbits. Powered by solar energy, the early communication satellites used relatively little current, less than 100 watts, about the strength of a light bulb. The signal could be picked up and amplified only by a sensitive, large, and expensive earth station located far from the electrical interference of cities.

INTELSAT

The opening ceremony of the Tokyo Olympic Games in 1964 was broadcast live to much of the northern hemisphere by *Syncom 3,* the first satellite to be placed into *geostationary* (also known as *geosynchronous*) orbit. A year later came the Comsat satellite, *Intelsat I,* nicknamed *Early Bird*, a 76-pound workhorse parked in geostationary orbit over the Atlantic Ocean to link countries around the North Atlantic. Designed to work for 18 months, it lasted four years carrying 240 telephone circuits, more than six times as many as the Atlantic cable laid on the ocean floor nine years earlier.

Early Bird initiated commercial communications. Satellites over the Pacific and Indian oceans began full global coverage in 1969, three weeks before the first moon landing, the most widely seen event in

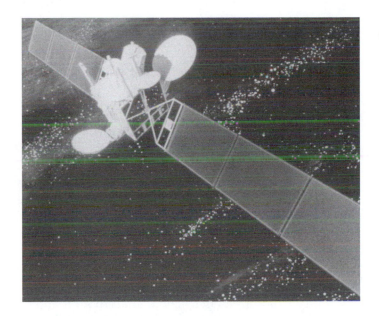

Figure 6.4
Communication satellites
in the Intelsat VII and
VII-A series are in orbit
beaming audio, video,
and data streams.
(Courtesy Comsat.)

history, which included a telephone call from President Nixon in the Oval Office to Neil Armstrong on the surface of the moon.

A consortium of more than 100 countries formed the International Telecommunications Satellite Organization. Owning more communication satellites in space than any other provider, Intelsat rents its services for television, radio, computer data, and telephone circuits to about 300 state-run and large private organizations around the world. The arrangement is profitable for its member countries—136 by 1996. Intelsat prices are relatively steep, even though the cost of transmitting telephone, telex, radio, and television signals has dropped sharply.

Video Teleconferencing

Video teleconferencing by satellite grew out of an experiment that began in 1974. A NASA Applications Technology Satellite, quickly nicknamed the *Teacher-in-the-Sky*, pointed its antenna toward Appalachia, where it fed graduate college courses to teachers whose remote locations gave them no opportunity for advancement. When the evening classes were over, the antenna shifted to the Rockies to beam vocational classes for junior high schools. When those classes ended, the antenna

once again shifted west, this time to Alaska, with two-way televised medical advice for people in remote areas who had called with specific problems. In one case, a health worker at a construction site got stitch-by-stitch guidance from a physician as he sewed up the face of a man who had been badly injured. During its five-year lifetime, the Teacher-in-the-Sky beamed programs to southern Asia on health, agriculture, and family planning to people who had never before seen television. It started India on its own satellite programming. In the United States, it led in 1979 to The Learning Channel. Its success advanced the realization that people could, in a sense, meet face-to-face without expensive travel.

Business and professional video teleconferencing has become a booming field. As for education, the phrase *distance learning* is heard with growing frequency, everything from graduate study to allowing bedridden children to attend class.

Direct Broadcasting

Three types of communication satellites are in orbit. *MSS (mobile satellite service)*, which serves ships at sea, has been expanded to include mobile satellite service like the system Peter Arnett used in covering the Gulf War. *FSS (fixed satellite service)*

Figure 6.5
To receive DBS service, customers need an 18-inch antenna dish, a remote control unit, and a receiver. (Courtesy USSB.)

is the standard commercial C-band and Ku-band service for telephone, television, radio, and data transmission. *BSS (broadcast satellite service)* is used for *DBS (direct broadcast satellite)* transmission. DBS may prove to be the ideal way to transmit *HDTV (high definition television)* pictures. In 1996, Hughes Electronics, a subsidiary of General Motors, offered about 175 channels of its DirecTv. USSB offered about 25 channels of DBS. Primestar expected to expand to about 150 channels of FSS. A fourth competitor, Echo Star Communications, promised about 200 channels of DBS, including international channels.

All types of DBS satellite-to-home service are also designated as *DTH (direct to home)*. A disadvantage of DBS services lies in being national and international only, not local. To hear a local newscast, some other means are needed, such as cable or even rabbit ears. And unless a technological breakthrough provides a way, interactive capability will not be available by satellite; it could be available by two-way cable service in competition with DBS for the viewer's dollar.

DBS employs a satellite transmitter that bypasses a ground television station to beam directly into homes equipped with relatively inexpensive (about $500) satellite dishes of 18 to 39 inches diameter. Far smaller than the $2,000 C-band dishes 8 feet or more wide that dot the rural landscape, the DBS dishes, either parabolic or flat, placed on a roof or window ledge, are no more conspicuous than rooftop antennas. It is expected that the dish will connect not only to the TV set for programs and to the VCR for movies, but to the home computer for data.

C-Band and Ku-Band

A transmitter on Earth uplinks signals 22,300 miles to a satellite transponder, which amplifies them, changes their frequencies to avoid interference with the incoming signals, and retransmits them back to Earth to satellite dishes. These downlinks are wired to receiver-decoder units about the size of small VCRs, each connected to a television set. C-band and Ku-band frequencies in the electromagnetic spectrum can be used for telephone, computer data, radio, and television transmission. DBS, using Ku-band frequencies, transmits television directly to homes.

Each band has its own advantages and problems. The C-band signal is not as affected as Ku-band by torrential rainstorms. However, C-band downlink frequencies must be shared with microwave systems on the ground, limiting the satellite's power and the location of earth stations. Ku-band does not interfere with microwave transmission, and the earth stations can be located in the middle of cities. The stronger the signal that the satellite returns, the higher the wavelength, and the wider the separation from other orbiting satellites, the smaller need be the collecting dish.

Scrambling the Signal

Although C-band transmission was not planned for direct-to-home use, as many as five million homes have installed receiving dishes on rooftops and backyards. Program suppliers and cable operators were shocked by their growing popularity because dish owners were getting free what others were paying for. What was more, the dish owners felt justified in doing what they wanted on their own property despite court decisions that receiving these programs was a theft of service. Threats of legal action were made, but the cable industry had no stomach for dragging tens of thousands of citizens to court.

Trying to put dish manufacturers out of business was no solution because some dishes are sold to people who live where no cable is available. This is a legitimate industry. The practical solution was to encrypt, or scramble, the satellite signals so they could be received only with a descrambler that could be rented for a monthly fee. Fabricating descramblers to evade the fee was a clear violation of the law.

The International Standards Organization met from time to time to deal with other problems, such as unrelated video standards, like NTSC, PAL, SECAM, D-2 Mac, Beta, and VHS, plus incompatible audio technologies.

Teleports

Beyond dishes serving homes and motels, there are multi-million dollar teleports offering a convergence of television, radio, and data services, including video teleconferencing, using satellite and ground communication. As an airport is a transportation hub for passengers and cargo, a modern teleport is a transportation hub for information.[42]

VSAT, which stands for *Very Small Aperture Terminal*, a private networking system, uses a satellite to replace terrestrial lines. Operating outside the telephone system, large corporations communicate with their branch offices through VSATs because they are cheap, reliable, fast, and of high quality.[43] Some developing countries use VSATs as a relatively inexpensive way to communicate over large distances when other means prove unreliable or unavailable.[44]

Three types of satellite communication can now be held with any number of participants. Video teleconferencing, which can appear like something out of Orwell's *1984*, is the least used and most expensive method because of the equipment and wideband transmission lines needed, but it is growing. Audio conferencing, a fancier version of the familiar telephone conference call, uses a clearer audio line and sometimes includes some limited visuals. Computer conferencing is a multi-participant version of e-mail; unlike the other versions, it is asynchronous; participants do not have to be present when messages arrive.[45]

A Limit to Infinite Space

Among the newest satellites, those in the Intelsat VII-A series carry 40 transponders each, which, with digital technology, can transmit 112,500 telephone conversations plus three television channels at once. Yet, space is not infinite where communication bandwidth is concerned. Despite ingenuity in expanding the available frequencies, limits exist. One way to get around the saturation is to change from normal analog television signals to digital signals, which can be compressed so a transponder that is sending one movie will be able to send ten in the same amount of spectrum. DBS signals are already digital.

A portion of the scientific and engineering talent devoted to improving communication satellites is engaged in trying to shovel more entertainment into the toolshed homes in which we live. Because consumers respond to ever greater choice, an advertisement for a home satellite dish read:

Electronic Commuting

Electrons are replacing cars as transportation to work and school. Consider these examples:

- A parole judge presides at a hearing as a convict wearing an orange prison jumpsuit stands penitently before a monitor. The judge no longer has to ride the circuit from prison to prison.
- Two cardiologists in a major hospital check over the cardiogram and X-rays of a heart patient in a rural clinic 70 miles away. Images, sounds, and data crisscross Iowa as digital pulses over fiber optic lines. Some discomfort may be felt by the patient because the warm physical presence and the touch of another person is missing, but the advantages are greater. Construction of telecommunications facilities can hardly keep up.
- A reporter beams live reports from the scene of a murder minutes after she and an engineer drive up in their satellite truck. The distance of an event from the television station has become less significant, and reporters travel much further.
- A middle management executive has a cellphone by his side morning, noon, and night. There is no certain escape time in the work week, and the week now contains seven days, not five. Home has become just another place to deal with data.
- Consultants put a different spin on the home-office-car triangle by living and working in vans filled with communication and computation equipment. Their home address is a telephone number, a fax number, and an e-mail Internet address. They travel from city to city for their business. A boat serves just as well if business is done in coastal cities.
- A Spanish language teacher in Spokane gives lessons via satellite to 1,300 students as far away as Alaska and Guam. In Maine, students can earn a B.A. degree via interactive TV.
- English literature students who click on a poem are hyperlinked to a literary review and a biography of the author.
- Law students use an electronic bulletin board to ask professors about legal points that puzzle them. Software lets the students remain anonymous, so they are less afraid to ask "dumb" questions. Lec-

Figure 6.6   Satellite dishes on the roof of a university building make interactive distance learning possible.

Figure 6.7 A classroom equipped for interactive distance learning. Some students attend class by satellite.

ture notes, assignments, and a legal database are online. Supplemental readings are, too, so the professor spends less time at the copier. Students who don't own computers go to computer labs.

Who Works at Home?

One survey reported that fully one-third of the adult work force of the United States in 1993 did all or part of their work at home, a total of 41.1 million *homeworkers*, of whom 7.6 million were identified as *telecommuters* who commute to their jobs electronically.[46] Among them were accountants, architects, bankers, bookkeepers, clerical workers, computer operators, programmers, systems analysts, counselors, data entry clerks, engineers, lawyers, real estate agents, secretaries, brokers, travel agents, and, of course, writers.[47]

Doctors plug into a personal communication network that reaches them in an emergency and will allow the exchange of detailed information in real time. Children who have been compelled by lengthy illness to remain away from school have been able to participate in daily classroom activity by means of equipment at their bedside.

About 100 Minnesota school districts share classes with neighboring districts through telecommunications, saving money and, most important, permitting schools to offer courses that otherwise would be unavailable.[48]

> When transportation meant ships, people built Venice. When it meant trains, they built Chicago. When it meant cars, they built Los Angeles. Cities have always been fundamentally shaped by the dominant transportation of their time. It's one of the givens of urban planning. But today, planners are beginning to see that society is on the verge of building a new kind of city in an era driven not by transportation but by telecommunications...
>
> Since at least the Industrial Revolution, people who wanted to get paid to work needed to migrate to where the jobs were located...
>
> Telecommunications might create an urban Diaspora that spreads hundreds of miles from the core. Or it might lead to the revival of smaller towns that provide a safer more pastoral environment for residents.[49]

Advantages of Working from Home

One lane of the information highway—telecommunications—is cheap to ride on, local to global in scope, saving of real travel, and sometimes subversive. Our vehicle on this lane may be a facsimile machine, a videophone, a computer modem, or perhaps just an ordinary telephone. Our purpose is to avoid driving downtown to work.

Considering the cost of renting office space, it is cheaper for corporations to have some workers plug into a network from home. But telecommunication may change the employer-employee relationship, so permanent staff positions are eliminated. Part-time contract workers or consultants are substituted.

It is certainly more efficient for the employee to avoid the time and expense of a daily commute, to say nothing of child day care. The reality is freeing many employees on some days from the freeway crawl. In 1993, about 41 million Americans, one-third of the adult work force, worked at home at least part of the time.[50] Alvin Toffler in 1980 foresaw an increasing shift of work from office and factory to the home, which he labeled "the electronic cottage."[51] The metaphor differs only slightly from the metaphor introduced in this book of the toolshed home filled with the paper, photographic, and electronic tools of communication that we use for information and entertainment.

Increasingly, the communication toolshed office has melded with the communication toolshed home to accomplish the process called *telecommuting*, allowing some office workers to stay at home, but connected to their jobs.

Personal savings in expanding the toolshed home into a workplace can be considerable, including automobile wear and tear, gasoline, dry cleaning, and child care. The isolation of working away from other people is offset by the compensation of taking a break to watch a child at a neighborhood ball game or to go grocery shopping. However, the telephone allows for human interaction, and for higher level employees and consultants, the videophone call and the video teleconference call may increase the degree of communication with colleagues. Parents care for small children while on the job, but at a time when young mothers work because the paycheck is needed, little joy may attend data entry or piecework with no company but small children and perhaps none of the regular company employee pension and medical insurance benefits. Once again we shaped the tools and then the tools shape us.

The Telecenter

A hermit existence suits few of us. As a compromise between commuting to a distant job site and working from home, the *telecenter* offers a neighborhood location fully equipped with the tools of communication, where people working for different companies can work and also gather around the coffee machine. The telecenter obviates the long daily commute on a crowded freeway, yet allows some self-herding, for most people have a gregarious element to their nature and need the occasional presence of others. Along with these benefits come the obvious financial savings that accrue with not having to purchase copiers, facsimile machines, videophones, and other tools that are needed only occasionally. A well-equipped telecenter will have all the needed business tools of communication for rent. It provides communication with only a bit of transportation, not the long commute downtown.

Telecommunication expands the possibilities of replacing travel by electronic communication, and does so in an era of growing concern about the deleterious effects of the automobile. Computers and communication satellites assist in telecommuting, a word coined to encompass all types of transmission over distance. The concept reflects the convergence of the means of electronic interchange among persons and machines, encompassing telephone, computer, facsimile, broadcasting, cable, and satellite technologies.

Multi-million dollar telecenters may offer a convergence of television, radio, and data services, including video teleconferencing, using satellite and ground communication. Just as an airport is a transportation hub for passengers and cargo, a modern teleport is a transportation hub for information.[52] Once again, people find new ways to communicate without actually going anywhere.

Where Will We Live?

The future promises even more replacement of transportation, with its demands on natural resources and its pollution. Shopping by electronic catalog, working at home via computer modem and facsimile, video teleconferencing in place of business travel, job interviewing, attending classes, and offering computer-assisted diagnostic medical care are all reporting success. Undoubtedly, they will expand. How that may affect future living patterns is challenging sociologists.

As for pollution, modern communication presents the least amount of pollution. It uses up the least amount of the earth's resources. In an era of recognized limits, it has found no limits. This powerful agent of change does its work by changing minds. It does not exhaust the land.

If significant parts of one's work, marketing, education, entertainment, and well-being can be accomplished without leaving home, how would that impinge on a choice of residence? Would more people choose to live in the countryside instead of in cities or suburbs? Would executives choose to live in San Francisco or Santa Fe and commute electronically to Omaha? The post-World War II shift of middle-class families from the city to the suburbs, a move partly determined by the technology of cars and super highways, altered American life. A new population shift based on the availability of the emerging communication technologies could shake up life as much as the move to the suburbs did.

What Will Happen to Cities?

Small towns in much of the United States suffered as high school graduates left for the opportunities and excitement of the cities. A few returned to raise their children, but only a few. With dwindling populations, businesses shuttered. Schools shut down. Towns essentially died, remaining home to a handful of elderly people living

on Social Security checks. Telecommuting could reverse at least some of that if concerns about urban crime and high living costs overcome a sense of the benefits of city life.

What kind of community would result if people could work from their homes and those homes could be anywhere in the city, in the state, in the world? Would a city even be necessary? Perhaps telecommunications will exert such a centrifugal force on populations that existing cities will decay, as Manuel Castells envisions, remaining as host mainly to populations who do not function in a society of electronic highways leading to toolshed homes. Those who lack opportunities to become part of the wired world, said Castells, "are not exploited; they are ignored. It's the shifting from exploitation to irrelevance. That's much worse."[53]

We have already been witness to a centrifugal movement to the suburbs, which has left behind a crumbling infrastructure marked by a declining tax base, rising expenses, and the other ills of modern cities. Matters could hardly improve if the most plugged-in members of a community had no reason whatever to enter the city where once they lived and worked. That has not happened yet, but the trend is accelerating.

The Internet

On the day in 1996 that President Clinton signed the Telecommunication Reform Act, users of the Internet around the world by coincidence cooperated in producing "24 Hours in Cyberspace." Internet browsers learned how rural doctors in Wales transmitted pictures to specialists 150 miles away for diagnosis, how a woman student in an Estonian university connected to a worldwide network of women, how relief workers in Cambodia went online to negotiate the language for a lending program, and on and on. But browsers also got a sense of the political battles that could swirl around such a powerful information tool when many home pages went black for the

day to protest the censorship implications of the Communications Decency Act.

The censors are not going away. In the borderless Internet world a game of cat and mouse may have been played in 1996 by restrictive Asian governments and those citizens who will risk arrest to gain free access. China and Singapore have been trying to block certain Web sites with political or sexual content they don't like. They limit the number of Internet service providers, then they set electronic filters to block unapproved sites. Other governments have been watching with more than curiosity. But dissidents may get around the blockage by setting up home pages overseas to serve as a kind of mail forwarder. Also, site addresses can be shifted. The Internet is not easy to block if someone is determined enough to get through, and access is growing.

Microsoft and Intel, the world's largest providers respectively of computer software and microchips, announced plans to make the Internet the dominant voice and video telephone system. Their announcement said computer users could reach each other for the price of a local phone call.

Around the world millions of people each day use the Internet, a network that links more than 40,000 (no one knows for certain) government, business, college, and private networks with more than two million host computers in 200 countries from Australia to Zambia, to tap into databases, swap e-mail messages, or chat with users who share a special interest.[54] A survey in late 1995 estimated 9.5 million users in the United States alone, spending an average of 6.6 hours weekly on the Internet.[55] Later surveys showed several times that number of users. At the end of 1995, Americans and Canadians on average spent as much time on the Internet as they did watching rented videotapes.[56]

Private corporations use the Internet for internal communication and to provide technical support for their customers. Politicians use it as a cheap way to get their messages to voters. Bored college students on different campuses can, via the Internet, tap into *MUDS*, which stands for *Multi-User Dungeons*, to battle villains and each other in medieval villages. It is all as anonymous as the senders wish. For everyone who can spare the time, there are soap operas. The proverbial fly upon the wall is now Everyman, who can buzz or watch as the mood strikes. Seductive, the Internet coaxes otherwise busy people to wile away hours, detoured by bulletin boards that catch their attention. One professor recalled, "One day I was looking at documents for a research project and found myself sidetracked to astrophysics documents from Lund, Sweden. The document was in Swedish and English translation. I ended up spending more than an hour

reading the document and its translations. At that point I said, 'That's it. I'm completely over the edge. I need to get out now!'"[57] Cases of Internet addiction have been reported, with users online for 18 hours a day racking up hundreds of dollars in monthly phone bills. The Internet Addiction Support Group had 300 members online, which seems a counterproductive way for "cyberaddicts" to meet.[58] Some companies try to keep employees from wasting time on their computers; a software program called *UnGame* blocks access to about 3,000 games.

Who Owns the Internet?

The Internet Society, based in Reston, Virginia, has been overseeing the Internet network, but, according to a computer specialist, "asking who is in charge of Internet is like asking who is in charge of the national sidewalk system."[59] The U.S. Defense Department set up the Internet in 1969 to promote communications between the military and the private sector. To be able to continue communication even in the event of a nuclear attack, the Internet was built to function without a central point of control. Each computer on the network shared equal responsibility. In 1984 a "backbone" of high-speed communication lines allowed supercomputers to exchange massive amounts of data for such tasks as weather forecasting without tying up the Internet. The National Science Foundation ran it as a research tool, although it was becoming clearer each year that the Internet had become much more. Because the service was subsidized by the U.S. government, it was cheaper than the telephone, the mails, or fax.

It has grown in such a chaotic fashion that some users have called for increased government control, a situation reminiscent of the mid-1920s, when U.S. broadcasters begged the federal government to step in to regulate the disorder that over-the-air broadcasting had become. In 1994, after 25 years of government management, the Internet was turned over to private enterprise. Naturally, the Internet free-for-all has its own appeal. Said one letter writer:

Don't touch my Internet. Keep the government out, and let us cyberjunkies regulate ourselves! The Internet stands for liberty and open expression. It is pure freedom of speech—the good, the bad and the ugly. And you don't have to get past magazine editors to be heard.[60]

An Internet address, a combination of letters and symbols, on an office card was a sign of being "with it" because the user functioned on a national, even global basis comfortably from within his or her toolshed home. The scope of the Internet seems to be as large as information itself. Programs and text can be downloaded with what is known as a *File Transfer Protocol*, referred to as *FTP*. Information stored on computers throughout the Internet can be accessed through a system called *Telnet*. A file access system known as *Gopher* arranges information by topic for easier access. Two other frequently encountered terms are *URL (Uniform Resource Locator)*, which means the address of a file, and *HTML (Hypertext Markup Language)*, which is the language used to write Web pages.

Internet, once the realm of scientists and computer experts, has become accessible to nearly everyone. Yet defining Internet, be it a democracy or anarchy, remains difficult, for it is just a computer network that connects to other computer networks. If that sounds dull, something of interest only to scientists and computer wizards, think again. Internet, because of its odd beginnings, is a relatively unregulated path through an electronic landscape filled with unimaginable treasures.

It can be a serious place, and indeed its electronic mail feature is one of the primary ways scientists and other academics talk to each other... It has its arty, intellectual side, with files that provide the complete works of Shakespeare, everything you could possibly want to know about classical music, and reviews of obscure and not-so-obscure movies...

Then there is the practical side. Hundreds of university and government library card catalogs are available, as well as the Central Intelligence Agency's latest review of the political climate of nearly every country in the world...

Finally, there is the fun stuff. Recipes for nearly every kind of dish, the lyrics of every song by Bob Dylan or 10,000 Maniacs, sex guides, games, magazines, chess clubs, the laws governing Hong Kong, and images from the space shuttle can all be pulled into your computer.[61]

A computer game that attracted attention was the National Budget Simulation, created at the University of California. Players saw a simplified model of the federal budget. They could reduce or cut programs ranging from national defense to elementary education. Many players discovered that balancing the budget was not so easy.

The World Wide Web

The World Wide Web, or WWW to its growing legions of devotees, is the most comprehensive part of the Internet. It combines words, graphics, video, and sound, adds colors, includes advertising, and downloadable text and programs. It gives a semblance of order to the Internet. It is possible to organize a search for information on any topic by a key word or phrase.

The Web is readily available to anyone with a modem and browser software. Each of more than 100,000 WWW sites (http://address/document name) welcomes you with a *home page* that includes a table of contents.[62] The home page serves as a front porch for the many rooms of the house inside (or a store front for a business). Each room may contain some combination of words, pictures, and sounds. Click on a small picture and it will grow to fill the screen. Click on a sound and it will pour through your computer speaker, be it a bit of country music or a lion's roar. The Web uses *hypertext*, or *hypermedia* software that lets users follow their own pathways, linking from topic to topic and cross-referencing.

Among the odder choices has been a video camera staring at a coffee machine, reminding anyone old enough to have been an early cable channel user of the video camera that panned among a clock, a thermometer, and a barometer. More interesting are the guides, including maps of subway routes around the world. Free software and electronic magazines are there for the downloading, along with pictures and sound.

Businesses use the Internet to communicate with each other. Has a Domino's franchise in Indianapolis run low on buffalo wings? Do they need more pizza dough in Little Rock? Get on the Domilink. It speeds cooking tips around the circuit and the recipes to make sure that the sauces taste the same in Minot, North Dakota, as they do in Miami.

Jim Clark, the manager of easy-to-use Web browsing software called Netscape Navigator, and Marc Andreessen, whose design of Mosaic provided the basic technology that led to Netscape, gave away millions of copies free and became wealthy in the process. By giving away the software they built a user base that businesses rightly saw as advertising targets and potential customers. A 1995 report estimated that the Netscape home page was being looked at more than three million times a day.

Electronic Cash

If anyone could create a home page, then anyone could be a publisher. Readership (visits to any portion of a Web site are called *hits*) could amount to the hundreds of thousands. Internet publishers have found ways to download money by offering a taste of their wares to the public, then asking for subscription fees to be sent to them the old fashioned way, with checks or credit cards. Many publishers are still paid only in reputation, but if current tests of electronic cash prove successful, a new publishing industry will be created.

Printed material that can be downloaded is a natural sales item to be paid by "e-cash," but in fact anything that is now sold by a mailed catalog could one day be advertised and ordered through the Web and paid for by a transfer of electronic cash from one account to another. David Chaum, the mathematician who founded Digicash, is convinced that thieves cannot get their fingers on anyone's electronic hoard.

Security of credit card and other financial information requires complex coding to foil thieves, but governments fear that such encryption will also protect the privacy of terrorists and child pornographers. In 1996 the U.S. government reluctantly eased some restrictions on selling coded Internet programs.

What is available on the Web can fill the Yellow Pages, so it was logical that someone would actually publish a book of yellow pages modeled after the telephone company book. It has the advantage of a quick look-up in a convenient form, but the disadvantage of relying on the static medium of a printed book to describe such a fast changing medium. Printed yellow pages are inevitably out of date before they reach the bookstore, yet they offer a useful service.

The Web itself carries free search tools, among them "Net Search," "Open Text Index," "Alta Vista," "Switchboard," "Deja News," "Excite," "The Lycos Home Page," "WebCrawler Searching," and "Yahoo." Anyone who logs on can reach what is available on a bewildering array of topics. For those willing to *subscribe*, with or without money changing hands, more detailed information is available. Subscribers are added to a *listserv*, an electronic mailing list. A subscription to a listserv may bring a periodic focused collection of news items, which is really a personalized electronic newspaper carrying stories gleaned from a variety of databases and online news services.

Bulletin Boards

The Los Angeles earthquake of 1994 tested the ingenuity of people outside the area who wanted to find out how their relatives had fared. To keep the lines clear, AT&T programmed its network to limit incoming calls. But the earthquake was not 20 minutes old when computer users plugged into the Internet to get messages in and out. The Associated Press reported:

A plea from Tobias Koehler in Denmark went out shortly after the quake hit.

"Hi there. Is everything OK in Ventura, California? My sister just went there, she is in California for the first time."

In an electronic version of a ham radio network, some computer users in various parts of of the country offered to relay messages to people in their areas from relatives and friends who couldn't make long-distance phone calls from the quake zone.[63]

By next day, 12,000 messages had been filed on a Prodigy bulletin board set up just for the earthquake.

Nothing on the chaotic Internet is more free-wheeling than the honky-tonk section of the Information Highway known as *newsgroups*, which vary from thoughtful to sleazy, even potentially dangerous. Unless someone exercises censorship, such as a decision in 1996 by CompuServe to shut down its member access to about 200 addresses identified with pornography, anything is available, including child pornography. Efforts are being made to stamp out sites dealing with child pornography, but the task isn't easy in the borderless world of the Internet. With dozens of neo-Nazi newsgroups at Web sites, confrontations have raged over First Amendment free speech issues. All arguments had to face the plain fact that the First Amendment is part of the U.S. Constitution, but the Internet is international. In Germany, for instance, displaying the swastika is illegal.

Anyone may start a newsgroup or add comments to someone else's comments about whatever, joining in with treasure or trash. An attack is known as *flaming*, just part of a free-wheeling anarchy. *Bulletin boards*, *forums*, and *chat lines* add to the ceaseless cacophony.

Electronic newspapers, or bulletin boards, for special interest groups (called *SIGs*), ignore geography in creating multiple versions of McLuhan's global village, but by no means a single village. Through a newsgroup BBS (bulletin board system), to cite one example out of thousands, the old tradition of quilting brings people together:

> …A group of quilters is turning a computer bulletin board into a back-fence quilting bee. Thirty-one subscribers to a general interest information and shopping service know as the Prodigy Service became acquainted when they tuned into the service's crafts bulletin board last summer to exchange quilting tips.
>
> Their first group activity was a scrap fabric swap by mail, which they planned on the computer bulletin board.[64]

Tens of thousands of bulletin boards serve millions of users in the United States alone with the electronic equivalent of tacking notes onto cork boards for anyone to read.[65] Many users also tap in for the free or shareware computer programs, there for the downloading.

Support groups use newsgroups to deal with problems relating to physical disabilities, eating disorders, drug use, AIDS, cancer, diabetes, and mental illness. At least one Alcoholics Anonymous group, which calls itself "One Byte at a Time," held bulletin board sessions. It is more convenient and decidedly less embarrassing to type in: "Hello, my name is Susan, and I'm an alcoholic," than to face others at a meeting. Sympathetic and understanding replies come flying back from members all over the world who are online. Online, distance becomes meaningless.

Women who do not identify their gender reported that they were being taken seriously for the first time and they were being appreciated for their ideas.

Boards devoted to devotion include not only religious discussion groups, but even prayer groups. Praying in a cyberchurch meets the special needs of people whose mobility is limited. It also brings together co-religionists who are a tiny minority in their own communities. Add one or two in this town to a handful in that town and you soon have the makings of a vigorous congregation. Yet, as already observed, such distant connections with unseen people separates the communicator from his or her immediate environment.

Exercising Control

Newsgroups allow communication both on a personal and a mass scale, so members may address their messages to one or all. Some boards provide information relating to computers themselves, but bulletin boards are also devoted to discussions of general topics, political topics, political causes, even hate propaganda on a few boards. The Prodigy online service established a policy to either accept or reject items for bulletin boards in order to remove offensive material, but decided not to get into the complications of editing material.

It may not be possible to stop militant groups from pouring out their messages of hate on the Internet. The United States, with its First Amendment protection, has long been hospitable to printing thoughts, no matter how vicious. Countries unaccustomed to anyone printing anything they like have no choice but to get used to it on the Internet.

All boards could be reached by anyone in the world with a computer, a modem, and a telephone. Some bulletin board *sysops* (system operators) allow free access, others set a nominal fee. Many sysops give themselves the authority to peek at any private messages and to censor messages. They are the policemen of the electronic communities they created.[66] They are also the landlords. The typical sysop needs little more than a computer, a modem, a leased telephone line, a network router, and some reason for existing, identified by a cyberspace address. Some sysops also figure out how to make money from the venture. For many others, it remains an expensive and time-consuming but enthralling hobby.

For the most part, newsgroups bring together cyberspace communities of common interest, uniting participants who are unlikely ever to meet face to face, a realignment of friendships through the gauze layers of tools of communication plus the further distancing of *handles*, reminiscent of citizen band radio, in place of real names. TERMIN A. TOR has whimsical confabulations with N. DROID to their hearts' content. No one in the group knows what N. DROID looks like, except DROID himself or herself.

Knowlege Groups

On a different level, the government-run National Research Education Network links universities by fiber optics to permit faculty and students to share information and super-computer resources, and to collaborate. It may be the genesis of a national information service.[67] Distant learning through video teleconferencing is a growing field, managed by both universities and private enterprises.

The days when the Internet was used by university faculty, business, and government staffers as a source of quick knowledge exchange are not gone. More serious groups, hoping to exchange valuable information, manage to convey a degree of orderliness by requiring interested parties to become subscribers. No cost is involved. Monitors decide who will be admitted to the ranks of subscribers and will thus be entitled to participate in the exchanges of data. The elect receive the privilege of wading through masses of data that arrive on every electronic breeze.

Tens of thousands of networks have been formed throughout the world. There are networks that serve private companies, networks that serve universities, networks for government agencies and for private agencies. Local-area networks, called *LANs*, allow computers to share files and such peripheral devices as printers. Super networks like Usenet for newsgroups and the World Wide Web interconnect many networks. These "networks of networks" allow a user to tap into an enormous range of bulletin boards and to reach e-mail users in other networks. Usenet, for example, connects several hundred thousand computer nodes for users exchanging everything from computer programs and cooking recipes to reviews of Japanese animation.

Advertising

Inevitably advertising came onto the Internet, at first as a free classified ad listing on a bulletin board of items for sale. But it was the World Wide Web that proved to be a vehicle for major advertisers. Typically, a company set up shop on the Web with a home page that acted as a store front. It looked attractive and displayed some of the wares available inside, just a mouse click away.

McDonald's led the caravan of major advertisers down the Information Highway by running ads in America Online's entertainment section. It should be noted that McDonald's Corp., the company with the golden arches, lost its name on the Internet to a company that got in first by registering its "domain name" with the Internet Network Information Center. The InterNIC is as close as the Internet comes to having a central administration.

Auto shoppers found not only information on the Web, but deals through discounters who signed up hundreds of dealers across the nation. Buyer and seller come together at what is purported to be a no-haggle price that might be thousands of dollars below usual dealer prices. The Internet has shaken up the automobile industry. It seems logical that appliance dealers and others would not be far behind. It was estimated that online purchases would reach $4 billion annually by 1999.

Chat Lines

There was no human contact, no "face time," unless you left it for an old-fashioned date, but some users found true love on what were called *Internet Relay Chat* lines, or *IRC*. These are ongoing conversations. "A" types something. "B" replies. "C" adds a comment. "A" can't let that remark pass. And so on into the night and the next morning. Conversations that began in anonymous safety online with names like "Fun," "Lips," and "Hot Sex" may have led, after the customary exchanges of e-mailed photographs, to actual meetings, where the cyberfantasy suddenly became, over hot coffee, cold reality. A few marriages have been reported from these cyberdates, but inevitably there have been a greater number of disappointments and not a few heartbreaks among lonely "computer-heads" who chose a social whirl of personal communication from the isolation of a keyboard. Still, hope sprang eternal down by the old bit stream.

The chat lines have been particularly addictive. Some students—mostly, but not exclusively, male—cannot tear themselves away even after 12 hours. A few students have gone without food or even bathroom breaks rather than risk missing some sharp retort. Through neglect of what was near and visible, more than one boy lost his flesh-and-blood girl friend and gained academic probation, which put chat lines firmly on the list of addictions.

A 34-year-old Seattle man wrote to "Dear Abby" that he had become "hooked on computer chat lines":

> I have been in contact with a young woman in Miami (computer only—no telephone, no mail). In recent weeks, our conversations have become very sexually explicit. (This is known as "computer sex.")
>
> Abby, in your opinion, am I being unfaithful to my wife—or just indulging in some harmless fun? Please bear in mind that there is no way to verify that the person you are chatting with on one of these lines is who she says she is (name, age, gender, etc.) You may be chatting with a 95-year-old grandfather.

Abby replied that computer sex could be damaging to his marriage and, if his wife found out, to his computer.

It should be noted that chat lines are also used by corporations for business purposes and by people interested in discussing special topics.

Social Implications

When we tie into the Internet from a home computer, we deny ourselves even the minimal contact with humans that we get by visiting the library and smiling a hello to a librarian. Howard Rheingold, a regular user of a computer bulletin board put the emotional connection and limitation into perspective:

> My virtual community, the WELL (Whole Earth 'Lectronic Link), is based in the San Francisco Bay Area, with members all over the world. Since I joined the WELL via my modem in 1985, I've spent more than two hours every day connected to the WELL and the larger Internet. My family and my flesh-and-blood community are living evidence that computer networks are not populated with that stereotype, the soulless geek. Sure, there are many lonely and

socially inept people who seek some kind of human contact that they lack in the real world. But there are plenty of people who are just like everyone else—we go to work, raise families, attend PTA meetings and baseball games...

Virtual communities are not utopias. People need to understand their limitations as well as their benefits. There are dark sides, just as every technology casts cultural shadows. Electronic bulletin-board systems can bring people together, but the computer screen can be a way of controlling relationships, keeping people at a distance.[68]

Supported by federal grants, public libraries and governments at various levels have been designing ways to use the Information Highway, including methods to provide open access to rich and poor alike. Governments expressed concern that poor people, deprived of means available to others to generate résumés or access employment databases, would fall still further behind.

With so many library card catalogs now in electronic files, accessible to users from office and home computers, it was only a matter of time that some universities would take the next step and allow users to order books by telephone or fax without setting foot into the library. The books are sent by post or the university's interoffice mailing service. The day may come when the books themselves will be downloaded. The books would then always remain on the library *shelf* in pristine condition. The user would be able to keep the books with no concern about overdue fines. Electronic databases already offer this option of communication without transportation. Hundreds exist, thanks to individuals and institutions willing and indeed eager to share compiled information.

Radio on the Internet

Nowhere is evidence of a potential explosion in the number of choices stronger than in the opportunity to put radio signals on the Internet.

Because the signals travel by wire, no demand is made on the electromagnetic spectrum. No permission is needed as yet from the Federal Communications Commission or any equivalent government agency anywhere. Because of the available technology, a radio program, a song, or speech can either be downloaded or heard in real time.

Most important, through the Internet a radio station is no longer local. Except for shortwave and clear channel broadcasting, radio had been basically a community technology except for some limited radio-by-satellite service. A broadcaster who cannot attract a large enough audience in his own city or town and the surrounding area cannot survive. With Internet radio, that limitation vanishes. Say that you want to specialize in patter songs—Gilbert & Sullivan, Tom Lehrer, Broadway show tunes, and the like. Perhaps no city in the United States could support such a radio broadcasting schedule. But with a hundred listeners in Memphis, a hundred more in Des Moines, two dozen each in Kuwait and Calcutta, and very low overhead, a radio entrepreneur could make some money at it.

Besides music, an Internet radio station could broadcast meetings, speeches, forums, conversation, or any other audio. In 1996, radio stations in Hong Kong, Taiwan, and Malaysia were reaching their nation and other listeners throughout the world. On the day in late 1995 that the net.radio site opened for business on the World Wide Web, it recorded more than 186,000 "hits."[69] Unlike radio broadcasting's imprecise ratings estimates, network radio stations can determine not only exactly how many people tuned in, but also their names, addresses, and phone numbers because listeners had to fill out a form in order to gain access.

Television signals can also be sent throughout the world via the Web, but their quality was a long way from broadcast standards as of 1996. Nevertheless, a start was made in 1996 by programs such as "Encarta on the Record," featuring former television journalist Linda Ellerbee with an audio track and video images.

Communication engineers use the metaphor of a pipe. A telephone line feeding into a computer modem is a narrow pipe. A coaxial cable feeding into a television set is a wide pipe. A fiber optic line feeding into a cable box is a Niagara of a pipe. Movies can be downloaded in seconds. Access via cable box to the Internet allows massive data transfer in fractions of a second, and that is expecially welcome in downloading Internet still and motion video.

Trying to explain the Internet recalls to mind the fable of the blind men describing an elephant. It is like the phone system, enabling anyone to reach anyone else immediately with a private message. No, it is like radio, enabling one person instantly to reach millions. No, it is like a newspaper, reporting fresh information, plus features, advertising, and a public forum. No, it is like the postal service with its private mail and junk mail. No, it is like television, with an ability on the World Wide Web to add pictures and sound to words. No, it is like the magazine industry, able to reach millions of readers self-selected in thousands of highly focused groups. It is a huge post office. It is a huge library. It is a huge soapbox. And on and on.

MAILBOX IN THE COMPUTER

E-mail, *electronic mail*, bypasses not only the post office, but also the telephone. It is total "communication without transportation," omitting even the trip to the corner mailbox, and without the accompanying effort of dealing with writing paper, envelopes, and stamps. A point-to-point communication system, it puts a mailbox in the home, inside any computer equipped with a modem and communications software. The owner of a computer so equipped can transmit a message—mail a letter—to one or many similarly equipped computers in offices down the hall or to a home halfway around the world.

To use a telephone, radio, or television requires an open channel of communication between sender and receiver. Even during periods of silence the channel remains open. By contrast, e-mail uses *store and forward* communications. A message is stored at the sending site, forwarded to the receiving site along channels shared by many other packets of information, and stored at the receiving site, to be read at leisure. E-mail in this way makes efficient and frugal use of communication bandwidth. For example, 15,000 people might be able to send one-page letters to 15,000 friends in a city one thousand miles away along the same channel that one person uses to telephone one other person for ten minutes. A disadvantage of e-mail has been that it has not worked well in sending vast amounts of real-time data such as a television program.

A mail receiver can reply easily and quickly to e-mail, bypassing the postal system and "telephone tag." In Great Britain, you can send e-mail to a friend even if your friend does not own a computer. With a service called *Electronic Post*, you send your e-mail to the post office nearest your friend's home. The local postman will laser print the letter, put it in an envelope and deliver it.

Along with newsgroup bulletin boards, e-mail links people with special interests, including the political, no matter how removed from centrist tendencies, all of it free of the censor. Government censors in scores of nations probably do not know what is going on, and, even if they did, could scarcely halt the exchange of information across their borders, short of copying all letters, seizing all computer modems or tracking down all international phone calls.

The transmission system of e-mail resembles a telephone network in its ability to connect one transmission node—a telephone—with another in seconds, and it resembles the postal service in its ability to transmit written information. Yet, e-mail "is just too democratic" for some addressees.[70] Matters have reached the point that movie stars and other well-known names would rather not have their e-mail addresses made public because their electronic mailboxes become cluttered with messages from the star-struck and anyone else with a yen to contact the famous. Unlisted e-mail addresses may be possible, but will certainly present an attractive challenge to a hacker who would enjoy digging out the address and *spamming* it on electronic bulletin boards far and wide.

Continued

Mailbox in the Computer *(continued)*

E-mail can be addressed to everyone on a list. The hacker as broadcaster. The hacker as junk mailer, anonymous as he wishes and free to say anything. The e-mailbox of everyone who belongs to a popular newsgroup is stuffed daily. Chain letters are among the nuisances, although they are as illegal on the Internet as they are through the postal system. Worse than a nuisance is the threat of a stalker who begins by "virtual stalking" on the Internet. Pedophiles have managed to locate the e-mail addresses of children to whom they send pornographic letters and pictures. Finding a way to stop them has not proved easy.

Writing Style   E-mail has also revived the art of letter writing, but has given it a spunky twist. These instant messages are shorter and more informal than the traditional "snail mail" wending its slow way through the postal system. Some users think that e-mail correspondence, like telephone conversations, lowers inhibitions. Messages are more direct and emotional.

People who "hate to write letters" say they encounter no such emotional impediments in tapping out a few words on a keyboard. Some observers have noted that the writing of faxed documents is more likely to be in the straightforward style of memos than in the more polite, more elaborate circumlocutions of letters, but philosopher David Glidden saw in bulletin boards a return to the days when letter writing was an art:

Although the art of letter-writing may have died, another form of writing has appeared: thinking people writing to each other on computer screens... Where the ancient forum was a place for making speeches, the computer forum is a place for written exchange.

With every new technology the art of writing changes. When Henry James switched from writing successive drafts on paper to dictation to a typist, his sentences grew longer and his fiction more diffuse. His writing became more like the way he talked. Composing by computer has had somewhat the opposite effect, making prose more focused and finessed, enabling—even encouraging—an endless series of revisions that would have strained the hand or forced the typist to quit.

Something that was lost in the age of telephone seems to be returning via the computer: literary friendship. Friendships formed through conversation are rather different from those written out. Verbal friendships are more transitory, thriving on the clever phrase, feeding off the facts of daily life—jobs, habits, shopping trips or sex stories. Friendships that come about through writing are far more intimate.[71]

Faxing

In the rain forests of Chiapas state, the Mexican army was in hot pursuit of the Zapatista rebels when the Zapatistas faxed out a communique that the federales were "killing children, beating and raping women." In the ensuing demand to know what was really going on, the offensive came to a halt and reporters were allowed into the area. They found no evidence of atrocities. Meanwhile, the Zapatistas had melted away into the rain forests, lugging their laptops.

Vice President Al Gore predicted an electronic battlefield where every soldier will be equipped with a cell telephone, computer, and fax:

During lulls they can arrange a date, they can settle on what they want to have fixed for dinner, and they can remind their home computer that it's time to water the plants.[72]

Speaker of the House Newt Gingrich predicted that armchair generals

...will be able to see the battle in real time. You'll then be able to pick up your telephone and call your son or daughter who you are watching real time in a firefight.

You will chat with them about your view of how they are conducting their squad operations.

Anyone listening to such speculations might be inclined to dismiss them as science fiction foolishness, but they were said in all seriousness by the United States Vice President and the Speaker of the House of Representatives, two men who agree with each other on almost nothing.

Speed of Facsimile

Facsimile is faster by far than the government postal system or Federal Express, using ordinary telephone lines. For many people, fax is easier to use than e-mail because it does not require a computer. Unlike e-mail, a fax message can carry graphics as easily as text, which was wonderful news for people writing in Chinese or Japanese. Because their written languages rely on complex ideographs that defeated the teletype machine, facsimile proved to be an ideal way to transmit writing. It is little wonder that the Japanese, the largest manufacturers of fax machines, have also been its largest market.

E-mail and fax are both transmitted in seconds from one location to another, or from one location to many others. Each method has its advantages. Totally electronic, e-mail does not require paper. Its alphanumeric characters can be written by one person, edited by another, and returned to the writer; for example, co-authors can send a document back and forth without ever committing the words to paper. However, e-mail cannot transmit pictures. Fax transmits *bit-mapped* images, essentially a pattern of dots that duplicates a page; words and pictures are all the same to a fax machine. The original fax message can be on paper or in a computer file.

The modern facsimile machine transmits what is on a page by scanning it using a light source, like a laser beam, to read the dark and light points, which are converted into digital data then sent over a phone line to the receiving machine, where the page is reproduced. Much of the function of a stand-alone facsimile machine can be re-placed by a computer containing an internal fax board capable of communicating with any fax machine, or by fax software. A laser printer at the receiving end can produce a hard copy.

"Fax" Is More Than a Noun

The word started as a noun: *facsimile*. That was shortened: *fax*. Then, a sure sign of popularity and diffusion into society, the noun *fax* became the adjective *fax* ("a fax report") and also a verb ("Fax it to me") with a past tense ("I faxed it to you yesterday"). A century ago, *telephone* started down the same path. Facsimile (from the Latin "to make similar") can also refer either to the output or to the machine that sends images of documents, including photographs, to the other side of town or across continents or oceans, point-to-point to anyone with another facsimile machine. The newspaper that will arrive at your computer printer instead of outside your door is still mostly a futurist's dream, but facsimile technology is bringing it closer. For documents and letters, including newsletters, the fax bypasses the postman. It is a photocopier hooked to a telephone. Delivery anywhere in the world takes seconds.

The fax machine and the computer modem turned out to be magic boxes for *telecommuters* who decided they no longer must drive to work each day for the sole purpose of writing, drawing, or examining what their colleagues were writing, drawing, or examining.

Facsimile's Origins

Although the facsimile machine, which rapidly diffused into society during the last decade of the twentieth century, was widely considered to be among the newest of the tools of communication, its origins can be traced to 1842, when the telegraph was being invented and long before Alexander Graham Bell invented the telephone. Credit is given to another Scottish inventor, Alexander Bain, who used a metallic brush sweeping over a raised copper letter of the alphabet to transmit a signal over an electric wire that resulted in a rough copy of that letter drawn by a pendulum swinging over a sheet of chemically treated paper. About the same time, F.C. Bakewell in London was developing an electrochemical copying telegraph that he demonstrated by transmitting handwriting and sketches. In 1865, the Italian Abbe Jean Caselli sent an actual photograph—of the Empress of France— over a wire, using a scanning cylinder, a stylus, and coated paper, a basic technology that was carried well into modern times by AP and UP for transmitting photographs to member newspapers.

In the late nineteenth century, the *telautograph* at railroad stations recorded seat reservations. It could transmit a handwritten message over a telegraph line for 250 miles. The device was invented by Elisha Gray, who had filed for a telephone patent on the same day as Alexander Graham Bell. In 1902, a photoelectric scanning system developed by Dr. Arthur Korn was able to transmit and reproduce images. The Associated Press began regular photoelectric service to member newspapers in 1934. AT&T and RCA transmitted photographs and weather maps by radio.

An early effort to send facsimile newspapers directly to homes and businesses had little success. These were slow, expensive machines that printed poorly.[73] To make matters worse, machines from different manufacturers were incompatible. A half century later the experiment was revived for people willing to pay the charges for having a newspaper delivered inside their homes instead of to their front doors.

Xerox introduced the Telecopier, the first paper facsimile machine for business, in 1966. The device, manufactured by Magnavox, produced poor quality faxes, but nothing else was available until the Japanese entered the marketplace in 1984. Their facsimile machines produced images of higher resolution transmitted in less time than the Telecopier. Demand by business firms grew at an astonishing rate, soon augmented by a home demand, the business-first-then-home pattern followed by the telephone a century ago and more recently by the computer and the copier.

The fax popularity explosion began after a court ruling in 1968, the Carterphone Decision, that allowed customers to connect fax machines and other non-Bell devices to the Bell System. Improvements in technology plus the agreement on a single worldwide standard for transmission did the rest.

One victim of the boom has been the telex business. Another is likely to be overnight mail delivery by the U.S. Postal Service and such private couriers as Federal Express. If there is a fax machine to receive a document, facsimile is cheaper, faster, and much more convenient than any method that involves transportation. In fact, fax rates dropped as first class postage rates rose, so that by 1990, it was sometimes cheaper to fax a letter than to mail it with a stamp.

A Variety of Uses

Faxes are used in seemingly infinite ways, including tasks involved in mass communication processes, such as an advertising agency sending a layout to a client for approval, the U.S. National Weather Service faxing forecast maps to television stations, or a newspaper bureau reporter sending a story to a distant city desk instead of telephoning for the rewrite desk.

While principally employed in business-to-business communication, the fax is used in ways that should be surprising only to those who underestimate the imagination of people who have a means of modern mass communication technology in their grasp.

> First we were faxing memos. Then birthday greetings. Then lunch orders for a ham-and-cheese to go. And now there is an art show of more than 70 works, all of which were faxed from around the globe... As it has done for the business world—eliminating such time-consuming problems as lead-footed couriers and post-office blunders— the fax machine has made the task of putting on an art show of more than 70 wildly different works a snap.[74]

At least one radio station encouraged fax requests for songs. Restaurants delivered faxed orders for lunch. Bowling teams each comprising a Japanese and an American competed across the Pacific with the partners faxing scores, strategy, and encouragement.

The fax machine is another communication technology with unintended consequences. Owners of fax machines find junk mail—copied on their own paper, no less—clogging their "in" trays.

> There's a dark side to this fax boom, too, of course: junk fax. Some outfits have taken to...rewarding office workers with tote bags and sometimes cash in exchange for lists of all the fax numbers the office machine has communicated with on a given day. They're gathering fax numbers to sell to direct marketers... Junk fax threatens to swamp many offices' fax machines, so now the trick is to conceal your fax number; don't spread it around.[75]

One advertiser offered for sale the very type of paper his ads were using up! Some persistent junk fax advertisers have combined fax transmission with automatic redial, so that nothing else can get through before their messages do, meanwhile churning out a repetitive series of beeps, clicks, and dial tones, the plaintive cry of one fax machine yearning for another.

Facsimile technology, which has been spreading year by year, has given the United States a truly national press when pages of major newspapers can be transmitted by satellite to regional printing plants so Wednesday's edition is available on Wednesday, not only in New York City and Washington, D.C., but in cities across the United States and overseas. As the facsimile machine has been diffused into society, prices dropped and the number of attractive features rose. Letters, photographs, and drawings are being sent anywhere in the world there is a telephone. As the twentieth century draws to a close, that means *anywhere* in the world.

Going Up the Highway

In the Coliseum of ancient Rome, spectators voted thumbs up or thumbs down on whether a gladiator lived or died. In 1982, *Saturday Night Live* comedian Eddie Murphy held up a live lobster he had named Larry. Viewers could call one number if they wanted Larry to live, another if they wanted Larry to go into the pot. At 50 cents a call, 123 thousand phoned to say Larry should live, and 117 thousand voted for the pot. At least that was the announced result. The rumor was that the vote went the other way, but the producers felt it would not do to cook Larry the Lobster, so they cooked the election returns instead.

The future may not hold more lobsters for us, but it will certainly hold more chances for such electronic plebiscites. Nothing is more likely to add to our choices in the communication toolsheds that we call home than two-way cable, also known as *interactive television (ITV)*. Many promises about cable's interactive potential have been made by futurists and by cable companies in franchise applications to city councils. Cable would supposedly do the shopping, perk the coffee, and protect the home, thanks to its two-way transmission capability downstream from a central location to a home and upstream from the home to the central location.

Does the public want interactive capacity? While the computer terminal-based Internet system is hugely popular, so far the everyday answer for a television terminal-based operation seems to be "No!" GTE spent millions in the prosperous Los Angeles suburb of Cerritos to test an interactive system that would permit residents to bank and shop at home, study, play games, and access movies. The experiment failed. "Quite frankly, I don't know of anyone who uses it," said the mayor.[76] Actually, hotels increasingly offer movies on instant demand instead of informing guests that a movie will start at the top of the hour. And the Sega cable channel lets young players choose among 50 interactive games. When interactive systems become more user friendly, use should grow.

The Qube Experiment

The same lack of interest led to the death of the Qube experiment. In 1977, Warner-Amex introduced the much publicized interactive system, Qube, in its Columbus, Ohio, cable system, and later incorporated it into several of its other systems. Qube subscribers had a keypad with numbers from 0 to 9 that could send an electronic signal to a central bank of computers that analyzed all responses. To elicit replies, an announcer or a written message across the screen questioned subscribers on various issues, such as whether a particular congressional bill should be passed. Subscribers selected the appropriate button in a multiple choice fashion. A computer calculated the calls and printed the percentage for each choice on screen.

The interactive system also polled the households to discover what programs they were watching. Qube expanded its interactive capability in 1981 to give subscribers access to a computer data bank that held such useful information as news, weather, and consumer tips. Viewers could compete against one another for prizes. Viewers could also scan a shopping catalog and place orders, and they could select programs. Unfortunately, either the interactive programs were less appealing than the designers predicted or Warner-Amex did not foresee Qube as becoming anything more than a loss leader to sell its cable service. In any case, the service lost more than $30 million in seven years and the company ended its ambitious experiment.

Figure 6.9 The remote control unit for the set-top box. (Courtesy Time Warner.)

However, Warner must have been impressed with the concept. Merged with Time, Inc. as Time Warner, it began an even bigger interactive experiment in 1994 with a digital video-on-demand service in Orlando, Florida, for 4,000 homes. At any time, 1,000 homes could simultaneously access any services of the Full Service Network, including any of about 100 movies, which viewers could fast-forward, rewind, or pause as if they had the videotape. Viewers could shop, bank, and order pizza. Time Warner and other American media giants have invested millions of dollars in developing new interactive and multimedia services. A major goal was to combine the bandwidth of fiber optic cable with the flexibility and storage of computers.

Other interactive efforts have been tried and sometimes abandoned. ACTV Interactive Television in the 1990s ran games for New York subscribers who competed for

Figure 6.8 A set-top box gives a television set interactivity capacity. (Courtesy Time Warner.)

prizes. Viewers played push-button black-jack with a dealer who sassed them ("I have your measly little bet"). A similar combination allowed an interactive "psychiatrist" to ask questions, nod his head, take notes, and accuse the viewer of "hiding something." Some California viewers could play along with *Wheel of Fortune* and *Jeopardy*. Singapore Airlines, in 1996, installed real gambling programs on seat back screens of some of its planes. Passengers used their credit cards to play.

Ultimately, users will decide if interactive television has a future. If the subscriber base fails to reach a critical mass, it cannot survive. Several American companies abandoned plans to launch such services, although France, Great Britain, Japan, and Canada provided two-way systems that ranged from experimental to actively profitable, including *teletext* and *videotex*.[77]

Teletext and Videotex

Newspapers eat forests. *Teletext* and *videotex* do not. Cynics refer to "the dead tree media." Newspapers are transported, requiring trucks and cars, sometimes buses and airplanes. All use gasoline. Teletext and videotex are communicated electronically, requiring none of these. A daily urban newspaper can easily weigh two pounds; its Sunday version, twice that. In virtually every household, much of it goes unread, a sheer waste. In a world of decreasing resources and increasing pollution, the electronic communication of news and information makes sense.

Teletext is the one-way transmission of text to viewers via a television signal's unused scanning lines, or vertical blanking interval (the horizontal bar on a television screen that becomes visible when the set isn't tuned perfectly). Special decoding equipment attached to the set deciphers the information, and it appears in the form of pages of text that the viewer can select.

Videotex is a computer-based interactive system that allows viewers access to a data bank containing information. Viewers can also conduct transactions. There is a greater practical application of this system

than of teletext because more information can be stored. Teletext users, using a television monitor, must also wait for a "page" to roll by before they capture it, whereas videotex users, using a computer monitor, can access frames of information immediately. To confuse matters, the terms are sometimes used interchangeably.

A criticism of online videotex, besides the discomfort of accessing words by sitting in front of a screen, has been the difficulty of getting an overall picture of the day's news, unlike the relaxed and common method of sprawling on the sofa and scanning the front page of the daily newspaper or watching a newscast. Using videotex has been compared to looking at a football field through a drinking straw.[78]

The idea for a commercial videotex service began when British scientists visiting the 1964 New York World's Fair came upon the AT&T Picturephone. Although they saw little immediate value in face-to-face telephone conversation, the idea of hooking television screens to the telephone network fascinated them. They wanted to show not faces, but information. Originally called *viewdata*, videotex service was first offered to consumers by the British Post Office in 1979 under the commercial name *Prestel*. Using the Prestel system, someone with a television set attached to a modem, a keypad, and a telephone could access computers loaded with information ranging from the stock market to horoscope readings. However, Prestel did not catch on with the British public. Fewer than 2 percent took the service, although it was popular with certain businesses like travel agents. Meanwhile, Great Britain's Ceefax and Oracle systems, both teletext, offered news, puzzles, fiction, and information for special groups.

France, Japan, and Canada also developed teletext and videotex systems. France's national system, Teletel, reaching one in every five households, became by far the most successful use of interactive television. The French government's postal service, PTT, gave telephone customers a free monitor and keyboard unit, or *Minitel*, then charged for access to about 10,000 private services listed in an electronic directory. The public use the Minitels to both shop and pay for goods, pay other bills, check airplane and train schedules, make hotel reservations, learn the latest news, the weather or what their horoscope advised, play computer games, or chat with fellow hobbyists. Subscribers also used it for e-mail. The 1996 Telecommunication Act will probably result in similar services in the United States as telephone and cable systems merge.

Online Services

America Online, also called AOL, tries to look slick and hip for a young, with-it clientele. CompuServe, which began as a consumer videotex service, provides Associated Press news on demand, access to many kinds of bulletin boards, e-mail, and a variety of information, just as AOL does. CompuServe established a niche among professional and business users as a serious, international network with access to local numbers in industrialized countries. Users also are given access to specialized libraries and databases. The Dow Jones News Retrieval began as a business information service before reaching out to the general public. Many of the features offered by commercial services were also available through independent gateway servers to the World Wide Web and the rest of the Internet through such navigation software as Netscape's Navigator.

One criticism of online services was that it was designed by men and most of its use is by men, not by women. More than four out of five subscribers in its formative years were men. Prodigy learned a lesson from this and hired women to help design and market its product in order to increase the number of women customers. Its goal was a family-oriented service with graphics and bulletin boards to which beginners could navigate fairly easily. However, it captured only a small portion of the market.

Other Interactive Operations

Meeting the strong public desire for communication without transportation, one of the potentially popular forms of interactive television is home shopping, which was the cable programming phenomenon of the 1980s. In the interactive version, subscribers purchase merchandise by keying in their account information on two-way cable systems. Teleshopping combines television and telephone, plus computers to process the orders. In the Chicago suburb of Deerfield, viewers in an experiment can order from several dozen local stores by punching into the phones the catalog numbers of the items displayed on the screen.

Cable's two-way capability allows burglar, fire, and medical alarm devices to connect to a cable system. Each participating home is scanned about every ten seconds by a computer in a central monitoring station to see if everything is in order. If any problems are detected, a signal is sent back to the cable company, which notifies police. At the community level, interactive cable systems provide services like traffic light control, energy management, and meter reading.

Not all varieties of interactive cable have fared well. What the public likes best is a smorgasbord of possibilities, including bulletin boards, e-mail, computer games, and videotex access to news headlines, sports scores, stock market reports, and the weather forecast. Knight-Ridder's Viewtron and similar services from the *Los Angeles Times-Mirror* and the *New York Times*, which offered only news-on-demand, failed. The public would not pay for a special terminal that did not provide entertainment. Online terminals by non-profit groups and bank-at-home terminals connected to personal computers did no better. Faring even worse were online terminals in shopping malls and airports that provide information if you pushed a button or touched a screen. They were vandalized. Teenage boys, it seems, could not resist them. Nevertheless, they are still in use.

Interactive Possibilities

Interactive cable can be hooked up without complex technology. A transceiver in the home gives the viewer upstream capability, anything from a simple "yes or no" response with a couple of pushbuttons to a keypad for a variety of choices all the way to conversation via computer keyboard or a speech recognition device.

The telephone works well enough if just a few people call, but on a national basis if millions of people called at once to express an opinion, most would not get through. The Bell system is not set up to handle such traffic. After President Bush's State of the Union Address in January 1992, CBS viewers were asked to phone in their opinions; 25 million tried, but only 315,000 got through.[79]

The home hooked by fiber optics to a computer can receive school lessons and send back the student's answers to a test, an electronic variation of the old familiar home study course. At Laurel Springs High School in Ojai, California, for example, students could elect online courses in which all the reading material, including course instructions and study guides, were fed to the students' homes electronically. Everything from social studies to science was online, although admittedly an assigned English novel was easier to read when it was in the old-fashioned form of a book. Homework was handed in online using software written for each course. Other kinds of information might be found in information-laden databases.

A daily listing of classified ads in direct competition with newspapers is a reality in many cities. Rental apartments can be located by tapping into a real estate database that is constantly updated. That makes a business for real estate firms that become not only customers of newspapers, but competitors.

Auto sales can be dealt with in a similar manner. By 1995, about 50 different makes of automobiles were advertised on World Wide Web sites and on a CD-ROM called the *New Car Buyers Guide*, which gives an alternative to car buyers who do not like to visit showrooms where they expect pressure from salesmen.

Manipulating Television Programs

The interactive possibilities of fiber optics had visionaries talking of giving viewers not only choices of programs, but choices within programs. Montreal interactive cable subscribers chose among camera angles in baseball and hockey games. Following the Montreal example, a viewer watching a football game potentially could choose at any moment to see the action from high above, from the 50-yard line, or from the end zone, the same choices now available only to the television director. A game show viewer could play against the studio contestants, answer multiple choice questions, and, after punching in an incorrect answer, hear the game show moderator say, "You at home are wrong." A homesick viewer who identified the place where she grew up could receive the latest home town news. In the future, a viewer watching a drama might be able to choose the path the story will take; children may find this prospect more appealing than adults would, but who knows?

A system called L-VIS (Live Video Insertion System) has been slipping customized billboard-like ads onto the walls of ballparks, using electronic imaging "occlusion technology" to mask for viewers at home what is actually on the wall. It is expected that static images will soon be replaced by moving pictures and even 3-D, and that advertising will be moved from the wall to the middle of the playing field.

Tests were also conducted to determine the feasibility of targeting commercials to reach homes fitting certain demographic profiles. If such a use of interactive television can be made to work, an elderly couple and a young single woman watching the same program might see different commercials. More ominously, one day registered Democrats might not hear the same version of a political speech as registered Republicans. Young and old might receive different messages.

According to George Gerbner, "What we are facing with cable is a transformation of our world similar to the one brought about by the printing press."[80]

News Online

Newspapers are no longer what they once were. They are more than black ink on white paper. They are a voice on the telephone, a matrix of pixels on a computer screen, a CD-ROM disk. American newspapers are going to multimedia. They are reinventing themselves to offer not a single product for all readers, but a variety of products for a diverse audience: people of every age and color and religion and ethnicity and language and sexual orientation and, above all, of every possible interest. Again, narrowcasting and choice.

The Electronic Newspaper

The paperless newspaper, whose roots go back to the late 1970s, is finally arriving at our homes through online database services like Prodigy, which was designed to be a national online newspaper, and from many newspapers themselves that have gone into the online business. For a few dollars a month, a daily newspaper, particularly those in large cities, offers its readers such fare as 24-hour news updates and more information than the printed edition carries on major stories, plus Internet access. For an extra charge, the reader gets sports scores, horse racing results, crossword puzzle solutions, an extended horoscope, and soap opera updates.

The *interactive* newspaper creates a living editorial page and *op-ed* page (the opinion page opposite the editorial page) unlike anything that exists on paper today. It resembles an Internet chat line or listserv that runs parallel *threads* (ongoing discussions on a topic) on several subjects at once. Many discussions are linked to news and editorial content.

In the realm of opinion, it may be possible to create a continuous interactive symposium that will make the current editorial and op-ed pages seem as though they belong in the Stone Age.[81]

Those who know where to look on the Internet can find news summaries from newspapers around the world. For example, ClariNet provides news from news services divided by region and topic. The Associated Press and CNN have separate news sites. So do hundreds of newspapers, television stations, radio stations, magazines, and newsletters. Their numbers grow daily.

Telcos, Newspapers, and Newscasts

In 1995, eight of the biggest American newspaper companies—owning 185 daily newspapers—joined to create a national network of online local newspapers, and they invited all daily newspapers in the United States to join them to set up a clearinghouse of information and sales between information providers and users. The announced goal was to offer for sale a vast array of information: news, features, sports, plus ticket purchases, home shopping, e-mail, and bulletin boards.

Telephone companies and newspapers may in future make excellent partners. The newspapers can produce a responsible editorial product, and the telephone companies can deliver it electronically over cable to the home.

Here would be a new way to get news, without a newspaper's built-in restriction of space. Anything that any wire service or major newspaper carried on a topic could be online.

A television newscast has an inherent limitation of time. Experiments were underway to combine a newspaper and a newscast so that a story would contain text *and* sound bites. The process would eliminate the wasteful practice of throwing away, unread, much of a Sunday newspaper that lands on the doorstep. In the United States, that can be several pounds of mostly wasted paper. Automobile bumper stickers once carried the message: "Save Our Forests. Don't read The Sunday New York Times."

We have not achieved the dream that our daily news*paper* will become paperless. In this vision, the information will come into our homes electronically, saving the

Figure 6.10 An online page from the Minneapolis *Star Tribune* features headlines leading to extensive story coverage, special services like classified ads, plus a directory to other newspapers. (Courtesy Minneapolis *Star Tribune*.)

world's dwindling forests, to say nothing of energy resources, such as the gas that fuels the trucks that deliver the lumber, the newsprint, and the newspaper that lands at the front door.

Aware of the inevitable waste of paper in delivering each day's news and advertising, futurists have long predicted an on-demand news service through telephone or cable lines onto television or computer screens. The electronic newspaper would not only bring news without paper, it could provide far more information about any subject of interest than an ordinary newspaper could provide. It would rival specialty magazines.

Selling News Instead of Newspapers

Newspapers are just one means of news delivery. If news can be delivered electronically, its cost will be in gathering and preparing, not in getting it into our homes. Huge, expensive presses, newsprint, and the complex infrastructure of home delivery would be unnecessary in a purely electronic world.

If the day comes that self-employed reporters can sell their stories, perhaps accompanied by sound and pictures, worldwide over the Internet for a few cents directly to each reader using digital cash, the entire basis of journalism will shake itself into new forms. An astrologer named Jean Dixon provided Prodigy subscribers on the Internet with horoscopes for the day they were born. Of every dollar that Prodigy charged, a portion went to the astrologer. At least one respected journalist, Robert Parry, formerly of the Associated Press and *Newsweek*, offered his investigative reports free on the Web and by subscription to readers who preferred direct delivery via e-mail, fax, or the postal service.

At MIT's Media Lab, NewsPeek (which sounds like "New Speak") was organized to receive only those news stories of interest to the user. Other researchers envisioned readers keying in a request to a portable computer hooked to a telephone line. The latest news would be downloaded to be read at leisure.

The volume of unedited, unorganized information available via the Internet today is so huge that only a determined reader with a lot of free time will pick through it looking for an understanding of the day's news. Inevitably, readers will seek organized reports, and that is the work of journalists.

The Computerized Newspaper

Modern newspapers rely on computers at every step. Reporters type their stories on keyboards using word processing programs plus spelling checkers and online library databases, including electronic records of past newspaper stories, which have replaced the old *morgue* of newspaper clippings. Using their terminals, reporters access computerized government records. Associated Press and other news agency wire copy pours in on high-speed data lines via modem. Copy editors call up stories on video display terminals to edit them and add headlines. Photographs enter computers as a digitized stream of dots to be sized and cropped. Makeup editors design each edition using page layout software. Classified ads, taken by phone, go right into the computer. Display ads arrive on diskette. The finished page comes out as a thin plate ready for the press, which is also under computer control. Circulation lists on database speed the home delivery.

The untidy piles of loose sheets of paper, once the hallmark of every newspaper office, are less evident. Gone at many newspapers are the noise, the grime, and the smell of ink, replaced by pastel carpet. Even small weeklies and free suburban shoppers have taken advantage of computers.

By the mid-1990s several hundred newspapers in the United States and Canada did their page makeup on computers. While many of them pasted graphics and pictures in manually, a few included all visual matter in the pagination.

Some reporters, especially sports reporters on tight deadlines, drive to their assignments with modem-equipped notebook computers. At the stadium, they write their stories as the game develops. The lead, with its score, is written last. The story is transmitted back to the newspaper office or the Associated Press bureau by the touch of a button. Portable computers are attached to cellular telephones, so the reporter does not have to go searching for a public telephone. Foreign correspondents, confronting uncertain telephone connections, have been grateful for equipment that can transmit an entire dispatch in just a minute or two with fidelity. It is much more efficient than shouting over a bad line, "No, that's 'B' as in 'Baker'."

National Distribution

For local newspaper readers dissatisfied with the rationing of serious news from around the world, a national press has emerged in the United States that rivals the national presses of Europe, whose geographically smaller countries have always liked national newspapers. Modern communications technology has made possible a national press in the United States.

For a newspaper with national distribution, a satellite uplink transmits images of each page to receiving dishes located at printing plants of cities chosen as regional distribution points. The Tuesday edition of such national newspapers as the *New York Times* and the *Wall Street Journal* arrives at most doorways in the nation on Tuesday.

As if all this were not enough, some *smart* newspaper vending racks signal the circulation department when they run low. As the song says, the *Times* they are a'changing.

Notes

1 Mark Poster, *The Mode of Information: Post-structuralism and Social Context* (The University of Chicago Press, 1990), 7.

2 Leo Bogart, "Highway to the Stars or Road to Nowhere?," *Media Studies Journal: The Race for Content*, (Winter 1994): 1.

3 *Newsweek*, 8 June 1992, 22.

4 Ithiel de Sola Pool, *Technology and Culture* (Cambridge: Harvard University Press, 1990), 261.

5 *Newsweek*, 22 January 1996, 60.

6 James W. Carey, "The Communications Revolution and the Professional Communicator," *Sociological Review*. Monograph No., 13, University of Keele, (1969), 26

7 Associated Press, Minneapolis *Star Tribune*, 7 October 1993, sec. 19A.

8 George Gilder, *Life After Television* (Columbus: Whittle Direct Books, 1990), 24.

9 *TV Guide*, 10 April 1993, 3.

10 Alvin Toffler, *The Third Wave* (New York: William Morrow, 1980), 369.

11 Minneapolis *Star Tribune*, 12 September 1993, sec. 27A

12 Peter Leyden interview with Manuel Castells, Minneapolis *Star Tribune*, 15 April 1994, sec. 16A.

13 *New Scientist*, 136:1850 (5 December 1992): 22.

14 *The Economist*, 13 February 1994, 4.

15 Lawrence Tessler, Vice President, Advanced Technology Apple Corp.

16 *Newsweek*, 27 February 1995, 27.

17 Alvin Toffler, 226.

18 Donald R. Katz, "Are Newspapers Yesterday's News?", *Esquire*, January, 1990, 40.

19 John Halton, "The Anatomy of Computing" in Tom Forester (ed.), *The Information Technology Revolution* (Cambridge: The MIT Press, 1985), 3-4.

20 David Bunnell, "Tracking the Revolution," *Publish!*, (September/October, 1986): 9.

21 Anthony Smith, *Books to Bytes: The Computer and the Library* (New York: Gannett Center for Media Studies, 1988), 3.

22 John Vivian, *The Media of Mass Communication*, 3rd ed. (Boston: Allyn and Bacon, 1995), 64.

23 *Newsweek*, 30 January 1995, 62.

24 Fred T. Hofstetter, "Is Multimedia the Next Literacy?" *Educators Tech Exchange*, (Winter 1994), 7.

25 *MacUser*, November 1993, 91.

26 Op. cit.: 98.

27 Op. cit.: 96.

28 *Newsweek*, 27 February 1995, 29.

29 Matt Stump and Harry Jessell, "Cable: The First Forty Years," *Broadcasting*, 21 November 1988, sec. 42.

30 Sydney W. Head, Christopher H. Sterling, and Lemuel B. Schofield, *Broadcasting in America: A Survey of Electronic Media*, seventh ed. (Boston: Houghton Mifflin Co., 1994), 574., and Minneapolis *Star Tribune*, 26 February 1994, sec. 3E.

31 Larry King, *On the Line* (New York: Harcourt Brace & Co., 1993), 176.

32 Tichenor, P.J., G.A. Donahue and C.N. Olien, "Mass Media Flow and Differential Growth in Knowledge," *Public Opinion Quarterly* (Summer 1970): 159-60.

33 Joan Van Tassel, "Electronic Retailing," in Grant, August E., and Kenton T. Wilkinson, eds., *Communication Technology Update, 1993-1994* (Austin: Technology Futures, Inc., 1993), 92-93.

34 Kelly S. Baldwin, "Wireless Cable (MMDS)," in Grant et. al, 67-68.

35 *Newsweek*, 17 October 1988, 95.

36 The *Wall Street Journal*, July 10, 1990: A1.

37 Joseph N. Pelton, Interlsat director of special projects, *21st Century Satellite Communications*.

38 Paul Kennedy, *Preparing for the Twenty-First Century* (Toronto: HarperCollins Publishers Ltd., 1993), 63.

39 The *Wall Street Journal*, 1 February 1990, sec. A1.

40 The *Economist*, 3 February 1996, sec. 54.

41 Extra-Terrestrial Relays: Can Rocket Stations Give World-Wide Radio Coverage?" *Wireless World*, October 1945.

42 Karen J.P. Howes, "Teleports — Satellites, Fiber and Compression," *Via Satellite*, August 1993, 26-34.

43 S. Chase, "The VSAT Revolution — Doing Business at Home and Abroad," *Via Satellite*, November 1991, 58-63.

44 P. McDougal, "VSATs and Developmental Communications," *Space Communication and Broadcasting*, June 1989, 445-455.

45 Rogers, Everett M., *Communication Technology: The New Media in Society* (New York: The Free Press, 1986), 50-51.

46 Based on a survey of 2,500 respondents nationwide by Link Resources, reported in Peter Leyden, "Teleworking could turn our cities inside out," Minneapolis *Star Tribune*, 5 September 1993, sec. 16A.

47 Marcia Kelly, "Work-at-home," *The Futurist*, (Nov/Dec 1988): 32.

48 Leonard Inskip, "Electronic 'Highways' of the Future," Minneapolis *Star Tribune*, 21 December 1988, sec. 21A.

49 Peter Leyden, "Teleworking could turn our cities inside out," Minneapolis *Star Tribune*, 5 September 1993, sec. 1A, 16A.

50 New York market research firm Link Resources, reported in the Minneapolis *Star-Tribune*, 14 May 1994, sec. 1E.

51 Toffler, 210-23.

52 Karen JP Howes, "Teleports — Satellites, Fiber and Compression," *Via Satellite*, August 1993, 26-34.

53 Peter Leyden interview, Minneapolis *Star Tribune*, 15 April 1994, sec. 16A.

54 The Internet Society estimated two million host computers as of January 1995, with the number climbing rapidly.

55 American Internet User Survey data available at http://etrg.findssvp.com/surveys/inetshrt.html

56 *Casro Communicator* (Winter 1995): 1.

57 The *Minnesota Daily,* 31 May 1994, 13.

58 *Newsweek,* 18 December 1995, 60.

59 Mark McCahill, quoted in the Minneapolis *Star Tribune*, 22 August 1993, sec. 5B.

60 *Time,* 15 August 1994, 6.

61 Minneapolis *Star-Tribune*, 22 August 1993, sec. 5B.

62 Scott Bourne, "Spicing Up Your Web Site with Audio," *InfoNation*, November 1995, reported an estimate of 55,000 sites as of October 10, 1995, with the number growing rapidly.

63 San Francisco dateline, 18 June 1994.

64 Associated Press, 19 January 1990.

65 *Newsweek,* 6 March 1995, 75.

66 Rogers, Everett M., *Communication Technology: The New Media in Society* (New York: The Free Press, 1986), 42.

67 Media, Democracy and the Information Highway. Conference report of The Freedom Forum Media Studies Center, Columbia University, 24.

68 Howard Rheingold, "Cold Knowledge and Social Warmth," *Newsweek*, 6 September 1993, 49.

69 Data supplied by net.radio, Minneapolis, Minnesota.

70 The *Wall Street Journal,* 22 June 1994, sec. A10.

71 David Glidden, professor of philosophy, University of California, in Minneapolis *Star Tribune,* 30 May 1989.

72 Vice President Al Gore, Speech to Armed Forces Communications and Electronics Association, February 1995.

73 Eli Wathne and Carlos Reos, "Facsimile Machines," in Grant, et al., *Communication Technology Update, 1993-1994* (Austin: Technology Futures, Inc., 1993), 286.

74 Leslie Guttman, San Francisco *Chronicle*, 12 January 1990.

75 Jim Seymour, "PCs and the Fax Culture," *PC Magazine*, 13 June 1989, 77.

76 Lawrence K. Grossman, "Reflections on Life Along the Electronic Superhighway," *Media Studies Journal* (Winter 1994): 32.

77 Chong Min Lee, "Videotex," in Grant, et al., *Communication Technology Update, 1993-1994* (Austin: Technology Futures, Inc., 1993), 155.

78 Rogers, 49.

79 Eli Wathney, "Interactive Television," in Grant, et al 80.

80 Waters, Harry F., "Cable TV: Coming of Age," *Newsweek*, 24 August 1981, 49.

81 Everette Dennis, "Values and Value Added for the New Electronic Journalism," *Vital Speeches*, 1 September 1995, 677.

A Summing Up

During all six information revolutions, in some region active with the ferment for change, at least one new means of producing communication messages was combined with at least one new means of distributing those messages to a wide audience. The result was the change that can be characterized as a revolution, sometimes slow and sometimes rapid, but always inexorable. Simultaneously, the ferment for change has led to the spread of the new media themselves.

An inseparable connection has always existed between the tools of communication and the social fabric. Throughout history they have developed together in an intertwined, mutual cause and effect relationship, each giving impetus to the other.

A rational explanation for such a consistent pattern of symbiotic activity is not hard to come by. The pattern that leads to such societal change has depended on more than an inventor's genius. A *Eureka!* moment has always been a necessary but insufficient basis.

An explanation can be stated as a series of logical steps that begin by recognizing that ferment in a society is carried on by people seeking change of some sort, perhaps political or perhaps for personal gain where a reasonable expectation of success exists. In order to induce the desired change, those people seek to convince others, using whatever means they can, particularly the media of communication. Where success depends upon convincing large populations, they use means of mass communication. If newly invented means of communication prove successful, the receivers of the communication are introduced not only to the message, but to the means of its delivery. Their effectiveness becomes self-evident.

Some of the receivers of communication in turn adapt these new means for their own purposes, becoming the new movers and shakers of their society. The result is an expansion into an information revolution that not only alters an existing political, social, or economic situation, but widens the use of the new tools of communication. The lesson of history is that the tools of communication will be used by those who want to better their society or their own fortunes, pleasures, or convenience.

It has been said that a society that has guns will find ways to use them. It is even truer that a society that possesses tools of communication will use them and will do so in unstructured ways. Unlike weapons, the tools of communication were never intended to remain on the shelf awaiting their hour of need. Distributed for active employment in commerce, education, information transfer, personal communication, and leisure activities, the tools of communication are potentially at hand for those dissatisfied enough with the status quo to make the effort or take the risk to use them. No shortage of the dissatisfied exists anywhere.

Revisiting the Six Information Revolutions

In the first of the six identified revolutions, writing, the combining of the phonetic alphabet for the production of communication with papyrus for its delivery led to a sharing of knowledge around the Mediterranean and to the beginnings of recorded history, plus tremendous advances in the arts and sciences. It was the true start of the movement of information across time and space. The mind would no longer be constrained by memory, for information could be stored.

The second information revolution, printing, combined the movable type printing system of Gutenberg, which produced the messages, with paper, which provided the delivery mechanism. Together, printing and paper gave words that took wing for the Renaissance, humanism, the Reformation, the Counter-Reformation, and mercantilism, and helped to end the static feudal age. The printing revolution aided and was aided by the spread of literacy. With printing the modern world began.

Mass media, the third information revolution, combined a soaring production of paper and of printing for newspapers and magazines to stimulate a responding rise in literacy. The public school, the public library, the telegraph, and photography joined this revolution to bring knowledge and current information for the first time to masses of people. Advertising kept the industrial revolution humming by expanding the markets for the output of the factories. Because of mass communication, the roots of democracy and capitalism sank deep.

The fourth information revolution, entertainment, brought escape in a package. Tales real and fictional of other places and other times took masses of people away from the dull, uncomfortable, and unhappy here and now. Delivered were music on a phonograph record; the novel in the pages of a bound book; the story and the article in a magazine; news and travel photographs; the affordable personal camera, which preserved memories; music, drama, and humor delivered by radio; and the handsome men and beautiful women, whose faces loomed in the mystical darkness of the nickelodeon and the movie theater. People no longer had to create their own daydreams. They came ready made.

We are living through the fifth information revolution, the transformation of the home into a communication toolshed. For millions of people, a home is no longer primarily a place in which a family lives in the traditional sense of gathering to eat, sleep, and share the small intimacies that constitute family. Instead, it is the place where the tools of communication are stored and communication beyond the home is received and sent. It is here that people spend many of their hours mentally or physically isolated from one another, mostly with television, but also with videotapes, radio, telephone, books, magazines, newspapers, and computers, brought by such devices as the modem, answering machine, fax, cable, and satellite dish. We have discovered the power of mass communication to part us from each other, and we appear to be contented.

Finally, we are entering the sixth information revolution, the journey filled with choices along the Information Highway. The dimensions of this revolution are not fully clear, but it promises to more completely separate communication from transportation. Working from home, learning from home, communicating with distant people from home, and receiving most of life's pleasures at home allows the individual to function while seldom venturing out of the front door. Home may no longer need to be within physical reach of job, school, entertainment sources, or loved ones. It can be anywhere we desire. That could in time reverse the industrial revolution's centripetal flow of populations and wealth into cities during the past two centuries. Tremendous social consequences both positive and negative would attend such a shifting of population. Further, the values inhering in information threaten economic stagnation for huge areas of the globe where communication tools are not abundant.

On a personal level, when any communication technology is used, it displaces some other means of communication or behavior that had been satisfactory until the new technology became available. True of writing in Socrates' era that replaced memorizing, it will be equally true of the Information Highway. Whether e-mail replaces Post Office "snail mail," the downloading of a movie replaces an evening out, or hours at a bulletin board replace a date, some other technology or activity is displaced. Something desirable such as direct human contact may be lost. Despite the effortless international reach of new media, isolation frequently accompanies the acquisition of information and entertainment, whether through the reading of a book or the online connection with an Internet database. That isolation began with the shift from an oral to a written culture and has expanded ever since to the extent that social dysfunction is a worrisome part of riding along the Information Highway.

Communication in Three Eras

Let us consider three human beings, one from a tribal civilization, one from a medieval world, and one from the modern world who lives in the midst of the latest tools of communication. Although they can be men or women, we must recognize the individual differences accorded by gender as well as by culture, education, and position. That is, we must acknowledge the weakness of generalization in what follows.

Let us say that Tribal Human belongs mostly to pre-history, although a few members still dwell in remote desert, jungle, and icy pockets of Earth. Medieval Human continues to exist in many places. Toolshed Human lives next door, or perhaps stares out of the mirror at you each morning.

Tribal Human lacked most tools of communication other than those that came with birth. Only a few other people composed Tribal Human's lifetime circle of acquaintances. For all we know, Tribal Human may have recognized those intimates by smell as much as by sight. Tribal Human's life in the natural state, lacking arts, letters, and a larger society, and surrounded by fear and danger, Thomas Hobbes summarized as solitary, poor, nasty, brutish, and short. However, poor, nasty, brutish, and short though Tribal Human's life was, it might have been less solitary than the life of plugged-in Toolshed Human, who, surrounded by and dependent upon the modern tools of communication, can live a very solitary life indeed. As for Tribal Human, surely with danger around and dependence upon other members of the tribe for very existence, all five senses and the sixth sense were kept sharp enough to know fellow tribal members intensely and intimately. If someone were to suggest that Tribal Human should think about what life must be like elsewhere, this human of a tribal world would probably snort in derision and go about the day's work.

Depending upon where on Earth and to what social stratum Medieval Human was born, this person probably lived much closer to the time of Toolshed Human, but in terms of communication, was closer to the spirit and the daily life of Tribal Human. If born to village life, Medieval Human may have met few others. An ordinary person in the French province of Normandy during the tenth century probably met between 100 and 200 people in a lifetime, and had a vocabulary of 600 words.[1]

Although aware of a world outside, Medieval Human knew that it was not to be examined. If born to a village, Medieval Human stayed in the village unless there came the rare opportunity to join a Crusade. Medieval Human's scant knowledge of the world beyond the village came from travelers passing through, but if they brought reports of strange and different worlds, as Marco Polo once did, Medieval Human had no reason to do anything but snort in derision and go about the day's work. Almost all the tools of communication that we take for granted did not exist in Medieval Human's time. Of those that did—parchment, maybe paper, the book copied in a monastery, the newsbook, postal service, the stained glass church window or monastery wall telling a Biblical story—awareness of any of them depended upon Medieval Human's place in life. In any event, they hardly mattered. It was unlikely that Medieval Human could read and certainly could not write. What did matter was Medieval Human's relationship with fellow villagers, with the lord of the land, and with the all-knowing, all-seeing God who ruled in this world and the world to come. Like Tribal Human, Medieval Human probably used the five senses to their fullest, at least when sober.

Toolshed Human, fully attuned to the world, is aware of millions of people, sees them in movies and videotapes, watches them on television, hears their music on a CD, reads about them in newspapers, books, and magazines, talks to a few of them on the telephone and exchanges chit-chat with others by mail and e-mail. Toolshed Human has knowledge through written, aural, and visual media of far more fictional people than Tribal Human or Medieval Human were aware of actual people. Like these ancestors, Toolshed Human has a need for intimacy, but seldom acquires it through close, direct, physical contact. If anyone were to speak of the pleasure of smelling another person, not the perfume but the unwashed skin, Toolshed Human would snort in derision and go about the day's work, for Toolshed Human's meetings with others are always preceded by generous applications of well-advertised deodorant.

If Toolshed Human has a physical impairment, such as blindness, deafness, or limited mobility, compassionate hardware and software such as braille, audio services, sensor equipment, and closed-captioning are available to switch the flow of information and entertainment to alternate senses.

Yet, although aware of millions of others, Toolshed Human may have in fact fewer touching contacts than Tribal Human or Medieval Human and may greet and be greeted by fewer people who know Toolshed Human's name. Desiring a large measure of non-involvement and anonymity, Toolshed Human may sublimate any need for emotional stimulation through transmitted forms of sex, violence, and gambling, all readily available by the various means of communication at the touch of a button. In fact, having read breathless reports that one of the earliest applications of three-dimensional virtual reality will be rated XXX, Toolshed Human can hardly wait for techno-romance to arrive. As for the five senses, only two of them, sight and hearing, are kept sharp. Toolshed Human's sense of smell hardly kicks in unless some offensive odor comes along. A keen touch has little value outside non-virtual romance or safe-cracking. As for taste, TV packaged dinners took care of that a long time ago.

The tools of communication will not guarantee Toolshed Human power or wealth, but without the tools power and wealth are not likely at all. Should the government lock up the tools, Toolshed Human certainly will lack power. Should Toolshed Human own the tools that can bring both information and entertainment, but use them only for the latter, wealth will not arrive.

If Toolshed Human chooses to live alone, a spider in an electronic web, it may be because living alone is the least bothersome lifestyle, with the fewest intrusions on connect time and no quarrels about media choice. Toolshed Human revels in media choice. If the history of communication tells us anything, it is that more choices come along all the time.

Notes

1   George C. Coulton, *Medieval Village, Manor and Monastery* (New York: Harper & Bros., Torchbooks, 1960), 15.

Bibliography

Abrahamson, Albert. *Electronic Motion Pictures: A History of the Television Camera*. Berkeley: University of California Press, 1955.

Aitken, Hugh G. *Syntony & Spark: The Origins of Radio*. New York: Wiley, 1976.

Aldgate, Anthony. *Cinema And History*. London: Scholar Press, 1979.

Aldridge, B.L. *The Victor Talking Machine Company*. Camden, NJ: RCA Sales Corp., 1964.

Allen, Marti Lu. *The Beginning of Understanding: Writing in the Ancient World*. Ann Arbor: Kelsey Museum of Archaeology, 1991.

American Heritage of Invention & Technology; "Laying a Cable Across the Sea," Fall, 1987.

Amphlett, James. *The Newspaper Press*. London: Whittaker & Co., 1860.

Angelakos, Diogenes and Everhart, Thomas E. *Microwave Communications*. New York: McGraw-Hill, 1968.

Anderson, Benedict. *Imagined Communities: Reflections on the Origin and Spread of Nationalism*. London: Verso, 1991.

Archer, Gleason. *The History of Radio to 1926*. New York: American Historical Society, 1938.

Asimov, Isaac. *Asimov's Biographical Encyclopedia of Science and Technology.*, 2nd revised ed. Garden City, N.Y.: Doubleday, 1982.

_____. *Is Anyone There?* Garden City, N.Y.: Doubleday, 1967.

Augarten, Stan. *Bit by Bit*. New York: Ticknor & Fields, 1984.

Bachlin, Peter. *Newsreels Across The World*. Paris: UNESCO, 1952.

Baker, W.J. *The History of the Marconi Company*. London: Methuen, 1970.

Bardeche, Maurice. *The History of Motion Pictures*. New York: W.W. Norton & Co., 1938.

Barker, Joel A. *Paradigms: The Business of Discovering the Future*. New York: Harper Business, 1992.

Barnouw, Erik. *A History of Broadcasting In the United States*. 3 vols. New York: Oxford University Press, 1966-70.

_____. *The Sponsor*. New York: Oxford University Press, 1978.

Basalla, George. *The Evolution of Technology*. Cambridge: Cambridge University Press, 1988.

Batra, Rajeev, and Glazer, Rashi, eds.. *Cable TV Advertising*. New York: Quorum Books, 1989.

Baxter, Sylvester. "The Telephone Girl," *The Outlook*, 26 May 1906.

Beaton, Cecil W.H. *The Magic Image*. Boston: Little, Brown, 1975.

Beaver, Frank E. *On Film: A History of the Motion Picture*. New York: McGraw-Hill, 1983.

Beck, Kirsten. *Cultivating the Wasteland*. New York: American Council for the Arts, 1983.

Begun, S.J. *Magnetic Recording*. New York: Rinehart, 1949.

Beith, John Hay. *The Post Office Went To War*. London: H.M. Stationery Office, 1946.

Beniger, James R. *The Control Revolution*. Cambridge, Mass.: Harvard University Press, 1986.

Bijker, Wiebe E., Hughes, Thomas P., and Pinch, Trevor, eds. *The Social Construction of Technological Systems*. Cambridge: MIT Press, 1987.

Blake, G.G. *History of Radio Telegraphy & Telephony*. New York: Arno Press, 1974.

Bliss, Edward, Jr. *Now the News*. New York: Columbia University Press, 1991.

Blumenthal, Howard J. *The Media Room*. New York: Penguin Books, 1983.

Boorstin, Daniel J. *The Americans: The Democratic Experience*. New York: Random House, 1973.

Brand, Stewart. *The Media Lab*. New York: Viking Press, 1987.

Braun, E. *Revolution In Miniature: The History and Impact of Semiconductor Electronics*. Cambridge: Cambridge University Press, 1982.

Brewer, Roy. *The Man Who Loved Letters*. New York: Rowman and Littlefield, 1973.

Bright, Charles. *Telegraphy, Aeronautics and War*. London: Constable & Co., 1918.

Brittain, James E. *Turning Points In American Electrical History*. New York: IEEE Press, 1977.

Brock, Gerald W. *The Telecommunications Industry*. Cambridge: Harvard University Press, 1981.

Broecker, William L., ed. *Encyclopedia of Photography*. New York: Crown Publishers, 1984.

Brooks, John. *Telephone: The First 100 Years*. New York: Harper & Row, 1976.

Brothers, Alfred. *Photography: Its History*, 2nd ed. London: C. Griffin & Co., 1899.

Bruns, James H. *Mail on the Move*. Polo, Ill: Transportation Trails, 1992.

Buckland, Gail. *Fox Talbot And The Invention of Photography*. Boston: D.R. Godine, 1980.

Bunnell, David. "Tracking the Revolution," *Publish!*, September/October, 1986.

Burch, Robert M. *Colour Printing & Color Printers*. London: Pitman & Sons, 1910.

Burckhardt, Jacob. *History of Greek Culture*. Trans. Palmer Hilty. New York: Frederick Ungar Publishing Co., 1963.

Burke, James. "Communication in the Middle Ages," in David Crowley and Paul Heyer, *Communication in History*. New York: Longman, 1991.

————. *Connections*. Boston: Little, Brown & Co., 1978.

Burrows, A.R. *The Story of Broadcasting*. New York: Cassell & Co., Ltd., 1924.

Bush, Wendell T. "An Impression of Greek Political Philosophy," *Studies in the History of Ideas*, vol. 1. New York: Columbia University Press, 1918.

Butler, Pierce. *The Origin of Printing In Europe*. Chicago: University of Chicago Press, 1940.

Butterworth, William E. *Hi Fi: From Edison's Phonograph To Quad Sound*. New York: Four Winds Press, 1977.

Cameron, E.W., ed. *Sound and the Cinema*. New York: Redgrave Publishing Co., 1980.

Cantor, Norman, and Werthman, Michael. *The History of Popular Culture*. New York: Macmillan, 1968.

Carey, James. "Harold Adams Innis and Marshall McLuhan," *The Antioch Review*, vol. 27, 1967.

Carpenter, Edmund. *Explorations in Communication*. Boston: Beacon Press, 1960.

Carruthers, George. *Paper in the Making*. Toronto: The Garden City Press Cooperative, 1947.

Carter, Harry. *A View of Early Typography*. Oxford: Clarendon Press, 1969.

Carter, Hodding, III. *The Black American and the Press*. Orinda, CA: Ward Ritchie Press, 1967.

Carter, John. *Printing And The Mind of Man*. New York: Holt, Rinehart & Winston, 1967.

Carter, T.F. *The Invention of Printing in China and Its Spread Westward*. New York: Ronald Press, 1955.

Casmir, Fred L., ed. *Communication in Development*. Norwood, N.J.: Ablex Publishing Corp., 1991.

Centerwall, Brandon S. "Television and Violent Crime," *The Public Interest*, (Spring 1993): 61.

Chanan, Michael. *The Dream That Kicks*. Boston: Routledge & Kegan Paul, 1980.

Chappell, Warren. *A Short History of the Printed Word*. New York: Alfred A. Knopf, 1970.

Chase, Scott, "22,300 Miles Closer to Heaven," *Via Satellite*, December 1988.

Christie, Linda Gail. *The Simon & Schuster Guide to Computer Peripherals*. New York: Simon & Schuster, 1985.

Clark, David G. and Blankenburg, William B. *You & Media*. San Francisco: Canfield Press, 1973.

Clark, Kenneth. *Civilization*. New York: Harper & Row, 1969.

Clarke, Arthur C. *Voice Across The Sea*. New York: Harper & Row, 1958.

Clarkson, Leslie. *Death, Disease and Famine in Pre-industrial England*. Dublin: Gill and Macmillan, 1975.

Coe, Brian. *The Birth of Photography*. New York: Taplinger Publishing Co., 1977.

_____. *History of Motion Picture Photography*. New York: Zoetrope, Inc., 1981.

Cohn, Angelo. *The Wonderful World of Paper*. London: Abelard-Schuman, 1967.

Collins, Douglas. *The Story of Kodak*. New York: Harry Abrams, Inc., 1990.

Cooke, Philip. *Back to the Future*. London: Unwin Hyman, 1990.

Corn, Joseph J., ed. *Imagining Tomorrow* . Cambridge: The MIT Press, 1986.

Cornish, Edward. "The Coming of an Information Society," *The Futurist*, (April 1981): 14.

Costigan, Daniel M. *Fax: The Principles And Practice of Facsimile Communication*. Philadelphia: Chilton Book Co., 1971

Cottrell, Leonard. *The Quest for Sumer*. New York: G.P. Putnam's Sons, 1965.

Coulton, George C. *Medieval Village, Manor and Monastery*. New York: Harper & Bros., Torchbooks, 1960.

Coursey, Philip R. *Telephony Without Wires*. New York: Wireless Press, Ltd., 1919.

Crawford, William. *The Keepers of Light: A History*. Dobbs Ferry, N.Y.: Morgan & Morgan, 1979.

Crosby, John. *Out of The Blue*. New York: Simon & Schuster, 1952.

Crowley, David, and Heyer, Paul, *Communication in History*. New York: Longman, 1991.

Cullinan, Gerald. *The United States Postal Service*. New York: Praeger, 1973.

Curran, James, ed. *Mass Communications and Society*. London: Edward Arnold, Ltd., 1977.

Czitrom, Daniel J. *Media and the American Mind*. Chapel Hill, N.C.: University of North Carolina Press, 1982.

Davis, Charles. *The Manufacture of Paper*. New York: Arno Press, 1972.

Darnton, Robert, and Roche, Daniel, eds. *Revolution in Print: The Press in France 1775-1800*. Berkeley: University of California Press, 1989.

Davis, Natalie Zemon. "Printing and the People: Early Modern France," in *Literacy and Social Development in the West: A Reader*, ed. Harvery J. Graff. Cambridge: Cambridge University Press, 1981.

Dayan, Daniel, and Katz, Elihu. *Media Events*. Cambridge: Harvard University Press, 1992.

DeForest, Lee. *Television Today and Tomorrow*. New York: Dial Press, 1942.

DeLuca, Stuart M.*Television's Transformation: The Next 25 Years*. San Diego: A.S. Barnes, 1980.

Denman, Frank. *Television: The Magic Window*. New York: Macmillan, 1952.

Deslandes, Jacques. *Histoire Comparee du Cinema*. Paris: Casterman, 1966.

Didsbury, Howard F. ed., *Communications and the Future*. Bethesda, Md., World Future Society, 1982.

"The Difficult Birth of the Typewriter," *American Heritage of Invention & Technology*; Spring/Summer, 1988.

Dilts, Marion May. *The Telephone in a Changing World*. New York: Longman's Green, 1941.

Disraeli, Isaac. *The Invention of Printing*. New York: The American Institute of Graphic Arts, 1940.

Dizard, Wilson P. *The Coming Information Age*. New York: Longman, 1982.

Dominick, Joseph R., Sherman, Barry, and Copeland, Gary, eds. *Broadcasting/Cable and Beyond*. New York: McGraw-Hill, 1993.

Donovan, Robert J. and Scherer, Ray. *Unsilent Revolution: Television News and American Public Life*. New York: Cambridge University Press, 1992.

Douglas, Susan J. *Inventing American Broadcasting, 1899-1922*. Baltimore: The Johns Hopkins University Press, 1987.

Driver, G.R. *Semitic Writing: From Pictograph to Alphabet*. London: Oxford University Press, 1948.

Dryer, Sherman H. *Radio In Wartime*. New York: Greenberg, 1942.

Dunlap, Orrin E. *Communications In Space: From Wireless to Satellite Relay*. New York: Harper, 1962.

_____. *Communications In Space: From Marconi to Man on the Moon*. New York: Harper & Row, 1970.

_____. *Radio's 100 Men of Science*. New York: Harper & Bros., 1944.

Dunn, John, ed. *Democracy: The Unfinished Journey, 508 BC to AD 1993*. New York: Oxford University Press, 1992.

Durant, Will and Ariel. *The Story of Civilization*, Vol 1-5. New York: Simon & Schuster, 1939-1957.

Dyer, Frank and Martin, Thomas. *Edison, His Life and Inventions*. New York: Harper & Bros., 1929.

Eaglesfield, Charles. *Laser Light: Fundamentals and Optical Communications*. New York: St. Martin's Press, 1967.

Eargle, John. *Handbook of Recording Engineering*. New York: Van Nostrand Reinhold, 1986.

Edgerton, Harold E. *Moments of Vision: The Stroboscopic Revolution in Photography*. Cambridge: MIT Press, 1979.

Eisenstein, Elizabeth. *The Printing Press As An Agent Of Change*. Cambridge: Cambridge University Press, 1979.

_____. *The Printing Revolution in Early Modern Europe*. Cambridge: Cambridge University Press, 1983.

Ellis, Jack C. *A History of Film*, 2nd ed. Englewood Cliffs, N.J.: Prentice-Hall, 1979.

Emery, Edwin and Michael. *The Press and America*, Sixth Edition. Englewood Cliffs, N.J.: Prentice Hall, 1988.

Engels, Friederich. *The Conditions of the Working Class in English Tradition*. Trans. & ed. W. Ottenderson and W.H. Chaloner. Oxford: Oxford University Press, 1958.

Ennes, Harold E. *Television Broadcasting: Tape Recording Systems*. Indianapolis: Howard W. Sams & Co., 1979.

Everson, George. *The Story of Television: The Life of Philo T. Farnsworth*. New York: W.W. Norton, 1949.

Faber, Ronald J. and O'Guinn, Thomas C. "Expanding the View of Consumer Socialization," *Research in Consumer Behavior*, vol. 3 (1988): 58.

Fabre, Maurice. *A History of Communications*. New York: Hawthorne Books, 1963.

Fahie, John J. *A History of Electric Telegraphy to the Year 1837*. London: E.& F. Spon, 1884.

Fang, Irving E. *The Computer Story*. St. Paul: Rada Press, 1987.

_____. *Pictures*. St. Paul: Rada Press, 1993.

_____. *Those Radio Commentators!* Ames: Iowa State University Press, 1977.

Febvre, Lucien and Martin, Henri-Jean. *The Coming of the Book*. Trans. David Gerard, ed. Geoffrey Nowell-Smith and David Wooten. London: Verso, 1984.

Fedida, Sam. *Viewdata Revolution*. New York: Wiley, 1979.

Fenster, J.M. "How Bing Crosby Brought You Audiotape," *Invention and Technology*, (Fall 1994): 58.

Fielding, Raymond. *The American Newsreel 1911-1967*. Norman: University of Oklahoma Press, 1972.

_____. *A Technological History of Motion Pictures And Television*. Berkeley: University of California Press, 1967.

Finley, M.I., ed. *The Legacy of Greece*. Oxford: Oxford University Press, 1984.

Foque, Victor. *The Truth Concerning the Invention of Photography*. New York: Tennant & Ward, 1979.

Forester, Tom. *High-Tech Society*. Cambridge: MIT Press, 1983.

_____, ed. *The Information Technology Revolution*. Cambridge: MIT Press, 1985.

Forkert, Otto. *From Gutenberg To The Cuneo Press: An Historical Sketch*. Chicago: Cuneo Press, 1933.

Fornatele, Peter. *Radio In The Television Age*. Woodstock, N.Y.: Overlook Press, 1980.

Franklin, Harold B. *Sound Motion Pictures*. Garden City, N. J.: Doubleday, Doran, 1929.

Friedman, Joseph S. *History of Color Photography*. Boston: American Photographic Publishing Co., 1944.

Friedman, Thomas L. *From Beirut to Jerusalem*. New York: Farrar, Straus & Giroux, 1989.

Fuller, Wayne E. *The American Mail, Enlarger of the Common Life*. Chicago: University of Chicago Press, 1972.

Gabler, Edwin. *The American Telegrapher: A Social History, 1860–1900*. New Brunswick, N. J.: Rutgers University Press, 1988.

Ganley, Gladys D. *The Exploding Political Power of Personal Media*. Norwood, N. J.: Ablex Publishing, 1992.

Garrett, Albert E. *The Advance of Photography*. London: K. Paul, Trench, Trubner & Co., 1911.

Garson, Barbara. *The Electronic Sweatshop: How Computers Are Transforming the Office of the Future into the Factory of the Past*. New York: Bantam Books, 1988.

Gaur, Albertine. *A History of Writing*. London: The British Library, 1987.

Geck, Elisabeth. *Johannes Gutenberg: From Lead Letter to the Computer*. Bad Godesberg: Inter Nationes, 1968.

Geldud, Harry M. *The Birth of the Talkies: From Edison to Jolson*. Bloomington: Indiana University Press, 1975.

Gernsheim, Helmut and Alison. *The History of Photography*. London: Oxford University Press, 1955.

Gernsheim, Helmut. *The Origins of Photography*. New York: Thames and Hudson, 1982.

Gibson, James M. and Hall, James C. Jr., *Damn Reading!: A Case Against Literacy*. New York: Vantage Press, 1969.

Glasser, Theodore. "The Role of the Press, and the Value of Journalism," *Focus*, University of Minnesota, (Fall 1988).

Goldberg, Robert and Gerald Jay. *Anchors: Brokaw, Jennings, Rather and the Evening News*. New York: Carol Publishing Group, 1990.

Goldsmith, Alfred N. *This Thing Called Broadcasting*. New York: H. Holt & Co., 1930.

Goldsmith, Arthur. "Reinventing the Image," *Popular Photography*, March 1990.

Goldstine, Herman H. *The Computer from Pascal to von Neumann*. Princeton, N. J.: Princeton University Press, 1972.

Goody, Jack. *Literacy in Traditional Societies*. Cambridge: Cambridge University Press, 1968.

Gorham, Maurice A.C. *Broadcasting and Television*. London: Dakers, 1952.

Gouldner, Alvin W. *The Dialectic of Ideology and Technology*. Oxford: Oxford University Press, 1976.

Grant, August E. and Wilkinson, Kenton T., eds. *Communication Technology Update, 1993-1994*. Austin: Technology Futures, Inc., 1993.

Gray, Thomas. *The Inventors of the Telegraph and Telephone*. Washington: Smithsonian Institution, 1892.

Green, Fitzhugh. *The Film Finds Its Tongue*. New York: G.P. Putnam's Sons, 1929.

Gumpert, Gary. *Talking Tombstones and Other Tales of the Media Age*. Oxford: Oxford University Press, 1987.

Hamilton, Frederick W. *The Invention of Typography*. Chicago: The Committee of Education. United Typothetae, 1918.

Hammargren, Russell James. *The Impact Of Radio On The Newspaper*. M.A. thesis, University of Minnesota, 1934.

Hammer, Mina F. *History of the Kodak and its Continuations*. New York: Pioneer Publications, 1940.

Hammond, John H. *The Camera Obscura: A Chronicle*. Bristol, England: Adam Hilger, Ltd., 1981.

Hansen, Miriam. *Babel and Babylon: Spectatorship in American Silent Film*. Cambridge: Harvard University Press, 1991.

Hanson, Jarice. *Connections: Technologies of Communication*. New York: Harper Collins, 1994.

Harlow, Alvin F. *Old Post Bags*. New York: D. Appleton, 1938.

_____. *Old Wires and New Waves*. New York: D. Appleton-Century, 1936.

Harpur, Patrick, ed. *The Timetable of Technology*. New York: Hearst Books, 1982.

Harris, William V. *Ancient Literacy*. Cambridge: Harvard University Press, 1989.

Hartmann, Heidi I., Kraut, Robert E., and Tilly, Louise A. eds. *Computer Chips and Paper Clips: Technology and Women's Employment*. Washington, D. C.: National Academy Press, 1986.

Haskins, Charles H. *Studies in Medieval Culture*. Oxford: The Clarendon Press, 1929.

Hassard, John R.G. *The Wonders Of The Press*. New York: The Tribune Association, 1878.

Havelock, Eric A. *Preface to Plato*. Cambridge, Mass.: Belknap Press, 1963.

Hawks, Ellison. *Pioneers of Wireless*. London: Methuen & Co., 1927.

Haynes, Merritt W. *The Students' History of Printing*. New York: McGraw-Hill, 1930.

Head, Sydney W., Sterling, Christopher H., and Schofield, Lemuel B. *Broadcasting in America*, 7th ed. Boston: Houghton-Mifflin, 1994.

Hellemans, Alexander and Bunch, Bryan. *The Timetables of Science: A Chronology of the Most Important People and Events in the History of Science*. New York: Simon & Schuster, 1991.

Hendricks, Gordon. *The Edison Motion Picture Myth*. Berkeley: University of California Press, 1961.

Herodotus. *The History*. Trans. David Grene. Chicago: University of Chicago Press, 1987.

Hessel, Alfred. *A History of Libraries*. Trans. Reuben Peiss. New Brunswick, N. J.: The Scarecrow Press, 1955.

Hiebert, Ray. *Impact of Mass Media: Current Issues*, New York: Longman, 1985.

Hindle, Brooke. *Emulation and Invention*. New York: New York University Press, 1981.

A History of Engineering and Science in the Bell System. Vol. 7, Bell Laboratories Series. New York, AT&T, 1975.

Hoe, Robert. *A Short History of the Printing Press*. New York: R. Hoe, 1902.

Hofstadter, Richard. *The Progressive Movement, 1900-1915*. New York: Simon & Schuster, 1963.

Hofstetter, Fred T. "Is Multimedia the New Literacy?" *Educators Tech Exchange* (Winter 1994): 7.

Hollander, Richard. *Video Democracy*. Mt. Airy, Md.: Lomond Publications, 1985.

House, William C. *Laser Beam Information Systems*. New York: Petrocelli Books, 1978.

Hubbard, Geoffrey. *Cooke & Wheatstone & the Invention of the Electric Telegraph*. London: Routledge & K. Paul, 1956.

Hubbell, Richard W. *4,000 Years of Television*. New York: G.P. Putnam's Sons, 1942.

Hughbanks, Leroy. *Talking Wax or the Story of the Phonograph*. New York: Hobson Book Press, 1945.

Hunter, Dard. *Papermaking: The History and Technique of an Ancient Craft*. New York: Dover Publications, 1978.

Huss, Richard E. *The Development of Printers' Mechanical Typesetting Methods, 1822–1925*. Charlottesville: University Press of Virginia, 1973.

Hutt, Allen. *The Changing Newspaper*. London: Gordon Fraser Gallery., 1973.

Inglis, Andrew F. *Behind the Tube*. Stoneham, Mass.: Focal Press, 1990.

Innis, Harold A. *The Bias of Communication*. Toronto: University of Toronto Press, rev. ed., 1972.

________. *Empire and Communications*. Toronto: University of Toronto Press, revised ed., 1972.

Isaacs, George A. *The Story of the Newspaper Printing Press*. London: Cooperative Printing Society, 1931.

Jaggard, William. *Printing: Its Birth And Growth*. Liverpool: The Shakespeare Press, 1908.

Jeffrey, Ian. *Photography: A Concise History*. New York: Oxford University Press., 1981.

Jenkins, Reese. *Images & Enterprise: Technology & the American Photography Industry*. Baltimore: Johns Hopkins University Press, 1975.

Jennings, Mary-Lou and Madge, Charles, eds. *Pandæmonium: 1660-1886*. New York: The Free Press, 1985.

Jespersen, James and Fits-Randolph, Jane. *Mercury's Web: The Story of Telecommunications*. New York: Atheneum, 1981.

Johnson, Paul. *A History of the Jews*. New York: Harper & Row, 1987.

Jones, Alexander. *Historical Sketch of the Electric Telegraph*. New York: George P. Putnam, 1852.

Jussim, Estelle. *Visual Communication and the Graphic Arts: Photographic Techniques in the 19th Century*. New York: R.R. Bowker, 1984.

Katz, Donald R. "Are Newspapers Yesterday's News?" *Esquire* (January 1990): 40.

Keith, Michael C. and Krause, Joseph M. *The Radio Station*, 3rd ed. Boston: Focal Press, 1993.

Kelley, Marcia. "Work-at-home," *The Futurist* (November/December 1988): 32.

Kennedy, Paul. *Preparing for the Twenty-First Century*. Toronto: Harper Collins Publishers Ltd., 1993.

Kenyon, Frederic G. *Books and Readers in Ancient Greece and Rome*, 2nd ed. Oxford: Clarendon Press, 1951.

Kielbowicz, Richard. "News Gathering by Mail in the Age of the Telegraph: Adapting to a New Technology," *Technology and Culture*, January 1987.

King, Larry. *On the Line*. New York: Harcourt Brace & Co., 1993.

Kingslake, Rudolf. *A History of the Photographic Lens*. Boston: Academic Press, 1989.

Koestler, Arthur. *The Sleepwalkers: A History of Man's Changing Vision of the Universe*. New York: Penguin Books, 1964.

Kosinski, Jerzy. *Being There*. New York: Harcourt Brace Jovanovich, 1970.

Kozol, Jonathan. *Illiterate America*. Garden City, N. Y.: Anchor Press, 1985.

Kramarae, Cheris, ed. *Technology and Women's Voices: Keeping in Touch*. New York: Routledge & Kegan Paul, 1988.

Kramer, Samuel. *From the Tablets of Sumer*. Indian Hills, Colo.: Falcon's Wing Press, 1956.

Lakshmanan, T.R. "Social Change Induced by Technology: Promotion and Resistance," in

Nordal Akerman, ed. *The Necessity of Friction*. Heidelberg: Physica-Verlag, 1993.

Lander, David. "Technology Makes Music," *Invention and Technology*, Spring/Summer, 1990.

Lardner, James. *Fast Forward*. New York: W.W. Norton, 1987.

Lascia, J.D. "Photographs That Lie," *Washington Journalism Review*, June 1989.

Laufer, Berthold. *Paper and Printing in Ancient China*. Chicago: Printed for the Caxton Club, 1931.

Layton, Edwin T. Jr. *Technology and Social Change in America*. New York: Harper & Row, 1973.

Lehman, Maxwell. *Communication Technologies and Information Flow*. New York: Pergamon Press, 1981.

Leinwoll, Stanley. *From Spark to Satellite*. New York: Charles Scribner's Sons, 1979.

Lenmark, Barbara G. *Some Effects of the Teletypesetter on the Newspaper*. M.A. thesis, University of Minnesota, 1954.

Lewis, Tom. *Empire of the Air: The Men Who Made Radio*. New York: HarperCollins, 1991.

Lichty, Lawrence. *American Broadcasting: A Source Book on the History of Radio and Television*. New York: Hastings House, 1975.

Lloyd, G.E.R. "Science and Mathematics," in M.I. Finley (ed.), *The Legacy of Greece*. Oxford: Oxford University Press, 1984.

Logan, Robert K. *The Alphabet Effect: The Impact of the Phonetic Alphabet on the Development of Western Civilization*. New York: William Morrow and Co., 1986.

Lowman, Charles E. *Magnetic Recording*. New York: McGraw-Hill, 1972.

Lown, Edward. *An Introduction To Technological Changes In Journalism*. Ann Arbor, Mich.: Published for the Journalism Program, State University of New York at New Paltz by University Microfilms International, 1977.

MacDonald, J. Fred. *Blacks and White TV—Afro-Americans in Television since 1948*. Chicago: Nelson-Hall Publishers, 1983, p. 89.

_____. *Don't Touch That Dial: Radio Programming in American Life, 1920-1960*. Chicago: Nelson-Hall Publishers, 1979.

Macgowan, Kenneth. *Behind The Screen: History and Techniques of the Motion Picture*. New York: Delacorte Press, 1965.

Maclaurin, William R. *Invention & Innovation in the Radio Industry*. New York: Macmillan, 1949.

MacNeil, Robert. *The People Machine*. New York: Harper & Row, 1968.

Manchester, William. *A World Lit Only by Fire: The Medieval Mind and the Renaissance*. Boston: Little, Brown and Company, 1992.

Mander, Jerry. *Four Arguments for the Elimination of Television*. New York: Morrow, 1978.

Marchand, Philip. *Marshall McLuhan*. New York: Ticknor & Fields, 1989.

Marcus, Alan I. and Segal, Howard P. *Technology in America: A Brief History*. New York: Harcourt Brace Jovanovich, 1990.

Marek, Kurt W. *Archaeology of the Cinema*. New York: Harcourt, Brace & World, 1965.

Marland, E.A. *Early Electrical Communication*. London: Abelard-Schuman, 1964.

Marrou, H.I. "Education and Rhetoric," in M.I. Finley (ed.), *The Legacy of Greece*. Oxford: Oxford University Press, 1984.

Martin, Henri-Jean. *The History and Power of Writing*. Trans. Lydia G. Cochrane. Chicago: University of Chicago Press, 1994.

Martin, James. *Future Developments In Telecommunications*. Englewood Cliffs, N. J.: Prentice-Hall, 1977.

_____. *Telecommunications and the Computer*, 3rd ed. Englewood Cliffs, N. J.: Prentice-Hall, 1990.

_____. *Telematic Society: A Challenge for Tomorrow*. Englewood Cliffs, N. J.: Prentice-Hall, 1981.

Marvin, Carolyn. *When Old Technologies Were New*. Oxford: Oxford University Press, 1988.

Mason, William A. *A History of the Art of Writing*. New York: Macmillan Co., 1920.

Maspero, Gaston. *The Dawn of Civilization: Egypt and Chaldæa*. Trans. M.T. McClure. London: Society for Promoting Christian Knowledge, 1922.

Matusow, Barbara. *The Evening Stars*. New York: Ballantine Books, 1984.

Maurer, Allan. *Lasers: Light Wave of the Future*. New York: Arco Publishing, Inc., 1982.

McClure, M.T. "Appearance and Reality in Greek Philosophy," *Studies in the History of Ideas*, vol. 1. New York: Columbia University Press, 1918.

McLean, Mick. *The Information Explosion: The New Electronic Media in Japan and Europe.* Westport, Conn.: Greenwood Press, 1985.

McLuhan, Marshall. *Understanding Media: The Extensions of Man.* New York: McGraw-Hill, 1964.

_____. *The Gutenberg Galaxy: The Making of Typographic Man.* Toronto: University of Toronto Press, 1962.

_____, and Powers, Bruce. *The Global Village.* Oxford: Oxford University Press, 1989.

McMurtie, Douglas C. *The Book.* New York: Dorset Press, 1989.

Mees, C.E.K. *From Dry Plates To Ektachrome Film.* New York: Ziff-Davis Publishing Co., 1961.

Meggs, Philip B. *A History of Graphic Design.* New York: Van Nostrand Reinhold, 1983.

Merriam, C. *Telegraphing Among the Ancients.* Cambridge: Cambridge University Press, 1890.

Michaelis, Anthony. *From Semaphore to Satellite.* Geneva: International Telecommunication Union, 1965.

Mingo, Jack. *The Official Couch Potato Handbook.* Santa Barbara, CA: Capra Press, 1983.

Momigliano, Arnaldo. "History and Biography," in M.I. Finley (ed.), *The Legacy of Greece.* Oxford: Oxford University Press, 1984.

Moran, James. *Printing Presses: History and Development.* Berkeley: University of California Press, 1973.

Moreau, R. *The Computer Comes of Age.* Cambridge, Mass.: The MIT Press, 1986.

Morison, Stanley. *Politics and Script.* Oxford: The Clarendon Press, 1972.

Morris, Lloyd R. *Not So Long Ago.* New York: Random House, 1949.

Morse, Arthur H. *Radio: Beam & Broadcast.* London: Benn, 1925.

Moseley, Maboth. *Irascible Genius: A Life of Charles Babbage, Inventor.* London: Hutchinson, 1964.

Nasaw, David. *Going Out: The Rise and Fall of Public Amusements.* New York: Basic Books, 1993.

Neale, Steve. *Cinema and Technology: Image, Sound, Color.* Bloomington: Indiana University Press, 1985.

Newhall, Beaumont. *Latent Image: The Discovery of Photography.* Garden City, N. Y.: Doubleday, 1967.

Newhall, Beaumont. *On Photography: A Sourcebook of Photo History.* Watkins Glen, N. Y.: Century House, 1956.

North, Joseph H. *The Early Development of the Motion Picture.* New York: Arno Press, 1973.

O'Brien, John E. *Telegraphing in Battle.* Scranton, Pa.: The Reader Press, 1910.

Ogburn, William F. *Social Change.* New York: Viking Press, 1950.

_____, and Nimkoff, M.F. *Sociology.* New York: Houghton-Mifflin, 1950.

Ong, Walter S. *The Presence of the Word: Some Prolegomena for Cultural and Religious History.* New Haven: Yale University Press, 1967.

Oslin, George P. *The Story of Telecommunications.* Macon, Ga.: Mercer University Press, 1992.

Pask, Gordon. *Microman: Computers and the Evolution of Consciousness.* New York: Macmillan, 1982.

Pattison, Robert. *On Literacy.* Oxford: Oxford University Press, 1982.

Pease, Edward C., ed. *Radio: The Forgotten Medium.* New York: Columbia University, The Freedom Forum Media Studies Center, Summer 1993.

Peckman, Morse. *Beyond the Tragic Vision.* New York: George Braziller, 1962.

Peterson, Theodore. *Magazines in the Twentieth Century.* Urbana: University of Illinois Press, 1964.

Petrie, W.M. Flinders. *The Formation of the Alphabet.* London: MacMillan & Co., 1912.

Plato. *Phaedo.* Trans. and ed. David Gallop. Oxford: Oxford University Press, 1993.

_____. *Phaedrus.* Trans. C.J. Rowe, (2nd corrected ed.). Warminster, England: Aris & Rowe, 1988.

Plum, William R. *The Military Telegraph During The Civil War.* Chicago: Jansen, McLurg & Co., 1882.

Polscher, Andrew A. *The Evolution of Printing Presses from Wood to Metal.* Harper Woods, Mich.: Adagio Press, 1968.

Pool, Ithiel de Sola. *Technologies of Freedom.* Cambridge: Harvard University Press, 1983.

Poster, Mark. *The Mode of Information: Poststructuralism and Social Context.* Chicago: The University of Chicago Press, 1990.

Postman, Neil. *Amusing Ourselves to Death.* New York: Viking Penguin, 1985.

Pound, Arthur. *The Telephone Idea: 50 Years After*. New York: Greenberg, 1926.

Pratt, William K. *Laser Communications Systems*. New York, Wiley, 1969.

Presbrey, Frank.*The History and Development of Advertising*. Garden City, N. Y.: Doubleday, Doran, 1929.

Prescott, George B. *Bell's Speaking Telephone: Its Invention, Construction*. New York: Arno Press, 1972.

_____. *History, Theory & Practice of the Electronic Telegraph*. Boston: Ticknor & Fields, 1860.

Putnam, Robert D. "Bowling Alone: America's Declining Social Capital," *Journal of Democracy* (January 1995): 65-78.

Quigley, Martin. *Magic Shadows: The Story of the Origin of Motion Pictures*. Washington: Georgetown University Press, 1948.

Read, Oliver and Welch, Walter L. *From Tin Foil To Stereo*, 2nd ed. Indianapolis: Howard W. Sams & Co., 1976.

Redmond, James. *Broadcasting: The Developing Technology*. London: British Broadcasting Corp., 1974.

Reid, James D. *The Telegraph in America*. Boston: Derby Bros., 1879.

Rhode, Eric. *A History of the Cinema*. New York: Hill and Wang, 1976.

Rhodes, Frederick L. *Beginnings of Telephony*. New York: Harper & Bros., 1929.

Ritchie, David. *The Computer Pioneers*. New York: Simon & Schuster, 1986.

Robinson, David. *The History of World Cinema*. New York: Stein and Day, 1973.

Rogers, Everett M. *Communication Technology*. New York: The Free Press, 1986.

Rolo, Charles. *Radio Goes to War*. New York: G.P. Putnam's Sons, 1942.

Rosenblum, Naomi. *A World History of Photography*. New York: Abbeville Press, 1989.

Rose, Albert. *Vision: Human & Electronic*. New York: Plenum Press, 1973.

Rosewater, Victor. *History of Cooperative News-Gathering in the United States*. New York: D. Appleton & Co. 1930.

Rosten, Leo. *Hollywood, the Movie Colony and the Movie Makers*. New York: Harcourt Brace & Co., 1941.

Roszak, Theodore. *The Cult of Information*. New York: Pantheon, 1986.

Russell, James. *The Impact of Radio on the Newspaper*. Unpublished M.A. Thesis, University of Minnesota, 1934.

Rybczynski, Witold. *Taming the Tiger: The Struggle to Control Technology*. New York: Viking Press, 1983.

Safley, Thomas and Rosenband, Leonard eds., *The Workplace before the Factory: Artisans and Proletarians, 1500-1800*. Ithaca: Cornell University Press, 1993.

Salt, Barry. *Film Style and Technology: History and Analysis*. London: Starword, 1983.

Sanderson, Richard A. *A Historical Study*. New York: Arno Press, 1971.

Scarborough, John. *Facets of Hellenic Life*. Boston: Houghton Mifflin Co., 1976.

Scheele, Carl H. *A Short History of the Mail Service*. Washington: Smithsonian Institute Press, 1970.

Schiffer, Michael Brian. *The Portable Radio in American Life*. Tucson: University of Arizona Press, 1991.

Schmandt-Besserat, Denise. *Before Writing*. Austin: University of Texas Press, 1992.

Schramm, Wilbur. *The Story of Human Communication: Cave Painting to Microchip*. New York: Harper & Row, 1988.

Schroeder, Peter B. *Contact at Sea*. Ridgewood, N. J.: Gregg Press, 1967.

Schubert, Paul. *The Electric Word: The Rise of Radio*. New York: Macmillan, 1928.

Schubert, Steven. "The Oriental Origins of the Alexandrian Library," *Libri* 43.2, (1993): 163.

Schudson, Michael. *Discovering the News*. New York: Basic Books, Inc., 1978.

Settel, Irving and Lass, William. *A Pictorial History of Television*. New York: Grosset & Dunlap, 1969.

Shaffner, Taliaferro P. *The Telegraph Manual*. New York: Pudney & Russell, 1859.

Shapiro, Neil. *The Small Computer Connection*. New York: McGraw-Hill, 1983.

Shaw, Donald L. "News Bias and the Telegraph," *Journalism Quarterly*, Spring, 1967, pp. 3-12.

Shaw, Thomas. *The Conquest of Distance by Wire Telephony*. New York: AT&T, 1944.

Shiers, George. *The Development of Wireless to 1920*. New York: Arno Press, 1977.

_____.*The Electric Telegraph: An Historical Anthology*. New York: Arno Press, 1977.

_____.*Technical Development of Television*. New York: Arno Press, 1977.

_____.*The Telephone: An Historical Anthology*. New York: Arno Press, 1977.

Shipman, David. *The Story of Cinema*. New York: St. Martin's Press, 1982.

Shurkin, Joel. *Engines of the Mind: A History of the Computer*. New York: Norton, 1984.

Sigel, Efrem. *The Future of Videotext*. White Plains, N.Y.: Knowledge Industry Publications, 1983.

_____.*Videodiscs: The Technology, the Application & the Future*. New York: Van Nostrand, 1981.

Simon, Irving B. *The Story of Printing: From Woodblocks to Electronics*. New York: Harvey House, 1965.

Singer, et. al., (eds). *A History of Technology; Vol. 5, The Late 19th Century*. Oxford: The Clarendon Press, 1958.

Singleton, Loy. *Telecommunications in the Information Age*. Cambridge, Mass.: Ballinger Publishing Co., 1983.

Sloan, William, et al, eds. *The Media in America: A History*. Worthington, Ohio: Publishing Horizons, 1989.

Smith, Adele M. *Printing And Writing Materials: Their Evolution*. Philadelphia, published by the author, 1912.

Smith, Anthony. *Books to Bytes: The Computer and the Library*. New York: Gannett Center for Media Studies, 1988.

_____. *Goodbye Gutenberg*. New York: Oxford University Press, 1986.

Smith, F. Leslie. *Perspectives on Radio and Television*. New York: Harper & Row, 1985.

Soley, Lawrence C. *Clandestine Radio Broadcasting*. New York: Praeger, 1987.

Speliotis, Dennis E. and Johnson, Clark E. *Advances In Magnetic Recording*. New York: N.Y. Academy of Sciences, 1972.

Starr, Chester G. *The Origins of Greek Civilization: 1100 - 650 B.C.* Alfred A. Knopf, 1961.

Stearns, Peter N. *The Industrial Revolution in World History*. Boulder: Westview Press, 1993.

Stein, Dorothy. *Ada: A Life and a Legacy*. Cambridge: The MIT Press, 1987.

Steinberg, S.H. *Five Hundred Years of Printing*, 2nd ed.. Baltimore: Penguin Books, 1962.

Stephens, Mitchell. *A History of News*. New York: Viking Press, 1988.

Sterling, Christopher H. and Kittross, John M. *Stay Tuned: A Concise History of American Broadcasting*, 2nd ed.. Belmont, Calif.: Wadsworth, 1990.

Still, Alfred. *Communication through the Ages*. New York: Murray Hill Books, 1946.

"The Stormy Birth of the FM Radio," *American Heritage of Invention & Technology*; fall, 1985.

Stump, Matt and Jessell, Harry. "Cable: The First Forty Years," *Broadcasting*, 21 November 1988.

Swift, John. *Adventure in Vision: The First 25 Years of Television*. London: J. Lehman, 1950.

Tedesch, James T., ed. *The Social Influence Process*. Chicago: Aldine Atherton Publishing, 1972.

Thomas, Lowell. *Magic Dials: The Story of Radio and Television*. New York: L. Furman, 1939.

Thomas, Sari, ed. *Studies in Mass Communication and Technology*. Norwood, N. J.: Ablex Publishing, 1984.

Thompson, James W. *Ancient Libraries*. Berkeley: University of California Press, 1940.

Thompson, John S. *History of Composing Machines*. New York: Arno Press, 1972.

Thompson, S.P. *Philipp Reis: Inventor of the Telephone*. Reprint of 1883 edition. New York: Arno Press, 1974.

Toffler, Alvin. *Future Shock*. New York: Bantam Books, 1971.

_____.*The Third Wave*. New York: William Morrow, 1980.

Towers, Walter K. *From Beacon Fire to Radio*. New York: Harper & Bros., 1924.

Trethowan, Ian. *The Development of Radio*. London: British Broadcasting Corp., 1975.

Tsien, Tsuen-Hsien. *Written on Bamboo and Silk*. Chicago: University of Chicago Press, 1962.

Tubbs, Douglas B. *The Illustrated History of the Camera from 1839 to the Present*. Boston: New York Graphic Society, 1975.

Tuchman, Barbara. *A Distant Mirror: The Calamitous 14th Century*. New York: Alfred A. Knopf, 1978.

Turkle, Sherry. *The Second Self*. New York: Simon & Schuster, 1984.

Bryan S. Turner, ed. *Theories of Modernity and Postmodernity*. London: Sage Publications, 1990.

Vattimo, Gianni. *The Transparent Society*, trans. David Webb. Baltimore: The Johns Hopkins University Press, 1992.

Vivian, John. *The Media of Mass Communication*, 3rd ed. Boston: Allyn and Bacon, 1995.

Vogt, Ernest. *Radio Technology: Telegraphy, Telephony, Television*. New York: Pitman Publishing, 1949.

Vyvyan, Richard N. *Wireless Over 30 Years*. London: G. Routledge & Sons, Ltd., 1922.

Waterhouse, James. *The Beginnings of Photography*. Washington: Smithsonian Institution, 1903.

Watson, Thomas A. *The Birth and Babyhood of the Telephone*. New York: AT&T, 1940.

Weaver, David H. *Videotex Journalism*. Hillsdale, N. J.: L. Erlbaum Associates, 1983.

Westcott, Charles G., and Dubbe, Richard F. *Tape Recorders - How They Work*. Indianapolis: Howard W. Sams & Co., The Bobbs Merrill Co., 1974.

Wheeler, Leslie J. *Principles of Cinematography*, 4th ed. London: Fountain Press, 1969.

Wheen, Francis. *Television*. London: Century Publishing, 1985.

White, Roy B. *Telegrams in 1889-and Since!* Princeton, N. J.: Princeton University Press, 1939.

Wiborg, Frank B. *Printing Ink: A History*. New York: Harper & Bros., 1926.

Wicklein, John. *Electronic Nightmare: The New Communications and Freedom*. New York: The Viking Press, 1981.

Wile, Frederic W. *Emile Berliner, Maker of the Microphone*. Indianapolis: Bobbs-Merrill, 1926.

Wilkinson, Paul. *Terrorism and the Liberal State*. New York: New York University Press, 1986.

Williams, Frederick. *The Communications Revolution*. Beverly Hills: Sage Press, 1982.

Williams, Raymond, ed. *Contact: Human Communication and Its History*. New York: Thames and Hudson, 1981.

Williams, Raymond. *Televison: Technology and Cultural Form*. New York: Schockben Books, 1975.

Williams, Rosalind. *Notes on the Underground*. Cambridge: MIT Press, 1990.

Willis, Edgar E. and Aldridge, Henry B. *Television, Cable and Radio*. Englewood Cliffs: Prentice-Hall, 1992.

Wilson, Carmen. *Magnetic Recording 1900-1949*. Chicago: John Crerar Library Bibliographic Series, no. 1, 1950.

Winn, Marie. *The Plug-In Drug*. New York: Viking Press, 1985.

Winsbury, Rex. *New Technology and the Press*. London: H.M. Stationery Office, 1975.

Winston, Brian. *Misunderstanding Media*. Cambridge: Harvard University Press, 1986.

Wood, Henry A. *Progress in Newspaper Manufacture*. New York: Wood Newspaper Machinery Corp., 1932.

Wood, James P. *Magazines in the United States*, 2nd ed. New York: Ronald Press, 1956.

Wrigley, Maurice J. *The Cinema: Historical, Technical, & Bibliographical*. London: Grafton & Co., 1939.

Wulforst, Harry. *Breakthrough to the Computer Age*. New York: Scribner, 1982.

Wymer, Norman. *From Marconi to Telstar*. London: Longmans, 1966.

Young, L.C. *Materials in Printing Processes*. New York: Hastings House, 1973.

Zilliacus, Laurin. *Mail for the World*. New York: John Day, 1953.

Communication Timeline

3500: In Sumer pictographs of accounts written on clay tablets.

2600: Scribes employed in Egypt.

2400: In India, engraved seals identify the writer.

2200: Date of oldest existing document written on papyrus.

1500: Phoenician alphabet.

1400: Oldest record of writing in China, on bones.

1270: Syrian scholar compiles an encyclopedia.

900: China has an organized postal service for government use.

775: Greeks develop a phonetic alphabet, written from left to right.

530: In Greece, a library.

500: Greek telegraph: trumpets, drums, shouting, beacon fires, smoke signals, mirrors.

500: Persia has a form of pony express.

500: Chinese scholars write on bamboo with reeds dipped in pigment.

400: Chinese write on silk as well as wood, bamboo.

200: Books written on parchment and vellum.

200: Tipao gazettes are circulated to Chinese officials.

59: Julius Caesar orders postings of Acta Diurna.

A.D.

100: Roman couriers carry government mail across the empire.

105: T'sai Lun invents paper.

175: Chinese classics are carved in stone that will later be used for rubbings.

180: In China, an elementary zoetrope.

250: Paper use spreads to central Asia.

350: In Egypt, parchment book of Psalms bound in wood covers.

450: Ink on seals is stamped on paper in China. This is true printing.

600: Books printed in China.

700: Sizing agents are used to improve paper quality.

751: Paper manufactured outside of China, in Samarkand by Chinese captured in war.

765: Picture books printed in Japan.

868: The Diamond Sutra, a block-printed book in China.

950: Paper use spreads west to Spain.

950: Folded books appear in China in place of rolls.

950: Bored women in a Chinese harem invent playing cards.

1000: Mayas in Yucatan, Mexico, make writing paper from tree bark.

1035: Japanese use waste paper to make new paper.

1049: Pi Sheng fabricates movable type, using clay.

1116: Chinese sew pages to make stitched books.

1140: In Egypt, cloth is stripped from mummies to make paper.

1147: Crusader taken prisoner returns with papermaking art, according to a legend.

1200: European monasteries communicate by letter system.

1200: University of Paris starts messenger service.

1282: In Italy, watermarks are added to paper.

1298: Marco Polo describes use of paper money in China.

1300: Wooden type found in central Asia.

1305: Taxis family begins private postal service in Europe.

1309: Paper is used in England.

1392: Koreans have a type foundry to produce bronze characters.

1423: Europeans use block printing.

1443: The simplifed Korean phonetic alphabet, hangul.

1450: A few newsletters begin circulating in Europe.

1451: Johnannes Gutenberg uses a press to print an old German poem.

1452: Metal plates are used in printing.

1453: Gutenberg prints the 42-line Bible.

1464: King of France establishes postal system.

1477: An advertisement appears in English.

1490: Printing of books on paper becomes more common in Europe.

1495: A paper mill is established in England.

1500: Arithmetic + and – symbols are used in Europe.

1500: By now, approximately 35,000 books have been printed, some 10 million copies.

1500: Spectacles balance on the noses of Europe's educated.

1533: A postmaster in England.

1545: Garamond designs his typeface.

1550: Wallpaper brought to Europe from China by traders.

1560: In Italy, the portable camera obscura allows precise tracing of an image.

1560: Legalized, regulated private postal systems grow in Europe.

1565: The pencil.

1609: First regularly published newspaper appears in Germany.

1627: France introduces registered mail.

1631: A French newspaper carries classified ads.

1639: In Boston, someone is appointed to deal with foreign mail.

1639: First printing press in the American colonies.

1640: Kirchner, a German Jesuit, builds a magic lantern to project images.

1650: Leipzig has a daily newspaper.

1653: Parisians can put their postage-paid letters in mail boxes.

1655: The word "advertising" is introduced.

1659: Londoners get the penny post.

1661: Postal service within the colony of Virginia.

1673: Mail is delivered on a route between New York and Boston.

1689: Newspapers are printed, at first as unfolded "broadsides."

1696: By now, England has 100 paper mills.

1698: Public library opens in Charleston, S.C.

1704: A newspaper in Boston prints advertising.

1710: German engraver Le Blon develops three-color printing.

1714: Henry Mill receives patent in England for a typewriter.

1719: Reaumur proposes using wood to make paper.

1725: Scottish printer develops stereotyping system.

1727: Schulze begins science of photochemistry.

1732: In Philadelphia, Ben Franklin starts a circulating library.

1755: Regular mail ship runs between England and the colonies.

1770: The eraser.

1774: Swedish chemist invents a paper whitener.

1775: Continental Congress authorizes Post Office; Ben Franklin first Postmaster General.

1780: Steel pen points begin to replace quill feathers.

1784: French book is made without rags, from vegetation.

1785: Stagecoaches carry the mail between towns in U.S.

1790: In England, the hydraulic press is invented.

1792: Mechanical semaphore signaler built in France.

1792: In Britain, postal money orders.

1792: Postal Act promises mail regularity throughout U.S.

1794: First letter carriers appear on American city streets.

1794: Panorama, forerunner of movie theaters, opens.

1794: Signaling system connects Paris and Lille.

1798: Senefelder in Germany invents lithography.

1799: Robert in France invents a paper-making machine.

1800: Letter takes 20 days to reach Savannah, Georgia from Portland, Maine.

1801: Semaphore system built along the coast of France.

1801: Joseph-Marie Jacquard invents a loom using punch cards.

1803: Fourdrinier continuous web paper-making machine.

1807: Camera lucida improves image tracing.

1808: Turri of Italy builds a typewriter for a blind contessa.

1810: An electro-chemical telegraph is constructed in Germany.

1810: Postal services consolidated under uniform private contracts.

1813: Congress authorizes steam boats to carry mail.

1814: In England, a steam-powered rotary press prints *The Times*.

1815: 3,000 post offices in U.S.

1816: Newspapers carried for less than 2 cents postage.

1816: Niépce captures image with 8-hour exposure.

1818: Stamped letter paper is sold in Sardinia.

1818: In Sweden, Berzelius isolates selenium; its electric conductivity reacts to light.

1819: Napier builds a rotary printing press.

1820: Arithmometer, forerunner of the calculator.

1821: In England, Wheatstone reproduces sound.

1823: Babbage builds a section of a calculating machine.

1823: In England, Ronalds builds a telegraph in his garden; no one is interested.

1825: Persistence of vision shown with Thaumatrope.

1827: Niépce makes a true photograph.

1827: In London, Wheatstone constructs a microphone.

1829: Daguerre joins Niépce to pursue photographic inventions.

1829: Burt gets the first U.S. patent for a typewriter.

1830: Calendered paper is produced in England.

1832: Phenakistoscope in Belgium and Stroboscope in Austria point to motion pictures.

1833: A penny buys a New York newspaper, opening a mass market.

1833: In Germany, a telegraph running nearly two miles.

1834: Babbage conceives the analytical engine, forerunner of the computer.

1836: Rowland Hill starts to reform British postal system.

1837: Wheatstone and Cooke patent an electric telegraph in England.

1837: Morse exhibits an electric telegraph in the U.S.

1837: Pitman publishes a book on shorthand in England.

1837: Daguerre cuts photo exposure time to 20 minutes.

1838: In England, Wheatstone's Stereoscope shows pictures in 3-D.

1838: Daguerre-Niépce method begins photography craze.

1839: Fox Talbot in England prints photographs from negatives.

1839: Herschel invents hypo fixative.

1839: In Russia, Jacobi invents electrotyping, the duplicating of printing plates.

1839: Electricity runs a printing press.

1840: In Britain, first postage stamps are sold.

1841: Petzval of Austria builds an f/3.6 lens.

1841: The advertising agency is born.

1841: The first type-composing machine goes into use in London.

1842: *Illustrated London News* appears.

1842: Another use for paper: the Christmas card.

1843: In the U.S., the photographic enlarger.

1843: Ada, Lady Lovelace publishes her Notes explaining a computer.

1844: Morse's telegraph connects Washington and Baltimore.

1845: Postal reform bill lowers rates and regulates domestic and international service.

1845: The typewriter ribbon.

1846: In Germany, Zeiss begins manufacturing lenses.

1846: Double cylinder rotary press produces 8,000 sheets an hour.

1847: First use of telegraph as business tool.

1847: In England, Bakewell constructs a "copying telegraph."

1848: Forerunner of the Associated Press is founded in New York.

1849: The photographic slide.

1850: The paper bag arrives.

1851: In the U.S., paper is made from wood fiber.

1851: The Erie railroad depends on the telegraph.

1851: Telegraph cable is laid across the English Channel.

1851: Archer invents wet-plate photography process.

1851: Newspaper postage cut in half; free distribution within county.

1852: Postage stamps are widely used.

1853: Envelopes made by paper folding machine.

1854: Telegraph used in Crimean War.

1854: Bourseul in France builds an experimental telephone.

1854: Carte-de-visite process simplifies photography.

1854: Curved stereotype plate obviates column rules; wide ads soon.

1855: Printing telegraph invented in the U.S.

1855: Prepayment of letters made compulsory.

1855: Registered letters enter service.

1856: Poitevan starts photolithography.

1856: Blotting paper replaces sand boxes.

1856: Machine folds newspapers, paper for books for drying ink.

1857: A machine to set type is demonstrated.

1857: In France, Scott's phonautograph is a forerunner of Edison's phonograph.

1858: Mail boxes appear on American streets.

1858: First effort at transatlantic telegraph service fails.

1858: Eraser is fitted to the end of a pencil.

1858: An aerial photograph is taken.

1859: Camera gets a wide-angled lens.

1860: Pony Express carries mail between St. Joseph, Mo. and Sacramento.

1861: Telegraph brings Pony Express to an abrupt end.

1861: First chemical means to color photography.

1861: Oliver Wendell Holmes invents stereoscope.

1862: In Italy, Caselli sends a drawing over a wire.

1862: In U.S., paper money.

1863: Large U.S. cities get free home delivery of mail.

1863: First international postal conference held in Paris.

1864: Workers in "railway post office" sort mail on trains.

1864: Postal money orders sold in U.S; $1.3 million in 6 months.

1865: Atlantic cable ties Europe and U.S. for instant communication.

1866: Western Union dominates U.S. wires.

1867: In U.S., Sholes builds a working typewriter.

1869: Color photography, using the subtractive method.

1869: From Austria, postcards.

1870: Stock ticker comes to Wall Street.

1871: Halftone process allows newspaper printing of pictures.

1872: Simultaneous transmission from both ends of a telegraph wire.

1873: U.S. postcard debuts; costs one penny.

1873: Illustrated daily newspaper appears in New York.

1873: Maxwell publishes theory of radio waves.

1873: Remington starts manufacturing Sholes' typewriters.

1873: Typewriters get the QWERTY pseudo-scientific keyboard.

1873: In Ireland, May uses selenium to send a signal through the Atlantic cable.

1874: Universal Postal Union formed.

1875: Edison invents the mimeograph.

1875: In the U.S., Carey designs a selenium mosaic to transmit a picture.

1876: Bell invents the telephone.

1877: In France, Charles Cros invents the phonograph.

1877: In America, Edison also invents the phonograph.

1878: Muybridge photographs a horse in motion.

1878: Cathode ray tube is invented by Crookes, English chemist.

1878: The dynamic microphone is invented in the U.S. and Germany.

1878: Telephone directories are issued.

1878: Full page newspaper ads.

1878: In France, praxinoscope, an optical toy, a step toward movies.

1878: Dry-plate photography.

1879: Benday process aids newspaper production of maps, drawings.

1880: First photos in newspapers, using halftones.

1880: Edison invents the electric light.

1880: France's Leblanc theorizes transmitting a picture in segments.

1880: First parcel post.

1881: Women enter the business world via the typewriter.

1881: Business offices begin to look modern.

1882: In England, the first wirephotos.

1883: Edison stumbles onto "Edison effect"; later, basis of broadcast tubes.

1884: In Germany, Nipkow scanning disc, early version of television.

1884: People can now make long distance phone calls.

1884: Electric tabulator is introduced.

1884: Waterman's fountain pen blots out earlier versions.

1885: Dictating machines are bought for offices.

1885: Eastman makes coated photo printing paper.

1885: U.S. Post Office offers special delivery.

1885: Trains are delivering newspapers daily.

1886: Graphophone's wax cylinder and sapphire stylus improve sound.

1886: Mergenthaler constructs the Linotype machine for setting type.

1887: Celluloid film; it will replace glass plate photography.

1887: Montgomery Ward mails out a 540-page catalog.

1887: Berliner gets music from a flat disc stamped out by machine.

1887: Comptometer multi-function adding machine is manufactured.

1887: Ads appear in magazines.

1888: "Kodak" box camera makes picture taking simple.

1888: Heinrich Hertz proves the existence of radio waves.

1888: The coin-operated public telephone.

1888: Edison's phonograph is manufactured for sale to the public.

1888: Oberlin Smith sets forth theory of magnetic recording.

1889: Herman Hollerith counts the U.S. population with punch cards.

1890: A.B. Dick markets the mimeograph.

1890: Typewriters are in common use in offices.

1890: In England, Friese-Greene builds the kinematograph camera and projector.

1890: In France, Branly's coherer conducts radio waves.

1891: Large press prints and folds 90,000 4-page papers an hour.

1891: Telephoto lens is attached to the camera.

1891: Edison's assistant, Dickson, builds the Kinetograph motion picture camera.

1892: Edison and Dickson build the peepshow Kinetoscope.

1892: 4-color rotary press.

1892: Portable typewriters.

1892: Automatic telephone switchboard comes into service.

1893: Dickson builds a motion picture studio in New Jersey.

1893: Addressograph joins the office machinery.

1894: Marconi invents wireless telegraphy.

1895: France's Lumière brothers build a portable movie camera.

1895: Paris audience sees movies projected.

1895: In England, Friese-Greene invents phototypesetting.

1896: Underwood model permits typists to see what they are typing.

1896: The monotype sets type by machine in single characters.

1896: Electric power is used to run a paper mill.

1896: In Britain, the motion picture projector is manufactured.

1896: X-ray photography.

1896: Rural free delivery (RFD) inaugurated.

1897: In England, postmen deliver mail to most homes.

1897: In Germany, Braun improves cathode ray tube with fluorescence.

1897: General Electric creates a publicity department.

1898: Photographs taken by artificial light.

1898: New York State passes a law against misleading advertising.

1899: Sound is recorded magnetically by Poulsen of Denmark.

1899: American Marconi Company incorporated; forerunner of RCA.

1900: Kodak Brownie makes photography cheaper and simpler.

1900: Pupin's loading coil reduces telephone voice distortion.

1901: Sale of phonograph disc made of hard resinous shellac.

1901: First electric typewriter, the Blickensderfer.

1901: Marconi sends a radio signal across the Atlantic.

1902: Germany's Zeiss invents the four-element Tessar camera lens.

1902: Etched zinc photoengraving.

1902: U.S. Navy installs radio telephones aboard ships.

1902: Photoelectric scanning can send and receive a picture.

1903: Technical improvements in radio, telegraph, phonograph, movies, and printing.

1903: London *Daily Mirror* illustrates only with photographs.

1903: Cheap crayons are mass produced in the United States.

1904: A telephone answering machine is invented.

1904: Fleming invents the diode to improve radio communication.

1904: Offset lithography becomes a commercial reality.

1904: A photograph is transmitted by wire in Germany.

1904: Hine photographs America's underclass.

1904: *The Great Train Robbery* creates demand for fiction movies.

1904: The comic book.

1904: Music is recorded on both sides of a phonograph disc.

1905: In Pittsburgh, the first nickelodeon opens.

1905: Photography, printing, and post combine in the year's craze, picture postcards.

1905: In France, Pathé colors black and white films by machine.

1905: In New Zealand, the postage meter is introduced.

1905: The Yellow Pages.

1905: The juke box; 24 choices.

1906: The Victrola turns the phonograph into furniture.

1906: In Britain, new process colors books cheaply.

1906: A program of voice and music is broadcast in the U.S.

1906: Lee de Forest invents the three-element vacuum tube.

1906: Dunwoody and Pickard build a crystal-and-catwhisker radio.

1906: An animated cartoon film is produced.

1906: Fessenden plays violin for startled ship wireless operators.

1906: An experimental sound-on-film motion picture.

1907: Bell and Howell develop a film projection system.

1907: Lumière brothers invent still color photography process.

1907: DeForest begins regular radio music broadcasts.

1907: In Russia, Rosing develops theory of television.

1908: In U.S., Smith introduces true color motion pictures.

1909: Radio distress signal saves 1,700 lives after ships collide.

1910: Sweden's Elkstrom invents "flying spot" camera light beam.

1911: Rotogravure aids magazine production of photos.

1911: "Postal savings system" inaugurated.

1912: U.S. passes law to control radio stations.

1912: Motorized movie cameras replace hand cranks.

1912: Feedback and heterodyne systems usher in modern radio.

1912: First mail carried by airplane.

1913: The portable phonograph is manufactured.

1914: Radio message is sent to an airplane.

1914: In Germany, the 35mm still camera, a Leica.

1914: In the U.S., Goddard begins rocket experiments.

1914: First transcontinental telephone call.

1915: Wireless radio service connects U.S. and Japan.

1915: Radio-telephone carries speech across the Atlantic.

1915: *Birth of a Nation* sets new movie standards, but is racist.

1915: The electric loudspeaker.

1916: Cameras get optical rangefinders.

1916: Radios get tuners.

1917: Photocomposition begins.

1917: Frank Conrad builds a radio station, later KDKA.

1917: Condenser microphone aids broadcasting, recording.

1918: First regular airmail service: Washington, D.C. to New York.

1919: Shortwave radio is invented.

1919: Flip-flop circuit invented; will help computers to count.

1920: First cross-country airmail flight in the U.S.

1920: Sound recording is done electrically.

1920: KDKA in Pittsburgh broadcasts first scheduled programs.

1921: Quartz crystals keep radio signals from wandering.

1921: The word "robot" enters the language.

1921: Western Union begins wirephoto service.

1922: A commercial is broadcast.

1922: Technicolor introduces two-color process for movies.

1922: Germany's UFA produces a film with an optical sound track.

1922: Singers desert phonograph horn mouths for acoustic studios.

1922: *Nanook of the North,* the first documentary.

1923: Zworykin's electronic iconoscope camera tube.

1923: Ribbon microphone becomes the studio standard.

1923: A picture, broken into dots, is sent by wire.

1923: 16mm nonflammable film makes its debut.

1923: Kodak introduces home movie equipment.

1923: Neon advertising signs.

1924: Low tech achievement: notebooks get spiral bindings.

1924: *The Eveready Hour* is the first sponsored radio program.

1924: At KDKA, Conrad sets up a short-wave radio transmitter.

1924: Daily coast-to-coast air mail service.

1924: Pictures are transmitted over telephone lines.

1924: Two and a half million radio sets in the U.S.

1925: Commercial picture facsimile radio service across the U.S.

1925: All-electric phonograph is built.

1925: A moving image, the blades of a model windmill, is telecast.

1925: From France, a wide-screen film.

1926: Commercial picture facsimile radio service across the Atlantic.

1926: Baird demonstrates an electro-mechanical TV system.

1926: Some radios get automatic volume control, a mixed blessing.

1926: The Book-of-the-Month Club.

1926: In U.S., first 16mm movie is shot.

1926: Goddard launches liquid-fuel rocket.

1926: Permanent radio network, NBC, is formed.

1926: Bell Telephone Labs transmits film by television.

1927: NBC begins second radio network; CBS formed.

1927: Farnsworth assembles a complete electronic TV system.

1927: Jolson's *The Jazz Singer* is the first popular "talkie."

1927: Movietone offers newsreels in sound.

1927: U.S. Radio Act declares public ownership of the airwaves.

1927: Negative feedback makes hi-fi possible.

1928: The teletype machine makes its debut.

1928: Television sets are put in three homes, programming begins.

1928: Baird invents a video disc to record television.

1928: In an experiment, television crosses the Atlantic.

1928: In Schenectady, N.Y., the first scheduled television broadcasts.

1928: *Steamboat Willie* introduces Mickey Mouse.

1928: Times Square gets moving headlines in electric lights.

1928: IBM adopts the 80-column punched card.

1929: Experiments begin on electronic color television.

1929: Telegraph ticker sends 500 characters per minute.

1929: Ship passengers can phone relatives ashore.

1929: Brokers watch stock prices on an automated electric board.

1929: Something else new: the car radio.

1929: In Germany, magnetic sound recording on tape in the lab.

1929: Television studio is built in London.

1929: Air mail flown from Miami to South America.

1930: Photo flashbulbs replace dangerous flash powder.

1930: "Golden Age" of radio begins in U.S.

1930: Lowell Thomas begins first regular network newscast.

1930: TVs based on British mechanical system roll off factory line.

1930: AT&T tries the picture telephone.

1931: Commercial teletype service.

1931: Electronic TV broadcasts in Los Angeles and Moscow.

1931: Exposure meters go on sale to photographers.

1931: Bell Labs experiment with stereo recording.

1931: NBC experimentally transmits 120-line screen.

1932: Disney adopts three-color Technicolor process for cartoons.

1932: Kodak introduces 8mm film for home movies.

1932: *The Times* of London uses its new Times Roman typeface.

1932: Stereophonic sound in a motion picture, Napoleon.

1932: Zoom lens is invented, but a practical model is 21 years off.

1932: The light meter.

1932: NBC and CBS allow prices to be mentioned in commercials.

1933: Armstrong invents FM, but its real future is 20 years off.

1933: Multiple-flash sports photography.

1933: Singing telegrams.

1934: Drive-in movie theater opens in New Jersey.

1934: Associated Press starts wirephoto service.

1934: In Germany, a mobile television truck roams the streets.

1934: In Scotland, teletypesetting sets type by phone line.

1934: Three-color Technicolor used in live action film.

1934: Communications Act of 1934 creates FCC.

1934: Half of the homes in the U.S. have radios.

1934: Mutual Radio Network begins operations.

1935: German single lens reflex roll film camera synchronized for flash bulbs.

1935: IBM's electric typewriter comes off the assembly line.

1935: The Penguin paperback book.

1935: All-electronic VHF television comes out of the lab.

1935: Eastman-Kodak develops Kodachrome color film.

1935: Nielsen's Audimeter tracks radio audiences.

1935: Tweeter and woofer reduce loudspeaker distortion.

1936: In London, scheduled television broadcasts begin.

1936. A magnetic tape recorder, the Magnetophone, is built in Germany.

1936: Berlin Olympics are televised closed circuit.

1936: Bell Labs invents a voice recognition machine.

1936: Kodachrome film sharpens color photography.

1936: Coaxial cable connects New York to Philadelphia.

1936: Alan Turing's "On Computable Numbers" describes a general purpose computer.

1937: Stibitz of Bell Labs invents the electrical digital calculator.

1937: Pulse Code Modulation points the way to digital audio transmission.

1937: NBC sends mobile TV truck onto New York streets.

1937: A recording, the *Hindenburg* crash, is broadcast coast to coast.

1937: Carlson invents the photocopier.

1937: *Snow White* is the first feature-length cartoon.

1938: Strobe lighting.

1938: Two brothers named Biro invent the ballpoint pen in Argentina.

1938: *CBS World News Roundup* ushers in modern newscasting.

1938: DuMont markets electronic television receiver for the home.

1938: Radio drama, "War of the Worlds," causes national panic.

1939: Mechanical television scanning system abandoned.

1939: New York World's Fair shows television to public.

1939: Regular electronic TV broadcasts begin in the U.S.

1939: Air mail service across the Atlantic.

1939: Many televised firsts including sports coverage, variety show, feature film.

1940: *Fantasia* introduces stereo sound to American movie public.

1941: FCC sets U.S. TV standards.

1941: CBS and NBC start commercial transmission: WW II intervenes.

1941: Goldmark at CBS experiments with electronic color TV.

1941: Microwave transmission.

1941: Zuse's Z3 in Germany is the first computer controlled by software.

1942: Atanasoff and Berry in Iowa build the first electronic digital computer.

1942: Kodacolor process produces the color print.

1943: Repeaters on phone lines quiet long distance call noise.

1943: Wire recorders help Allied radio journalists cover WWII.

1944: Harvard's Mark I, first digital computer to be put into service.

1944: IBM offers a typewriter with proportional spacing.

1945: American G.I.s find tape recorders in German radio stations.

1945: Clarke envisions geosynchronous communication satellites.

1945: It is estimated that 14,000 products are made from paper.

1946: Jukeboxes go into mass production.

1946: Pennsylvania's ENIAC heralds the modern electronic computer.

1946: Automobile radio telephones connect to telephone network.

1946: French engineers build a photo-typesetting machine.

1947: Hungarian engineer in England invents holography.

1947: The transistor is invented, will replace vacuum tubes.

1947: The zoom lens covers baseball's world series for TV.

1948: The LP record arrives on a vinyl disk.

1948: Shannon and Weaver of Bell Labs propound information theory.

1948: Land's Polaroid camera prints pictures in a minute.

1948: Hollywood switches to nonflammable film.

1948: Public clamors for television; FCC freezes new licenses.

1948: Airplane re-broadcasts TV signal across nine states.

1949: Network TV established in U.S.

1949: RCA offers the 45 rpm record.

1949: Community Antenna Television, forerunner to cable.

1949: Whirlwind at MIT is the first real time computer.

1949: Magnetic core computer memory is invented.

1950: Regular color television transmission.

1950: Vidicon camera tube improves television picture.

1950: A.C. Nielsen's Audimeters track viewer watching.

1951: One and a half million TV sets in U.S., a tenfold jump in one year.

1951: Cinerama will briefly dazzle with a wide, curved screen and three projectors.

1951: Computers are sold commercially.

1951: Still cameras get built-in flash units.

1951: Coaxial cable reaches coast to coast.

1951: Bing Crosby's company tests video recording.

1952: 3-D movies offer thrills to the audience.

1952: Sony offers a miniature transistor radio.

1952: EDVAC takes computer technology a giant leap forward.

1952: Univac projects the winner of the presidential election on CBS.

1952: Telephone area codes.

1952: Sony offers a miniature transistor radio.

1953: NTSC color standard adopted.

1953: CATV system uses microwave to bring in distant signals.

1954: U.S.S.R. launches *Sputnik*.

1954: Radio sets in the world now outnumber newspapers printed daily.

1954: Regular color TV broadcasts begin in U.S. using NTSC standard.

1954: Sporting events are broadcast live in color.

1954: Transistor radios are sold.

1955: Tests begin to communicate via fiber optics.

1956: Ampex builds a practical videotape recorder.

1956: Bell tests the picture phone.

1956: First transatlantic telephone calls by cable.

1957: Soviet Union's *Sputnik* sends signals from space.

1957: FORTRAN becomes the first high-level computer programming language.

1957: A surgical operation is televised.

1957: First book to be entirely phototypeset is offset printed.

1958: Videotape delivers color.

1958: Stereo recording is introduced for public sale.

1958: Data moves over regular phone circuits.

1958: Broadcast bounced off rocket, pre-satellite communication.

1958: The laser.

1958: Cable carries FM radio stations.

1959: Local announcements, weather data, and local ads go on cable.

1959: The microchip is invented.

1959: Xerox manufactures a plain paper copier.

1959: Bell Labs experiments with artificial intelligence.

1959: French SECAM and German PAL systems introduced.

1960: *Echo I*, a U.S. balloon in orbit, reflects radio signals to Earth.

1960: In Rhode Island, an electronic, automated post office.

1960: A movie gets Smell-O-Vision, but the public just sniffs.

1960: The Post Office experiments with facsimile mail.

1960: Zenith tests subscription TV; unsuccessful.

1961: Boxing match test shows potential of pay-TV.

1961: FCC approves FM stereo broadcasting; spurs FM development.

1961: Bell Labs tests communication by light waves.

1961: IBM introduces the "golf ball" typewriter.

1961: Letraset setting makes headlines at home simple.

1961: The time-sharing computer is developed.

1962: Cable companies import distant signals.

1962: FCC requires UHF tuners on TV sets.

1962: Comsat created to launch and operate global satellite system.

1962: *Telstar* satellite transmits an image across the Atlantic.

1963: From Holland comes the audio cassette.

1963: Zip codes.

1963: CBS and NBC TV newscasts expand to 30 minutes in color.

1963: PDP-8 becomes the first popular minicomputer.

1963: Polaroid camera instant photography adds color.

1963: Communications satellite is placed in geosynchronous orbit.

1963: TV news "comes of age" in reporting JFK assassination.

1964: Olympic Games in Tokyo telecast live globally by satellite.

1964: Touch Tone telephones and Picturephone service.

1964: From Japan, the videotape recorder for home use.

1964: Russian scientists bounce a signal off Jupiter.

1964: Intelsat, international satellite organization, is formed.

1965: Electronic phone exchange gives customers extra services.

1965: Satellites begin domestic TV distribution in Soviet Union.

1965: Computer time-sharing becomes popular.

1965: Color news film.

1965: Communications satellite *Early Bird (Intelsat I)* orbits above the Atlantic.

1965: Kodak offers Super 8 film for home movies.

1965: Cartridge audio tapes go on sale for a few years.

1965: Most broadcasts are in color.

1965: FCC rules bring structure to cable television.

1965: Solid-state equipment spreads through the cable industry.

1966: Linotron can produce 1,000 alphanumeric characters per second for printing.

1966: Fiber optic cable multiplies communication channels.

1966: Xerox sells the Telecopier, a fax machine.

1967: Dolby eliminates audio hiss.

1967: Computers get the light pen.

1967: Pre-recorded movies on videotape sold for home TV sets.

1967: Cordless telephones get some calls.

1967: Approx. 200 million telephones in the world, half in U.S.

1968: TV photographers lug two-inch-tape portable videotape recorders.

1968: FCC approves non-Bell equipment attached to phone system.

1968: Intelsat completes global communications satellite loop.

1968: Approx. 200 million TV sets in the world, 78 million in U.S.

1968: The RAM microchip reaches the market.

1969: Astronauts send live photographs from the moon.

1970: Postal Reform Bill makes U.S. Postal Service self-supporing.

1970: In Germany, a videodisc is demonstrated.

1970: U.S. Post Office and Western Union offer Mailgrams.

1970: The computer floppy disc is an instant success.

1971: Intel builds the microprocessor, "a computer on a chip."

1971: Sony's 3/4 inch "U-Matic" cassette VCR makes TV news photography easier.

1971: Wang 1200 is the first word processor.

1972: HBO starts pay-TV service for cable.

1972: New FCC rules lead to community access channels.

1972: Polaroid camera can focus by itself.

1972: Digital television comes out of the lab.

1972: The BBC offers "Ceefax," two-way cable information system.

1972: "Open Skies": any U.S. firm can have communication satellites.

1972: *Landsat I*, "eye-in-the-sky" satellite, is launched.

1972: Sony's Port-a-Pak, a much more portable video recorder.

1972: "Pong" starts the video game craze.

1973: The microcomputer is born in France.

1973: IBM's Selectric typewriter is now "self-correcting."

1974: In England, the BBC transmits Teletext data to TV sets.

1974: Electronic News Gathering, or ENG.

1974: Satellite transmission of mailgrams.

1974: "Teacher-in-the-Sky" satellite begins educational mission.

1975: The microcomputer, in kit form, reaches the U.S. home market.

1975: "Thrilla' from Manila"; substantial original cable programming.

1976: Sony's Betamax and JVC's VHS battle for acceptance in the home.

1976: Apple I.

1976: Dolby stereo goes into movie theaters.

1976: Ted Turner delivers programming nationwide by satellite.

1976: Still cameras are controlled by microprocessors.

1977: Columbus, Ohio, residents try 2-way cable experiment, QUBE.

1978: From Konica, the point-and-shoot camera.

1978: PBS goes to satellite for delivery, abandoning telephone lines.

1978: Electronic typewriters go on sale.

1979: Speech recognition machine has a vocabulary of 1,000 words.

1979: Videotext provides data on command.

1979: From Holland comes the digital videodisc read by laser.

1979: In Japan, first cellular phone network.

1979: Computerized laser printing is a boon to Chinese printers.

1980: In France, a holographic film shows a gull flying.

1980: *Intelsat V* relays 12,000 phone calls, 2 color TV channels.

1980: Public international electronic fax service, Intelpost, begins.

1980: Atlanta gets first fiber optics system.

1980: CNN 24-hour news channel.

1980: Addressable cable T.V. converters pinpoint individual homes.

1981: 450,000 transistors fit on a silicon chip 1/4-inch square.

1981: Hologram technology improves, now in video games.

1981: Sony Walkman tape player starts a fad.

1981: The IBM PC.

1981: The laptop computer is introduced.

1981: The first mouse pointing device.

1982: From Japan, a camera with electronic picture storage, no film.

1982: *USA Today* typeset in regional plants by satellite command.

1982: Kodak camera uses film on a disc cassette.

1982: Optical character readers identify city, state, and ZIP Code on envelopes.

1983: Cellular phone network starts in U.S.

1983: Lasers and plastics improve newspaper production.

1983: Computer chip holds 288,000 bits of memory.

1983: *Time* names the computer as "Man of the Year."

1983: ZIP + 4, expanded 9-digit ZIP codes and postal bar codes are introduced.

1983: AT&T forced to break up; 7 Baby Bells are born.

1983: American videotext service starts; fails in three years.

1984: Trucks used for SNG transmission.

1984: Experimental machine can translate basic Japanese into basic English but with mistakes.

1984: Portable compact disc player arrives.

1984: *National Geographic* puts a hologram on its cover.

1984: A television set can be worn on the wrist.

1984: Japanese introduce high quality facsmile.

1984: Camera and tape deck combine in the camcorder.

1984: Apple Macintosh, IBM PC AT.

1984: The 32-bit microprocessor.

1984: The one-megabyte memory chip.

1984: CONUS relays news feeds for stations on Ku-Band satellites.

1985: Digital image processing for editing stills bit by bit.

1985: CD-ROM can put 270,000 pages of text on a CD record.

1985: Cellular telephones go into cars.

1985: Synthetic text-to-speech computer pronounces 20,000 words.

1985: Television broadcasts can be heard in stereo.

1985: U.S. TV networks begin satellite distribution to affiliates.

1985: At Expo, a Sony TV screen measures 40x25 meters.

1985: Sony builds a radio the size of a credit card.

1985: In Japan, 3-D television; no spectacles needed.

1985: Pay-per-view channels open for business.

1986: HBO scrambles its signals.

1986: Cable shopping networks.

1987: Half of all U.S. homes with TV are on cable.

1987: Government deregulates cable industry.

1988: Government brochure mailed to 107 million addresses.

1989: Tiananmen Square demonstrates power of media to inform the world.

1989: Pacific Link fiber optic cable opens, can carry 40,000 phone calls.

1990: Flyaway SNG aids foreign reportage.

1990: IBM sells its Selectric division, a sign of the typewriter's passing.

1990: Most 2-inch videotape machines are also gone.

1990: Videodisc returns in a new laser form.

1991: *Beauty and the Beast*, a cartoon, Oscar nominee as best picture.

1991: CNN dominates news coverage worldwide during Gulf War.

1991: Live TV news switching between world capitals during Gulf War looks simple.

1991: Denver viewers can order movies at home from list of more than 1,000 titles.

1991: Moviegoers astonished by computer morphing in *Terminator 2*.

1991: Baby Bells get government permission to offer information services.

1991: Collapse of Soviet anti-Gorbachev plot aided by global system called the Internet.

1991: More than 4 billion cassette tape rentals in U.S. alone.

1991: 3 out of 4 U.S. homes own VCRs; fastest selling domestic appliance in history.

1992: Cable TV revenues reach $22 billion.

1992: At least 50 U.S. cities have competing cable services.

1992: After President Bush speaks, 25 million viewers try to phone in their opinions.

1993: Dinosaurs roam the earth in *Jurassic Park*.

1993: Unfounded rumors fly that cellphones cause brain cancer.

1993: Demand begins for "V-chip" to block out violent television programs.

1993: 1 in 3 Americans does some work at home instead of driving to work.

1994: After 25 years, U.S. government privatizes Internet management.

1994: Rolling Stones concert goes to 200 workstations worldwide on Internet "MBone."

1994: To reduce Western influence, a dozen nations ban or restrict satellite dishes.

1994: Prodigy bulletin board fields 12,000 messages after L.A. quake.

1994: Magazines—known as "'zines"—are published on CD-ROM disks.

1994: Competitors agree on a standard for high definition TV.

1995: Experimental CD-ROM disk can carry a full-length feature film.

1995: Sony demonstrates flat TV set.

1995: DBS feeds are offered nationwide in U.S.

1995: Denmark announces plan to put much of the nation online within 5 years.

1995: Major U.S. dailies create national on-line newspaper network.

1995: Lamar Alexander chooses the Internet to announce presidential candidacy.

1995: Audio of live events can be heard on the Internet.

1996: The stripped-down Net computer arrives.

1996: More than 100,000 World Wide Web sites, and growing fast.

1996: There are 60 million Internet users worldwide, and growing fast.

1996: The TV-top box connects television sets to the Internet.

1996: The Advanced Photo System provides drop-in film loading, choice of print formats.

1996: Phone, cable, broadcast companies compete under the Telecommunication Reform Act.

1996: U.S. Postal Service handles nearly 600 million pieces of mail daily.

1996: A pocket telephone/computer comes on the market.

Index

A

Acta Diurna, 3, 30
Actors, 127–128, 132–133, 140
ACTV Interactive Television, 230–231
Advanced Photo System, 121
Advertising, 60–65
  children and, 162
  ethics and, 65
  interactive TV and, 233
  Internet, 222–223
  and multimedia, 200–201
  newspapers and, 52, 56
  origins of, 61–62
  radio, 64, 117–118
  television, 64–65, 161–162
  tools, 64
Advertising agencies, 62–63
Agenda setting, 163
Agitprop trains, 129
Alexanderson, E.F.W., 93
Alexandria, library of, 13
Alpha state trance, 141
Alphabets, 7–8
AM radio, 151
America Online (AOL), 232
American Federation of Musicians, 183
American Revolution, 44–45
Ampex, 176
Andreessen, Marc, 220
Answering machines, xxiii, 147, 175
Aquino, Benigno, xxvi
Archer, Frederick, 72
Aristotle, 9
Armstrong, E. Howard, 91, 93, 94, 150
Arnett, Peter, 168
Associated Press, 56, 67, 82
  objective reporting and, 53–54
Assyria, 13
AT&T (American Telephone and
    Telegraph), 86, 117–118, 145, 155

Audience fragmentation, 169–170,
  190–191
Audion, 93, 94
Audiophiles, 150
Audiotape, 112–114, 164
  books on, 199
  digital, 114, 185
Auteur tradition, 129
Authors, 26
Avant-garde movies, 129

B

Babbage, Charles, 195
Baby Bells, 145–146
Babylon
  libraries in, 13
  writing in, 2–3
Bain, Alexander, 154, 227–228
Baird, John Logie, 154, 155, 175
Bakewell, F.C., 228
Battleship Potemkin, 129
Beato, Felice, 73
Being There (Kosinski), 139–140
Bell, Alexander Graham, 84–85, 107, 108
Bell Laboratories, 85, 111
Berliner, Emile, 85, 109
Berzelius, Jon, 154
Betahans, 179–180
Betamax VCRs, 177
Bible
  Gutenberg, 23
  translation restrictions on, 19, 26–27
  vernacular translations of, 33–34, 36
Billboards, 61–62
Birth of a Nation, The, 128–129
Bit-mapped images, 227
Black Death, 18
Blay, Andre, 177
Bleak House (Dickens), 193

Blender, 200
Bly, Nellie, 103
Boiler plate, 54
Bookmobiles, 186
Booknet, 186
Book-of-the-Month Club, 185
Books, 22–27, 185–186
  on audiotape, 199
  censorship of, 26–27
  early, 36–37, 39–40
Boorstin, Daniel J., 75
Bradford, Andrew, 104
Brady, Mathew, 73
Brainerd, Paul, 195–196
Brand loyalty, 60
Brand names, 63–64
Branly, Édouard, 90
Braun, Ferdinand, 93
Braun, Karl, 154
Briggs, Joseph, 142
Britain
  movies in, 130
  Prestel system, 231
British Broadcasting Corporation (BBC),
    118, 154
Broadcasting, 93, 95, 162. *See also* Radio;
    Television
Broadsides, 31
Brownie cameras, 121
BSS (broadcast satellite service), 212
Bubonic plague, 18
Bulletin board systems (BBSs), 220–221

C

Cable TV, 169–174, 201–207
  fiber optics and, 205–207
  franchises, 173–174, 203–204
  interactive, 191–192, 204, 229–233
  narrowcasting in, 201–203
  pay, 204–205
  piracy, 205
  specialized channels on, 201–203
  and video rentals, 179
  wireless, 205
Calhoun, John, 68
Caller ID, 147
Camera lucida, 70
Camera obscura, 69–70
Camera Work, 119
Cameras, 119–121. *See also* Photography
  video, 136, 181–182
Canaanite alphabet, 8
Canards, 31. *See also* Pamphlets
Carey, Philip, 154

Carlson, Chester, 75
Carlyle, Thomas, 45
Carson, Rachel, 186
Carter, Jimmy, xxvii
Carterphone Decision, 145, 228
Caselli, Abbe Jean, 154, 228
Castells, Manuel, 193, 217
Catalogs, 63, 143–144
Catholic Church, 40
Caxton, William, 25
CB (citizen's band) radio, 151
C-band, 212–213
CD-ROMs, 199–201
Cellular phones, 146–147
Censorship
  books and, 26–27
  Internet and, 217–218, 221–222
  movies and, 125–126, 133
  news and, 51
  satellite communications and, xxv,
      207–208
  videos and, 181
Change, societal. *See* Society, change and
Channel One, 202
Chaplin, Charlie, 127, 128, 131
Chat lines, 221, 223
Chaum, David, 220
Child labor, 45–46, 74
Children of the Poor, 74
Children's programming, 160–161
China
  censorship and, xxix, 37, 208
  lack of information revolutions in, 22
  movies in, 130
  news in, 30
  paper invented in, 21–22
  postal system in, 15
  printing in, 35–38
  Tiananmen Square uprising, xxiv–xxvi
Christianity, 18–19, 26–27, 33–34, 40
  written tradition of, 6, 8
Cinematographe, 97
Cities, 43–44, 216–217
City Mercury, 61
Civil Rights movement, 165–166
Civil War, American, 62, 73
Civil War, The, 161
Clark, Jim, 220
Clarke, Arthur, 207, 210
Class consciousness, 44–45
Clay tablets, 1–2, 3
Cleisthenes, 11
CNN (Cable News Network), 168, 169, 202
CNN syndrome, xxxi
Codexes, 6

Coherers, 90, 93
Coinage, 10–11
Columbia Broadcasting System (CBS), 108
Comics, newspaper, 103
Commerce
    14th century, 19, 23
    changes due to, 10–11
Commercial press, 52
Common Sense, 49
Communication
    history of, 1–3, 77–78
    three eras of, 241–242
Communication Act of 1934, 117
Communication toolshed, xvii, 138–188,
    240
Communications Decency Act, 217
Communications Satellite Act (1962), 209
Community antenna television (CATV),
    170, 172. *See also* Cable TV
Compact discs (CDs), 114, 136, 185
    erasable, 179
    video, 178–179
Composographs, 122
CompuServe, 232
Computers, 194–196
Conrad, Frank, 114–115
Contact photography, 71
Continuous web paper, 106
CONUS, 165, 209
Cooke, William, 78
Courier, 210
Crookes, Sir William, 154
Crosby, Bing, 113, 175–176, 183
Crusades, 36
Crystal-and-cat-whisker detectors, 93–94
Cultural imperialism, xxix–xxx, 181
Cuneiform writing, 2–3, 4
Curiosi, 15
Cursus publicus, 15

D

Daguerre, Louis, 70–72
Daguerreotypes, 71
Daley, Richard, 167
Dance crazes, 110
Dark Ages, 18–19
Dayan, Daniel, 168
de Forest, Lee, 91, 93, 151, 175
Declaration of the Rights of Man, 49
Defoe, Daniel, 104
Democracy, 11
Demotic writing, 3
Denmark, computerization in, 193
Department stores, 102

Desktop publishing, 191, 194–196
Desktop video, 136, 182
Diamond Sutra, 36
Dickens, Charles, 106, 193
Dickson, W.K.L., 97
Dictating machines, 111
Digicash, 220
Digital audio broadcasting (DAB), 151
Digital audio tape (DAT), 115, 185
Digital compact cassettes (DCC), 114, 185
Digital compression, 206
Digital imaging, 121–122
Digital video discs (DVD), 178, 199
Diodes, 92–93
Direct broadcast satellites (DBS), 207,
    211–213
    movie distribution and, 136
    radio and, 151
Direct to home (DTH) service. *See* Direct
    broadcast satellites (DBS)
DiscoVision, 178
Dockwra, William, 30
Doctorow, E.L., 186
Dolby, Ray, M., 176
Double chaining, 164
Doublier, Francis, 98
Dove, Rita, 191–192
Drive time, 150
Drive-in movies, 134
Drummers, 60
DuMont, Allen, 156
Durant, Will, 6, 11

E

Early Bird, 210–211
Eastman, George, 97, 120–121
E-cash, 220
Echo, 210
Economist, The, xxx
Ediphone, 111
Edison, Thomas
    movies and, 97
    phonograph and, 107–109
    radio and, 90
    telegraph and, 82
    telephone and, 85
Edison effect, 92
Education. *See also* Literacy; Universities
    free public, 44, 48
    videos and, 179–180
Egypt
    libraries in, 12
    and papyrus, 4–5
    postal system in, 15

scribes in, 6
writing in, 3
Eisenstein, Elizabeth, 25
Eisenstein, Sergei, 129
Electrical transcriptions. *See* Recording
Electronic news gathering (ENG), 164–165, 176–177
Electronic voice messaging (EVM), 147
Electrotyping, 48
E-mail, 225–226, 227
Engels, Friedrich, 46
Entertainment media, xvii, 101–137, 240
    cultural imperialism in, xxix–xxx
    magazines, 104–106
    movies, 123–136
    newspapers, 103–104
    photography, 119–123
    the poor and, 98, 102, 124
    radio, 114–118
    recordings, 107–114
Erasmus, Desiderius, 20
Ethics, advertising and, 65
Evening Transcript, 52
EVR cartridges, 177

F

Family structure
    computers and, 194
    Industrial Revolution and, 46
    media and, 192–193
Family Viewing Hour, 160
Faraday, Michael, 90, 154
Farming, 46–47
Farnsworth, Philo, 155
Fax machines, xxv, 226–229
Federal Communications Commission (FCC), 117
    and cable TV, 172–173
    and phone company reorganization, 145–146
    and television standards, 157
Federal Food and Drugs Act (1906), 63
Feminine Mystique, The, 186
Fêng Tao, 35
Fenton, Roger, 73
Fessenden, Reginald, 91, 93
Fiber optics, 205–207, 233
    cable TV and, 206–207
    movie distribution and, 136
    telephone and, 145
Film, 97, 120
    color, 121
Fixed satellite service (FSS), 211–212
Flaming, 221

Fleming, John Ambrose, 92–93
Fleming valves, 93
Footprints, satellite, 208
Forums, Internet, 221
Fourdrinier machine, 48, 49–50
France, movies in, 129
Franklin, Benjamin, 49, 53, 66, 104
Fred Ott's Sneeze, 127
Freed, Alan, 182–183
French Revolution, 44–45, 46, 47, 49
Friedan, Betty, 186
Friese-Greene, William, 97
FSS (fixed satellite service), 211–212
FTP (file transfer protocol), 219

G

Gazettes, 31. *See also* Newspapers
Geosynchronous orbit, 210
Gerbner, George, 233
Germany, movies in, 129, 130
Glidden, David, 226
Global village, 168–169, 189
Godey's Lady's Book, 105
Goldmark, Peter, 184
Goldwyn, Samuel, 98
Gopher, 219
Gorbachev, Michail, xxiv
Graphophone, 108, 111
Gray, Elisha, 84, 85, 107, 228
Gray, William, 88
Great Train Robbery, The, 126
Greece
    alphabet of, 7
    knowledge/learning in, 7–14
    libraries in, 13
    papyrus and, 5–6
    postal system in, 15
Greek language, 10
Greene, Graham, xvi
Griffith, D.W., 128
Gulf War, xxxi–xxxii, 167–168, 180
Gutenberg, Johannes, 23, 38–40

H

Halftone process, 48, 63, 74
Hammurabi's code, 3
Handwriting, 34
Harris, Benjamin, 31
Hartley, R.V.L., 175
Harvest of Shame, 165
Havas, Charles, 81
Hays Office, 133
HBO (Home Box Office), 201, 206

Helical scan VCRs, 176
Heliographs, 78
Henry, Joseph, 90
Herodotus, 15
Herschel, Sir John, 71
Hertz, Heinrich, 90
Hieratic language, 3
Hieroglyphics, 3
High definition television (HDTV), 158,
    206, 212
  movie distribution and, 136, 158
High fidelity, 111, 184–185
Hill Street Blues, 159
Hindenberg, 183
Hine, Lewis, 74, 75
"His Master's Voice," 110
Hitler, Adolf, 149
Hits, Internet, 220
Hoardings, 62
Hoe, Richard, 48
Hogan's Alley, 103
Hollerith, Herman, 195
Holograms, 122–123
Home pages, 219
Home shopping, 203, 232
Homeworkers, 215. *See also*
    Telecommuting
House Un-American Activities
    Committee, 134
How the Other Half Lives, 74
HTML (Hypertext Markup Language), 219
Humanism, 20, 34, 36
Hussein, Saddam, xxviii
Hyksos, 5
Hypermedia, 219
Hypertext, 219
Hypo, 71

I

Iconoscope, 155
Illustrated London News, 74
Image dissector, 155
Incunabula, 24
India, movies in, 130
Industrial Revolution, xvi–xvii, 43–47
  advertising and, 60–61, 62
  mass entertainment and, 101–102
Information Age, xvi
Information highway, xvii–xviii, 189–201,
    229–238, 240–241. *See also* Internet;
    World Wide Web
  information rich/poor and, 194,
    202–203
  interactivity and, 190, 191–192

  multimedia and, 198–201
Information revolutions
  defining, xv–xvii
  lifestyle changes due to, xxii–xxiii
  shared characteristics of, xviii–xix
Infotainment, 161
Ink, 4
Inquisition, the, 27
Instant print process, 121
Integrated services digital network
    (ISDN), 145
INTELSAT, 210–211
Intelsat I, 210–211
Interactivity, 190, 191–192
  TV and, 229–233
International Telecommunications
    Satellite Organization, 211
Internet, 217–226
  advertising on, 222–223
  bulletin boards, 220–221
  censorship and, 217–218, 220–221
  chat lines, 223
  e-mail, 225–226
  extremists on, xxxi, 222
  history of, 218–219
  knowledge groups on, 222
  news on, 234–236
  newsgroups, 221–222
  politics on the, xxxi, 217–218
  radio on, 224–225
  shopping on, 203, 220
  social implications of, 223–224
  World Wide Web and, 219–220
Internet Network Information Center, 223
Internet Society, 218
Inventions, dissemination/integration of,
    xxii
Iran, censorship in, 208
IRC (Internet relay chat) lines, 223
Islamic civilization, 22
Italy, movies in, 130
Ives, Frederick, 74
Ives, Herbert, 155, 175

J

Jackson, William Henry, 73
Jane Fonda's Workout, 177
Japan
  movies in, 130
  papermaking in, 7, 22
  writing/alphabet in, 7
Jazz Singer, The, 131
Jenkins, Charles Francis, 155
Jerrold Electronics, 171–172

Jingles, 64
Johnson, Eldridge, 109–110
Journal of Public Notices, 61
Journalism, 56, 103. *See also* News;
    Newspapers
Jukeboxes, 111
Junk mail, 143–144, 229

K

Kalmus, Herbert, 131
Katz, Elihu, 168
Keillor, Garrison, 192
Kennedy, John F., assassination of, 165
Keystone Kops, 127
Khomeini, Ayatollah, xxviii
Kinescope, 175
Kinetograph, 97
Kinetoscope, 97
King, Larry, 202
King, Martin Luther, 166
King, Rodney, 180
Klein, Paul, 153
Knowledge gap, 202
Kodak camera, 120–121
Koenig, Friedrich, 48
Koppel, Ted, xxvi
Korea, printing in, 38
Korn, Arthur, 228
Kosinski, Jerzy, 140–141
Ku-band, 212–213
Kurosawa, Akira, 130

L

Labor unions, 45, 46
Land, Edwin, 121
Lantern slide shows, 73
Lasker, Albert, 64
Latin language, 32–33
Letterpress printing, 49
Libraries, 3
    ancient, 9, 12–13
    free public, 44
License fees, 161
Life, 74
Lights, electric, 101–102
Lindbergh, Charles, 144
Linotype machines, 48–49
Listservs, 220
Literacy
    in the 14th century, 19–20
    in ancient Greece, 10
    middle-class, 24
    newspapers and, 55

paper's effects on, 23
    vernacular printing's effects on, 32–35
Local area networks (LANs), 87, 222
Lodge, Oliver, 90, 91
Logan, Robert, 8
Lollards, 27
L.O.P. (least objectionable program)
    policy, 153
Lord & Thomas, 64
Loudspeakers, 95
Low power television (LPTV), 162
Lower case letters, 40
LPs, 184
Luddites, 46
Lumière, Auguste, 97
Lumière, Louis, 97
Luther, Martin, 15, 20, 36
L-VIS (live video insertion system), 233

M

Magazines, 104–106, 197–198
    and advertising, 62–63, 104, 106
    audience fragmentation in, 106, 191,
        197–198
    delivery of, 68, 104
    early, 26, 104–105
    electronic, 197–198
    illustrations in, 54, 74–75, 105
    mass circulation, 56, 105–106, 197
    plagiarism in, 105–106
Malarkey, Martin, 172
Manutius, Aldus, 34
Marconi, Guglielmo, 90–91
Marcos, Ferdinand, xxvi
Marey, Etienne Jules, 96–97
Marketing, xix, 150
Marketing research, 64
Mass media, xvii, 43–100, 240
    content vs. medium in, xx–xxi
    Industrial Revolution and, 43–47
    power of, xix–xx
    and social fragmentation, 190–194
    and social protest, xix
Master antenna television (MATV), 170,
    171–172. *See also* Cable TV
Materialism, advertising and, 65
Maxwell, James Clerk, 85, 90
May, Joseph, 154
McClure, S.S., 56
McClure's Magazine, 56
MCI Decision, 145
McLuhan, Marshall, xxi, 7, 135, 152–153,
    189
Medicines, patent, 63

Medieval Human, 241–242
Méliès, George, 123
Merganthaler, Ottmar, 48
Mesopotamia, 6
Mexican War, 81
Microphones, 108
Middle class
    literacy and, 24
    movies and, 98, 125–126
    and working class, 44
Mill, Henry, 58
Milton, John, 53
Minidiscs (MDs), 114, 185
Modernism, 47
Monasteries
    books produced by, 23–24
    knowledge maintained by, 7
    postal systems of, 28
Money
    coinage, 10–11
    electronic, 220
    paper, 21–22, 37
Mongols, 37
Morita, Akio, 177
Morris, Lloyd, 102
Morrison, Herbert, 183
Morse, Samuel F.B., 71, 78–79
Movie palaces, 125–126
Movies, 95–98, 123–136
    and censorship, 125–126, 133
    color, 131–132
    colorizing, 131–132
    as communication, 95–96
    and desktop video, 136
    development of, 96–97
    distribution of, 135–136
    escapist, 126–127
    impact of, 95–96
    musicals, 132
    nickelodeons, 123–125
    non-American, 129–130
    political issues in, 133–134
    projection of, 97–98
    racism and, 124–125, 128–129
    sound in, 130–131
    the star system and, 127–128, 132–133
    and television, 134–135, 158–159
    visual language of, 126, 128
    vs. videos, 174–175, 177–178
    westerns, 132–133, 159
    women and, 124
MSS (mobile satellite service), 211
Muckrakers, 56, 74
MUDs (multi-user dungeons), 218
Mullin, John, 113

Multimedia, 198–201, 204
Multiple systems operators (MSOs),
    203–204
Munsey, Frank, 106
Murrow, Edward R., 160–161, 164, 165
Music. See also Recording
    fragmentation and, 190–191
    radio and, 182–183
Music videos, 184
Mutoscopes, 97
Muybridge, Eadweard, 96
Muzak, 111

N

Narrowcasting, 150, 169–170, 201–203
Nation, The, 65
National Biscuit Company, 63–64
National Board of Censorship of Motion
    Pictures, 133
National Cable Television Association,
    172
National Community Television Council,
    172
National Public Radio (NPR), 158
National Research Education Network,
    222
Nationalism, 33, 89
Neorealism, 130
Netscape Navigator, 220
Networks
    Internet, 222
    radio, 118, 149, 150
    satellite, 213
    satellites and, 209
    television, 162, 165
New Wave movies, 129
New World Information and
    Communication Order (NWICO), xxix
New York Sun, 52
News
    concept of, 51–52
    electronic news gathering, 164–165,
        176–177
    history of, 30–32
    local, 67, 168–169
    online, 234–236
    public appetite for, 81–82, 168–169
    radio, 149, 163–164
    satellite news gathering, 165, 208–209
    television, 162–163, 164–169
    timeliness of, 65–66
News agencies, 81–82
    and objective reporting, 53–54, 82
News expresses, 68

News gathering
   audiotape and, 113–114
   cooperative, 53
   electronic, 164–165, 176–177
   satellite, 165, 208–209
   telegraph and, 80–81
   videotape and, 164–165,
      176–177
Newsbooks, 31
Newsgroups, 221–222
Newsletters, 31
Newspapers, 51–56
   advertising in, 62–63
   business of, 51–52
   censorship and, 51
   chains, 55
   colonial American, 65–66
   color in, 103
   effects on reading, 103
   entertainment in, 103–104
   faxes and, 227, 228
   free exchange of, 66–67
   free vs. controlled, 55–56
   illustrations in, 51, 54–55, 74–75
   inverted pyramid style in, 82
   local news in, 67
   mass circulation, 103
   news sources of, 52–54
   online, 234–236
   origins of, 30–32
   postal delivery of, 65–69, 142–144
   technical improvements in, 54
   telegraph and, 77, 80–82
   telephone-based services by, 148
Newsreels, 164
Newssheets, 31
Newsweek, xxv
Niche marketing, 150
Nickelodeons, 123–125
Niépce, Joseph, 70
Nipkow, Paul, 154
Novels, 106
NTSC (National Television System
    Committee) standard, 157

O

Objectivity
   Greek concept of, 12
   in reporting, 53–54, 167
   telegraph and, 77
Offices, business, 57–58
Offset lithography, 49, 55
Oldcastle, Sir John, 27
Olympic games, 168, 208

Online services, 232
Oral culture
   television as, 152–153
   writing and, 11–12

P

Packaging, 63–64
Pagers, 146
Pahlevi, Shah Reza, xxvii
Paine, Tom, 49
PAL standard, 157
Pamphlets, 31, 49
Paper, 19, 20–23
   invention of, 21
   manufacture of, 48, 49–50, 106
   newsprint, 74
   westward spread of, 22–23
Paperless society/office, 21
Papyrus, 4–6, 19
Parcel post, 30, 143
Parchment, 6–7
Parry, Robert, 235
Parsons, L.E., 171
Party press, 52
Pathé, Charles, 110
Pathé, Emile, 110
Pathégraphe, 111
Pay-per-view (PPV), 204
Pay-TV, 174
PCS (personal communication service),
    146–147
Peel, Sir Robert, 46
Peephole machines, 97
Penny Magazine, The, 105
Penny press, 50, 52, 54. *See also*
    Newspapers
Persistence of vision, 96, 154
Peter Pan Clock, 111
Petites Affiches, Les (Little Notices), 61
Petzval, Josef, 71
Pfleumer, Fritz, 113
Phoenicians, 7, 8
Phonautograph, 107
Phonevision, 174
Phonofiddle, 111
Phonograph parlors, 109
Phonographs, 108–111
Phonopostal, 111
Photoconductivity, 75
Photocopying, 75–76
Photoengraving, 74–75
Photogenic drawing, 71. *See also*
    Photography
Photographic revolver, 97

Photographs/illustrations
  half-tone printing, 48
  manipulation of, 121–122
  in newspapers, 54–55
Photography, 69–76
  camera improvements and, 119–121
  chemistry of, 70
  digital, 121–122
  dry-plate, 119–120
  as a hobby, 120–121
  holograms, 122–123
  muckrakers and, 74
  photoengraving and, 74–75
  roots of, 69–70
  wet-plate, 72
Photojournalism, 74
Physical activity, media's effects on,
    140, 141
Pi Shêng, 38
Pickford, Mary, 128
Pictographs, 2
Picturephones, 147
Points (type size), 40
Poland, media in, xxx–xxxi
Polaroid cameras, 121
Police, 46
Politics
  in America, xxxi
  censorship in, 26–27, 207–208
  economic freedom vs political control
      and, xxx–xxxi
  and mass media, xxiii–xxxii
  newspapers and, 32, 55–56
  photography and, 72–73
  radio and, 90, 149
  television and, 165, 166–167
  written documents, 9–10
Poniatoff, Alexander M., 176
Pony Express, 68, 81
Population transfers
  the Industrial Revolution and, 43–44
  technology and, xxi, 216–217
Porter, Edwin, 126
Post roads, 68
Postal Reform Act (1970), 144
Postal systems, 65–69, 142–144
  air mail, 144
  as businesses, 29–30
  e-mail and, 225–226
  free home delivery by, 142–143
  governments and, 30
  history of, 14–15
  international agreements in, 68–69
  mail transportation in, 67–68
  Middle Ages, 28–30

newspapers/magazines and, 65–66,
    67–68, 142–144
  postage stamps and, 62, 80
  postmasters and, 29–30, 66–67
  Tasso family, 19
Poster, Mark, 189
Postmodernism, 35, 47, 189
POTS (plain old telephone service), 146
Poulsen, Valdemar, 113
Powers, John E., 65
Preece, Sir William, 85, 91
Press-radio war, 163
Prestel system, 231
Prices, uniformity in, 80
Prime time, 150
Printing, xvii, 18–42, 47–49, 240
  block, 26, 36, 37
  books and, 23–27
  censorship and, 26–27
  European knowledge of Chinese,
      35–38
  literacy and, 34–36
  as mass medium, 47–49
  movable type, 38–40
  newspapers and, 31–32
  stereotyping, 48
  typesetting in, 48–49
  vernacular, 25–26, 32–33
Printing presses, 48
Printing telegraph. See Teletype
Privacy, computers and, 195
Private branch exchanges (PBXs), 87
Private cable, 205
Private express companies, 68, 143
Prodigy, 232, 234
Producers, independent, 135, 136
Production Code Administration, 133
Programming
  cable TV and, 170, 172
  fiber optics and, 206–207
  interactive TV and, 233
Projection, motion picture, 96, 97–98
Public access stations, 173, 174, 204
Public affairs, 47–48
Public Broadcasting System (PBS), 158
Public Radio International, 158
Publick Occurrences, 31
Publishers, as postmasters, 66–67
Pulitzer, Joseph, 54

Q

Quadraphonic sound, 184–185
Qube, 230–231
QWERTY keyboards, 59–60

R

Racism, in movies, 124–125
Radio, 89–95, 114–118, 148–152
  advertising, 64, 117–118
  amateurs in, 93–94
  broadcasting, 93, 114–118
  CB, 151
  clandestine, xxvii
  competition in, 91–92, 115–116
  cultural influence of, 149
  FM, 150
  future of, 151
  golden age of, 149
  homogenization by, 148–149, 189–190
  on the Internet, 151, 191, 224–225
  national policies on, 118
  networks, 118, 149, 150
  origins of, 90–91
  political broadcasts, 149
  receivers, early, 94–95
  regulation of, 92, 116–117
  scheduled programming in, 114–115
  societal effects of, 89–90, 115–116
  stations, early, 94, 115
  telephone used as, 86–87
  television and, 150–151
  voice transmission in, 92–93
Radio Act of 1912, 92
Radio Act of 1927, 116–117
Radio group, 117
Railroads
  mail delivery and, 68, 80
  and newspapers, 52–53
  telegraph and, 79–80
Rashomon, 130
Reading. *See also* Literacy
  as listening, 25, 33
  spread of, 33–34
Ready prints, 54
Réaumur, Rene de, 50
Receivers, radio, 93–95, 118
Recording, 107–114, 182–186
  audiotape, 112–114, 164
  digital, 114, 185
  high fidelity, 111, 184–185
  invention of, 107–109
  music and, 182–183
  phonographs and, 109–111
  portable, 112–114
  radio and, 149, 183–184
Recreation, public, 101–102. *See also*
  Entertainment media
Reformation, the, 20, 34, 36
Registered mail, 30

Religion
  censorship and, 26–27
  in the Dark Ages, 18–19
  television as, 168–169
  vernacular printing and, 33–34
  written tradition in, 6, 8
Renaissance, the, 20, 34, 36
Reporting, 52–54, 77, 167. *See also* News;
    Newspapers
Reuter, Julius, 30
Reuters, 81
Review, The, 104
Rheingold, Howard, 223–224
Righi, Auguste, 90
Riis, Jacob, 74
Robert, Nicholas, 49
Robertson, James, 73
Rock 'n' roll, 182–183
Romans, 12, 15
Ronephone, 111
Roosevelt, Franklin, 149
Rosing, Boris, 154–155
Rotary cylinder press, 48
Rotula, 28
Rural free delivery (RFD), 142–143
Russia
  Gorbachev's arrest, xxiv
  movies in, 129–130
  VCRs in, 180
Rybczynski, Witold, xix–xx

S

Samizdat, 198
Sarnoff, David, 150, 155, 156
SATCOM, 201
Satellite communications, 207–213
  bandwidth limits and, 213
  cable TV and, 200–201, 204
  C-band/Ku-band, 212–213
  censorship and, xxv
  direct broadcasting and, 211–212
  future of, 213
  history of, 209–211
  news and, 208–209
  phone service and, 146
  politics and, 207–208
  radio and, 151
  television and, 170
Satellite master antenna television
    (SMATV), 205
Satellite news gathering (SNG), 165,
    208–209
Satellites, types of, 211–212
Schawlow, Arthur, 206

Schulze, Johann, 70
Schwarzkopf, Gen. Norman, xxxi, 167–168
Scott, Leon, 107
Scrambling signals, 213
Scribes, 6, 7
Scriveners, 25
SECAM standard, 157
Sejong, King, 38
Selectavision, 177–178
Semaphore, 78
Sennett, Mack, 127
Shapp, Milton Jerrold, 171–172
Sholes, Christopher, 58–59, 60
Silent Spring, 186
Siquis, 61
Sitcoms, 160
Smith, Oberlin, 112–113
Soap operas, 159–160
Social interaction
    communication tools effect on, xix, xxi,
        95–96, 139–140, 175, 239–241
    Internet and, 223–224
    printed materials effect on, 32
Social structure
    Greek, 10–11
    Industrial Revolution and, 43–44, 46
    printing/literacy and, 34–35
    village/rural vs. urban, 44
Society
    change and, xvi, 239–240
    fragmentation in, 190–193
    wireless communication and, 152
Socrates, 12
Spamming, 225
Sparta, 11
Special interest groups (SIGs), 221
Spectator, The, 104
Spielberg, Steven, 95
Sputnik, 209
Stamp Act of 1765, 32
Stanford, Leland, 96
Stanton, Edwin, 82
Steichen, Edward, 119
Stereo, 111, 150
Stereo mats, 54
Stereotyping (printing), 48
Stern, Howard, 151
Stibitz, George, 195
Stieglitz, Alfred, 119
Stone, John, 91
Store and forward communications, 225
Stroh, Augustus, 111
Stromer, Ulman, 23
Strowger, Almon, 87–88
Subscription television (STV), 174

Sumerians
    libraries of, 13
    numerals invented by, 2
    writing and, 1–2, 4
Superstations, 201–202
Syllabaries, 2

T

Tabloids, 103–104
Talbot, William Fox, 71–72
Talk shows, 161
Tarlton, Robert, 172
Tasso postal system, 19, 29
Tatler, The, 104
Teacher-in-the-Sky, 211
Technicolor, 131
Technology
    developing countries and, 193
    pattern of progress in, 9
Telautograph, 228
Telecenters, 216
Telecommunication Reform Act (1996),
        146, 159, 204
Telecommunications, 195
Telecommuting, 193, 214–217
    advantages of, 215–216
    and population transfers, xxi, 216–217
Teleconferencing, 147, 211
Telefon Hirmondo, 86–87, 170
Telegraph, 77–83
    development of, 77–79
    news and, 55
    newspapers and, 77, 80–82
    telephone competition with, 85
    typewriters and, 58, 59
Telegraph reporters, 53
Telegraphone, 113
Telemarketing, 147
Telephone, 83–89, 145–148
    automatic translation, 148
    cellular/pocket, 146–147
    development of, 84–85
    dial, 88
    early perceptions of, 83–84
    long distance and, 88
    news and, 55
    operators/switchboards, 86–88
    picturephones, 147
    as public utility, 86
    as radio, 86–87
    reorganization of phone companies,
        145–146
    telegraph competition with, 85
Telephone group, 117

Teleports, 213
Teleprinters, 82
Teletel system, 231–232
Teletext, 231–232
Teletype, 55, 59, 82, 89
Teletypewriter exchange service (TWX), 89
Teletypewriters. *See* Teletype
Television, 152–162
  advertising, 64–65, 158
  and books, 185–186
  cable, 169–174
  Civil Rights movement and, 165–166
  color, 155, 157
  HDTV, 136, 158, 206, 212
  interactive, 229–233
  on the Internet, 224–225
  invention of, 154–156
  knowledge gap and, 202–203
  movies and, 134–135
  news, 162–163, 164–169
  pay, 174
  paying for, 161–162
  problems with heavy usage of, 141
  programming, 158–161
  and radio, 150–151
  spread of, 156–157
  standards, 156, 157
  stations, early, 155–156
  time spent watching, xxiii, 152–153, 202–203
  videotape and, 175–177, 180
Telnet, 219
Telstar, 210
Terrorism, xxvii
Third World countries, xxviii–xxix, 181, 194, 202–203
Thomas, Lowell, 163
Thomson, Sir J.J., 154
Thoreau, Henry David, 83
Threads, 234
Thurn and Taxis postal system, 29
Tiananmen Square uprising, xxiv–xxvi
Tielines, 82
Tipao (palace report), 30
Titanic, 92
Tocqueville, Alexis de, 47
Toffler, Alvin, 194, 216
Toll broadcasting, 117. *See also* Advertising
Tombstone page makeup style, 48
Toolshed Human, 241–242
Townes, Charles, 206
Transatlantic cables, 80, 88
Transponders, 210
Tribal Human, 241–242

Trip to the Moon, A, 123
Ts'ai Lun, 21
Turner, Ted, 169, 201–202
Tyndale, William, 27
Type, movable, 38–40
Type sizes, 40
Typewriters, 57–60
  keyboards, 59–60
  Sholes, 58–59

U

UHF (ultra-high frequency), 157
U-matic, 176–177
UNESCO, xxviii–xxix
United States
  Civil War, 62, 73
  first newspapers in, 31–32
  private media development in, 79, 92
Univac, 195
Universal Postal Union, 69
Universities, 24–25, 34
  Internet and, 222
  postal systems of, 28–29
University of Paris, postal system, 28–29
Upper case letters, 40
URLs (uniform resource locators), 219
U.S. v. Paramount, 158
Usenet, 222

V

Vacuum tubes, 92–93
Vail, Alfred, 78–79
Vail, Theodore, 86
V-chips, 159
Vellum, 6
VHF (very-high frequency), 157
VHS format, 177
Victor Talking Machine Company, 109–110
Video camcorders, 136, 181–182
Video piracy, 180–181
Video teleconferencing, 147, 211
Videocassette recorders (VCRs), 174–176, 177–178
  political power of, xxvi–xxvii, 179–180
  video piracy and, 180–181
Videodiscs, 178
Video-on-demand, 230
Videos, music, 184
Videotape, 164, 174–182
  color, 176
  development of, 175–176
  news gathering and, 176–177

Videotex, 231–232
Vietnam War, 167–168
Viewdata, 231–232
Village Video Network, 179
Violence
    rock/rap music and, 183
    television/movies and, 140, 159
Voice mail, 147
Voice of America, 90
VSAT (very small aperture terminal), 213

W

Walesa, Lech, xxxi
Walkie-Talkies, 146
Walkman, 112, 140
Wall Street Journal, xxvi
Walson, John, 171
Wanamaker, John, 64
Wang, An, 195
War of the Worlds, 149
Warfare
    photography and, 46
    technology and, 46
    television and, 167–168
Warner, Harry M., 130–131
Watergate scandal, 168
Watts riots, 166
Wedgewood, Thomas, 70
Western Union, 79–80. *See also* Telegraph
Wet-plate photography, 72
Wheatstone, Charles, 78
White, E.B., 156
Whitney, Eli, 50
Wireless cable, 205
Wolff, Bernard, 81–82
Women
    Internet and, 221, 232
    literacy and, 33
    as telephone operators, 87–88
    typewriters and, 57–60
    work and, 44, 45–46
"World News Roundup," 149
World War I
    movies and, 129

radio and, 92, 94, 95
    telephone and, 88
World War II
    audiotape and, 113–114
    television and, 156–157
World Wide Web, 219–220
    advertising and, 222–223
    choices and, 192
    links on, 198–199
    radio on, 151, 191, 224–225
    search tools, 220
Worldwide Television News (WTN), 165
Writing, xvii, 1–17, 240
    Chinese, 21
    on clay tablets, 1–2
    handwriting, 34
    ideographic, 2
    knowledge advances and, 2–3, 7–14
    media for, 3–7
    oral cultures and, 11–12
    phonetic, 2
    resistance to, 11, 12
WTBS, 201

X

Xerography, 75–76
X-ray photography, 75
Xylographic printing, 26
Xylography, 35

Y

Yellow journalism, 103
Yellow Kid, The, 103
Young, Thomas, 107

Z

Zenger, John Peter, 51
Zines, 197–198, 200–201
ZIP (Zoning Improvement Plan) codes, 144
Zukor, Adolph, 128
Zworykin, Vladimir, 155